Study Guide

for use with

Macroeconomics

Seventh Edition

David Colander
Middlebury College

Prepared by
David Colander
Douglas Copeland
Jenifer Gamber

 **McGraw-Hill
Irwin**

Boston   Burr Ridge, IL   Dubuque, IA   Madison, WI   New York   San Francisco
Bangkok   Bogotá   Caracas   Kuala Lumpur   Lisbon   London   Madrid   Mexico
Milan   Montreal   New Delhi   Santiago   Seoul   Singapore   Sydney   Taipei   To

Study Guide for use with
MACROECONOMICS
David Colander

Published by McGraw-Hill/Irwin, an imprint of The McGraw-Hill Companies, Inc., 1221 Avenue of the Americas, New York, NY 10020. Copyright © 2008 by The McGraw-Hill Companies, Inc. All rights reserved.

1 2 3 4 5 6 7 8 9 0 PAT/PAT 0 9 8 7

ISBN   978-0-07-334372-3
MHID 0-07-334372-2

www.mhhe.com

Contents

Preface

We wrote this study guide to help you do well in your economics courses. We know that even using a great book such as the Colander textbook, studying is not all fun. The reality is: most studying is hard work and a study guide won't change that. Your text and lectures will give you the foundation for doing well. So the first advice we will give you is:

1. Read the textbook.
2. Attend class.

We cannot emphasize that enough. Working through the study guide will not replace the text or lectures; this study guide is designed to help you retain the knowledge from the text and classroom by practicing the tools of economics. It is not an alternative to the book and class; it is **in addition to them**.

Having said that, we should point out that buying this guide isn't enough. You have to *use* it. Really, if it sits on your desk, or even under your pillow, it won't do you any good. Osmosis only works with plants. This study guide should be well worn by the end of the semester—dog-eared pages, scribbles beneath questions, some pages even torn out. It should look used.

WHAT CAN YOU EXPECT FROM THIS BOOK?

This study guide concentrates on the terminology and models in your text. It does not expand upon the material in the textbook; it reinforces it. It primarily serves to give you a good foundation to understanding principles of economics. Your professor has chosen this study guide for you, suggesting that your economics exams are going to focus on this kind of foundational understanding. You should be sure of this: if your professor is going to give you mainly essay exams, or complex questions about applying the foundations (such as the more difficult end-of-chapter questions in your textbook) this study guide will not be enough to ace that exam.

To get an idea of what your exams will be like, ask your professor to take a look at these questions and tell the class whether they are representative of the type of questions that will be on the exam. And if they will differ, how.

HOW SHOULD YOU USE THIS STUDY GUIDE?

As we stated above, this book works best if you have attended class and read the book. Ideally, you were awake during class and took notes, you have read the textbook chapters more than once, and have worked through some of the questions at the end of the chapter. (So, we're optimists.)

Just in case the material in the book isn't fresh in your mind, before turning to this study guide it is a good idea to refresh your memory about the material in the text. To do so:

1. Read through the margin comments in the text; they highlight the main concepts in each chapter.
2. Turn to the last few pages of the chapter and reread the chapter summary.
3. Look through the key terms, making sure they are familiar. (O.K., we're not only optimists, we're wild optimists.)

Even if you do not do the above, working through the questions in the study guide will help to tell you whether you really do know the material in the textbook chapters.

STRUCTURE OF THE STUDY GUIDE

This study guide has two main components: (1) a chapter-by-chapter review and (2) pretests based upon groups of chapters.

Chapter-by-chapter review
Each chapter has eight elements:

1. A chapter at a glance: A brief exposition and discussion of the learning objectives for the chapter.
2. Short-answer questions keyed to the learning objectives.
3. A test of matching the terms to their definitions.

4. Problems and applications.
5. A brain teaser.
6. Multiple choice questions.
7. Potential essay questions
8. Answers to all questions.

Each chapter presents the sections in the order that we believe is most beneficial to you. Here is how we suggest you use them:

Chapter at a Glance: These should jog your memory about the text and lecture. If you don't remember ever seeing the material before, you should go back and reread the textbook chapter. The numbers in parentheses following each learning objective refer to the page in the text that covers that objective. Remember, reading a chapter when you are thinking about a fantasy date is almost the same as not having read the chapter at all.

Short-Answer Questions: The short-answer questions will tell you if you are familiar with the learning objectives. Try to answer each within the space below each question. Don't just read the questions and assume you can write an answer. Actually writing an answer will reveal your weaknesses. If you can answer them all perfectly, great. But, quite honestly, we don't expect you to be able to answer them all perfectly. We only expect you to be able to sketch out an answer.

Of course, some other questions are important to know. For example, if there is a question about the economic decision rule and you don't remember that it excludes past costs and benefits, you need more studying. So the rule is: Know the central ideas of the chapter; be less concerned about the specific presentation of those central ideas.

After you have sketched out all your answers, check them with those at the end of the chapter and review those that you didn't get right. Since each question is based upon a specific learning objective in the text, for those you didn't get right, you may want to return to the textbook to review the material covering that learning objective.

Match the Terms and Concepts to Their Definitions: Since the definitions are listed, you should get most of these right. The best way to match these is to read the definition first, and then find the term on the left that it defines. If you are not sure of the matching term, circle that definition and move on to the next one. At the end, return to the remaining definitions and look at the remaining terms to complete the matches. After completing this part, check your answers with those in the back of the chapter and figure out what percent you got right. If that percent is below the grade you want to get on your exam, try to see why you missed the ones you did and review those terms and concepts in the textbook.

Problems and Applications: Now it's time to take on any problems in the chapter. These problems are generally more difficult than the short-answer questions. These problems focus on numerical and graphical aspects of the chapter.

Working through problems is perhaps one of the best ways to practice your understanding of economic principles. Even if you are expecting a multiple choice exam, working through these problems will give you a good handle on using the concepts in each chapter.

If you expect a multiple choice exam with no problems, you can work through these fairly quickly, making sure you understand the concepts being tested. If you will have a test with problems and exercises, make sure you can answer each of these questions accurately.

Work out the answers to all the problems in the space provided before checking them against the answers in the back of the chapter. Where our answers differ from yours, check to find out why. The answers refer to specific pages in the textbook so you can review the text again too.

Most of the problems are objective and have only one answer. A few are interpretative and have many answers. We recognize that some questions can be answered in different ways than we did. If you cannot reconcile your answer with ours, check with your professor. Once you are at this stage—worrying about different interpretations—you're ahead of most students and, most likely, prepared for the exam.

A Brain Teaser: This section consists of one problem that is generally one step up in the level of difficulty from the "Problems and Applications" exercises or is a critical–thought question. It is designed to provide a challenge to those students who have studied the way we have suggested.

Multiple Choice Questions: The next exercise in each chapter is the multiple choice test. It serves to test the breadth of your knowledge of the text material. Multiple choice questions are not the final arbiters of your understanding. They are, instead, a way of determining whether you have read the book and generally understood the material.

Take this test after having worked through the other questions. Give the answer that most closely corresponds to the answer presented in your text. If you can answer these questions you should be ready for the multiple choice part of your exam.

Work through all the questions in the test before grading yourself. Looking up the answer before you try to answer the questions is a poor way to study. For a multiple choice exam, the percent you answer correctly will be a good predictor of how well you will do on the test.

You can foul up on multiple choice questions in two ways—you can know too little and you can know too much. The answer to knowing too little is obvious: Study more— that is, read the chapters more carefully (and maybe more often). The answer to knowing too much is more complicated. Our suggestions for students who know too much is not to ask themselves "What is the answer?" but instead to ask "What is the answer the person writing the question wants?" Since, with these multiple choice questions, the writer of many of the questions is the textbook author, ask yourself: "What answer would the textbook author want me to give?" Answering the questions in this way will stop you from going too deeply into them and trying to see nuances that aren't supposed to be there.

For the most part questions in this study guide are meant to be straightforward. There may be deeper levels at which other answers could be relevant, but searching for those deeper answers will generally get you in trouble and not be worth the cost.

If you are having difficulty answering a multiple choice question, make your best guess. Once you are familiar with the material, even if you don't know the answer to a question you can generally make a reasonable guess. What point do you think the writer of the question wanted to make with the question? Figuring out that point and then thinking of incorrect answers may be a way for you to eliminate wrong answers and then choose among the remaining options.

Notice that the answers at the end of the chapter are not just the lettered answers. We have provided an explanation for each answer — why the right one is right and why some of the other choices are wrong. If you miss a question, read that rationale carefully. If you are not convinced, or do not follow the reasoning, go to the page in the text referred to in the answer and reread the material. If you are still not convinced, see the caveat on the next page.

Potential Essay Questions: These questions provide yet another opportunity to test your understanding of what you have learned. Answering these questions will be especially helpful if you expect these types of questions on the exams. We have only sketched the beginning of an answer to these. This beginning should give you a good sense of the direction to go in your answer, but be aware that on an exam a more complete answer will be required.

Questions on Appendixes: In the chapters we have included a number of questions on the text appendixes. To separate these questions from the others, the letter A precedes the question number. They are for students who have been assigned the appendixes. If you have not been assigned them (and you have not read them on your own out of your great interest in economics) you can skip these.

Answers to All Questions: The answers to all questions appear at the end of each chapter. They begin on a new page so that you can tear out the answers and more easily check your answers against ours. We cannot emphasize enough that the best way to study is to answer the questions yourself first, and then check out our answers. Just looking at the questions and our answers may tell you what the answers are but will not give you the chance to see where your knowledge of the material is weak.

Pretests

Most class exams cover more than one chapter. To prepare you for such an exam, we provide multiple choice pretests for groups of chapters. These pretests consist of 20-40 multiple choice questions from the selected group of chapters. These questions are identical to earlier questions so if you have done the work, you should do well on these. We suggest you complete the entire exam before grading yourself.

We also suggest taking these under test conditions. Specifically,

Use a set time period to complete the exam.
Sit at a hard chair at a desk with good lighting.

Each answer will tell you the chapter on which the question is based, so if you did not cover one of the chapters in the text for your class, don't worry if you get that question wrong. If you get a number of questions wrong from the chapters your class has covered, worry.

There is another way to use these pretests that we hesitate to mention, but we're realists so we will. That way is to forget doing the chapter-by-chapter work and simply take the pretests. Go back and review the material you get wrong.

However you use the pretests, if it turns out that you consistently miss questions from the same chapter, return to your notes from the lecture and reread your textbook chapters.

A FINAL WORD OF ADVICE

That's about it. If you use it, this study guide can help you do better on the exam by giving you the opportunity to use the terms and models of economics. However, we reiterate one last time: The best way to do well in a course is to attend every class and read every chapter in the text as well as work through the chapters in this study guide. Start early and work consistently. Do not do all your studying the night before the exam.

THANKS AND A CAVEAT

We and our friends went through this book more times than we want to remember. All the authors proofed the entire book, as did our good friends, Pam Bodenhorn and Helen Reiff. We also had some superb students, Rachel Butera, Yunfei Ren, Yun Min Choo, John Meyer, Hassat Cukkalkurt, Tom Brush, Dinesh Palhak, Tizzy Dominguez, Zhen Chen Wu, Yan Oak, and Tugce Erten go through it. (Our sincere thanks go to them for doing so.) Despite our best efforts, there is always a chance that there's a correct answer other than the one the book tells you is the correct answer, or even that the answer the book gives is wrong. If you find a mistake, and it is a small problem about a number or an obvious mistake, assume the error is typographical. If that is not the case, and you still think another answer is the correct one, write up an alternative rationale and e-mail Professor Colander the question and the alternative rationale. Professor Colander's e-mail is:

colander@middlebury.edu.

When he gets it he will send you a note either thanking you immensely for finding another example of his fallibility, or explaining why we disagree with you. If you're the first one to have pointed out an error he will also send you a copy of an honors companion for economics—just what you always wanted, right?

David Colander
Douglas Copeland
Jenifer Gamber

ECONOMICS AND ECONOMIC REASONING

CHAPTER AT A GLANCE

This review is based upon the learning objectives that open the chapter.

1a. Economics is the study of how human beings coordinate their wants and desires, given the decision-making mechanisms, social customs, and political realities of the society. (4)

1b. Three central coordination problems any economy must solve are: (5)
- What, and how much, to produce.
- How to produce it.
- For whom to produce it.

Most economic coordination problems involve scarcity.

2. If the marginal benefits of doing something exceed the marginal costs, do it. If the marginal costs of doing something exceed the marginal benefits, don't do it. This is known as the economic decision rule. (7)

You really need to think in terms of the marginal, or "extra" benefits (MB) and marginal, or "extra" costs (MC) of a course of action. Also, ignore sunk costs.

Economic decision rule:
If MB>MC → Do more of it *because "it's worth it."*

If MB<MC→ Do less of it *because "it's not worth it."*

NOTE: The symbol "→" means "implies" or "logically follows."

3. Opportunity cost is the basis of cost/benefit reasoning; it is the benefit forgone, or the cost of the next-best alternative to the activity you've chosen. That cost should be less than the benefit of what you've chosen. (8)

Opportunity cost → "What must be given up in order to get something else." Opportunity costs are often "hidden." You need to take into consideration all *opportunity costs when making a decision.*

4. Economic reality is controlled by economic forces, social forces, and political forces. (9-11)

What happens in a society can be seen as the reaction and interaction of these 3 forces.

- *Economic forces: The market forces of demand, supply, prices, etc.*

- *Social and cultural forces: Social and cultural forces can prevent economic forces from becoming market forces.*

- *Political and legal forces: Political and legal forces affect decisions too.*

5. Microeconomics considers economic reasoning from the viewpoint of individuals and builds up; macroeconomics considers economic reasoning from the aggregate and builds down. (14)

Microeconomics (micro) → concerned with some particular segment of the economy. Macroeconomics (macro) → concerned with the entire economy.

6a. Positive economics is the study of what is, and how the economy works. (16)

Deals with "what is" (objective analysis).

6b. Normative economics is the study of what the goals of the economy should be. (16)

Deals with "what ought to be" (subjective).

6c. The art of economics is the application of the knowledge learned in positive economics to the achievement of the goals determined in normative economics. (16)

The art of economics is sometimes referred to as "policy economics."

"Good" policy tries to be objective. It tries to weigh all the benefits and costs associated with all policy options and chooses that option in which the benefits outweigh the costs to the greatest degree.

● SHORT-ANSWER QUESTIONS

1. What are the three central problems that every economy must solve?

2. What is scarcity? What are two elements that comprise scarcity? How do they affect relative scarcity?

3. State the economic decision rule.

4. Define opportunity cost.

5. What is the importance of opportunity cost to economic reasoning?

6. What is an economic force? What are the forces that can keep an economic force from becoming a market force?

7. How does microeconomics differ from macroeconomics? Give an example of a macroeconomic issue and a microeconomic issue.

8. Define positive economics, normative economics, and the art of economics. How do they relate to one another?

MATCHING THE TERMS
Match the terms to their definitions

___ 1.	art of economics	a.	Additional benefit above what you've already derived.
___ 2.	economic decision rule	b.	Additional cost above what you've already incurred.
___ 3.	economic force	c.	If benefits exceed costs, do it. If costs exceed benefits, don't.
___ 4.	economic model	d.	The study of individual choice, and how that choice is influenced by economic forces.
___ 5.	economic policy	e.	Necessary reactions to scarcity.
___ 6.	economic principle	f.	The benefit forgone, or the cost, of the next-best alternative to the activity you've chosen.
___ 7.	economics	g.	The study of what is, and how the economy works.
___ 8.	efficiency	h.	The insight that a market economy, through the price mechanism, will allocate resources efficiently.
___ 9.	invisible hand	i.	The study of the economy as a whole, which includes inflation, unemployment, business cycles, and growth.
___ 10.	invisible hand theory	j.	The study of how human beings coordinate their wants.
___ 11.	macroeconomics	k.	Goods available are too few to satisfy individuals' desires.
___ 12.	marginal benefit	l.	The application of the knowledge learned in positive economics to the achievement of the goals determined in normative economics.
___ 13.	marginal cost		
___ 14.	market force	m.	An economic force that is given relatively free rein by society to work through the market.
___ 15.	microeconomics	n.	The price mechanism.
___ 16.	normative economics	o.	A framework that places the generalized insights of theory in a more specific contextual setting.
___ 17.	opportunity cost	p.	A commonly-held economic insight stated as a law or general assumption.
___ 18.	positive economics	q.	Achieving a goal as cheaply as possible.
___ 19.	scarcity	r.	Action taken by government to influence economic actions.
___ 20.	sunk cost	s.	Study of what the goals of the economy should be.
		t.	Cost that has already been incurred and cannot be recovered.

PROBLEMS AND APPLICATIONS

1. State what happens to scarcity for each good in the following situations:

    a. New storage technology allows college dining services to keep peaches from rotting for a longer time. (Good: peaches).

    b. More students desire to live in single-sex dormitories. No new single-sex dormitories are established. (Good: single-sex dormitory rooms).

2. State as best you can:
   a. The opportunity cost of going out on a date tonight that was scheduled last Wednesday.

   b. The opportunity cost of breaking the date for tonight you made last Wednesday.

   c. The opportunity cost of working through this study guide.

   d. The opportunity cost of buying this study guide.

3. Assume you have purchased a $15,000 car. The salesperson has offered you a maintenance contract covering all major repairs for the next 3 years, with some exclusions, for $750.

   a. What is the sunk cost of purchasing the maintenance contract? Should this sunk cost be considered when deciding to purchase a maintenance contract?

   b. What is the opportunity cost of purchasing that maintenance contract?

   c. What information would you need to make a decision based on the economic decision rule?

   d. Based upon that information how would you make your decision?

4. State for each of the following whether it is an example of political forces, social forces, or economic forces at work:

   a. Warm weather arrives and more people take Sunday afternoon drives. As a result, the price of gasoline rises.

   b. In some states, liquor cannot be sold before noon on Sunday.

   c. Minors cannot purchase cigarettes.

   d. Many parents will send money to their children in college without the expectation of being repaid.

● A BRAIN TEASER

1. Suppose you are a producer of hand-crafted picture frames. The going market price for your frames is $250 a piece. No matter how many frames you sell your revenue per unit (equal to the selling price per unit) is constant at $250 per frame. However, your per unit costs of producing each additional picture frame are not constant. Suppose the following table summarizes your costs of producing picture frames. Use cost/benefit analysis to determine the most economical (profit maximizing) number of frames to produce given the price per unit and the accompanying cost schedule shown. What are your total profits per week?

# of Frames	Price	Total Cost
0	$250	$0
1	$250	$25
2	$250	$75
3	$250	$150
4	$250	$300
5	$250	$560

● MULTIPLE CHOICE

Circle the one best answer for each of the following questions:

1. Economic reasoning:
   a. provides a framework with which to approach questions.
   b. provides correct answers to just about every question.
   c. is only used by economists.
   d. should only be applied to economic business matters.

2. Scarcity could be reduced if:
   a. individuals work less and want fewer consumption goods.
   b. individuals work more and want fewer consumption goods.
   c. world population grows and world production remains the same.
   d. innovation comes to a halt.

3. In the textbook, the author focuses on coordination rather than scarcity as the central point of the definition of economics because:
   a. economics is not really about scarcity.
   b. scarcity involves coercion, and the author doesn't like coercion.
   c. the author wants to emphasize that the quantity of goods and services depends upon human action and the ability to coordinate that human action.
   d. the concept "scarcity" does not fit within the institutional structure of the economy.

4. In the U.S. economy, who is in charge of organizing and coordinating overall economic activities?
   a. Government.
   b. Corporations.
   c. No one.
   d. Consumers.

5. You bought stock A for $10 and stock B for $50. The price of each is currently $20. Assuming no tax issues, which should you sell if you need money?
   a. Stock A.
   b. Stock B.
   c. The price at which you bought it doesn't matter.
   d. You should sell an equal amount of both.

6. In deciding whether to go to lectures in the final weeks the semester, you should:
   a. include tuition as part of the cost of that decision.
   b. not include tuition as part of the cost of that decision.
   c. include a portion of tuition as part of the cost of that decision.
   d. only include tuition if you paid it rather than your parents.

7. In making economic decisions you should consider:
   a. marginal costs and marginal benefits.
   b. marginal costs and average benefits.
   c. average costs and average benefits.
   d. total costs and total benefits, including past costs and benefits.

8. According to the economic decision rule, if MB>MC, one should:
   a. do less.
   b. do more.
   c. do nothing
   d. exit the market.

9. In arriving at a decision, a good economist would say that:
   a. one should consider only total costs and total benefits.
   b. one should consider only marginal costs and marginal benefits.

c. after one has considered marginal costs and benefits, one should integrate the social and moral implications and reconsider those costs and benefits.

d. after considering the marginal costs and benefits, one should make the decision on social and moral grounds.

10. In making decisions economists primarily use:
    a. monetary costs.
    b. opportunity costs.
    c. benefit costs.
    d. dollar costs.

11. The opportunity cost of reading Chapter 1 of a 34-chapter text:
    a. is about 1/34 of the price you paid for the book because the chapter is about 1/34 of the book.
    b. is zero since you have already paid for the book.
    c. has nothing to do with the price you paid for the book.
    d. is 1/34 the price of the book plus 1/34 the price of tuition for the course.

12. Rationing devices that our society uses include:
    a. the invisible hand only.
    b. the invisible hand and social forces only.
    c. the invisible hand and political forces only.
    d. the invisible hand, the social forces, and political forces.

13. If at Female College there are significantly more females than males (and there are not a significant number of gays or off-campus dating opportunities), economic forces:
    a. will likely be pushing for females to pay on dates.
    b. will likely be pushing for males to pay on dates.
    c. will likely be pushing for neither to pay on dates.
    d. are irrelevant to this issue. Everyone knows that the males always should pay.

14. Individuals are prohibited from practicing medicine without a license. The legal prohibition is an example of:
    a. the invisible hand.
    b. social forces.
    c. political forces.
    d. market forces.

15. Which of the following is most likely an example of a microeconomic topic?
    a. The effect of a flood in the Midwest on the price of bottled water.
    b. How a government policy will affect inflation.
    c. The relationship between unemployment and inflation.
    d. Why an economy goes into a recession.

16. Which of the following is most strongly an example of a macroeconomic topic?
    a. The effect of a frost on the Florida orange crop.
    b. Wages of cross-country truckers.
    c. How the unemployment and inflation rates are related.
    d. How income is distributed in the United States.

17. The statement, "The distribution of income should be left to the market," is:
    a. a positive statement.
    b. a normative statement.
    c. an art-of-economics statement.
    d. an objective statement.

18. "Given certain conditions, the market achieves efficient results" is an example of:
    a. a positive statement.
    b. a normative statement.
    c. an art-of-economics statement.
    d. a subjective statement.

● POTENTIAL ESSAY QUESTIONS

You may also see essay questions similar to the "Problems & Applications" and "A Brain Teaser" exercises.

1. Respond to the following statement: "Theories are of no use to me because they are not very practical. All I need are the facts because they speak for themselves."

2. The United States is one of the wealthiest nations on earth, yet our fundamental economic problem is scarcity. How can this be?

3. Does economics help teach us how to approach problems, or does it give us a set of answers to problems?

ANSWERS

SHORT-ANSWER QUESTIONS

1. The three central problems that every economy must solve are (1) what and how much to produce, (2) how to produce it, and (3) for whom to produce it. (5)

2. Scarcity occurs when there are not enough goods available to satisfy individuals' desires. Scarcity has two elements, our wants and our means of fulfilling those wants. Since each of these two elements can change, relative scarcity can also change. If we can reduce our wants, relative scarcity will be reduced. Likewise if we can increase our efforts to produce more goods or if technological changes allow people to produce more using the same resources, relative scarcity will be reduced. (5)

3. If the marginal benefits of doing something exceed the marginal costs, do it. If the marginal costs of doing something exceed the marginal benefits, don't do it. (7)

4. Opportunity cost is the benefit forgone by undertaking an activity. Indeed, it is the benefit forgone of the next best alternative to the activity you have chosen. Otherwise stated, it is what must be given up in order to get something else. (8-9)

5. Opportunity cost is the basis of cost/benefit economic reasoning. It takes into account benefits of all other options, and converts these alternative benefits into costs of the decision you're now making. In economic reasoning, opportunity cost will be less than the benefit of what you have chosen. (8-9)

6. An economic force is the necessary reaction to scarcity. All scarce goods must be rationed in some way. If an economic force is allowed to work through the market, that economic force becomes a market force. The invisible hand is the price mechanism, the rise and fall of prices that affects our incentives and guides our actions in a market. Social and political forces can keep economic forces from becoming market forces. (9-11)

7. Microeconomics is the study of how individual choice is influenced by economic forces. Microeconomics focuses on a particular segment of the economy, like how a specific market price and quantity sold is determined. Macroeconomics is the study of the economy as a whole. It considers the problems of inflation, unemployment, business cycles, and growth. (14)

8. Positive economics is the study of what is and how the economy works. Normative economics is the study of what the goals of the economy should be. The art of economics is the application of the knowledge learned in positive economics to the achievement of the goals determined in normative economics. (16)

ANSWERS

MATCHING

1-l; 2-c; 3-e; 4-o; 5-r; 6-p; 7-j; 8-q; 9-n; 10-h; 11-i; 12-a; 13-b; 14-m; 15-d; 16-s; 17-f; 18-g; 19-k; 20-t.

ANSWERS

PROBLEMS AND APPLICATIONS

1. a. Scarcity will fall because fewer peaches will rot. (5)
   b. Scarcity of single-sex dorm rooms will rise since the number of students desiring single-sex dorm rooms has risen, but the number available has not. (5)

2. a. The opportunity cost of going out on a date tonight that was scheduled last Wednesday is the benefit forgone of the best alternative. If my best alternative was to study for an economics exam, it would be the increase in my exam grade that I would have otherwise gotten had I studied. Many answers are possible. (8-9)
   b. The opportunity cost of breaking the date for tonight that I made last Wednesday is the benefit forgone of going out on that date. It would be all the fun I would have had on that date. Other answers are possible. (8-9)

c. The opportunity cost of working through this study guide is the benefit forgone of the next-best alternative to studying. It could be the increase in the grade I would have received by studying for another exam, or the money I could have earned if I were working at the library. Many answers are possible. (8-9)

d. The opportunity cost of buying this study guide is the benefit forgone of spending that money on the next-best alternative. Perhaps it is the enjoyment forgone of eating two pizzas. Other answers are possible. (8-9)

3. a. The sunk cost of purchasing the maintenance contract is the $15,000 cost of the car because it is a cost that has already been incurred and cannot be recovered. Sunk costs should always be ignored when making a current decision because only marginal costs are relevant to the current decision. (6)

b. The opportunity cost of purchasing the maintenance contract is the benefit I could receive by spending that $750 on something else, such as a moon roof. (8-9)

c. I would need to know the benefit of the maintenance contract to assess whether the cost of $750 is worthwhile. (6-7)

d. For me the benefit of the maintenance contract is the expected cost of future repairs that would be covered and the peace of mind of knowing that future repairs are covered by the contract. The cost is the opportunity cost of using the $750 in another way. Notice that the cost of a decision includes opportunity costs only; it does not include count sunk costs because they are not relevant. If the benefit exceeds the cost, do it. If the cost exceeds the benefit, do not do it. (6-7)

4. a. This is an example of an economic force. (9)

b. This is an example of political forces. Some states have laws, called blue laws, against selling liquor on Sundays altogether or selling it before noon. (9-11)

c. This is an example of a political force. This is a federal law. (9-11)

d. This is an example of a social force. (9-11)

ANSWERS

A BRAIN TEASER

1. The most economical (profit-maximizing) quantity of frames to produce is 4 frames. This is because the marginal benefit of producing frames (the revenue per unit equal to the price per unit of $250) exceeds the marginal (extra) cost of producing frames through the first 4 frames produced. The 5th frame should not be produced because the marginal benefit (the price received) is less than the marginal (extra) cost of production. You would be adding more to your costs than to your revenues and thereby reducing your profits. Your profit would total $700 per week if you produce 4 frames. (6-7)

(Q)	Price = Marginal Benefit	Total Cost (TC)	Marginal Cost	Total Revenue (TR=PQ)	Profit TR−TC
0	$250	$0	—	$0	$0
1	$250	$25	$25	$250	$225
2	$250	$75	$50	$500	$425
3	$250	$150	$75	$750	$600
4	$250	$300	$150	$1000	$700
5	$250	$560	$260	$1250	$690

ANSWERS

MULTIPLE CHOICE

1. **a** As discussed on pages 5 and 6, the textbook author clearly believes that economic reasoning applies to just about everything. This eliminates c and d. He also carefully points out that it is not the only reasoning that can be used; hence b does not fit. So the correct answer must be a.

2. **b** On page 5 of the textbook, the author states that the problem of scarcity depends upon our wants and our means of fulfilling those wants. An implication of this is that scarcity could be reduced if individuals worked more and wanted less.

3. **c** On page 5 of the textbook the author emphasizes the human action reason for focusing on coordination. He explicitly points out that scarcity is important, but that the concept of coordination is broader.

4. c   As discussed on page 9, the invisible hand of the market coordinates the activities and is a composite of many individuals rather than just any one individual. If you were tempted to say b, corporations, your instincts are right, but the "overall" eliminated that as a possible answer.

5. c   As is discussed on page 6 of the book, in making economic decisions you consider that only costs from this point on are relevant; historical costs are sunk costs and therefore have no relevance. Since the prices of the stocks are currently the same, it doesn't matter which you sell.

6. b   As discussed on page 6, in economic decisions, you only look at costs from this point on; sunk costs are sunk costs, so tuition can be forgotten. Economic decisions focus on forward-looking marginal costs and marginal benefits.

7. a   The economic decision rule is "If marginal benefits exceed marginal costs, do it." As is discussed on pages 6 and 7 of the text, the relevant benefits and relevant costs to be considered are *marginal* (additional) costs and *marginal* benefits. The answer d is definitely ruled out by the qualifying phrase referring to past benefits and costs. Thus, only a is correct.

8. b   The economic decision rule is "If marginal benefits exceed marginal costs, do it." See page 7 of the text.

9. c   As the textbook points out on page 6, economists use a framework of costs and benefits initially, but then later they add the social and moral implications to their conclusions. Adding these can change the estimates of costs and benefits, and in doing so can change the result of economic analysis, so there is an integration between the two. (This was a hard question that required careful reading of the text to answer correctly.)

10. b   As discussed on page 8 of the text, opportunity costs include measures of nonmonetary costs. The other answers either do not include all the costs that an economist would consider, or are simply two words put together. The opportunity costs include the benefit forgone by undertaking an activity and should always be included in measuring marginal costs.

11. c   As discussed on pages 6 and 8-9, the correct answer is that it has nothing to do with the price you paid since that is a sunk cost that has already been paid, so a and d are wrong. The opportunity cost is not zero, however, since there are costs of reading the book. The primary opportunity cost of reading the book is the value of the time you're spending on it, which is determined by what you could be doing with that time otherwise.

12. d   As discussed on page 9 of the text, all of these are rationing devices. The invisible hand works through the market and thus is focused on in economics. However, the others also play a role in determining what people want, either through legal means or through social control.

13. a   As discussed on page 10 of the text, if there are significantly more of one gender than another, dates with that group must be rationed out among the other group. Economic forces will be pushing for the group in excess quantity supplied (in this case women) to pay. Economic forces may be pushing in that direction even though historical forces may push us in the opposite direction. Thus, even if males pay because of social forces, economic forces will be pushing for females to pay.

14. c   As discussed on pages 10 and 11, laws are political forces.

15. a   As discussed on page 14, macroeconomics is concerned with inflation, unemployment, business cycles and growth. Microeconomics is the study of individuals and individual markets.

16. c   As discussed on page 14, macroeconomics is concerned with inflation, unemployment, business cycles, and growth. Microeconomics is the study of individuals and individual markets. The distribution of income is a micro topic because it is concerned with the distribution of income among individuals.

17. b   As discussed on pages 16 and 17, this could be either a normative or an art-of-economics statement, depending on whether there is an explicit "given the way the real-world economy operates." This qualifier is not there, so "normative" is the preferable answer. After all, normative economics deals with what *should* be.

18. a   As discussed on page 16 this is a positive statement. It is a statement about *what is,* not about what should be.

ANSWERS

POTENTIAL ESSAY QUESTIONS

The following are annotated answers. They indicate the general idea behind the answer.

1.   Theories are practical because they are generalizations based on real-world observations or facts. They enable us to predict and to explain real-world economic behavior. Because they are generalizations, they enable us to avoid unnecessary details or facts. The drawback, however, is that because they are generalizations, at times there will be exceptions to the prediction we would generally expect to observe.

  Facts, on the other hand, do not always speak for themselves. One can often be overwhelmed by a large set of data or facts. Not until one systematically arranges, interprets, and generalizes upon facts, tying them together, and distilling out a theory (general statement) related to those facts, do they take on any real meaning. In short, theory and facts are inseparable in the scientific process because theory gives meaning to facts and facts check the validity of theory.

2.   The United States is still faced with scarcity because we are unable to have as much as we would like to have. Our resources (as vast as they are) are still scarce relative to the amount of goods and services we would like to have (indeed, our wants appear to be unlimited).

3.   Economics is a methodology, or an approach to how we think about the world. It does not come to us equipped with a whole set of solutions to complex real-world problems. However, it may help shed some light on the complexities of real-world issues and thus help us to find solutions.

THE PRODUCTION POSSIBILITY MODEL, TRADE, AND GLOBALIZATION

CHAPTER AT A GLANCE

This review is based upon the learning objectives that open the chapter.

1. The production possibilities curve shows the trade-off (or opportunity cost) between two things. (23-26)

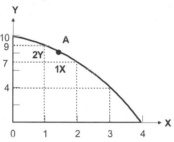

The slope tells you the opportunity cost of good X in terms of good Y. In this particular graph you have to give up 2 Y to get 1 X when you're around point A.

2. The principle of increasing marginal opportunity cost states that opportunity costs increase the more you concentrate on the activity. In order to get more of something, one must give up ever-increasing quantities of something else. (25-26)

The following production possibility curve and table demonstrate the principle of increasing marginal opportunity cost.

Production Possibility Curve

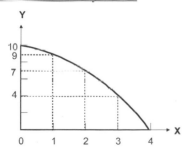

Production Possibility Table

X	Y	Opportunity cost of X (amount of Y which must be forgone)
0	10	
		1
1	9	
		2
2	7	
		3
3	4	
		4
4	0	

Note: As you get more of X you have to give up larger amounts of Y.

3. In general, the production possibility curve is bowed outward, meaning that in order to get more and more of something, we must give up ever-increasing quantities of something else. The outward bow of the production possibility curve is the result of comparative advantage. (26-27)

Some resources are better suited for the production of certain goods than they are for the production of other goods. The outward bow of the production possibility curve reflects that when more and more of a good is produced, we must use resources whose comparative advantage is in the production of the other good.

4. Countries can consume more if they specialize in those goods for which they have a comparative advantage and trade. (30-34)

Country A can produce 30Y or 10X, or any combination thereof, while Country B can produce 20Y or 30X or any combination thereof. Since country A has a comparative advantage in Y, it should produce 30Y and Country B should produce 30X. If they divide the goods equally, each can consume 15 units of each good, or point C in the graph on the next page. Each can consume beyond its individual production possibilities.

Constructing a production possibility curve that shows the combination of goods these two countries can produce together is useful. You can draw this curve by connecting three points: if both produce good X, if both produce good Y, and if each specializes in the good in which it has a comparative advantage. This is done below.

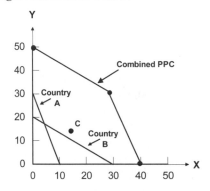

5. Globalization and outsourcing is a response to the forces of the law of one price. (35-37)

    The law of one price states that wages of workers in one country will equal the wages of equal workers in countries with similar institutions. If wages differ sufficiently, companies will relocate jobs to a low-wage country until parity is reestablished.

    Remember: all jobs cannot be outsourced. Every country has, by definition, a comparative advantage in the production of some good if the other country has a comparative advantage in the production of another good.

    See also, Appendix A: "Graphish: The Language of Graphs."

SHORT-ANSWER QUESTIONS

1. Design a grade production possibility curve for studying economics and English, and show how it demonstrates the concept of opportunity cost.

2. State the principle of increasing marginal opportunity cost.

3. What would the production possibility curve look like if opportunity cost were constant?

4. What happens to the production possibility curve when people specialize and trade? Why do specialization and trade make individuals better off?

5. What is the positive effect of globalization for firms? What is the negative effect?

6. State the law of one price. How is it related to globalization and outsourcing?

MATCHING THE TERMS
Match the terms to their definitions

___ 1. comparative advantage

___ 2. globalization

___ 3. laissez-faire

___ 4. law of one price

___ 5. outsourcing

___ 6. principle of increasing marginal opportunity cost

___ 7. productive efficiency

___ 8. production possibility curve

___ 9. production possibility table

a. A curve measuring the maximum combination of outputs that can be obtained from a given number of inputs.

b. Achieving as much output as possible from a given amount of inputs or resources.

c. An economic policy of leaving coordination of individuals' actions to the market.

d. In order to get more of something, one must give up ever-increasing quantities of something else.

e. Table that lists a choice's opportunity cost by summarizing alternative outputs that can be achieved with your inputs.

f. The advantage that attaches to a resource when that resource is better suited to the production of one good than to the production of another good.

g. The relocation to foreign countries of production once done in the United States.

h. Wages of (equal) workers in one country will not differ significantly from wages in another institutionally similar country.

i. The increasing integration of economies, cultures, and institutions across the world.

PROBLEMS AND APPLICATIONS

1. Suppose a restaurant has the following production possibility table:

Resources devoted to pizza in % of total	Output of pizza in pies per week	Resources devoted to spaghetti in % of total	Output of spaghetti in bowls per week
100	50	0	0
80	40	20	10
60	30	40	17
40	20	60	22
20	10	80	25
0	0	100	27

a. Plot the restaurant's production possibility curve. Put output of pizza in pies on the horizontal axis.

b. What happens to the opportunity cost of making spaghetti as the number of bowls of spaghetti made increases?

c.   What would happen to the production possibility curve if the restaurant found a way to toss and cook pizzas faster?

d.   What would happen to the production possibility curve if the restaurant bought new stoves and ovens that cooked both pizzas and spaghetti faster?

2.   Suppose Ecoland has the following production possibility table:

% resources devoted to production of guns	Number of guns	% resources devoted to production of butter	Pounds of butter
100	50	0	0
80	40	20	5
60	30	40	10
40	20	60	15
20	10	80	20
0	0	100	25

a.   Plot the production possibility curve for the production of guns and butter. Put the number of guns on the horizontal axis.

b.   What is the per unit opportunity cost of increasing the production of guns from 20 to 30? From 40 to 50?

c.   What happens to the opportunity cost of producing guns as the production of guns increases?

d.   What is the per unit opportunity cost of increasing the production of butter from 10 to 15? From 20 to 25?

e.   What happens to the opportunity cost of producing butter as the production of butter increases?

f.   Given this production possibility curve, is producing 26 guns and 13 pounds of butter possible?

g.   Is producing 34 guns and 7 pounds of butter possible? Is it efficient?

3. Using the following production possibility tables and using production possibility curves, show how the United States and Japan would be better off specializing in the production of either food or machinery and then trading rather than producing both food and machinery themselves and not trading.

United States Production per year		Japan Production per year	
Food (tons)	Machinery (1000 units)	Food (tons)	Machinery (1000 units)
10	0	12.5	0
8	5	10.0	1
6	10	7.5	2
4	15	5.0	3
2	20	2.5	4
0	25	0.0	5

4. Assume that France can produce wine for 25 euros per bottle and can produce butter for 5 euros per pound. Assume that Italy can produce wine for 16,000 euros per bottle and butter for 10,000 euros per pound.

   a. In terms of pounds of butter, what is the opportunity cost of producing wine in each country?

   b. Who has the comparative advantage in producing butter?

   c. To obtain the greatest combined production possibilities, which country should specialize in wine and which should specialize in butter?

d. What is likely to happen to each country's consumption possibilities if each specializes in the good for which it has a comparative advantage and then trades?

● A BRAIN TEASER

1. Consider the production possibilities for an entire nation. Within any national economy there are only two general kinds of products that can be produced–consumer products and capital products. Consumer products (e.g., food, clothes, medical services, etc.) satisfy our wants directly when we use them and while we consume them. Capital products (e.g., machines and other plant and equipment) satisfy our wants indirectly and in the future because they increase our productivity and help us produce even more products over time. Answer the following questions based on the production possibilities of consumer and capital products for a national economy shown in the following graph.

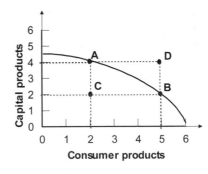

   a. Does production possibility A or B provide the greatest amount of current consumption? Why?

   b. What is the opportunity cost of moving from point B to point A?

c.   Consider the choice of currently producing a
     relatively large amount of consumer products
     shown at point B (which means, given limited
     resources, relatively few capital products can
     be produced), compared to producing a
     relatively large amount of capital products
     now, shown at point A (which means relatively
     few consumer products can be produced).
     Which of these two points (or combinations of
     consumer and capital goods production) do
     you think will increase the production possi-
     bilities (shift the curve to the right) the most
     over time, giving rise to the greatest rate of
     economic growth? Why? *(Hint: Whenever
     workers have more capital, such as factories
     and machinery, to work with, they become
     more productive.)*

● MULTIPLE CHOICE

Circle the one best answer for each of the following questions:

1.   If the opportunity cost of good X in terms of
     good Y is 2Y, so you'll have to give up 2Y to
     get one X, the production possibility curve
     would look like:
     a. a.
     b. b.
     c. c.
     d. a, b and c.

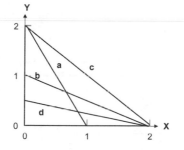

2.   If the opportunity cost of good X in terms of
     good Y is 2Y, so you'll have to give up 2Y to
     get one X, the production possibility curve
     would look like:
     a. a.
     b. b.
     c. c.
     d. d.

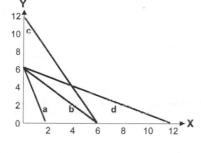

3.   If the opportunity cost of good X in terms of
     good Y is 2Y, so you'll have to give up 2Y to
     get one X, the production possibility curve
     could look like:
     a. A only.
     b. B only.
     c. C only.
     d. A, B, or C.

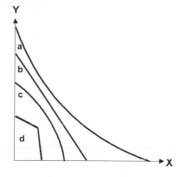

4.   If the opportunity cost is constant for all
     combinations, the production possibility
     curve will look like:
     a. a.
     b. b.
     c. c.
     d. d.

5.   If the principle of increasing marginal opportu-
     nity cost applies at all points, using the
     graph for question 4, the production
     possibility curve looks like:
     a. a.
     b. b.
     c. c.
     d. d.

6.   Given the accompanying production possibil-
     ity curve, when you're moving from point C
     to point B the opportunity cost of butter in
     terms of guns is:
     a. 1/3.
     b. 1.
     c. 2.
     d. 3/2.

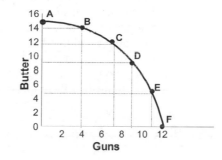

7. In the graph for question 6, in the range of points between A and B there is:
   a. a high opportunity cost of guns in terms of butter.
   b. a low opportunity cost of guns in terms of butter.
   c. no opportunity cost of guns in terms of butter.
   d. a high monetary cost of guns in terms of butter.

8. In the accompanying production possibility diagram, point A would be:

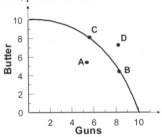

   a. an efficient point.
   b. a superefficient point.
   c. an inefficient point.
   d. a non-attainable point.

9. The efficiency of producing computers is increasing each year. Which of the four arrows would demonstrate the appropriate shifting of the production possibility curve?

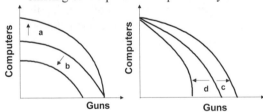

   a. a.
   b. b.
   c. c.
   d. d.

10. Say that methods of production are tied to particular income distributions, so that choosing one method will help some people but hurt others and that the society's income distribution is one of its goals. Say also that method A produces significantly more total output than method B. In this case:

   a. method A is more efficient than method B.
   b. method B is more efficient than method A.
   c. if method A produces more and gives more to the poor people, method A is more efficient.
   d. one can't say whether A or B is more efficient.

11. If the United States and Japan have production possibility curves as shown in the diagram below, at what point would their consumption possibilities most likely be after trade?
   a. A.
   b. B.
   c. C.
   d. D.

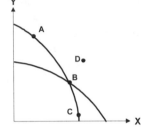

12. If countries A and B have production possibility curves A and B respectively, country A has a comparative advantage in the production of:
   a. no good.
   b. both goods.
   c. good X only.
   d. good Y only.

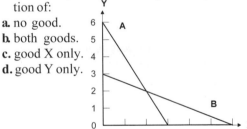

13. If countries X and Y have production possibility curves I and II respectively, which curve represents their combined production possibilities if they specialize and trade?
   a. I
   b. II
   c. III
   d. IV

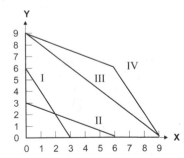

14. Suppose country A can produce either 100 cars or 50 tractors, or any combination thereof, while country B can produce either 200 cars or 50 tractors, or any combination thereof, and both countries consume both goods. Which of the following combination of goods can be produced only if the countries specialize and trade:
    a. 300 cars, 0 tractors.
    b. 0 cars, 100 tractors.
    c. 200 cars, 50 tractors.
    d. 300 cars, 100 tractors.

15. When trade is allowed between two countries, the slope of the combined production possibility curve is determined by the country with the:
    a. highest output.
    b. lowest output.
    c. highest opportunity cost.
    d. lowest opportunity cost.

16. Outsourcing in the United States is evidence that:
    a. the United States does not have any comparative advantages.
    b. the U.S. dollar is valued too low.
    c. the law of one price doesn't hold.
    d. the law of one price is affecting global production.

17. Globablization:
    a. is decreasing in importance.
    b. increases competition.
    c. reduces the need to specialize.
    d. reduces productivity.

18. According to the law of one price:
    a. wages will eventually be the same for every industry.
    b. wages will eventually be the same in every country.
    c. wage differences cannot continue unless they reflect differences in productivity.
    d. wage differences can continue as long as product prices can differ among countries.

19. Assuming productivity differentials diminish, the law of one price will likely result in:
    a. a decline in nominal U.S. wages.
    b. a rise in nominal U.S. wages.
    c. a decline in the value of the U.S. dollar.
    d. a rise in the value of the U.S. dollar.

20. Because of international competition and the ease with which technology is transferable among many nations with similar institutional structures, we can expect the wages for workers with similar skills to:
    a. increase in developing countries faster than they increase in developed nations.
    b. decrease in developing countries while they increase in developed nations.
    c. increase in developing countries while they decrease in developed nations.
    d. decrease in both developed and developing countries.

A1. In the graph below, point A represents:

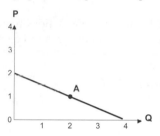

    a. a price of 1 and a quantity of 2.
    b. a price of 2 and a quantity of 2.
    c. a price of 2 and a quantity of 1.
    d. a price of 1 and a quantity of 1.

A2. The slope of the line in the graph below is
    a. 1/2.
    b. 2.
    c. minus 1/2.
    d. minus 2.

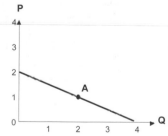

A3. At the maximum and minimum points of a nonlinear curve, the value of the slope is equal to
    a. 1.
    b. zero.
    c. minus 1.
    d. indeterminate.

A4. Which of the four lines in the graphs below has the largest slope?

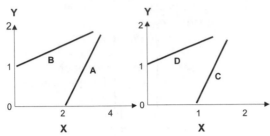

   a. A.
   b. B.
   c. C.
   d. A and C.

A5. Which of the following equations represents the line depicted in the graph to question A2?
   a. $P = 2 - .5Q$.
   b. $P = 2 - 2Q$.
   c. $Q = 4 - 2P$.
   d. $Q = 2 - .5P$.

A6. Suppose the demand curve is represented by $P = -2Q + 8$. Which of the following equations represents a *shift to the right* in that demand curve, with no change in slope?
   a. $P = -Q + 8$.
   b. $P = -2Q + 10$.
   c. $P = -2Q + 6$.
   d. $P = -4Q + 8$.

● POTENTIAL ESSAY QUESTIONS

You may also see essay questions similar to the "Problems & Applications" and "A Brain Teaser" exercises.

1.   What did Adam Smith mean when he said, "It is not from the benevolence of the butcher, the brewer, or the baker, that we expect our dinner, but from their regard to their own interest" (*Wealth of Nations*, Book 1, Chapter 2)? How does this quotation relate to specialization?

2.   Your study partner tells you that because wages are higher in the United States than in many other countries, eventually all U.S. jobs will be outsourced. How do you respond?

ANSWERS

SHORT-ANSWER QUESTIONS

1. The production possibility curve below shows the highest combination of grades you can get with 20 hours of studying economics and English. The grade received in economics is on the vertical axis and the grade received in English is on the horizontal axis. The graph tells us the opportunity cost of spending any combination of 20 hours on economics and English. For example, the opportunity cost of increasing your grade in economics by 6 points is decreasing your English grade by 4 points (a 2/3-point reduction in English grade for each one-point improvement in economics grade). (24-26)

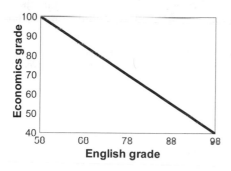

2. The principle of increasing marginal opportunity cost states that in order to get more of something, one must give up ever-increasing quantities of something else. (25-26)

3. Such a production possibility curve would be a straight line connecting the maximum number of units of each product that could be produced if all inputs were devoted to one or the other good. (24-25)

4. The production possibility curve shifts out with trade. By concentrating on those activities for which one has a comparative advantage and trading those goods for goods for which others have a comparative advantage, individuals can end up with a combination of goods to consume that would not be attainable without trade. (30-34)

5. The rewards for winning in a global market are bigger because the market is larger. The negative effect is that the firm faces more competitors, some of which may have lower costs. (35-37)

6. The law of one price is that wages of workers in one country will not differ significantly from the wages of equal workers in another institutionally similar country. Globalization means that firms will seek low-cost areas for production throughout the world. Outsourcing is the result of differing wages among countries. As the high-wage country outsources jobs to lower-wage countries, wages will tend to equalize. So, outsourcing is the result of the law of one price in action. (39)

ANSWERS

MATCHING

1-f; 2-i; 3-c; 4-h; 5-g; 6-d; 7-b; 8-a; 9-e.

ANSWERS

PROBLEMS AND APPLICATIONS

1. a. The restaurant's production possibility curve is shown below. (23-26)

   b. The opportunity cost of spaghetti increases because the number of pizza pies that must be given up to make an additional bowl of spaghetti increases as the number of bowls of spaghetti produced increases. (25-26)

   c. If the restaurant found a way to toss and cook pizzas faster, the production possibility curve would rotate out along the pizza axis as shown below. (27-29)

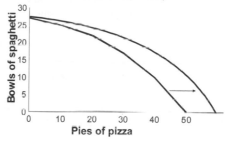

d. The production possibility curve would shift out to the right as shown in the figure below. (27-29)

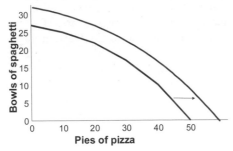

2. a. The production possibility curve is a straight line as shown below. (26-29)

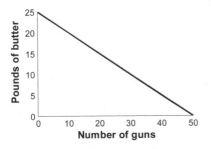

b. The opportunity cost of increasing the production of guns from 20 to 30 is 0.5 pounds of butter per gun. The opportunity cost of increasing the production of guns from 40 to 50 is also 0.5 pounds of butter per gun. (24-26)

c. The opportunity cost of producing guns stays the same as the production of guns increases. (24-26)

d. The opportunity cost of increasing the production of butter from 10 to 15 is 2 guns per pound of butter. The opportunity cost of increasing the production of butter from 20 to 25 is also 2 guns per pound of butter. (24-26)

e. The opportunity cost of producing butter stays the same as the production of butter increases. (24-26)

f. Producing 26 guns and 13 lbs of butter is not attainable given this production possibility curve. We can produce 20 guns and 15 lbs of butter. To produce six more guns, Ecoland must give up 3 lbs of butter. Ecoland can produce only 26 guns and 12 lbs of butter. (24-26)

g. Ecoland can produce 34 guns and 7 pounds of butter. To see this, begin at 30 guns and 10 pounds of butter. To produce 4 more guns, 2 pounds of butter must be given up. Ecoland can produce 34 guns and 8 pounds of butter, which is more than 34 guns and 7 pounds of butter. 34 guns and 7 pounds of butter is an inefficient point of production. (25-29)

3. The production possibility of producing food and machinery for both Japan and the United States is shown in the graph below. The United States has a comparative advantage in the production of machinery. It must give up only 0.4 tons of food for each additional thousand units of machinery produced. Japan must give up 2.5 tons of food for each additional thousand units of machinery produced. If they specialize and trade, they could attain the combined production possibility curve shown below.

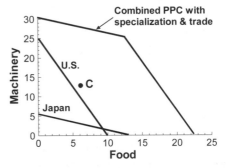

To draw the combined production possibility curve, connect these three points: (1) a point along the food axis when both produce food (22.5 units), (2) a point along the machinery axis when both produce machines (30 units), (3) a point where each produces only that good for which it has a comparative advantage (food = 12.5, machinery = 25). If each country specializes in their comparative advantage and equally divides that production they will each consume 6.25 units of food and 12.5 units of machinery (point C in the graph)—more than either could have consumed if they produced just for themselves. (30-34)

4. a. In France, the opportunity cost of producing wine is 5 pounds of butter. In Italy, the opportunity cost of producing wine is 1.6 pounds of butter. Calculate this by finding how much butter must be forgone for each bottle of wine in each country. (24-26)

b. France has the comparative advantage in producing butter because it can produce butter at a lower opportunity cost. (26-27)

c. To obtain the greatest combined production possibilities Italy should specialize in producing only wine and France should specialize in producing only butter. (30-34)

d. Each country's consumption possibilities increase. (32-34)

ANSWERS

A BRAIN TEASER

1. a. Production possibility B. Why? Because consumer products provide for *current* satisfaction, and at B we are getting a relatively larger amount of consumer products. (24-29)

b. 3 units of consumer products. (24-29)

c. Point A. Producing a relatively larger amount of capital products now means workers will have more plant and equipment to work with in the future. This will increase workers' productivity and the nation's production possibilities over time. Producing more capital is an ingredient for economic growth (greater production possibilities over time). (24-29)

ANSWERS

MULTIPLE CHOICE

1. a As discussed on pages 24-26, the production possibility curve tells how much of one good you must give up to get more of the other good; here you must give up 2Y to get one X, making a the correct answer.

2. c As discussed on pages 24-26, the production possibility curve tells how much of one good you must give up to get more of another good. Opportunity cost is a ratio; it determines the slope, not the position, of the production possibility curve. Thus, the correct answer is c because the 12 to 6 trade-off reduces to a 2 to 1 trade-off.

3. d As discussed on pages 24-26, the production possibility curve tells how much of one good you must give up to get more of

the other good. Opportunity cost is a ratio; it determines the slope, not the position, of the PPC curve. Since all have the same correct slope, all three are correct, so d is the right answer.

4. b As discussed in the "Reminder" box on page 27 of the book, if the opportunity costs are constant, the PPC is a straight line, so b must be the answer.

5. c As discussed on pages 25-26 of the book, with increasing marginal opportunity costs, as you produce more and more of a good, you will have to give up more and more of the other good to do so. This means that the slope of the PPC must be bowed outward, so c is the correct answer. See Figure 2-2, page 26 for an in-depth discussion.

6. d As discussed on pages 25-26, the slope of the PPC measures the trade-off of one good for the other. Since moving from point C to B means giving up 3 guns for 2 pounds of butter, the correct answer is 3/2 (d).

7. b As discussed on page 27, the flatter the slope, the higher the opportunity cost of the good measured on the vertical axis; alternatively, the flatter the slope the lower the opportunity cost of the good measured on the horizontal axis. In the AB range the slope is flat so guns have a low opportunity cost in terms of butter; one need give up only one pound of butter to get four guns.

8. c As discussed on page 29 (See Figure 2-3), point A is an inefficient point because it is inside the PPC.

9. a As discussed on page 29 (See Figure 2-3), technological change that improves the efficiency of producing a good shifts the PPC out for that good, but not for the other good. So a is the correct answer.

10. d The answer is "You can't say," as discussed on page 29. The term "efficiency" involves *achieving a goal as cheaply as possible.* Without specifying one's goal, one cannot say what method is more efficient. The concept of efficiency generally presumes that the goal includes preferring more to less, so if any method is more productive, it will be method A. But because there are distributional effects that involve making additional judgments, the correct answer is d. Some students may have been tempted to choose c because their goals involve more equity, but that is their particular judgment, and not all people may agree. Thus c would be incorrect, leaving d as the correct answer.

11. d   As discussed in Figure 2-7 on page 33, with trade, both countries can attain consumption possibilities outside their production possibility curves. The only point not already attainable by either country is D.

12. d   Country A must give up 2Y to produce an additional X while Country B must give up only 1/2 Y to produce an additional X. Therefore, Country A has a comparative advantage in good Y and Country B has a comparative advantage in good X. See pages 26- 27.

13. d   To construct the combined production possibilities with specialization and trade, sum the production if each country produced the same good (these are the axis intercepts). Connect these points with that point that represents the combination of goods if each country specialized in that good for which it has a comparative advantage. See pages 32-34, especially Figure 2-7 on page 33.

14. c   The greatest gains are when each country specializes in the good for which it has the lowest opportunity cost. If Country A specializes in tractors, producing 50 tractors, and Country B specializes in cars and produces 200 cars, production of 200 cars and 50 tractors is possible. The combination of 300 cars and 100 tractors is unattainable even with specialization and trade. The other combinations are possible without trade. See pages 32-34, especially Figure 2-7.

15. d   This is the principle of lowest cost rules. It is by producing where costs are lowest that countries can achieve gains from trade. See page 34.

16. d   The law of one price is that workers in one country are paid the same as equal workers in other countries with similar institutional structures. If this isn't true, the forces of this law will lead to outsourcing. The United States continues to have comparative advantages. The U.S. dollar is likely too high to equalize wages across nations. See pages 35-37.

17. b   Globalization is increasing in importance. It also increases specialization, productivity, and competition. See pages 35-37.

18. c   According to the law of one price wages of workers in one country will not differ substantially from <u>equal</u> workers in another country with similar institutions. That is, there will be pressure for equally productive workers to receive similar wages. See page 39 for a discussion of the law of one price.

19. c   The text suggests that it is unlikely that nominal wages will decline in the United States. It is more likely that the exchange value of the dollar will decline to offset wage differentials between the United States and other countries. See page 38.

20. a   According to the law of one price, wages of (equal) workers in one country will not differ significantly from the wages of workers in another institutionally similar country. It is unlikely that wages will fall, but if the law of one price holds then wages in developing countries will rise faster than wages in developed nations rise. See pages 37-39.

A1. a   As discussed in Appendix A, pages 44 and 45, a point represents the corresponding numbers on the horizontal and vertical number lines.

A2. c   As discussed on pages 46 of Appendix A, the slope of a line is defined as rise over run. Since the rise is −2 and the run is 4, the slope of the above line is minus 1/2.

A3. b   As discussed on page 47 of Appendix A, at the maximum and minimum points of a nonlinear curve the slope is zero.

A4. c   As discussed in Appendix A, pages 46 and 47, the slope is defined as rise over run. Line C has the largest rise for a given run so c is the answer. Even though, visually, line A seems to have the same slope as line C, it has a different coordinate system. Line A has a slope of 1 and line B has a slope of 1/4. Always be careful about checking coordinate systems when visually interpreting a graph.

A5. a To construct the equation, use the form $y = mx + b$ where m is the slope and b is the y-axis intercept. The y-axis intercept is 2 and the slope is -rise/run $= -2/4 = -.5$. Plugging in these values we get $y = -.5x + 2$. Since P is on the y-axis and Q is on the x axis, this can also be written as $P = 2 - .5Q$. See pages 48.

A6. b A change in the intercept represents a shift in the curve. A higher intercept is a shift to the right. See page 48.

POTENTIAL ESSAY QUESTIONS

The following are annotated answers. They indicate the general idea behind the answer.

1. Adam Smith was saying that it is not out of the kindness of producers that we are able to purchase what we want to consume, but the benefit that they will receive from selling their product. If each producer specializes in producing that good for which he receives the greatest benefit (produce at lowest cost) then the consumer will be able to consume the most goods at the lowest cost.

2. I would remind my study partner that the jobs that are being outsourced tend to be in the manufacturing industry. The U.S. does have a comparative advantage in creativity and innovation and jobs in industries such as advertising and marketing are being insourced to the United States. In addition, I would remind my partner that the very definition of comparative advantage means that if one country has a comparative advantage in one good, the other country has a comparative advantage in another good.

ECONOMIC INSTITUTIONS

● CHAPTER AT A GLANCE

This review is based upon the learning objectives that open the chapter.

1. A <u>market economy</u> is an economic system based on private property and the market. It gives private property rights to individuals, and relies on market forces to coordinate economic activity. (54)

   A market economy is characterized by:
   (I) mainly private ownership of resources
   (II) a market system that solves the What? How? and For whom? problems.

   A market economy's solutions to the central economic problems are:
   - *What to produce: what businesses believe people want, and what is profitable.*
   - *How to produce: businesses decide how to produce efficiently, guided by their desire to make a profit.*
   - *For whom to produce: distribution according to individuals' ability and/or inherited wealth.*

2. <u>Capitalism</u> is an economic system based on the market in which the ownership of the means of production resides with a small group of individuals called capitalists. (55)

   <u>Socialism</u> is, in theory, an economic system that tries to organize society in the same way that most families are organized—all people should contribute what they can, and get what they need. (55)

   A command, or centrally planned socialist economy's solutions to the three central economic problems are:
   - *What to produce: what central planners believe is socially beneficial.*
   - *How to produce: central planners decide, based on what they think is good for the country.*

   - *For whom to produce: central planners distribute goods based on what they determine are individuals' needs.*

   All economic systems are dynamic and evolve over time so the meaning of terms referring to economic systems is evolving. Ours has evolved from feudalism, mercantilism, and capitalism.

3. Businesses, households, and government interact in a market economy. (58)

   For a bird's-eye view of the U.S. economy, see Figure 3-1 (sometimes called the "circular flow of income model"). Be able to draw and explain it.

   Note: there are 3 basic economic institutions:
   - *Businesses:*
     a. Supply goods in a goods market.
     b. Demand factors in a factor market.
     c. Pay taxes and receive benefits from government.

   - *Households:*
     a. Supply factors.
     b. Demand goods.
     c. Pay taxes and receive benefits from government.

   - *Government:*
     a. Demands goods.
     b. Demands factors.
     c. Collects taxes and provides services.

   It will be important to remember who does the demanding and the supplying in goods and factor (resource) markets.

4. The advantages and disadvantages of the three forms of business are shown in a table on page 61.

✔ *Know the advantages and disadvantages of the three forms of business:*
- *Sole Proprietorship*
- *Partnership*
- *Corporation*

E-commerce is changing the nature of trade relationships among businesses and consumers.

5. Although, in principle, ultimate power resides with the people and households (consumer sovereignty), in practice the representatives of the people–firms and government–are sometimes removed from the people and, in the short run, are only indirectly monitored by the people. (60, 63-64)

Also note: Economics focuses on households' role as the suppliers of labor.

- *Do we control business and government, or do they control us?*
- *The distribution of income (rich vs. poor) determines the "for whom" question. If you're rich you get more.*
- *Social forces affect what business and government do or don't do.*

6. Six roles of government in a market economy are: (64-69)

- Provide a stable set of institutions and rules.
  The government specifies "the rules of the game."

- Promote effective and workable competition.

✔ *Know the different consequences associated with competition vs. monopoly power.*

- Correct for externalities.
  Government attempts to restrict the production and consumption of negative externalities, while promoting the production and consumption of positive externalities.

- Ensure economic stability and growth.
  Government tries to ensure: full employment, low inflation, economic growth (which increases the standard of living)

- Provide for public goods.
  Government provides public goods by collecting taxes from everyone to try to eliminate the free-rider problem.

- Adjust for undesired market results.
  Sometimes the market result is not what society wants. For example, an unequal distribution of income may be undesirable. Government can adjust for these failures, but when correcting for these failures, it may make matters even worse. These are called "government failures."

7. There is no central world government. Governments enter into voluntary agreements that perform the role of regulating international markets. (71)

Countries have developed international institutions to oversee global business as well as promote economic relations among countries. These include the UN, the World Bank, the WTO, and the IMF. Regional trade organizations such as the EU and NAFTA work to reduce trade barriers among member countries.

See also, Appendix A: "The History of Economic Systems."

● SHORT-ANSWER QUESTIONS

1. What is a market economy? How does it solve the three central economic problems?

2. What is socialism? In practice, how have socialist economies addressed the three central economic problems?

3. Draw a diagram of the U.S. economy showing the three groups that comprise the U.S. economy. What is the role of each group in the economy?

4. Your friend wants to buy a coin-operated laundromat. Her brother has offered to be a partner in the operation and put up half the money to buy the business. They have come to you for advice about what form of business to create. Of course you oblige, letting them know the three possibilities and the advantages and disadvantages of each.

5. What is consumer sovereignty? Why is much of the economic decision-making done by business and government even though households have the ultimate power?

6. Briefly distinguish between the two general roles of government.

7. What are the six roles of government?

8. Should government always intervene when markets fail?

9. Why are trade agreements important in the international market?

A1. Why did feudalism evolve into mercantilism?

A2. Why did mercantilism evolve into capitalism?

A3. Explain what is meant by the statement that capitalism has evolved into welfare capitalism.

MATCHING THE TERMS
Match the terms to their definitions

___ 1. consumer sovereignty		a.	A business with two or more owners.
___ 2. corporation		b.	Principle that the consumer's wishes rule what's produced.
___ 3. demerit good or activity		c.	Corporation with substantial operations on both production and sales in more than one country.
___ 4. c-commerce		d.	A business that has only one owner.
___ 5. entrepreneurship		e.	The stockholder's liability is limited to the amount that stockholder has invested in the company.
___ 6. externality		f.	Buying and selling over the Internet.
___ 7. free rider		g.	What's left over from total revenue after all appropriate costs have been subtracted.
___ 8. global corporation		h.	The ability to organize and get something done.
___ 9. government failure		i.	A business that is treated as a person, and is legally owned by its shareholders who are not liable for the actions of the corporate "person."
___ 10. institutions		j.	An economic system based on individuals' goodwill toward others, not on their own self-interest, in which society decides what, how, and for whom to produce.
___ 11. limited liability		k.	An economic system based on private property and the market, in which individuals decide how, what, and for whom to produce.
___ 12. market economy		l.	Certificate of ownership of a corporation.
___ 13. merit good or activity		m.	A good that if supplied to one person must be supplied to all and whose consumption by one individual does not prevent its consumption by another individual.
___ 14. partnership		n.	A good or activity that government believes is good for you even though you may not choose to engage in the activity or consume the good.
___ 15. profit		o.	A situation where the government intervenes and makes things worse.
___ 16. public good		p.	A person who participates in something for free because others have paid for it.
___ 17. socialism		q.	Good or activity that society believes is bad for people even though they choose to use the good or engage in the activity.
___ 18. sole proprietorship		r.	The effect of a decision on a third party not taken into account by the decision maker.
___ 19. stock		s.	The formal and informal rules that constrain human economic behavior.

● PROBLEMS AND APPLICATIONS

1. Fill in the blanks with the appropriate economic institution (households, businesses, or government).

   a. In the goods market, _____ and _____ buy goods and services from _____.

   b. In the goods market, _____ sell goods and services to _____ and _____.

   c. In the factor market, _____ and _____ buy (or employ) the resources owned by _____.

d. In the factor market, _____ supply labor and other factors of production to _____ and _____.

e. _____ redistributes income.

f. _____ provides services to the public with tax revenue.

2. For each of the following, state for which form or forms of business it is an advantage: Sole proprietorships, partnerships, corporations.

a. Minimum bureaucratic hassle.

b. Ability to share work and risks.

c. Direct control by owner.

d. Relatively easy (but not the easiest) to form.

e. Limited individual liability.

f. Greatest ability to get funds.

3. For each of the following, state for which form or forms of business it is a disadvantage: Sole proprietorships, partnerships, corporations.

a. Unlimited personal liability.

b. Possible double taxation of income.

c. Limited ability to get funds.

d. Legal hassle to organize.

4. State some of the benefits global corporations offer countries. What is one problem that global corporations pose for governments?

● A BRAIN TEASER

1. Why have some politicians who wish to significantly reduce federal government spending find it difficult to achieve that reduction in practice?

● MULTIPLE CHOICE

Circle the one best answer for each of the following questions:

1. For a market to exist, you have to have:
a. a capitalist economy.
b. private property rights.
c. no government intervention.
d. externalities.

2. In theory, socialism is an economic system:
a. that tries to organize society in the same ways as most families organize, striving to see that individuals get what they need.
b. based on central planning and government ownership of the means of production.
c. based on private property rights.
d. based on markets.

3. In practice, a command or socialist economy is an economic system:
a. that tries to organize society in the same ways as most families organize, striving to see that individuals get what they need.
b. based on central planning and government ownership of the means of production.
c. based on private property rights.
d. based on markets.

4. In a market economy, the "what to produce" decision in practice is most often made directly by:
a. consumers.
b. the market.
c. government.
d. firms.

5. In practice, in command or socialist economies, the "what to produce" decision is most often made by:
a. consumers.
b. the market.
c. government.
d. firms.

6. In the factor market:
   a. businesses supply goods and services to households and government.
   b. government provides income support to households unable to supply factors of production to businesses.
   c. households supply labor and other factors of production to businesses.
   d. households purchase goods and services from businesses.

7. The ability to organize and get something done generally goes under the term:
   a. the corporate approach.
   b. entrepreneurship.
   c. efficiency.
   d. consumer sovereignty.

8. In terms of numbers, the largest percentage of businesses are:
   a. partnerships.
   b. sole proprietorships.
   c. corporations.
   d. nonprofit companies.

9. The largest percentage of business receipts are by:
   a. partnerships.
   b. sole proprietorships.
   c. corporations.
   d. nonprofit companies.

10. A sole proprietorship has the advantage of:
    a. raising funds by selling stocks or bonds.
    b. limited personal liability.
    c. minimum bureaucratic hassle.
    d. sharing work and risks.

11. All of the following are reasons why e-commerce and the Internet increase competition *except*:
    a. they increase the size of the marketplace in which goods are sold.
    b. they increase the value of companies who can establish brand name first.
    c. they reduce the cost of obtaining information.
    d. they reduce the importance of geographical location.

12. The largest percentage of federal government expenditures is on:
    a. education.
    b. health and medical care.
    c. infrastructure.
    d. income security.

13. The largest percentage of state and local expenditures is on:
    a. education.
    b. health and medical care.
    c. highways.
    d. income security.

14. All of the following are examples of government's role as referee *except*:
    a. setting limitations on when someone can be fired.
    b. collecting Social Security taxes from workers' paychecks.
    c. setting minimum safety regulations for the workplace.
    d. disallowing two competitors to meet to fix prices of their products.

15. When government attempts to adjust for the effect of decisions on third parties not taken into account by the decision makers, the government is attempting to:
    a. provide for a stable set of institutions and rules.
    b. promote effective and workable competition.
    c. provide for public goods and services.
    d. correct for externalities.

16. The ability of individuals or firms currently in business to prevent others from entering the same kind of business is:
    a. comparative advantage.
    b. market failure.
    c. monopoly power.
    d. externality.

17. A good whose consumption by one individual does not prevent its consumption by another individual has a characteristic of:
    a. a public good.
    b. a private good.
    c. a macroeconomic good.
    d. a demerit good.

18. Global corporations:
    a. offer enormous benefits to countries but rarely any problems.
    b. are easy for governments to control.
    c. reduce competition in countries.
    d. have substantial operations on both the production and the sales sides in more than one country.

A1. In feudalism the most important force was:
     a. the price mechanism.
     b. cultural force.
     c. legal force.
     d. anarchy.

A2. In mercantilism, the guiding force is:
     a. the price mechanism.
     b. legal force.
     c. cultural force.
     d. anarchy.

A3. Mercantilism evolved into capitalism because:
     a. government investments did not pan out.
     b. the Industrial Revolution undermined the craft guilds' mercantilist method of production.
     c. the guilds wanted more freedom.
     d. serfs wanted more freedom.

A4. Marx saw the strongest tension between:
     a. rich capitalists and poor capitalists.
     b. capitalists and government.
     c. capitalists and the proletariat.
     d. government and the proletariat.

A5. State socialism is an economic system in which:
     a. business sees to it that people work for their own good until they can be relied upon to do that on their own.
     b. business sees to it that people work for the common good until they can be relied upon to do that on their own.
     c. government sees to it that people work for their own good until they can be relied upon to do so on their own.
     d. government sees to it that people work for the common good until they can be relied upon to do so on their own.

● POTENTIAL ESSAY QUESTIONS

You may also see essay questions similar to the "Problems & Applications" and "A Brain Teaser" exercises.

1. Contrast the market economy and the command economy in addressing the three fundamental economic problems.

2. Uglies is a brand of boxer shorts sold on the Internet. Their claim to fame is that the front of the shorts doesn't match the back. Their marketing ploy is the boxer-short-of-the-month club. Suppose you were the one who came up with the idea for Uglies and wanted to start the business. What form of business would you select and why? (Thinking about where the funds to start the business will come from, who will make the shorts, and how the shorts will be sold will help you answer this question.)

3. How are global economic issues different from national economic issues? How have governments attempted to grapple with global economic issues? What is a major drawback associated with these attempts?

ANSWERS

SHORT-ANSWER QUESTIONS

1. A market economy is an economic system based on private property and the market. It gives private property rights to individuals, and relies on market forces to coordinate economic activity. In a market economy businesses produce what they believe people want and think they can make a profit supplying. Businesses decide how to produce efficiently, guided by their desire to make a profit. Goods are distributed according to individuals' ability and/or inherited wealth. (54)

2. In theory, socialism is an economic system that tries to organize society in the same way as most families are organized—all people contribute what they can and get what they need. In practice, socialism is an economic system based on government ownership of the means of production, with economic activity governed by central planning. So, central planners (not market forces) decide *what* is produced, *how* it is produced, and *for whom* it is produced. (55-56)

3. As seen in the diagram below, the three groups that comprise the U.S. economy are households, businesses, and government. Households supply factors of production to businesses in exchange for money; businesses produce goods and services and sell them to households and government in exchange for money. The government taxes businesses and households, buys goods and services from businesses and labor services from households, and provides goods and services to each of them. (58)

4. I would advise each of them to think hard about their situation. There are three main possibilities: sole proprietorship, partnership

and a corporation. Each form of business has its disadvantages and advantages. If your friend wants to minimize bureaucratic hassle and be her own boss, the best form of business would be a sole proprietorship. However, she would be personally liable for all losses and might have difficulty obtaining additional funds should that be necessary. If her brother has some skills to offer the new business and is willing to share in the cost of purchasing the company, she might want to form a partnership with him. Beware, though: Both partners are liable for any losses regardless of whose fault it is. I would ask her if she trusts her brother's decision-making abilities.

As a partnership they still might have problems getting additional funds. What about becoming a corporation? Her liability would be limited to her initial investment, her ability to get funds is greater, and she can shed personal income and gain added expenses to limit taxation. However, a corporation is a legal hassle to organize, may involve possible double taxation of income, and if she plans to hire many employees she may face difficulty monitoring the business once she becomes less involved. I would tell her she needs to weigh the costs and benefits of each option and choose the one that best suits her needs. (60-61)

5. Consumer sovereignty is the notion that the consumer's wishes rule what's produced. It means that if businesses wish to make a profit, they will need to produce what households want. That is not to say that businesses don't affect the desires of consumers through advertising. However, in practice, business and government do much of the economic decision-making even though households retain the ultimate power. This is because people have delegated much of that power to institutions and representatives–firms and the government–that are sometimes removed from the people. In the short run, households only indirectly control government and business. (60-64)

6. Two general roles of government are as actor and as referee. As an actor, government collects taxes and spends money. As a referee, government sets the rules governing relations between households and businesses. (64)

7. Six roles of government are (1) provide a stable set of institutions and rules, (2) promote effective and workable competition, (3) correct for externalities, (4) provide public goods, (5) ensure economic stability and growth, and (6) adjust for undesirable market results. (66)

8. The fact that a market has failed does not mean that government intervention will improve the situation; it may make things worse. (69)

9. Ongoing trade requires rules and methods of trade. The international market has no central government to set rules and methods for trade. Governments enter into voluntary trade agreements to fulfill some of these roles. (71)

A1. Feudalism evolved into mercantilism as the development of money allowed trade to grow, undermining the traditional base of feudalism. Politics rather than social forces came to control the central economic decisions. (77)

A2. Mercantilism evolved into capitalism because the Industrial Revolution shifted the economic power base away from craftsmen toward industrialists and toward an understanding that markets could coordinate the economy without the active involvement of the government. (77-78)

A3. Capitalism has evolved into welfare capitalism. That is, the human abuses marked by early capitalist developments led to a criticism of the market economic system. Political forces have changed government's role in the market, making government a key player in determining distribution and in making the what, how, and for whom decisions. This characterizes the U.S. economy today. (78-79)

ANSWERS

MATCHING

1-b; 2-i; 3-q; 4-f; 5-h; 6-r; 7-p; 8-c; 9-o; 10-s; 11-e; 12-k; 13-n; 14-a; 15-g; 16-m; 17-j; 18-d; 19-l.

ANSWERS

PROBLEMS AND APPLICATIONS

1. a. In the goods market, **households** and **government** buy goods and services from **businesses**. (58)
   b. In the goods market, **businesses** sell goods and services to **households** and **government**. (58)
   c. In the factor market, **businesses** and **government** buy (or employ) the resources owned by **households**. (58)
   d. In the factor market, **households** supply labor and other factors of production to **businesses** and **government**. (58)
   e. **Government** redistributes income. (58)
   f. **Government** provides services to the public with tax revenue. (58)

2. a. Sole proprietorship. No special bureaucratic forms are required to start one. (60-61)
   b. Partnership. The owners have another one to work with and risks are shared. (60-61)
   c. Sole proprietorship. This is a firm of one person who controls the business. (60-61)
   d. Partnership. This is easy to form relative to the easiest (sole proprietorship) and the hardest (corporation). (60-61)
   e. Corporation. The individual liability is limited by individual investment. (60-61)
   f. Corporation. Because it can issue stock and has limited liability, it has more access to financial capital. (60-61)

3. a. Sole proprietorship and partnership. (60-61)
   b. Corporation. (60-61)
   c. Sole proprietorship and partnership. (60-61)
   d. Corporation. (60-61)

4. Global corporations can benefit countries by creating jobs, by bringing new ideas and new technologies to a country, and by providing competition to domestic companies, keeping them on their toes. But, global corporations, because they exist in many countries and there is no world government, may be difficult to regulate or to control. If they don't like one government's taxes, regulation, or other policies, they can shift operations to another country with more favorable policies. (70-71)

ANSWERS

A BRAIN TEASER

1. A significant reduction in federal government spending would require cuts in income security (like social security), national defense, and other major components of federal government expenditures that are politically popular. Many people applaud attempts to reduce government spending as long as there are no cuts in programs they support. See Figure 3-4 on page 65.

ANSWERS

MULTIPLE CHOICE

1. b   As discussed on page 54, markets require private property rights because these give people the framework within which they can trade and markets rely on trading. Markets also require government, but government and private property rights are not the same thing, which rules out a and c. And d is a throwaway answer.

2. a   As discussed on page 55, a is the correct answer. If the question had said "In practice," b would have been an acceptable answer.

3. b   As discussed on page 56, b is the correct answer. If the question had said "In theory, a socialist economy..." a would have been an acceptable answer.

4. d   Under a market economy, firms decide what to produce based on what they think will sell. See pages 59-60.

5. c   As discussed on page 56, in command economies, central planners decide what to produce based upon what they believe society needs.

6. c. In Figure 3-1 households supply labor and other factors of production while businesses demand these inputs used in the production process. See page 58.

7. b   Entrepreneurship is the ability to organize and get something done. See page 59.

8. b   Most businesses are sole proprietorships. See Figure 3-2 on page 60.

9. c   Corporations account for most business receipts (revenues). See Figure 3-2 on page 60.

10. c   Corporations have the advantages of options a and b. Partnerships have the advantage of option d. See page 61.

11. b   While it is true that e-commerce and the Internet can increase the value of companies that establish their brand names first, this characteristic decreases competition once that name brand is established. See pages 62-63.

12. d   The largest component of federal government spending is income security. See Figure 3-4 on page 65.

13. a   Most state and local government spending is on education. See Figure 3-3 on page 65.

14. b   Collecting Social Security taxes to fund the Social Security system is government as an actor. Government as referee refers to laws regulating interaction between households and businesses. See pages 64-66.

15. d   Economists call the effect of a decision on a third party not taken into account by the decision maker an externality. Government sometimes attempts to adjust for these effects. See pages 67-68.

16. c   Monopoly power is the ability of individuals or firms currently in business to prevent others from entering their businesses. Monopoly power gives existing firms or individuals the ability to raise their prices. See page 67.

17. a   A public good is a good that if supplied to one person must be supplied to all and whose consumption by one individual does not prevent its consumption by another individual. See page 68.

18. d   Option d is the definition of global corporations. They often create problems. Governments often find it difficult to control them and they increase competition, not decrease it. See pages 69-71.

A1. b   As discussed on page 76, in feudalism tradition reigned.

A2. b   As discussed on page 77, in mercantilism government directed the economy.

A3. b   Mercantilism evolved into capitalism because of the changes brought about by the Industrial Revolution. See pages 77-78.

A4. c   To the degree that government was controlled by capitalists, d would be a correct answer, but it is not as good an answer as c, which represents the primary conflict. Remember, you are choosing the answer that best reflects the discussion in the text. See pages 78-79.

A5. d   The author defines state socialism as option d. Socialists saw state socialism as a transition stage to pure socialism. See page 79.

ANSWERS

POTENTIAL ESSAY QUESTIONS

The following are annotated answers. They indicate the general idea behind the answer.

1. Both economic systems have to address the three central economic problems. (1) What to produce? In a market economy, firms produce what they believe people want and what will make them a profit. In socialism, or a command economy, central planners decide what is produced. (2) How to produce? In a market economy, firms decide how to produce efficiently, guided by their desire to make a profit. In socialism, central planners decide how to produce. (3) For whom to produce? In a market economy, distribution is decided according to ability and inherited wealth. In socialism, distribution is according to individuals' needs (as determined by central planners).

2. The answer to this question will vary from person to person and will depend on personal finances, how much risk one is able and willing to undertake, how much responsibility one wants to take on, and whether or not you want to share in any profits. Given limited financial resources, I'd find a partner I can trust who has the funds needed to launch a web site, hire a firm to carry out transactions, and build inventory. With a partnership I can share the work and the risks of the venture. Since the liability associated with selling boxer shorts is not too great, unlimited liability with a partnership is not a problem. I would not choose a corporation because establishing one is a legal hassle requiring even more money. I would not choose a sole proprietorship because I don't have the funds to start the company on my own.

3. Global economic issues differ from national economic issues because national economies have governments to referee disputes among players in the economy; global economies do not; no international government exists. Governments, however, have developed a variety of international institutions to promote negotiations and coordinate economic relations among countries. These include the UN, the World Bank, the World Court and the International Monetary Fund. Countries also have developed global and regional organizations whose jobs it is to coordinate trade among countries and reduce trade barriers. Some are the WTO, the EU and NAFTA. In addition to these formal institutions, there are informal meetings of various countries like the Group of Five and the Group of Eight. A major drawback associated with governmental attempts to deal with global economic issues is that because government membership in international organizations is voluntary, then the power of international organizations is limited. An individual government may simply choose to ignore an international ruling with little impunity.

SUPPLY AND DEMAND

CHAPTER AT A GLANCE

This review is based upon the learning objectives that open the chapter.

1. The <u>law of demand</u> states that the quantity of a good demanded is <u>inversely related</u> to the good's price. When price goes up, quantity demanded goes down. When price goes down, quantity demanded goes up. (82)

   Law of Demand (Inverse Relationship):
   arrows move in $\uparrow P \rightarrow \downarrow Q_d$
   opposite directions $\downarrow P \rightarrow \uparrow Q_d$

   Law of Demand expressed as a <u>downward-sloping curve</u>:

   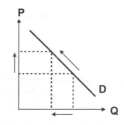

   To derive a demand curve from a demand table, plot each point on the demand table on a graph and connect the points.

   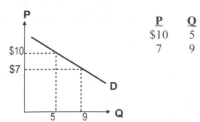

P	Q
$10	5
7	9

2a. The law of demand is based on opportunity cost and individuals' ability to substitute. If the price of a good rises, the opportunity cost of purchasing that good will also rise and consumers will substitute a good with a lower opportunity cost. (82)

   As the P of beef ↑s, we buy less beef and more chicken.

2b. The law of supply, like the law of demand, is based on opportunity cost and the individual firm's ability to substitute. Suppliers will substitute toward goods for which they receive higher relative prices. (88-89)

   If the P of wheat ↑s, farmers grow more wheat and less corn.

3. Changes in quantity demanded are shown by movements along a demand curve. Shifts in demand are shown by a shift of the entire demand curve. (83) *(Note: "Δ" means "change.")*

   Don't get this confused on the exam!

   ΔQ_d *is caused <u>only</u> by a Δ in the P of the good itself.*

   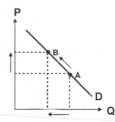

   $\Delta P \rightarrow \Delta Q_d \rightarrow$ *movement along a given D curve.*

   $\uparrow P \rightarrow \downarrow Q_d$: *movement along a curve (e.g. from point A to point B).*

   ΔD *is caused only by Δs in the shift factors of D (<u>not</u> a Δ in the P of the good itself!)*
   <u>Δ *in shift factors of D*→ΔD→ *shift of a D curve*</u>

   ✔ *Know what can cause an increase and decrease in demand:*
   ↑D→<u>*Rightward Shift*</u>   ↓D →<u>*Leftward Shift*</u>

   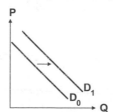 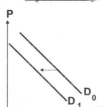

4. The <u>law of supply</u> states that the quantity of a good supplied is <u>directly</u> <u>related</u> to the good's price. When price goes up, quantity supplied goes up. When price goes down, quantity supplied goes down. (88-89)

Law of Supply (Direct Relationship):
arrows move in $\uparrow P \rightarrow \uparrow Q_s$
same direction $\downarrow P \rightarrow \downarrow Q_s$

Law of Supply expressed as an <u>upward-sloping curve</u>:

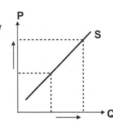

To derive a supply curve from a supply table, plot each point on the supply table on a graph and connect the points.

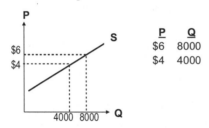

P	Q
$6	8000
$4	4000

5. Just as with demand, it is important to distinguish between a change in supply (due to a change in shift factors and reflected as a shift of the entire supply curve) and a change in the quantity supplied (due to a change in price and reflected as a movement along a supply curve). (89-90)
    Don't get this confused on the exam!

ΔQ_s *is caused <u>only</u> by a Δ in the P of the good itself.*

$\Delta P \rightarrow \Delta Q_s \rightarrow$ *movement along a given S curve.*

$\uparrow P \rightarrow \uparrow Q_s$*: movement along a curve (e.g. from point A to point B).*

ΔS *is caused only by Δs in the shift factors of S (<u>not</u> a Δ in the P of the good itself!)*

Δ in shift factors of S $\rightarrow \Delta S \rightarrow$ <u>shift of a S curve</u>

✔ *Know what can cause an increase and decrease in supply:*
    $\uparrow S \rightarrow$<u>Rightward Shift</u> $\downarrow S \rightarrow$<u>Leftward Shift</u>

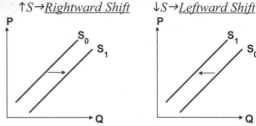

6. Equilibrium is where quantity supplied equals quantity demanded: (93-94)

- If quantity demanded is greater than quantity supplied (excess demand), prices tend to rise;
- If quantity supplied is greater than quantity demanded (excess supply), prices tend to fall.
- When quantity demanded equals quantity supplied, prices have no tendency to change.

✔ *Know this!*

- If $Q_d > Q_s \rightarrow$ Shortage $\rightarrow P$ will $\uparrow$.
- If $Q_s > Q_d \rightarrow$ Surplus $\rightarrow P$ will $\downarrow$.
- If $Q_s = Q_d \rightarrow$ Equilibrium $\rightarrow$ no tendency for P to change (because there is neither a surplus nor a shortage).

Shortage	**Surplus**	**Equilibrium**
$(Q_d > Q_s)$	$(Q_s > Q_d)$	$(Q_s = Q_d)$
P is below equilibrium	P is above equilibrium	

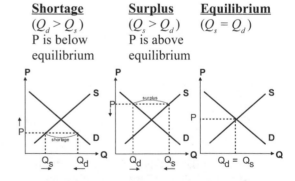

7. Demand and supply curves enable us to determine the equilibrium price and quantity. In addition, changes (shifts) in demand and supply curves enable us to predict the effect on the equilibrium price and quantity in a market. (96-97)

Anything other than price that affects demand or supply will shift the curves.

✔ *Know how a change in demand or supply affects the equilibrium price and quantity!*

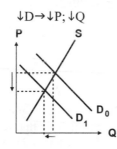
↑D→↑P; ↑Q

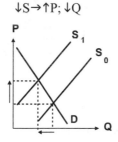
↑S→↓P; ↑Q

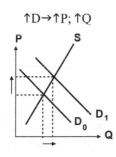
↓D→↓P; ↓Q

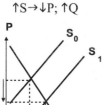
↓S→↑P; ↓Q

8. Simple supply and demand analysis holds other things constant. Sometimes supply and demand are interconnected, making it impossible to hold other things constant. When there is interdependence between supply and demand, a movement along one curve can cause the other curve to shift. Thus, supply and demand analysis used alone is not enough to determine where the equilibrium will be. (97-98)

When the "other things are constant" assumption is not realistic, feedback or ripple effects can become relevant. The degree of interdependence differs among various sets of issues. That is why there is a separate micro and macro analysis—microeconomics and macroeconomics.

The fallacy of composition is the false assumption that what is true for a part will also be true for the whole. This means that what is true in microeconomics may not be true in macroeconomics.

● SHORT-ANSWER QUESTIONS

1. What is the law of demand?

2. Draw a demand curve from the following demand table.

   Demand Table

Q	P
50	1
40	2
30	3
20	4

3. Demonstrate graphically a shift in demand and on another graph demonstrate movement along the demand curve.

4. State the law of supply.

5. What does the law of supply say that most individuals would do with the quantity of labor they supply employers if their wage increased? Explain the importance of substitution in this decision.

6. Draw a supply curve from the following supply table.

   Supply Table

Q	P
20	1
30	2
40	3
50	4

7. Demonstrate graphically the effect of a new technology that reduces the cost of producing Linkin Park CDs on the supply of Linkin Park CDs.

8. Demonstrate graphically the effect of a rise in the price of Linkin Park CDs on the quantity supplied.

9. What are three things to note about supply and demand that help to explain how they interact to bring about equilibrium in a market?

10. Demonstrate graphically what happens to the equilibrium price and quantity of M&Ms if they suddenly become more popular.

11. Demonstrate graphically what happens to the equilibrium price and quantity of oranges if a frost destroys 50 percent of the orange crop.

12. What is the fallacy of composition and how is it related to why economists separate micro from macro economics?

MATCHING THE TERMS
Match the terms to their definitions

___ **1.** demand

___ **2.** demand curve

___ **3.** equilibrium

___ **4.** equilibrium price

___ **5.** equilibrium quantity

___ **6.** excess demand

___ **7.** excess supply

___ **8.** fallacy of composition

___ **9.** law of demand

___ **10.** law of supply

___ **11.** market demand curve

___ **12.** movement along a demand curve

___ **13.** movement along a supply curve

___ **14.** quantity demanded

___ **15.** quantity supplied

___ **16.** shift in demand

___ **17.** shift in supply

___ **18.** supply

___ **19.** supply curve

a. A specific amount that will be demanded per unit of time at a specific price, other things constant.

b. Curve that tells how much of a good will be bought at various prices.

c. The effect of a change in a shift factor on the supply curve.

d. Curve that tells how much of a good will be offered for sale at various prices.

e. The graphic representation of the effect of a change in price on the quantity supplied.

f. Quantity demanded rises as price falls, other things constant.

g. Quantity supplied rises as price rises, other things constant.

h. A schedule of quantities of a good that will be bought per unit of time at various prices, other things constant.

i. Quantity supplied is greater than quantity demanded.

j. A concept in which opposing dynamic forces cancel each other out.

k. The effect of a change in a shift factor on the demand curve.

l. The price toward which the invisible hand (economic forces) drives the market.

m. The horizontal sum of all individual demand curves.

n. Amount bought and sold at the equilibrium price.

o. Quantity demanded is greater than quantity supplied.

p. The graphic representation of the effect of a change in price on the quantity demanded.

q. A specific amount that will be offered for sale per unit of time at a specific price.

r. A schedule of quantities a seller is willing to sell per unit of time at various prices, other things constant.

s. The false assumption that what is true for a part will also be true for the whole.

● PROBLEMS AND APPLICATIONS

1. Draw two linear curves on the same graph from the following table, one relating P with Q_1 and the other relating P with Q_2.

P	Q_1	Q_2
$30	60	100
35	70	90
40	80	80
45	90	70

   a. Label the curve that is most likely a demand curve. Explain your choice.

   b. Label the curve that is most likely a supply curve. Explain your choice.

   c. What is the equilibrium price and quantity? Choose points above and below that price and explain why each is not the equilibrium price.

2. Correct the following statements, if needed, so that the terms "demand," "quantity demanded," "supply," and "quantity supplied" are used correctly.

   a. As the price of pizza increases, consumers demand less pizza.

   b. Whenever the price of bicycles increases, the supply of bicycles increases.

   c. The price of electricity is cheaper in the northwestern part of the United States and therefore the demand for electricity is greater in the northwest.

   d. An increase in the incomes of car buyers will increase the quantity demanded for cars.

   e. An increase in the quantity demanded of lobsters means consumers are willing and able to buy more lobsters at any given price.

   f. A decrease in the supply of frog legs means suppliers will provide fewer frog legs at any given price.

3. You are given the following individual demand tables for compact discs.

Price	Juan	Philippe	Ramone
$7	3	20	50
$10	2	10	40
$13	1	7	32
$16	0	5	26
$19	0	3	20
$22	0	0	14

   a. Determine the market demand table.

   b. Graph the individual and market demand curves.

   c. If the current market price is $13, what is the total market quantity demanded? What happens to total market quantity demanded if the price rises to $19 a disc?

   d. Say that a new popular Usher compact disc hits the market that increases demand for compact discs by 25%. Show with a demand table what happens to the individual and market demand curves. Demonstrate graphically what happens to market demand.

4. The following table depicts the market supply
    and demand for oranges in the United States
    (in thousands of bushels).

Price per bushel	Quantity supplied	Quantity demanded
$15	7000	2000
$14	5500	3000
$13	4000	4000
$12	2500	5000
$11	1000	6000

a. Graph the market supply and demand for
    oranges.

b. What is the equilibrium price and quantity
    of oranges in the market? Why?

c. Suppose the price is $14. Would we
    observe a surplus (excess supply) or a
    shortage (excess demand)? If so, by how
    much? What could be expected to happen
    to the price over time? Why?

d. Suppose the price is $12. Would we
    observe a surplus or a shortage? If so, by
    how much? What could be expected to
    happen to the price over time? Why?

5. Draw a hypothetical demand and supply curve
    for cyber cafes — coffee houses with comput-
    ers hooked up to the Internet with access to
    daily newspapers (among other things) at each
    table. Show how demand or supply is affected
    by the following:

a. A technological breakthrough lowers the
    cost of computers.

b. Consumers' income rises.

c. A per-hour fee is charged to coffee houses
    to use the Internet.

d. The price of newspapers in print rises.

e. Possible suppliers expect cyber cafes to
    become more popular.

6. Use supply and demand curves to help you
    determine the impact that each of the follow-
    ing events has on the market for surfboards in
    Southern California.

a. Southern California experiences unusually
    high temperatures, sending an unusually
    large number of people to its beaches.

b. Large sharks are reported feeding near the
    beaches of Southern California.

c. Due to the large profits earned by surfboard producers there is a significant increase in the number of producers of surfboards.

d. There is a significant increase in the price of epoxy paint used to coat surfboards.

7. Use supply and demand curves to help you determine the impact that each of the following events has on the market for beef.

a. New genetic engineering technology enables ranchers to raise healthier, heavier cattle, significantly reducing costs.

b. The CBS program "60 Minutes" reports on the unsanitary conditions in poultry processing plants that may increase the chances of consumers getting sick by eating chicken.

c. In addition to developing new genetic engineering technology, highly credible new research results report that abundant consumption of fatty red meats actually prolongs average life expectancy.

d. Consumers expect the price of beef to fall in the near future.

● A BRAIN TEASER

1. The invention of a self-milking cow machine allows cows to milk themselves. Not only does this reduce the need for higher-cost human assistance in milking, but it also allows the cow to milk herself three times a day instead of two, leading to both a healthier cow and increased milk production.

a. Show the effect of this innovation on the equilibrium quantity and price of milk.

b. Show the likely effect on equilibrium price and quantity of apple juice (a substitute for milk).

● MULTIPLE CHOICE

Circle the one best answer for each of the following questions:

1. The law of demand states:
a. quantity demanded increases as price falls, other things constant.
b. more of a good will be demanded the higher its price, other things constant.
c. people always want more.
d. you can't always get what you want at the price you want.

2. There are many more substitutes for good A than for good B.
   a. The demand curve for good B will likely shift out further.
   b. The demand curve for good B will likely be flatter.
   c. You can't say anything about the likely relative flatness of the demand curves.
   d. The demand curve for good A will likely be flatter.

3. If the weather gets very hot, what will most likely happen?
   a. The supply of air conditioners will increase.
   b. Quantity of air conditioners demanded will increase.
   c. Demand for air conditioners will increase.
   d. The quality of air conditioners demanded will increase.

4. If the price of air conditioners falls, there will be:
   a. an increase in demand for air conditioners.
   b. an increase in the quantity of air conditioners demanded.
   c. an increase in the quantity of air conditioners supplied.
   d. a shift out of the supply for air conditioners.

5. An increase in demand:
   a. is reflected as a rightward (outward) shift of the demand curve.
   b. is caused by a decrease in price.
   c. means demanders are buying less at any price
   d. shifts the demand curve to the left (inward).

6. The demand curve will likely shift outward to the right if:
   a. society's income falls.
   b. the price of a substitute good falls.
   c. the price of the good is expected to rise in the near future.
   d. the good goes out of style.

7. The difference between the quantity demanded and demand is:
   a. the quantity demanded is associated with a whole set of prices, whereas demand is associated with a particular price.
   b. the quantity demanded is associated with a particular price, whereas demand is associated with a whole set of prices.

c. the quantity demanded is the whole demand curve, whereas demand is a particular point along a demand curve.
   d. a change in the quantity demanded is reflected graphically as a shift of the demand curve, whereas a change in demand is reflected as movement along a given demand curve.

8. If there is a flood, what will most likely happen in the market for bottled water?
   a. Demand will increase.
   b. Demand will fall.
   c. Supply will increase.
   d. Supply will decrease.

9. The movement in the graph below from point A to point B represents:

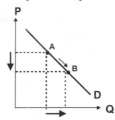

   a. an increase in demand.
   b. an increase in the quantity demanded.
   c. an increase in the quantity supplied.
   d. an increase in supply.

10. Using the standard axes, the demand curve associated with the following demand table is:

Demand Table

P	Q
7	5
9	4
11	3

   a. a
   b. b
   c. c
   d. d

11. To derive a market demand curve from two individual demand curves:
   a. one adds the two demand curves horizontally.
   b. one adds the two demand curves vertically.
   c. one subtracts one demand curve from the other demand curve.
   d. one adds the demand curves both horizontally and vertically.

12. The market demand curve will always:
   a. be unrelated to the individual demand curves and slope.
   b. be steeper than the individual demand curves that make it up.
   c. have the same slope as the individual demand curves that make it up.
   d. be flatter than the individual demand curves that make it up.

13. The law of supply states that:
   a. quantity supplied increases as price increases, other things constant.
   b. quantity supplied decreases as price increases, other things constant.
   c. more of a good will be supplied the higher its price, other things changing proportionately.
   d. less of a good will be supplied the higher its price, other things changing proportionately.

14. In the graph below, the arrow refers to:

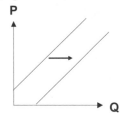

   a. a shift in demand.
   b. a shift in supply.
   c. a change in the quantity demanded.
   d. a change in the quantity supplied.

15. If there is an improvement in technology one would expect:
   a. a movement along the supply curve.
   b. a shift upward (or to the left) of the supply curve.
   c. a shift downward (or to the right) of the supply curve.
   d. a movement down along the supply curve.

16. You're the supplier of a good and suddenly a number of your long-lost friends call you to buy your product. Your good is most likely:
   a. in excess supply.
   b. in excess demand.
   c. in equilibrium.
   d. in both excess supply and demand.

17. At which point on the graph below will you expect the strongest downward pressure on prices?

   a. a.
   b. b.
   c. c.
   d. d.

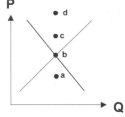

18. If at some price the quantity supplied exceeds the quantity demanded, then:
   a. a surplus (excess supply) exists and the price will fall over time as sellers competitively bid down the price.
   b. a shortage (excess demand) exists and the price will rise over time as buyers competitively bid up the price.
   c. the price is below equilibrium.
   d. equilibrium will be reestablished as the demand curve shifts to the left.

19. If the price of a good:
   a. rises, it is a response to a surplus (excess supply).
   b. falls, it is a response to a shortage (excess demand).
   c. is below equilibrium, then a shortage will be observed.
   d. is below equilibrium, then a surplus will be observed.

20. If the demand for a good increases, you will expect price to:
   a. fall and quantity to rise.
   b. rise and quantity to rise.
   c. fall and quantity to fall.
   d. rise and quantity to fall.

21. If the supply of a good decreases, you will expect price to:
   a. fall and quantity to rise.
   b. rise and quantity to rise.
   c. fall and quantity to fall.
   d. rise and quantity to fall.

22. Consider the market for bikinis. If bikinis suddenly become more fashionable, you will expect:
   a. a temporary shortage of bikinis that will be eliminated over time as the market price of

bikinis rises and a greater quantity is bought and sold.

b. a temporary shortage of bikinis that will be eliminated over time as the market price of bikinis rises and a smaller quantity is bought and sold.

c. a temporary surplus of bikinis that will be eliminated over time as the market price of bikinis falls and a smaller quantity is bought and sold.

d. a temporary surplus of bikinis that will be eliminated over time as the market price of bikinis rises and a greater quantity is bought and sold.

23. Compared to last year, fewer oranges are being purchased and the selling price has decreased. This could have been caused by:
    a. an increase in demand.
    b. an increase in supply.
    c. a decrease in demand.
    d. a decrease in supply.

24. If demand and supply both increase, this will cause:
    a. an increase in the equilibrium quantity, but an uncertain effect on the equilibrium price.
    b. an increase in the equilibrium price, but an uncertain effect on the equilibrium quantity.
    c. an increase in the equilibrium price and quantity.
    d. a decrease in the equilibrium price and quantity.

25. An increase in demand for a good will cause:
    a. excess demand (a shortage) before price changes.
    b. movement down along the demand curve as price changes.
    c. movement down along the supply curve as price changes.
    d. a higher price and a smaller quantity traded in the market.

26. The fallacy of composition is:
    a. the false assumption that what is false for a part will also be false for the whole.
    b. the false assumption that what is true for a part will also be true for the whole.
    c. the false assumption that what is false for a whole will also be false for the part.
    d. the false assumption that what is true for a whole will also be true for the part.

POTENTIAL ESSAY QUESTIONS

You may also see essay questions similar to the "Problems & Applications" and "A Brain Teaser" exercises.

1. Many university campuses sell parking permits to their students allowing them to park on campus in designated areas. Although most students complain about the relatively high cost of these parking permits, what annoys many students even more is that after having paid for their permits, vacant parking spaces in the designated lots are very difficult to find during much of the day. Many end up having to park off campus anyway, where permits are not required. Assuming the university is unable to build new parking facilities on campus due to insufficient funds, what recommendation might you make to remedy the problem of students with permits being unable to find places to park on campus?

2. Discuss how changes in demand or supply impact a market equilibrium price and quantity.

■ ANSWERS ■

SHORT-ANSWER QUESTIONS

1. The law of demand states that the quantity of a good demanded is inversely related to the good's price, other things constant. (82)

2. To derive a demand curve from a demand table, plot each point of the demand table on a graph and connect the points. This is shown on the graph below. (86)

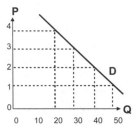

3. A shift in demand is shown by a shift of the entire demand curve resulting from a change in a shift factor of demand as shown in the graph below on the left (which illustrates an increase in demand because it is a rightward shift). A movement along a demand curve is shown on the right as a movement from point A to point B due to a price decrease. (83 and Figure 4-2 on page 85)

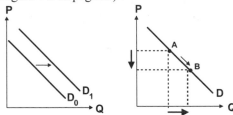

4. The law of supply states that the quantity supplied rises as price rises, other things constant. Or alternatively: quantity supplied falls as price falls. (88)

5. The law of supply states that quantity supplied rises as price rises; quantity supplied falls as price falls. According to this law, most individuals would choose to supply a greater quantity of labor hours if their wage increased. They will substitute work for leisure. (Figure 4-5 on page 89)

6. To derive a supply curve from a supply table, you plot each point on the supply table on a graph and connect the points. This is shown on the graph in the next column. (91)

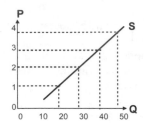

7. A new technology that reduces the cost of producing Linkin Park CDs will shift the entire supply curve to the right from S_0 to S_1, as shown in the graph below. (90)

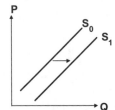

8. A rise in the price of Linkin Park CDs from P_0 to P_1 results in a movement up along a supply curve and the quantity of Linkin Park CDs supplied will rise from Q_0 to Q_1 as shown in the graph below. (89-90)

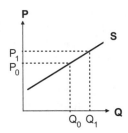

9. The first thing to note is that when quantity demanded is greater than quantity supplied, prices tend to rise and when quantity supplied is greater than quantity demanded, prices tend to fall. Each case is demonstrated in the graph below. Price tends away from P_1 and P_2 and toward P_0.

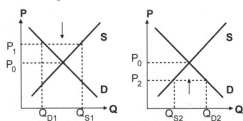

The second thing to note is that the larger the difference between quantity supplied and quantity demanded, the greater the pressure on prices to rise (if there is excess demand; a shortage) or fall (if there is excess supply; a surplus). This is demonstrated in the graph below. At P_2, the pressure for prices to fall toward P_0 is greater than the pressure at P_1 because excess supply (surplus) is greater at P_2 compared to excess supply at P_1.

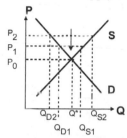

The third thing to note is that when quantity demanded equals quantity supplied, the market is in equilibrium. This is shown graphically at the point of intersection between the demand and supply curves. (93-94)

10. Increasing popularity of M&Ms means that at every price, more M&Ms are demanded. The demand curve shifts out to the right from D_0 to D_1, and both equilibrium price and quantity rise to P_1 and Q_1 respectively. (96-97)

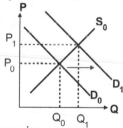

11. A frost damaging oranges means that at every price, suppliers will supply fewer oranges. The supply curve shifts in to the left from S_0 to S_1, and equilibrium price rises to P_1, and quantity traded falls to Q_1. (96-97)

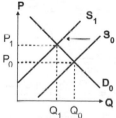

12. The fallacy of composition is the false assumption that what is true for a part will also be true for the whole. In micro, economists isolate an individual person's or firm's behavior and consider its effects, while the many side effects are kept in the background. In macro, those

side effects become too large and can no longer be held constant. These side effects are what account for the interdependence of supply and demand. Macro, thus, is not simply a summation of all micro results; it would be a fallacy of composition to take the sum of each individual's (micro) actions and say that this will be the aggregate (macro) result. (98)

ANSWERS

MATCHING

1-h; 2-b; 3-j; 4-l; 5-n; 6-o; 7-i; 8-s; 9-f; 10-g; 11-m; 12-p; 13-e; 14-a; 15-q; 16-k; 17-c; 18-r; 19-d.

ANSWERS

PROBLEMS AND APPLICATIONS

1. The linear curves are shown on the right. See Figure 4-8 on page 95.

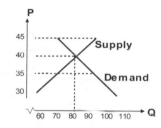

   a. As shown in the graph, the downward sloping curve is a demand curve. We deduce this from the law of demand: quantity demanded rises (falls) as the price decreases (increases). (82)

   b. As shown in the graph, the upward sloping curve is a supply curve. We deduce this from the law of supply: quantity supplied rises (falls) as the price rises (falls). (89)

   c. The equilibrium price and quantity are where the demand and supply curves intersect. This is at $P = \$40$, $Q = 80$. At a price above $40, such as $45, quantity supplied exceeds quantity demanded and there is pressure for price to fall. At a price below $40, such as $35, quantity demanded exceeds quantity supplied and there is pressure for price to rise. (93-94)

2. a. As the price of pizza increases, the *quantity demanded* of pizza decreases. (83)

Note that a change in the price of an item will cause a change in the quantity demanded; not a change in demand! A change in something else other than the price may cause a change in demand– such as a change in one of the shift factors of demand discussed in the textbook.

b. Whenever the price of bicycles increases, the *quantity of bicycles supplied* also increases. (90)

Note that a change in the price will cause a change in the quantity supplied; not supply! A change in something else other than the price–such as a change in one of the shift factors of supply discussed in the textbook–may cause a change in supply.

c. The price of electricity is cheaper in the NW part of the U. S. and therefore the *quantity demanded* of electricity is greater in the NW. (83)

d. An increase in incomes of car buyers will increase the *demand* for cars. (83-84)

Notice that a change in a shift factor of demand, such as income, will change demand; not the quantity demanded!

e. An increase in the *demand* for lobsters means consumers are willing and able to buy more lobsters at any given price (whatever the current price is). (83-84)

In order for there to be an increase in the quantity demanded there would have to be a decrease in the price. Moreover, recall that an increase in demand is reflected as a rightward shift of the demand curve. Upon viewing a graph where the demand curve has shifted to the right you will see that more will be purchased at any given price.

f. This is a correct use of the term "supply." Notice that a decrease in supply is reflected graphically as a leftward shift of the curve and less will be provided in the market at any given price. (89-90)

3. a. The market demand table is the summation of individual quantities demanded at each price as follows (86-87):

P	Q
$7	73
10	52
13	40
16	31
19	23
22	14

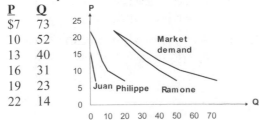

b. The individual and market demand curves are shown to the right of the demand table. (86-87)

c. At $13 a disc, total market quantity demanded is 40 discs. Total market quantity demanded falls to 23 when the price of discs rises to $19 per disc. (86-87)

d. Quantity demanded at each price rises by 25% for each individual and for the market as a whole. The new demand table is shown below. Graphically, both the individual and market demand curves shift to the right. The graph below shows the rightward shift in market demand. (86-87)

Price	Juan	Philippe	Ramone	Market
$7	3.75	25	62.50	91.25
$10	2.50	12.5	50	65
$13	1.25	8.75	40	50
$16	0	6.25	32.5	38.75
$19	0	3.75	25	28.75
$21	0	0	17.5	17.5

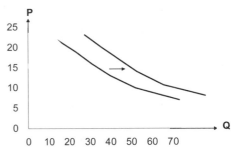

4. a. See the graph below. (See Figure 4-8 on page 95.)

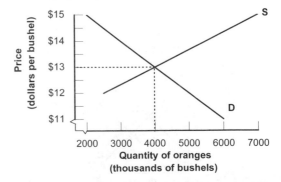

b. The equilibrium price is $13, the equilibrium quantity is 4000. This is an equilibrium because the quantity supplied equals the quantity demanded at this price. That is, there is neither a surplus (excess supply) nor a shortage (excess demand) and hence no tendency for the price to change. (93-94)

c. Because the quantity supplied exceeds the quantity demanded when the price is $14 per bushel, we would observe a surplus of 2,500 bushels (in thousands of bushels). We can expect the price of oranges per bushel to fall as sellers scramble to rid themselves of their excess supplies. (93-94)

d. Because the quantity demanded exceeds the quantity supplied at $12 per bushel, we would observe a shortage of 2,500 bushels (in thousands of bushels). We can expect the price of oranges per bushel to rise as some buyers competitively bid up the price just to get some oranges. (93-94)

5. A hypothetical market for cyber cafes shows an upward sloping supply curve, a downward sloping demand curve and an equilibrium price and quantity where the two curves intersect.

a. A technological breakthrough that lowers the cost of computers will shift the supply of cyber cafes to the right as shown in the graph below. (90)

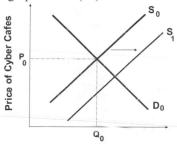

Quantity of Cyber Cafes

b. A rise in consumers' income will shift the demand for cyber cafes to the right as shown in the graph below. (84)

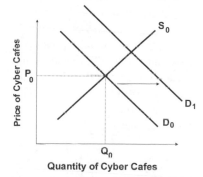

Quantity of Cyber Cafes

c. If a fee is charged to coffee houses to use the Internet, the supply of cyber cafes will shift to the left as shown in the accompanying graph. (90)

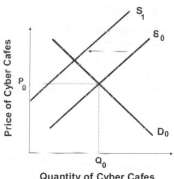

Quantity of Cyber Cafes

d. If the price of newspapers in print rises, the demand for cyber cafes will shift to the right as shown in the graph for answer (b). (90)

e. If possible suppliers expect cyber cafes to become more popular, the supply of cyber cafes will shift to the right as shown in the graph for answer (a). (90)

6. a. This will increase the demand for surfboards shifting the demand curve to the right. At the original price a temporary shortage would be observed putting upward pressure on price. We end up with a higher equilibrium price and a greater equilibrium quantity as illustrated in the graph below. (*When dealing with a change in D or S curves, just remember to go from the initial point of intersection will give you between the curves to the new point of intersection. The initial point of intersection will give you the initial equilibrium P and Q and the new point of intersection the new equilibrium P and Q. Then recall that if the price went up in the market, it was a response to a temporary shortage (excess demand). If the equilibrium price went down, then it was a response to a temporary surplus (excess supply)*). (96-97)

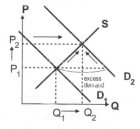

b. This would cause a decrease in the demand for surfboards shifting the demand curve to the left. At the original price a temporary surplus would be observed putting downward pressure on price. We end up with a lower equilibrium price and a lower equilibrium quantity, as illustrated in the graph below. (96-97)

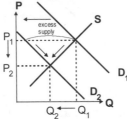

c. This would cause an increase in the supply of surfboards, shifting the supply curve to the right. At the original price a temporary surplus would be observed, putting downward pressure on price. We end up with a lower equilibrium price and a higher equilibrium quantity, as illustrated in the graph below. (96-97)

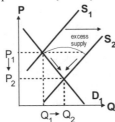

d. This would cause a decrease in the supply of surfboards ,shifting the supply curve to the left. At the original price a temporary shortage would be observed, putting upward pressure on price. We end up with a higher equilibrium price and a lower equilibrium quantity, as illustrated in the graph below. (96-97)

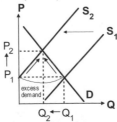

7. **a.** An increase in production technology will increase the supply of beef. The temporary surplus (excess supply) of beef at the original price will cause the market price to fall. Eventually we get a lower equilibrium price of beef and a greater amount bought and sold in the market. (96-97)

b. Chicken and beef are substitute goods– they can be used instead of each other. Therefore, this "60 Minutes" report will likely increase the demand for beef. The temporary shortage (excess demand) at the original price will cause the price to be competitively bid up. Eventually we observe a higher equilibrium price and a greater equilibrium quantity. (96-97)

c. The new development would increase the supply of beef while the reports of the health benefits of beef would increase the demand for beef. Quantity of beef sold would definitely rise. The impact on equilibrium price, however, depends upon the relative sizes of the shifts. (96-97)

d. Because people will postpone their purchases of beef until the price decreases, the demand for beef will fall today. A decrease in demand is reflected as a leftward shift of the demand curve. The temporary excess supply (surplus) that is created at the original price puts downward pressure on the market price of beef. Eventually we get a lower equilibrium price and quantity. (96-97)

ANSWERS

A BRAIN TEASER

1. **a.** This innovation will shift the supply curve to the right as shown in the graph on the left below. As a result, this creates excess supply and the equilibrium price falls while the equilibrium quantity rises. (96-97)

b. The market demand and supply for apple juice is shown below on the right. As a result of the fall in milk prices (assuming milk and apple juice are substitutes), the demand for apple juice shifts to the left. This creates excess supply of apple juice. The equilibrium price will fall. The equilibrium quantity will also fall. (96-97)

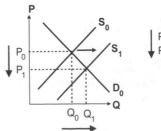

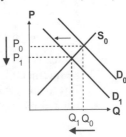

ANSWERS

MULTIPLE CHOICE

1. **a**   As discussed on page 82, the correct answer is a. A possible answer is d, which is a restatement of the law of demand, but since the actual law was among the choices, and is more precise, a is the correct answer.

2. **d**   An equal rise in price will cause individuals to switch more to other goods when there are more substitutes. See page 82.

3. **c**   As discussed on pages 83-84, it is important to distinguish between a change in the quantity demanded and a change in demand. Weather is a shift factor of demand, so demand, not quantity demanded, will increase. Supply will not increase; the quantity supplied will, however. Who knows what will happen to the quality demanded? We don't.

4. **b**   As discussed on page 83, when the price falls there is a movement along the demand curve which is expressed by saying the quantity demanded increased. Moreover, as the price falls, the quantity supplied falls.

5. **a**   As discussed on pages 83-84, an increase in demand is expressed as an outward (or rightward) shift of the demand curve. It is caused by something other than the price. It means people will buy more at any price or pay a higher price for a given quantity demanded.

6. **c**   All of these are shift factors of demand. However, only c will increase demand and shift the demand curve to the right. See pages 83-84.

7. **b**   As is discussed on page 83, b is the only correct response.

8. **a**   A flood will likely bring about a significant increase in the demand for bottled water since a flood makes most other water undrinkable. A flood would be a shift factor of demand for bottled water. See pages 83-84.

9. **b**   The curve slopes downward, so we can surmise that it is a demand curve; and the two points are on the demand curve, so

the movement represents an increase in the quantity demanded, not an increase in demand. Moreover, as price falls, the quantity demanded rises. A shift in demand would be a shift of the entire curve. See the figures on page 85.

10. **b**   This demand curve is the only demand curve that goes through all the points in the table. See page 86.

11. **a**   As discussed in the text on page 87 (Figure 4-4), market demand curves are determined by adding individuals' demand curves horizontally. That is, you add the quantities demanded at each price.

12. **d**   Since the market demand curve is derived by adding the individual demand curves horizontally, it will always be flatter. See pages 86-88 and Figure 4-4.

13. **a**   As discussed on pages 88-89, the law of supply is stated in a. The others either have the movement in the wrong direction or are not holding all other things constant.

14. **b**   It is a shift in supply because the curve is upward sloping; and it's a shift of the entire curve, so it is not a movement along. See pages 89-90 and Figure 4-6.

15. **c**   As discussed on page 90, technology is a shift factor of supply so it must be a shift of the supply curve. Since it is an improvement, it must be a shift rightward (or downward). See also Figure 4-6 on page 91.

16. **b**   When there is excess demand, demanders start searching for new suppliers, as discussed on pages 93-94.

17. **d**   The greater the extent to which the quantity supplied exceeds the quantity demanded, the greater the surplus (excess supply) and the greater the pressure for the price to fall. See pages 93-95.

18. **a**   As discussed on page 93, there is a surplus (excess supply) when the price is above equilibrium. A surplus will motivate sellers to reduce price to rid themselves of their excess supplies. As the price falls, the quantity demand rises and the quantity supplied falls; demand and supply curves do *not* shift.

19. c   As discussed on pages 93-94 whenever price is below equilibrium, a shortage is observed, and price rises.

20. b   Since this statement says demand increases, then the demand curve shifts rightward. There is no change in the supply curve. Assuming an upward sloping supply curve, that means that price will rise and quantity will rise. See pages 96-97.

21. d   Since this statement says supply decreases, then the supply curve shifts leftward. There is no change in the demand curve. Assuming a downward sloping demand curve, that means that price will rise and quantity will fall. See pages 96-97.

22. a   The demand for bikinis would rise shifting the demand curve to the right. The supply curve does not change. This creates a temporary shortage that is eliminated over time as the market moves to its new equilibrium at a higher price and a greater quantity traded. See pages 96-97.

23. c   Only a decrease in demand will result in a decrease in quantity and a decrease in price. See pages 96-97.

24. a   An increase in demand has a tendency to increase price and increase the quantity. An increase in supply has a tendency to *decrease* the price and increase the quantity. So, on balance, we are certain of an increase in the equilibrium quantity, but we are uncertain about the impact on the price in the market. See pages 96-97.

25. a   An increase in demand causes the quantity demanded to exceed the quantity supplied, creating excess demand (a shortage). This increases the price causing movement *up* along the demand and supply curves resulting in a *greater* quantity traded in the market. See pages 96-97.

26. b   The fallacy of composition is the false assumption that what is true for a part will also be true for the whole. See page 98.

═══ ANSWERS ═══

POTENTIAL ESSAY QUESTIONS

The following are annotated answers. They indicate the general idea behind the answer.

1.   The shortage of parking spaces implies that permit prices are below equilibrium. The price of a permit should be increased. At least with the purchase of a permit you could be reasonably certain that a space would be available.

2.   Suppose there is an increase in demand. The demand curve shifts out to the right, creating a temporary shortage (excess demand) at the original price. As a result, buyers competitively bid up the price. As the price rises, the quantity demanded falls (movement up along the demand curve toward the new point of intersection) and the quantity supplied rises (movement up along the supply curve toward the new point of intersection). Eventually, the price rises enough until the quantity demanded is once again equal to the quantity supplied. Because there is neither a shortage nor a surplus at this new point of intersection, the new market equilibrium price and quantity is obtained. The market equilibrium price and quantity will both increase as a result of an increase in demand. *You should be able to illustrate this graphically as well.*

USING SUPPLY AND DEMAND

● CHAPTER AT A GLANCE

This review is based upon the learning objectives that open the chapter.

1. Changes (shifts) in demand and supply are what cause changes in the price and the quantity traded in real-world markets. (104-109)

    Shifts in both demand and supply can be tricky. But remember, simply locate the new point of intersection. When both curves shift, the effect on either price or quantity depends on the relative size of the shifts. Moreover, the effect on either price or quantity (one of them) will be certain, while the effect on the other will be uncertain. Note:

    ↑D and ↑S→?P;↑Q   ↑D and ↓S→↑P;? Q

    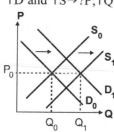   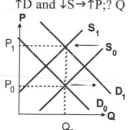

    ↓D and ↑S→↓P; ?Q   ↓D and ↓S→?P;↓ Q

    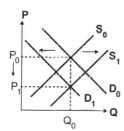   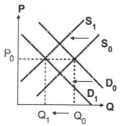

2. The determination of exchange rates—the price of currencies—can be determined by supply and demand analysis, in the same way supply and demand analysis applies to any other good. (105-107)

    Exchange rates reported daily in newspapers enable us to determine the dollar price of foreign goods.

3. Price ceilings cause shortages; price floors cause surpluses. (109-113)

    A price ceiling is a legal price set by government below equilibrium. An example is rent controls. A price floor (sometimes called a price support) is a legal price set by government above equilibrium. An example is the minimum wage.

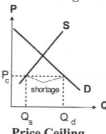

    Price Ceiling   **Price Floor**

4. Excise taxes and tariffs (excise taxes paid by foreign producers on imported goods) raise price and reduce quantity. Quantity restrictions also decrease supply (shift the supply curve up, to the left) raising the price and reducing the quantity. (113-115)

    Any excise tax imposed on suppliers shifts the supply curve up by the amount of the tax. Rarely is the tax entirely passed on to consumers in the form of a higher price. Quantity restrictions also decrease supply.

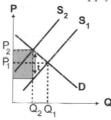

With tax t, price rises to P_2 and the government collects revenue shown by the shaded region. A quantity restriction of Q_2 has the same effect on price and quantity.

5. In a third-party payer system, the consumer and the one who pays the cost differ. In third-party payer systems quantity demanded, price, and total spending are greater than when the consumer pays. (115-116)

   The graph below shows the effects of a third-party payer market. In a free market, given the supply and demand curve shown, equilibrium price is P_1 and equilibrium quantity is Q_1. If the co-payment, however, is P_0, the consumer purchases quantity Q_2. The supplier will only sell that quantity at price P_2, so the third party pays the difference $(P_2 - P_0)$. Under a third-party payer system, total expenditures are larger—shown by the larger shaded square—than a free market—shown by the smaller and darker shaded square.

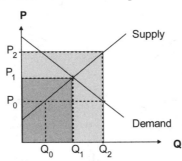

   Third-party payers are typically health insurance companies, Medicare or Medicaid. Consumers have little incentive to hold down costs when someone else pays. Much of the health care system in the United States today is a third-party payer system.

   See also, "Appendix A: Algebraic Representation of Supply, Demand, and Equilibrium."

● SHORT-ANSWER QUESTIONS

1. Demonstrate graphically what happens in the following situation: Income in the U.S. rose in the 1990s and more and more people began to buy luxury items such as caviar. However, about that same time, the dissolution of the Soviet Union threw suppliers of caviar from the Caspian Sea into a mire of bureaucracy, reducing their ability to export caviar. Market: Caviar sold in the United States.

2. What changes in demand or supply would increase the exchange rate value of the dollar?

3. What is a price ceiling? Demonstrate graphically the effect of a price ceiling on a market.

4. What is a price floor? Demonstrate graphically the effect of a price floor on a market.

5. Why are rent controls likely to worsen an existing shortage of housing?

6. Demonstrate graphically what happens to equilibrium price and quantity when a tariff is imposed on imports.

7. What is a third-party payer system? Name one example.

MATCHING THE TERMS
Match the terms to their definitions

___	**1.** euro	**a.**	The law that sets lowest wage a firm can legally pay an employee.
___	**2.** exchange rate	**b.**	Tax on an imported good.
___	**3.** excise tax	**c.**	Tax that is levied on a specific good.
___	**4.** minimum wage law	**d.**	The person who decides how much of the good to buy differs from the person paying for the good.
___	**5.** price ceiling		
___	**6.** price floor	**e.**	A government-imposed limit on how high a price can be charged.
___	**7.** rent control	**f.**	The price of one currency in terms of another currency.
___	**8.** tariff	**g.**	Price ceiling on rents set by government.
___	**9.** third-party payer market	**h.**	A government-imposed limit on how low a price can be charged.
		i.	The currency used by some members of the European Union.

● PROBLEMS AND APPLICATIONS

1. Suppose you are told that the price of Cadillacs has increased from last year, as has the number bought and sold. Is this an exception to the law of demand, or has there been a change in demand or supply that could account for this?

2. Suppose the exchange rate is one dollar for 125 Japanese yen. How much will a $50 pair of Levi jeans cost a Japanese consumer? How much will a 4,000,000 yen Toyota cost an American consumer?

3. The following table depicts the market supply and demand for milk in the United States.

Price in dollars per gal.	Quantity of gal. supplied in 1,000s	Quantity of gal. demanded in 1,000s
$1.50	600	800
$1.75	620	720
$2.00	640	640
$2.25	660	560
$2.50	680	480

a. Graph the market supply and demand for milk.

b. What is the equilibrium market price and quantity in the market?

c. Show the effect of a government–imposed price floor of $2.25 on the quantity supplied and quantity demanded.

d. Show the effect of a government–imposed price ceiling of $1.75 on the quantity supplied and quantity demanded.

e. What would happen to equilibrium price and quantity if the government imposes a $1 per gallon tax on the sellers and as a result, at every price supply decreases by 100,000? What price would the sellers receive?

4. Suppose the U.S. government imposes stricter entry barriers on Japanese cars imported into the United States. This could be accomplished by the U.S. government either raising tariffs or imposing a quantity restriction (such as a quota).

    a. What impact would this have on the market for Japanese cars in the United States?

    b. What impact would this likely have on the market for American-made cars in the United States?

    c. What do you think could motivate the U.S. government to pursue these stricter entry barriers on Japanese cars coming into the U.S.?

    d. Would Japanese car manufacturers prefer a tariff or a quota? Why?

5. Describe what likely happens to market price and quantity for the particular goods in each of the following cases:

    a. A technological breakthrough lowers the costs of producing tractors in India while there is an increase in incomes of all citizens in India. Market: tractors.

    b. The United States imposes a ban on the sale of oil by companies that do business with Libya and Iran. At the same time, very surprisingly, a large reserve of drillable oil is discovered in Barrington, Rhode Island. Market: Oil.

    c. In the summer of 2004, many people watched the Summer Olympics on television instead of going to the movies. At the same time, thinking that summer is the peak season for movies, Hollywood released a record number of movies. Market: Movie tickets.

    d. After a promotional visit by Michael Jordan to France, a craze for Nike Air shoes develops, while workers in Nike's manufacturing plants in China go on strike, decreasing the production of these shoes. Market: Nike shoes.

A1. The supply and demand equations for strawberries are given by $Q_s = -10 + 5P$ and $Q_d = 20 - 5P$ respectively, where P is price in dollars per quart, Q_s is millions of quarts of strawberries supplied, and Q_d is millions of quarts of strawberries demanded.

    a. What is the equilibrium market price and quantity for strawberries in the market?

b. Suppose a new preservative is introduced that prevents more strawberries from rotting on their way from the farm to the store. As a result, the supply of strawberries increases by 20 million quarts at every price. What effect does this have on market price and quantity sold?

c. Given the original supply, now suppose it has been found that the spray used on cherry trees has ill effects on those who eat the cherries. As a result, the demand for strawberries increases by 10 million quarts at every price. What effect does this have on market price for strawberries and quantity of strawberries sold?

A2. The supply and demand equations for roses are given by $Q_s = -10 + 3P$ and $Q_d = 20 - 2P$ respectively, where P is dollars per dozen roses and Q is dozens of roses in hundred thousands.

a. What is the equilibrium market price and quantity of roses sold?

b. Suppose the government decides to make it more affordable for individuals to give roses to their significant others, and sets a price ceiling for roses at $4 a dozen. What is the likely result?

c. Suppose the government decides to tax the suppliers of roses $1 per dozen roses sold. What is the equilibrium price and quantity in the market? How much do buyers pay for each dozen they buy for their significant others? How much do suppliers receive for each dozen they sell?

d. Suppose the government decides instead to impose a $1 tax on buyers for each dozen roses purchased. (Government has determined buying roses for love to be a demerit good.) What is the equilibrium price and quantity in the market? How much do the buyers pay and how much do the sellers receive?

● A BRAIN TEASER

1. Buchananland wants to restrict its number of auto imports from Zachstan. It is trying to decide whether it should impose a tariff or quantity restrictions (in this case called quotas) on Zachstani cars. With the help of a diagram, explain why auto makers in Zachstan have hired a lobbyist to persuade the government of Buchananland to set quotas instead of imposing tariffs.

● MULTIPLE CHOICE

Circle the one best answer for each of the following questions:

1. If a frost in Florida damages oranges, what will likely happen to the market for Florida oranges?
   a. Demand will increase.
   b. Demand will fall.
   c. Supply will increase.
   d. Supply will decrease.

2. Assume that the cost of shipping automobiles from the United States to Japan decreases. What will most likely happen to the selling price and quantity of cars made in the U.S. and sold in Japan?
   a. The price will rise, and quantity will fall.
   b. Both price and quantity will rise.
   c. The price will fall, and quantity will rise.
   d. The price will fall. What happens to quantity is not clear.

3. Assuming standard supply and demand curves, what will likely happen to the price and quantity of cricket bats in Trinidad as interest in cricket dwindles following the dismal performance of the national cricket team, while at the same time taxes are repealed on producing cricket bats?
   a. The price will decrease, but what happens to quantity is not clear.
   b. The price will decrease, and quantity will increase.
   c. The price will increase, but what happens to quantity is not clear.
   d. It is not clear what happens to either price or quantity.

4. A higher equilibrium price with no change in market equilibrium quantity could be caused by:
   a. supply shifting in and no change in demand.
   b. supply and demand both increasing.
   c. a decrease in supply and an increase in demand.
   d. demand and supply both shifting in.

5. A fall in the value of the euro relative to the dollar:
   a. could be caused by an increase in the demand for the euro.
   b. could be caused by an increase in the supply of the euro.
   c. will make American made goods cheaper for Europeans.
   d. will make European-made goods more expensive for Americans.

6. An increase in the value of the dollar relative to the euro could be caused by:
   a. an increase in the supply of the dollar.
   b. an increase in the demand for the dollar.
   c. a decrease in the demand for the dollar.
   d. an increase in U.S. imports.

7. An expected decline in the value of U.S. stocks will most likely:
   a. increase the supply of the euro and increase the demand for the dollar.
   b. increase the supply of the dollar and increase the demand for the euro.
   c. decrease the demand for the dollar and the euro.
   d. increase the demand for the dollar and the euro.

8. Referring to the graph below, if there is a price ceiling imposed on this market of P_2, consumers will pay:

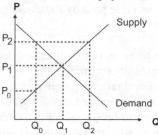

   a. P_1 and buy quantity Q_1.
   b. P_2 and buy quantity Q_2.
   c. P_0 and buy quantity Q_0.
   d. P_2 and buy quantity Q_0.

9. Referring to the graph below, if there is a price floor imposed on this market of P_2, consumers will pay:

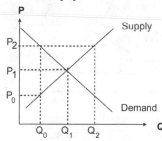

   a. P_1 and buy quantity Q_1.
   b. P_2 and buy quantity Q_2.
   c. P_0 and buy quantity Q_0.
   d. P_2 and buy quantity Q_0.

10. Effective rent controls:
    a. are examples of price floors.
    b. cause the quantity of rental occupied housing demanded to exceed the quantity supplied.
    c. create a greater amount of higher quality housing to be made available to renters.
    d. create a surplus of rental occupied housing.

11. An increase in the minimum wage can be expected to:
   a. cause unemployment for some workers.
   b. cause a shortage of workers.
   c. increase employment.
   d. help businesses by reducing their costs of production.

12. A tariff:
   a. is a tax imposed on an imported good.
   b. is a quantitative restriction on the amount that one country can export to another.
   c. imposed on a good will shift the supply of that good outward to the right.
   d. will reduce the price paid by the consumer of the good.

13. Quantity restrictions on supply imposed below equilibrium quantity on a market:
   a. increase price and reduce quantity traded.
   b. increase price and increase quantity traded.
   c. decrease price and reduce quantity traded.
   d. decrease price and increase quantity traded.

14. Referring to the graph below, suppose initial supply is represented by S_0. A tax T on suppliers will raise the price that:

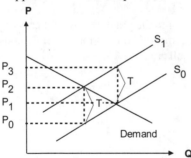

   a. suppliers receive net of the tax to P_1.
   b. suppliers receive net of the tax to P_2.
   c. consumers pay to P_2.
   d. consumers pay to P_3.

15. In a third-party payer system:
   a. the person who chooses the product pays the entire cost.
   b. the quantity demanded would be lower than it otherwise would be.
   c. the quantity demanded will be higher than it otherwise would be.
   d. consumers are hurt.

16. In the graph below that demonstrates a third-party payer market, suppose the consumer is required to make a co-payment of P_0. Which of the following areas represents the cost of the program to the third party?

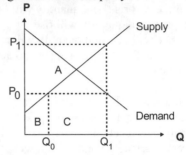

   a. rectangle A.
   b. retangle B.
   c. retangle C.
   d. the sum of rectangles A, B, and C.

17. Third-party payer markets result in:
   a. a lower equilibrium price received by the supplier.
   b. a smaller quantity supplied.
   c. a smaller quantity demanded
   d. increased total spending.

A1. The supply and demand equations for Nantucket Nectar's Kiwi-berry juice are given by $Q_s = -4 + 5P$ and $Q_d = 18 - 6P$ respectively, where price is dollars per quart and quantity is thousands of quarts. The equilibrium market price and quantity is:
   a. P = $2, Q = 6 thousand quarts.
   b. P = $3, Q = 5 thousand quarts.
   c. P = $14, Q = 66 thousand quarts.
   d. P = $22, Q = 106 thousand quarts.

A2. The supply and demand equations for sidewalk snow removal in a small town in Montana are given by $Q_s = -50 + 5P$ and $Q_d = 100 - 5P$ respectively, where price is in dollars per removal and quantity is numbers of removals per week. It snows so much that demand for sidewalk snow removals increases by 30 per week. The new equilibrium market price and quantity is:
   a. P = $15, Q = 6 sidewalk snow removals.
   b. P = $15, Q = 5 sidewalk snow removals.
   c. P = $18, Q = 66 sidewalk snow removals.
   d. P = $18, Q = 40 sidewalk snow removals.

A3. The supply and demand equations for Arizona Ice Tea in Arizona is given by $Q_s = -10 + 6P$ and $Q_d = 40 - 8P$; P is the price of each bottle in dollars; and quantity is in hundreds of thousands of bottles per month. Suppose the state government imposes a $1 per bottle tax on the suppliers. The market price the suppliers receive and the equilibrium quantity in the market are:

a. $3 per bottle and 8 hundred thousand bottles per month.

b. $3 per bottle and 16 hundred thousand bottles per month.

c. $4 per bottle and 8 hundred thousand bottles per month.

d. $4 per bottle and 16 hundred thousand bottles per month.

● POTENTIAL ESSAY QUESTIONS

You may also see essay questions similar to the "Problems & Applications" and "A Brain Teaser" exercises.

1. Discuss the impact on the relative price of American exports and imports if the exchange rate value of the dollar rises.

2. Explain why a third-party payer system results in a greater quantity demanded and increases total spending.

━━━━ ● ANSWERS ● ━━━━

SHORT-ANSWER QUESTIONS

1. The demand curve for Russian caviar shifts out; supply shifts in; the price rises substantially. What happens to quantity depends upon the relative sizes of the shifts. (108-109)

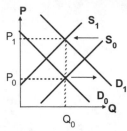

2. Either an increase in the demand or a decrease in the supply of the dollar could increase its price (exchange rate). (108-109)

3. A price ceiling is a government imposed limit on how high a price can be charged. An effective price ceiling below market equilibrium price will cause $Q_D > Q_S$ (a shortage) as shown in the graph below. (109-111)

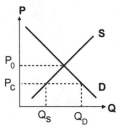

4. A price floor is a government imposed limit on how low a price can be charged. An effective price floor above market equilibrium price will cause $Q_S > Q_D$ (a surplus) as shown in the graph below. (111-113)

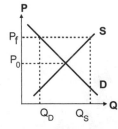

5. Rent controls are price ceilings and result in shortages in rental housing. As time passes and as the population rises, the demand for rental housing rises. On the supply side, other ventures become more lucrative relative to renting out housing. Owners have less incentive to repair existing buildings, let alone build new ones, reducing the supply of rental housing over time. As a result, the shortage becomes more acute over time (110-111)

6. A tariff is an excise tax paid by foreign producers on an imported good. As a tariff of t is imposed, the supply curve shifts upward to S_1 by the amount of the tariff. The equilibrium price goes up and quantity goes down. (113-114)

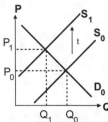

7. In a third-party payer system the person who decides how much of a good to buy differs from the person who pays for the good. One example is the health care system in the United States today. (115-116)

━━━━ ● ANSWERS ● ━━━━

MATCHING

1-i; 2-f; 3-c; 4-a; 5-e; 6-h; 7-g; 8-b; 9-d;

━━━━ ● ANSWERS ● ━━━━

PROBLEMS AND APPLICATIONS

1. This is not an exception to the law of demand (there are very few exceptions). Instead, an increase in demand could account for a higher price and a greater amount bought and sold, as is illustrated in the figure below. (108-109)

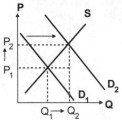

2. The Levi jeans will cost the Japanese consumer
    6,250 yen (125x50). The Toyota will cost the
    American consumer $32,000 (4,000,000/125).
    (105-107)

3. a. The market supply and demand for milk is
        graphed below. (box on 106, 108-109)

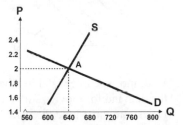

    b. The equilibrium market price is $2 and
        equilibrium quantity in the market is 640
        thousand gallons of milk because the
        quantity supplied equals the quantity
        demanded. This is point A on the graph
        above. (box on 106, 108-109)
    c. A government–imposed price floor of
        $2.25 is shown in the figure below. Since it
        is a price above market price, quantity
        supplied (660) exceeds quantity de-
        manded (560) by 100 thousand gallons.
        (111-113)

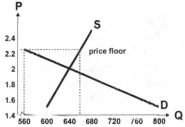

    d. A government-imposed price ceiling of
        $1.75 is below market price. Quantity
        supplied (620 thousand gallons) will be
        less than quantity demanded (720 thou-
        sand gallons) by 100 thousand gallons, as
        shown below. (109-111)

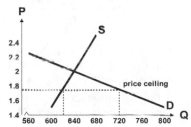

e. Because of the tax, the quantity supplied
    at every price level will decline by 100
    thousand gallons. The supply and demand
    table will change as follows:

Price in dollars per gal.	Quantity of gal. supplied 1,000s	Quantity of gal. demanded 1,000s
$1.50	500	800
$1.75	520	720
$2.00	540	640
$2.25	560	560
$2.50	580	480

The market equilibrium price would be
$2.25 and the equilibrium quantity would
be 560 thousand gallons. Since the sellers
will have to pay $1 tax on every gallon
they sell, they will receive $1.25 per gallon
of milk. (113-114)

4. a. A higher tariff or a stricter quota imposed
        on Japanese cars would decrease the
        supply of Japanese cars in the United
        States. The upward (leftward) shift of the
        supply curve, such as from S_1 to S_2 shown
        in the figure below, creates a temporary
        shortage (excess demand) at the original
        price that puts upward pressure on the
        prices of Japanese cars. The result over
        time will be higher prices for Japanese
        cars, as well as a decrease in the amount
        bought and sold in the U.S. market, as
        shown below. (113-115)

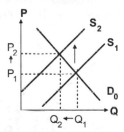

    b. Because Japanese and American-made
        cars are substitutes for each other, some
        people will switch from buying the now
        relatively more expensive Japanese cars
        (law of demand in action) to buying more
        American-made cars. (Notice that
        "relative" prices are what are relevant.)
        This increases the demand for American-
        made cars, increasing their prices as well

as the amount bought and sold. This is illustrated in the figure below. (113-115)

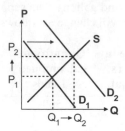

c. These trade barriers may be advocated by American car manufacturers. They could obviously benefit from the higher prices and greater sales. American automotive workers could also benefit from the greater job security that comes with more cars being produced and sold. These "special interest groups" may put political pressure on government, and the government may succumb to that pressure. (113-115)

d. The Japanese would prefer a quota over a tariff. This is because a tariff would require them to pay taxes to the U.S. government; while a quota would not. (113-115)

5. a. The supply curve will shift out from S_0 to S_1 as the new technology makes it cheaper to produce tractors. Increased incomes will shift the demand for tractors out from D_0 to D_1. Equilibrium price may go up, remain the same, or go down, depending on the relative shifts in the two curves. Equilibrium quantity, however, will definitely increase. (108-109)

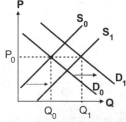

b. The ban on the companies doing business with Libya and Iran will shift the supply curve in from S_0 to S_1. The discovery of oil will, however, shift it back out to possibly S_2. Depending on the relative shifts, equilibrium price and quantity will change. In the case shown in the diagram, the shift resulting from the discovery of

the new oil source dominates the shift resulting from the ban, and the equilibrium price falls and quantity goes up. (108-109)

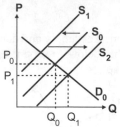

c. With more people watching the Olympics, the demand for movies shifts in from D_0 to D_1. At the same time the increased supply of movies will shift the supply curve out from S_0 to S_1. Equilibrium price will fall, while the change in equilibrium quantity will depend on the relative shifts in the curves. (108-109)

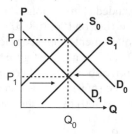

d. With more people demanding Nike Air shoes, the demand curve will shift out from D_0 to D_1. The worker strike will, however, reduce supply and shift it in from S_0 to S_1. The resulting equilibrium price will be higher, while the change in quantity depends on the relative shifts in the curves. (108-109)

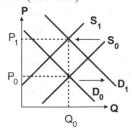

A1. a. Equating Q_s to Q_d and then solving for equilibrium price gives us $3 per quart. Substituting $3 into the demand and supply equations, we find that equilibrium quantity is 5 million quarts. (121)

h. Since supply increases by 20 million quarts, the new supply equation is $Q_s = 10 + 5P$. Equating this with the demand equation, we find the new equilibrium price to be $1 per quart. Substituting into either the new supply equation or the demand equation we find that equilibrium quantity is 15 million quarts. (122-123)

c. With demand increasing, the new demand equation is $Q_d = 30 - 5P$. Setting Q_s equal to Q_d and solving for price we find equilibrium price to be $4 per quart. Substituting this into either the new demand or the supply equation we find equilibrium quantity to be 10 million quarts. (122-123)

A2. a. Equating Q_s and Q_d, then solving gives equilibrium price $6 and quantity 8 hundred thousand dozen. (121)

b. If price ceiling is set at $4, $Q_s = 2$, and $Q_d = 12$; resulting in a shortage of ten hundred thousand dozen. (123)

c. If a $1 tax is imposed on suppliers, the new supply equation will be $Q_s = -10 + 3(P-1) = -13 + 3P$. Equating this with Q_d gives equilibrium price $6.60 and quantity 6.8 hundred thousand. Buyers pay $6.60 for each dozen they buy, and the sellers receive $1 less than that, or $5.60, for each dozen they sell. (123-124)

d. As a result of the tax, the new demand equation will be $Q_d = 20 - 2(P+1) = 18 - 2P$. Equating this with Q_s gives equilibrium price $5.60 and quantity 6.8 hundred thousand. Buyers pay $6.60 (P + 1) for each dozen they buy, and the sellers receive $5.60 for each dozen they sell. (123-124)

ANSWERS

A BRAIN TEASER

1. The supply and demand equilibrium are at price P_e and quality Q_e. If quotas for Zachstani cars are set at Q_2, the price received for each car sold is P_2, which is well above P_t, the price they would normally sell for at that quantity. A tariff of $t\,(P_2 - P_t)$ would have to be imposed to reduce imports to Q_2 reflected by the supply curve shifting in to S_1. In both cases, consumers pay Zachstan producers P_2 for each car. In the case of the quota, Zachstan producers keep P_2 for each car. In the case of the tariff, Zachstan producers must give up t to the government for each car sold. Because with quotas the price received (and therefore profits) are higher, they have the lobbyist lobbying for quotas. (113-115)

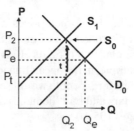

ANSWERS

MULTIPLE CHOICE

1. **d**   A frost will reduce the quantity of oranges available for sale at every price. Supply will decrease. See page 108-109.

2. **c**   The supply curve will shift out, market price will fall and the quantity will rise. See pages 108-109.

3. **a**   Demand for cricket bats will fall, shifting the demand curve in, while the tax repeal will shift the supply curve out. Price will fall, and quantity may change depending on the relative shifts of the supply and demand curves. See pages 108-109.

4. **c**   When the demand curve shifts out, while the supply curve shifts in, the price rises and the quantity can remain the same. See pages 108-109.

5. **b**   The analysis of currencies is the same as the analysis for any other good. A shift of supply out and to the right will result in a lower price. A fall in the value of the euro means it will take fewer dollars to purchase one euro, making European-made goods cheaper for Americans and American-made goods more expensive for Europeans. See pages 105-107.

6. b An increase in the price of anything would require an increase in demand or a decrease in supply. An increase in U.S. imports will increase the supply of dollars lowering the price of the dollar. See pages 105-107.

7. b Falling U.S. stock prices would encourage people to get out of the U.S. stock market and place their funds elsewhere, for example, in European financial markets. Therefore, people would sell (supply) dollars and buy (demand) more euros. See pages 105-107.

8. a As discussed on pages 109-111, a price ceiling above equilibrium price will not affect the market price or quantity. Equilibrium price and quantity, in this case will be determined by the intersection of the supply and demand curves—at price P_1 and quantity Q_1.

9. d At a price of P_2 the quantity demanded by consumers is Q_0. The quantity supplied by sellers would be Q_2 at price P_2. A surplus of $Q_2 - Q_0$ would put downward pressure on price. However, government does not allow a lower price. So, the equilibrium price and quantity of P_1 and Q_1 would not prevail when government intervenes with a price floor. See pages 111-113.

10. b Rent controls are price ceilings and therefore cause the quantity demanded to exceed the quantity supplied. Indeed, the quantity demanded rises while the quantity supplied falls creating a shortage. See pages 109-111.

11. a Because the minimum wage is a price floor it increases the quantity supplied and decreases the quantity demanded (*decreasing* employment) and creating a *surplus* of workers (causing some unemployment). The higher minimum wage would *increase* costs of production to businesses. See pages 111-113.

12. a The correct answer is a by definition. Also, a tariff will decrease supply, shifting the supply curve inward to the left. This causes the price consumers must pay to rise. See pages 113-114.

13. a Quantity restrictions reduce supply and create a higher price and lower quantity traded in a market. See pages 114-115.

14. c A tax shifts the supply curve up by the amount of the tax. The price consumers pay is determined by the price where the demand curve and the after-tax supply curve intersect. The after-tax price suppliers receive falls to P_0, the new equilibrium price less the tax ($P_2 - T$). See pages 113-114.

15. c In a third-party payer system the person who chooses the product pays some but not all of the cost. As a result of a lower effective price to the consumer, the quantity demanded will be higher than otherwise. See pages 115-116.

16. a At a price of P_0, the consumer demands quantity Q_1. The supplier requires a price of P_1 for that quantity. Therefore, total expenditures are P_1 times Q_1 or areas A, B, and C. Of this, consumers pay areas B and C. The third party pays area A. See pages 115-116.

17. d In third-party payer markets the quantity demanded, price, and total spending are greater than when the consumer pays. See pages 115-116.

A1. a Equating the supply and demand equations gives equilibrium P = \$2. Substituting this into either the supply or demand equation tells us that Q = 6 thousand quarts. See page 121.

A2. d The new demand becomes $Q_d = 130 - 5P$. Equating the supply and demand equations gives equilibrium P = \$18. Substituting this into either the supply or demand equation tells us that Q = 40 sidewalk snow removals. See pages 122-123.

A3. a A $1 per bottle tax on suppliers makes the supply equation $Q_s = -10 + 6(P-1) = -16 + 6P$. Equating this with the demand equation gives equilibrium $P = \$4$ and $Q = 8$ hundred thousand. The supplier receives $3 (\$4 - \$1)$. See pages 123-124.

ANSWERS

POTENTIAL ESSAY QUESTIONS

The following are annotated answers. They indicate the general idea behind the answer.

1. An increase in the exchange rate value of the dollar means that the dollar will buy more units of foreign currencies. Therefore, the relative price of foreign products imported into the United States will decrease and Americans will import more. Likewise, a stronger dollar will make American products relatively more expensive to foreigners. Foreigners will buy fewer American products and the United States will export less. If U.S. imports rise and exports fall, the U.S. trade deficit rises.

2. Because part of the costs of obtaining a good or service in a third-party payer system is paid by someone other than the consumer, the effective price to the consumer is lower and the quantity demanded is greater. At this higher quantity demanded the price charged by sellers is greater. The result is greater consumption at a higher price and therefore greater total spending on the good or service. See Figure 5-7 on page 115 for a graphic illustration of this.

Pretest
Chapters 1 - 5

I

Take this test in test conditions, giving yourself a limited amount of time to complete the questions. Ideally, check with your professor to see how much time he or she allows for an average multiple choice question and multiply this by 26. This is the time limit you should set for yourself for this pretest. If you do not know how much time your teacher would allow, we suggest 1 minute per question, or about 25 minutes.

1. Economic reasoning:
   a. provides a framework with which to approach questions.
   b. provides correct answers to just about every question.
   c. is only used by economists.
   d. should only be applied to economic business matters.

2. You bought stock A for $10 and stock B for $50. The price of each is currently $20. Assuming no tax issues, which should you sell if you need money?
   a. Stock A.
   b. Stock B.
   c. The price at which you bought it doesn't matter.
   d. You should sell an equal amount of both.

3. The opportunity cost of reading Chapter 1 of the text:
   a. is about 1/34 of the price you paid for the book because the chapter is about one 1/34 of the book.
   b. zero since you have already paid for the book
   c. has nothing to do with the price you paid for the book.
   d. is 1/34 the price of the book plus 1/34 the price of the tuition.

4. If at Female College there are significantly more females than males (and there are not a significant number of gays), economic forces:
   a. will be pushing for females to pay on dates.
   b. will be pushing for males to pay on dates.
   c. will be pushing for neither to pay on dates.
   d. are irrelevant to this issue. Everyone knows that the males always should pay.

5. The statement, "The distribution of income should be left to the market," is:
   a. a positive statement.
   b. a normative statement.
   c. an art-of-economics statement.
   d. an objective statement.

6. If the opportunity cost of good X in terms of good Y is 2Y, so you'll have to give up 2Y to get one X, the production possibility curve would look like:
   a. A only.
   b. B only.
   c. C only.
   d. A, B or C.

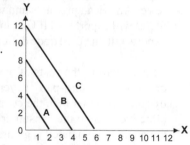

7. Given the accompanying production possibility curve, when you're moving from point C to point B the opportunity cost of butter in terms of guns is:
   a. 1/3.
   b. 1.
   c. 2.
   d. 3/2.

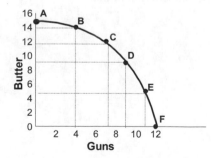

8. If countries A and B have production possibility curves A and B respectively, country A has a comparative advantage in the production of:
   a. no good.
   b. both goods.
   c. good X only.
   d. good Y only.

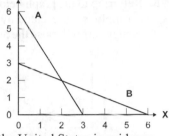

9. Outsourcing in the United States is evidence that:
   a. the United States does not have any comparative advantages.
   b. the U.S. dollar is valued too low.
   c. the law of one price doesn't hold.
   d. the law of one price is affecting global production.

10. Globalization:
    a. is decreasing in importance.
    b. increases competition.
    c. reduces the need to specialize.
    d. reduces productivity.

11. According to the law of one price:
    a. wages will eventually be the same for every industry.
    b. wages will eventually be the same in every country.
    c. wage differences cannot continue unless they reflect differences in productivity.
    d. wage differences can continue as long as product prices can differ among countries.

12. In theory, socialism is an economic system:
    a. that tries to organize society in the same ways as most families organize, striving to see that individuals get what they need.
    b. based on central planning and government ownership of the means of production.
    c. based on private property rights.
    d. based on markets.

13. In practice, in command or socialist economies, the "what to produce" decision in practice was most often made by:
    a. consumers.
    b. the market.
    c. government.
    d. firms.

14. The largest percentage of business receipts are by:
    a. partnerships.
    b. sole proprietorships.
    c. corporations.
    d. nonprofit companies.

15. The largest percentage of state and local expenditures is on:
    a. education.
    b. health and medical care.
    c. highways.
    d. income security.

16. There are many more substitutes for good A than for good B.
    a. The demand curve for good B will likely shift out further.
    b. The demand curve for good B will likely be flatter.
    c. You can't say anything about the likely relative flatness of the demand curves.
    d. The demand curve for good A will likely be flatter.

17. If the price of air conditioners falls, there will be:
    a. an increase in demand for air conditioners.
    b. an increase in the quantity of air conditioners demanded.
    c. an increase in the quantity of air conditioners supplied.
    d. a shift out of the demand for air conditioners.

18. The movement in the graph below from point A to point B represents:

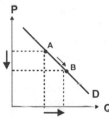

    a. an increase in demand.
    b. an increase in the quantity demanded.
    c. an increase in the quantity supplied.
    d. an increase in supply.

19. The law of supply states that:
   a. quantity supplied increases as price increases, other things constant.
   b. quantity supplied decreases as price increases, other things constant.
   c. more of a good will be supplied the higher its price, other things changing proportionately.
   d. less of a good will be supplied the higher its price, other things changing proportionately.

20. If at some price the quantity supplied exceeds the quantity demanded then:
   a. a surplus (excess supply) exists and the price will fall over time as sellers competitively bid down the price.
   b. a shortage (excess demand) exists and the price will rise over time as buyers competitively bid up the price.
   c. the price is below equilibrium.
   d. equilibrium will be reestablished as the demand curve shifts to the left.

21. An increase in demand for a good will cause:
   a. excess demand (a shortage) before price changes.
   b. movement down along the demand curve as price changes.
   c. movement down along the supply curve as price changes.
   d. a higher price and a smaller quantity traded in the market.

22. If a frost in Florida damages oranges, what will likely happen to the market for Florida oranges?
   a. Demand will increase.
   b. Demand will fall.
   c. Supply will increase.
   d. Supply will decrease.

23. A higher equilibrium price with no change in market equilibrium quantity could be caused by:
   a. supply shifting in and no change in demand.
   b. supply and demand both increasing.
   c. a decrease in supply and an increase in demand.
   d. demand and supply both shifting in.

24. Effective rent controls:
   a. are examples of price floors.
   b. cause the quantity of rental occupied housing demanded to exceed the quantity supplied.

   c. create a greater amount of higher quality housing to be made available to renters.
   d. create a surplus of rental occupied housing.

25. Referring to the graph below, suppose initial supply is represented by S_0. A tax T on suppliers will raise the price that:

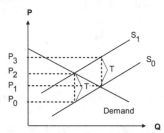

   a. suppliers receive net of the tax to P_1.
   b. suppliers receive net of the tax to P_2.
   c. consumers pay to P_2.
   d. consumers pay to P_3.

26. Third-party payer markets result in:
   a. a lower equilibrium price received by the supplier.
   b. a smaller quantity supplied.
   c. a smaller quantity demanded
   d. increased total spending.

━━━   ANSWERS   ━━━

1.	a	(1:1)	14.	c	(3:9)
2.	c	(1:5)	15.	a	(3:13)
3.	c	(1:11)	16.	d	(4:2)
4.	a	(1:13)	17.	b	(4:4)
5.	b	(1:17)	18.	b	(4:9)
6.	d	(2:3)	19.	a	(4:13)
7.	d	(2:6)	20.	a	(4:18)
8.	d	(2:12)	21.	a	(4:25)
9.	d	(2:16)	22.	d	(5:1)
10.	b	(2:17)	23.	c	(5:4)
11.	c	(2:18)	24.	b	(5:10)
12.	a	(3:2)	25.	c	(5:14)
13.	c	(3:5)	26.	d	(5:17)

Key: The figures in parentheses refer to multiple choice question and chapter numbers. For example (1:2) is multiple choice question 2 from chapter 1.

ECONOMIC GROWTH, BUSINESS CYCLES, UNEMPLOYMENT, AND INFLATION

CHAPTER AT A GLANCE

This review is based upon the learning objectives that open the chapter.

1. The long-run framework focuses on supply. The short-run framework focuses on demand. (128-129)

   Issues of growth are considered in a long-run framework. Business cycles are generally considered in a short-run framework. Unemployment and inflation fall within both frameworks.

2a. Growth is usually measured by changes in real GDP. U.S. economic output has grown at an annual rate of 2.5 to 3.5 percent. (129-130)

   Growth is desired because it increases standards of living.

2b. The range of growth rates among countries is wide. (130-131)

   Economies in Africa have consistently grown at below average rates. Japan and Western Europe grew quickly in the last half of the 20th century.

2c. Since 1945 the United States has had 10 recessions. (132-132)

2d. The target rate of unemployment is somewhere around 5 percent. (138)

   The target rate of unemployment has been called the "natural" rate of unemployment.

2e. Since World War II, the U.S. inflation rate has remained positive and relatively stable. (145)

3. The four phases of the business cycle are: the peak, the downturn, the trough, and the upturn. (133-134)

   Note!
   - *There is an overall upward secular growth trend of 2.5-3.5% shown by the dotted line.*
   - *We want to smooth out fluctuations because of the problems associated with them.*
   - *Two problems with a downturn (recession) are (a) cyclical unemployment and (b) low growth rate.*
   - *One problem with an upturn (expansion) is demand-pull inflation.*

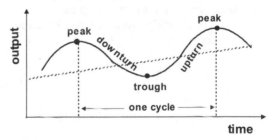

4a. Unemployment rate = $\dfrac{\text{unemployed}}{\text{labor force}} \times 100$. (136, 141)

   Unemployment measures are imperfect but are still a good gauge of the economy's performance.

4b. Some microeconomic categories of unemployment identified by: reason for unemployment, demographic unemployment, duration of unemployment, and unemployment by industry. (144)

   ✔ *Know the different types of unemployment.*

5. Potential output is defined as the output that will be achieved at the target rate of unemployment and the target level of capacity utilization. It is difficult to know precisely where potential output is. (143-144)

    Recession:
    Actual output (income) < Potential output.

    Expansion:
    Actual output (income) > Potential output.

    Target rate of unemployment (about 5%) is the lowest rate of unemployment that policymakers believe is achievable under existing conditions (where inflation is not accelerating). It is the rate of unemployment that exists when the economy is operating at potential.

6a. Inflation is a continual rise in the price level. (145)

    Price indexes are used to measure inflation; The most often used are the Producer Price Index (PPI), GDP deflator, and the Consumer Price Index (CPI).

6b. The "real" amount is the nominal amount adjusted for inflation. Real output is the nominal output divided by the price index multiplied by 100. (148-150)

    Real means "inflation-adjusted."

    $$Real\ Output = \frac{nominal\ output}{price\ index} \times 100$$

    Real interest rate = Nominal interest − Inflation

7. While inflation may not make the nation poorer, it does cause income to be redistributed and can reduce the amount of information that prices are supposed to convey. (151-152)

    Inflation hurts those who cannot or do not raise their prices, but benefits those who can and do raise their prices.

● SHORT-ANSWER QUESTIONS

1. What are the two frameworks economists use to analyze unemployment, inflation, growth, and business cycles? What distinguishes the two frameworks from one another?

2. What is the average growth rate of real output in the United States since 1890 to the present? What are the costs and the benefits of growth?

3. How long has the average expansion since mid-1945 lasted?

4. Since the late 1980s, what has been the target rate of unemployment?

5. What is the difference between pre-World War II and post-World War II (1945) inflation in the United States?

6. Label the four phases of the business cycle in the graph below.

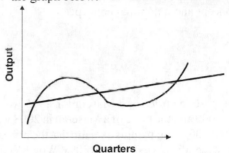

7. How is the unemployment rate calculated?

8. Who in the United States does not work and is nevertheless not counted as unemployed?

9. State two categories of unemployment for which microeconomic policies are appropriate. Why are such categories important to follow?

10. How is the target rate of unemployment related to potential output?

11. Define inflation. If there were no inflation what would happen to the distinction between a real concept and a nominal concept?

12. Suppose the price of a Maserati in 1975 was $75,000 and the price of a Maserati in 2008 was $210,000. Your parents exclaim that the prices of Maseratis have risen by 180%! Wow! You tell them that the price of a Maserati really hasn't risen that much. They are confusing real and nominal concepts. Explain what you mean.

13. What is the difference between expected and unexpected inflation?

14. What are two important costs of inflation?

MATCHING THE TERMS
Match the terms to their definitions

___ 1. business cycle

___ 2. consumer price index

___ 3. cyclical unemployment

___ 4. deflation

___ 5. frictional unemployment

___ 6. GDP deflator

___ 7. hyperinflation

___ 8. inflation

___ 9. labor force participation rate

___ 10. Okun's rule of thumb

___ 11. potential output

___ 12. real output

___ 13. recession

___ 14. structural unemployment

___ 15. target rate of unemployment

___ 16. unemployment rate

a. A downturn that persists for more than two consecutive quarters.

b. A continual rise in the price level.

c. A one percentage point change in the unemployment rate will cause output to change in the opposite direction by 2 percent.

d. Lowest sustainable rate of unemployment policymakers believe is achievable under existing conditions.

e. Index of inflation measuring prices of a fixed "basket" of consumer goods, weighted according to each component's share of an average consumer's expenditures.

f. Index of the average price of the components in GDP relative to a base year.

g. Labor force as a percentage of the total population at least 16 years old.

h. Inflation that hits triple digits (100 percent) or more per year.

i. Output that would materialize at the target rate of unemployment and the target rate of capacity utilization.

j. The total amount of goods and services produced, adjusted for price level changes.

k. The upward or downward movement of economic activity that occurs around the growth trend.

l. The percentage of people in the labor force who can't find a job.

m. Unemployment caused by new entrants to the job market and people who have left their jobs to look for and find other jobs.

n. Unemployment resulting from changes in the structure of the economy itself.

o. Unemployment resulting from fluctuations in economic activity.

p. A continual fall in the price level.

● PROBLEMS AND APPLICATIONS

1. State Okun's law (rule of thumb). For each of the following increases in the unemployment rate, state what will likely happen to output in the United States:

   a. Unemployment rate falls 2 percentage points.

   b. Unemployment rate falls 1 percentage point.

   c. Unemployment rate increases 3 percentage points.

2. For each, state whether the unemployment is structural or cyclical.

   a. As the United States becomes a more high-tech producer, labor-intensive factories relocate to low-wage countries. Factory workers lose their jobs and the unemployment rate rises.

   b. As it becomes more acceptable for mothers to work, more women enter the labor market looking for work. The unemployment rate rises.

   c. Foreign economics slow and demand fewer U.S. exports. Unemployment rate rises.

3. Calculate the following given the information about the economy in the table:

Total population	290 million
Noninstitutional population	220 million
Incapable of working	70 million
Not in the labor force	75 million
Employed	135 million
Unemployed	10 million

   a. Labor force.

   b. Unemployment rate.

4. Create a price index for New England Patriots fans using the following basket of goods with 2007 prices as the base year.

Quantities in 2007	Prices 2007	2008
12 packs of Pepsi	$2.50/pck	$2.00/pck
12 fan T-shirts	$15/shirt	$20/shirt
16 football tickets	$25/ticket	$30/ticket

   a. What is the price of the basket of goods in each year? Show how the price index is 100 in the base year 2007.

   b. Using 2007 as the base year, what is the price index in 2008? By how much have prices risen?

   c. What are some potential flaws of this price index?

5. Calculate the following given the following information about the economy in 1985, 1995, and 2006:

	1985	1995	2006
Nominal GDP (in billions of dollars)	4,220.3	____	12,246.6
GDP deflator (index,2000=100)	69.7	92.1	____
Real GDP (in billions of 2000 dollars)	____	8031.7	11,415.3
Population (in millions)	238	265	300

a. Nominal GDP in 1995.

b. Real GDP in 1985.

c. GDP deflator in 2006.

d. Rise in the price level from 1985 to 2006.

e. Growth in real output from 1985 to 2006.

f. Per capita real GDP in 1985, 1995, 2006. What was the growth in per capita real output from 1985 to 2006?

6. Answer each of the following questions about nominal output, real output, and inflation:
    a. Nominal output increased from $12,445.8 billion in 2005 to $13,246.6 billion in 2006. The GDP deflator rose over that same year by 2.9%. By how much did real output increase?

b. Real output increased from $9.19 trillion to $9.21 trillion from 2000 to 2001. The GDP deflator rose over that same year by 2.5%. By how much did nominal output increase?

c. Real output decreased from $6.70 billion in 1990 to $6.67 billion in 1991. Nominal output rose by 3.2%. By how much did the price level rise from 1990 to 1991?

● A BRAIN TEASER

1. How could output and unemployment rise in an economy at the same time?

● MULTIPLE CHOICE

Circle the one best answer for each of the following questions:

1. Inflation and unemployment:
    a. are best studied in the long-run framework.
    b. are best studied in the short-run framework.
    c. fall within both the short- and long-run frameworks.
    d. are not problems of today and therefore are not studied.

2. All of the following are long-run growth policies *except*:
    a. increasing government spending to spur consumer spending.
    b. reducing tax rates to increase incentives to work.
    c. providing funding for research.
    d. following policies to reduce interest rates and increase business investment.

3. If a country of 296 million people has a total income of $12 trillion, its per capita income is:
   a. $32.52.
   b. $35,520.
   c. $40.54.
   d. $40,541.

4. The secular trend growth rate in the United States is approximately:
   a. 1 to 1.5 percent per year.
   b. 2.5 to 3.5 percent per year.
   c. 5 to 5.5 percent per year.
   d. 7 to 7.5 percent per year.

5. Some people have argued that the two goals of (1) environmental protection and (2) economic growth that involves increased material consumption by individuals do not necessarily contradict each other because spending on the environment can create growth and jobs. This argument:
   a. offers great hope for the future.
   b. is incorrect because environmental issues are not as important as material consumption.
   c. is correct because material consumption is not as important as the environment.
   d. is incorrect because the environmental projects will use some of the resources generated from growth, leaving little or nothing for increased personal consumption.

6. From 1950 to 2007, which geographic area or country had the highest per capita growth rate?
   a. China.
   b. Western Europe.
   c. North America.
   d. Latin America.

7. The business cycle characterized by the Great Depression occurred in the early
   a. 1900s.
   b. 1930s.
   c. 1950s.
   d. 1960s.

8. Leading indicators include:
   a. manufacturing and trade sales volume.
   b. number of employees on non-agricultural payrolls.
   c. industrial production.
   d. new orders for goods and materials.

9. A Classical economist is most likely to support government intervention when an economy is:
   a. at a peak.
   b. at a trough.
   c. in a depression.
   d. in an upturn.

10. Under pure capitalism, the main deterrent of unemployment is:
    a. pure government intervention.
    b. pure market intervention.
    c. the fear of hunger.
    d. new immigrants entering the country.

11. Since the 1980s the target rate of unemployment generally has been:
    a. between 2 and 4 percent.
    b. between 3 and 5 percent.
    c. between 4 and 6 percent.
    d. between 7 and 9 percent.

12. Keynesians:
    a. generally favor activist government policies.
    b. generally favor laissez-faire policies.
    c. believe that frictional unemployment does not exist.
    d. believe that all unemployment is cyclical unemployment.

13. Classicals:
    a. generally favor activist government policies.
    b. generally favor laissez-faire policies.
    c. believe that frictional unemployment does not exist.
    d. believe that all unemployment is cyclical unemployment.

14. The level of output that would materialize at the target rate of unemployment and the target rate of capital utilization is called:
    a. nominal output.
    b. actual output.
    c. potential output.
    d. utilized output.

15. The real interest rate is equal to the:
    a. nominal interest rate minus the inflation rate.
    b. nominal interest rate plus the inflation rate.
    c. inflation rate minus the nominal interest rate.
    d. inflation rate plus the nominal interest rate.

16. Okun's rule of thumb states that:
    a. a 1 percentage-point change in the unemployment rate will cause output to change in the same direction by 2 percent.
    b. a 1 percentage-point change in the unemployment rate will cause output to change in the opposite direction by 2 percent.
    c. a 2 percentage-point change in the unemployment rate will cause output to change in the same direction by 1 percent.
    d. a 2 percentage-point change in the unemployment rate will cause output to change in the opposite direction by 1 percent.

17. Using Okun's rule of thumb, if unemployment rises from 5 to 6 percent, one would expect total output of $5 trillion to:
    a. rise by $5 billion.
    b. rise by $100 billion.
    c. fall by $100 billion.
    d. fall by $5 billion.

18. A one-time rise in the price level is:
    a. inflation if that rise is above 5 percent.
    b. inflation if that rise is above 10 percent.
    c. inflation if that rise is above 15 percent.
    d. not inflation.

19. Food and beverages make up about 15 percent of total expenditures. If food and beverage prices rise by 10 percent while the other components of the price index remain constant, approximately by how much will the price index rise?
    a. 1 percent.
    b. 1.5 percent.
    c. 15 percent.
    d. 25 percent.

20. Real output is:
    a. total amount of goods and services produced.
    b. total amount of goods and services produced adjusted for price level changes.
    c. total amount of goods produced, adjusted for services that aren't real.
    d. total amount of goods and services that are really produced as opposed to ones that are resold.

21. If the price level rises by 20 percent and real output remains constant, by how much will nominal output rise?
    a. 1 percent.
    b. 5 percent.
    c. 20 percent.
    d. 40 percent.

22. A cost of inflation is that:
    a. it makes everyone poorer.
    b. it makes the poor poorer but the rich richer.
    c. There are no costs of inflation because inflation does not make the society as a whole poorer.
    d. it reduces the informational content of prices.

23. Unexpected inflation:
    a. makes everyone poorer.
    b. redistributes income from those who raised their prices to those who did not.
    c. redistributes income from those who did not raise their prices to those who did.
    d. is impossible since firms always plan price increases.

● POTENTIAL ESSAY QUESTIONS

You may also see essay questions similar to the "Problems & Applications" and "A Brain Teaser" exercises.

1. Full employment, keeping inflation under control, and economic growth are among the major macroeconomic goals of all societies. Why is economic growth a major macroeconomic goal?

2. What is potential output and how is it related to the target rate of unemployment and the target level of capacity utilization? Which is greater: potential or actual output during a recession? During an economic boom?

3. What are some of the problems with the interpretation of unemployment statistics that can cause unemployment statistics to underestimate and to overestimate the true rate of unemployment? How do Classical and Keynesian economists differ in this regard?

ANSWERS

SHORT-ANSWER QUESTIONS

1. Economists use the long-run framework and the short-run framework to analyze macroeconomic problems. The long-run framework focuses on supply while the short-run framework focuses on demand. (128-129)

2. Real output has grown about 3.5% per year since 1890. In the 1970s and 1980s, the growth rate was more like 2.5 percent. In the late 1990s and early 2000s, it was again 3.5 percent. The benefits of growth are improvements in the standard of living, on average. The costs are pollution, resource exhaustion and destruction of natural habitat. (129-130)

3. The average expansion since mid-1945 has lasted 57 months. (133)

4. Since the late 1980s, the target rate of unemployment has been around 5 percent. (138)

5. The inflation rate in the U.S. before World War II fluctuated and was sometimes positive and sometimes negative. Since World War II the price level has continually risen. (145)

6. The four phases of the business cycle are: the peak, the downturn (recession), the trough, and the upturn. They are labeled in the graph below. (133-134)

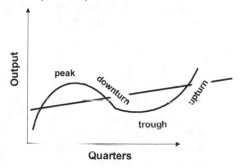

7. The unemployment rate is calculated by dividing the number of unemployed individuals by the number of people in the civilian labor force, and multiplying the result by 100. (141-142)

8. Those who are not in the labor force and those incapable of working are not employed and are not counted as unemployed. They include students, retirees, homemakers, those incapable of working, and those who choose not to participate in the labor force. (141-142)

9. Two microeconomic subcategories of unemployment include the reason for unemployment and demographic unemployment. Others are duration of unemployment and unemployment by industry. These categories are important to follow because policies affect different types of unemployment differently and sometimes macro policies should be supplemented by micro policies. (144)

10. Potential output is that level of output that will be achieved at the target rate of unemployment. (144)

11. Inflation is a continual rise in the price level. If there were no inflation there would be no difference between real and nominal concepts. A real concept is the nominal concept adjusted for inflation. (145, 148-149)

12. Nominally Maseratis have risen by 180% from 1975 to 2008, but all other prices have risen during that time period too, including wages. You must adjust the rise in the aggregate price level to find out how much Maseratis have risen in real terms. From 1975 to 2008, the price level rose by 147%. (We used the *Economic Report of the President* to find this information.) So, the real price of the Maserati rose by approximately 33% from 1975 to 2008. (148-151)

13. Expected inflation is the amount of inflation that people predict. Unexpected inflation is inflation that is a surprise. (150-151)

14. Two important costs of inflation are that it redistributes income from people who do not raise their prices to people who do raise their prices; and it can reduce the amount of information that prices are supposed to convey. (151-152)

━━━━ ● ANSWERS ● ━━━━

MATCHING

1-k; 2-e; 3-o; 4-p; 5-m; 6-f; 7-h; 8-b; 9-g; 10-c; 11-i; 12-j; 13-a; 14-n; 15-d; 16-l.

━━━━ ● ANSWERS ● ━━━━

PROBLEMS AND APPLICATIONS

1. Okun's rule of thumb states that a 1-percentage point change in the unemployment rate will cause output in the economy to change in the opposite direction by 2 percent.
   a. Output rises 4 percent. (144)
   b. Output rises 2 percent. (144)
   c. Output falls 6 percent. (144)

2. a. Structural because this is a structural change in the economy. (137)
   b. Structural because this is a change in social structure. (137)
   c. Cyclical because this is unemployment due to a change in economic activity. (137)

3. a. Labor force = employed + unemployed = 145 million. (141-142)
   b. Unemployment rate = (unemployed/labor force)×100=6.9%. (141-142)

4. a. The price of the basket in 2007 is $610 and in 2008 is $744. Since 2007 is the base year, the index must be 100. This is calculated as (price of the basket in 2007)/(price of the basket in 2007)=$610/$610 × 100=100. (146-147)
   b. The price index in 2008 is (price of the basket in 2008/(price of the basket in 2007) =$744/$610 × 100 = 122. Prices rose by 22%. (146-147)
   c. Some potential flaws are that (1) the basket of goods is small and might not reflect the true basket of goods purchased by Patriots fans, (2) the basket of goods is fixed (since the price of Pepsi fell, fans might be buying more Pepsi and fewer football tickets), (3) the basket does not reflect quality improvements (since the Patriots won the Super Bowl in 2007, the quality of subsequent games in 2008 might

improve, but the tickets are counted as if they were the same as in 2007). (149)

5. a. Nominal GDP in 1995 is $7,397.2 billion dollars. Calculate this by multiplying real GDP in 1995 by the GDP deflator and dividing by 100. (148-150)
   b. Real GDP in 2000 dollars in 1985 is $6,055 billion. Calculate this by dividing nominal GDP by the GDP deflator and multiplying by 100. (148-150)
   c. GDP deflator in 2006 is 107.3. Calculate this by solving for GDP deflator in the equation: Real GDP=(nominal GDP/GDP deflator) × 100. (148-150)
   d. The price level rose by 54% from 1985 to 2006. Calculate this by dividing the change in the GDP price deflator and multiplying by 100: (107.3 − 69.7)/69.7 × 100. (148-150)
   e. Real output grew by 89% from 1985 to 2006. Calculate this by dividing the change in real GDP from 1985 to 2006 and multiplying by 100: (11,415.3 − 6,055)/6,055 × 100. (148-150)
   f. Per capita real GDP in 1985 was $25,441; in 1995 it was $30,308; in 2006 it was $38,051. Calculate this by dividing real GDP by the population. Per capita real GDP rose by 50% from 1985 to 2006. (148-150)

6. a. Nominal output increased by 6.4% from 2005 to 2006. Since the GDP deflator rose over that same year, we know that real output increased by less—specifically by 3.5% from 2005 to 2006. Subtract inflation from the change in nominal output to get the change in real output: 6.4% − 2.9% = 3.5%. (148-150)
   b. Real output increased 0.2% from 2000 to 2001. Since the GDP deflator rose 2.5% over that same year, we know that nominal output increased 2.7% from 2000 to 2001. Add inflation to the change in real output to find the change in nominal output: 2.5% + 0.2%=2.7%. (148-150)
   c. Real output fell 0.45% from 1990 to 1991. Since nominal output rose by 3.2%, we know the price level rose 3.65% from 1990 to 1991. Subtract the change in real output from the change in nominal output to find the inflation rate: 3.2% − (−0.45%) =3.65%. (148-150)

━━ ANSWERS ━━

A BRAIN TEASER

1. Usually one would expect unemployment to fall as output rises because it takes more workers to produce more output. However, an increase in productivity of workers can cause an increase in output without any reduction in unemployment. Another possibility is that the labor force participation rate could be rising so that the labor force is rising at a faster pace than employment. This would cause unemployment to rise even though output is expanding and the economy is growing. (136-137)

━━ ANSWERS ━━

MULTIPLE CHOICE

1. c   As the text states on page 129, inflation and unemployment are both short- and long-run problems.

2. a   As stated on page 129, the long run focuses on supply issues that increase the incentive to work, create new technologies, and invest in capital.

3. d   Per capita income is calculated by dividing total income by total population as stated on page 130.

4. b   The secular trend is the long-term growth trend. See page 130.

5. d   As more material goods made available by growth are used for antipollution equipment, less is available for personal consumption. The added material goods have already been used. See page 132.

6. a   As seen in the table on page 130, China's per capita growth rate averaged 4.9 percent from 1950 to 2007. Western Europe's per capita growth rate was 2.2 percent, while North America's was 2.1 percent and Latin America's was 2.0 percent.

7. b   The Great Depression of the 1930s was the most severe downturn. See page 132.

8. d   The others are coincident indicators. Even if you didn't remember this, you should be able to figure out that the change in new orders predicts what firms think will be happening in the future, whereas the others tell what is happening now. See page 136.

9. c   Almost all economists believe government should intervene during a depression. See page 133.

10. c   As discussed on page 137, the fear of hunger was the main deterrent to unemployment. A second deterrent would have been emigration, but that would not be as good an answer. Since d says immigration (the flowing in of people), not emigration, d is definitely wrong.

11. c   The target rate of unemployment is around 5 percent. See page 138.

12. a   Classicals generally favor laissez-faire policies. See page 133.

13. b   Keynesians generally favor activist government policies. See page 133.

14. c   As discussed on page 144, the statement that begins the question is the definition of potential output.

15. a   The real interest rate is the nominal interest rate adjusted for inflation. See page 150.

16. b   This is the definition of Okun's rule of thumb. See page 144.

17. c   Total output moves in the opposite direction by 2% times $5 trillion, which equals a fall of $100 billion. See page 144.

18. d   As the text points out on page 145, inflation is a continual rise in the price level, so the use of the term "one-time" should have clued you that d is the answer.

19. b   To determine the price level rise you multiply each component by its price rise. Since only 15% of the total rose, you get 10% times 15% = 1.5%. See pages 146-147.

20. b See pages 148-150. A reminder: A service is considered just as much a good and a component of real output as is a physical good.

21. c If real output remains constant, then the nominal output must also rise by 20%, as discussed on page 148.

22. d Inflation does not make society richer or poorer, and the distributional consequences of inflation differ, eliminating answers a and b. While the second part of c is true, that doesn't mean that there are no costs of inflation and, as discussed on page 151, one of those costs is the reduction in the informational content of prices.

23. c As discussed on pages 150-151, unexpected inflation is inflation that surprises people. Those people who didn't raise their prices are surprised. Income is redistributed from those people who didn't raise their prices to those who did.

ANSWERS

POTENTIAL ESSAY QUESTIONS

The following are annotated answers. They indicate the general idea behind the answer.

1. Economic growth is a major macroeconomic goal because it provides more jobs for a growing population. If output increases more than population increases then per capita growth occurs. Assuming there is no change in the distribution of the nation's income then everybody gets a "bigger piece of the pie." In this way economic growth increases the average absolute standard of living for people. *Remember, economic growth is valued by all nations because it raises the standard of living.*

2. Potential output is the output that would materialize at the target rate of unemployment and the target level of capacity utilization. Potential output grows at the secular (long-term) trend rate of 2.5 to 3.5 percent per year. When the economy is in a recession, actual output is below potential output. When the economy is in a boom, actual output is above potential output.

3. The Bureau of Labor Statistics (BLS) estimates the rate of unemployment. Underestimation can occur because discouraged workers are not counted as unemployed. Also, many people may work part-time but would like to work full-time. This "underemployment" is not reflected in unemployment statistics and suggests that the official unemployment statistics underestimate the true problem. Alternatively, some people may be counted as being unemployed when they are working in the underground economy–working for "cash under the table." In this case, the official statistics will overestimate true unemployment. The Classicals and Keynesians differ most when it comes to the number of discouraged workers. Some Keynesians argue that the BLS underestimates unemployment significantly because a great number of discouraged workers are not counted as being unemployed.

MEASURING THE AGGREGATE ECONOMY

CHAPTER AT A GLANCE

This review is based upon the learning objectives that open the chapter.

1a. Gross domestic product (GDP): Aggregate final output of residents and businesses in an economy in a one-year period. (157)

GDP is total market ($) value of all __final__ goods and services produced in a one-year period.

1b. GDP = C + I + G + (X − M) is an accounting identity because it is defined as true. (157-159)

The above identity is really the expenditures approach, which states:

Total output = Total expenditures;
Total output = GDP;
Total expenditures=C+I+G+(X−M);
By substitution: GDP = C + I + G + (X−M).

✔ *Know what C, I, G, and X−M stand for!*

Also note:
(X − M) = Net exports.
If (X−M) is positive, then X>M→Trade surplus.
If (X−M) is negative, then X<M→Trade deficit.
If (X−M) is zero, then X=M→Trade balance.

2. To avoid double counting, you must eliminate intermediate goods, either by calculating only final output (expenditures approach), or by calculating only final income (income approach) by using the value added approach. (159-161)

✔ *Know what is and what is not included when calculating GDP.*

__GDP does not include:__
- *intermediate goods (sold for resale or further processing);*
- *second-hand sales;*
- *government transfers, housespouse production, or any other non-market activity;*
- *underground economic activity.*

3a. Net investment is gross investment less depreciation. (163)

Depreciation is the wear and tear of machines that happens during production. Some production goes to replacing depreciated machinery and is therefore unavailable for consumption.

3b. National output (GNP) is production by citizens of a country, whether the production happens within the geographic borders of a country or not. Domestic output (GDP) is production that occurs within the geographic borders of a country, whether it is done by citizens of the country or not. (164)

GNP = GDP + Net foreign factor income where:

Net foreign factor income is the foreign income of a country's citizens less the income of residents who are not citizens.

4. Aggregate income is the sum of compensation of employees, rents, interest, and profit. (164-165)

The largest component of aggregate income is compensation of employees.

5. Aggregate income = Aggregate production.
    (165-166)

    *Profit is the key to the equality between
    aggregate output and aggregate income. It is
    what remains after all the other firm's income
    is paid out.*

6. Real GDP is nominal GDP adjusted for inflation.
    (167-169)

    *GDP is a price times quantity (P×Q) phenom-
    enon. GDP can rise due to an increase in P
    (price level) and/or an increase in Q (real
    quantity of output).*

    *Real GDP, in essence, holds prices (P)
    constant. Hence, real GDP is inflation (or
    deflation) adjusted.*

7a. Limitations of national income accounting
    include: (169-171)

    • GDP measures economic activity, not welfare;
    • Measurement problems exist; and
    • Subcategories are often interdependent.

    *GDP is not and was never intended to be a
    measure of social well-being.*

7b. Using GDP to compare standards of living
    among countries has its problems. (166-167)

    *GDP only measures market activity. In
    developing countries individuals often
    produce and trade outside the market.*

    *Market prices often vary considerably among
    countries making the value of the same
    income in terms of purchasing power different.*

● SHORT-ANSWER QUESTIONS

1. What is GDP?

2. What are the four components of aggregate output?

3. Calculate the contribution of Chex cereal (from seeds to consumer) to GDP, using the following information:

Participants	Cost of materials	Value of Sales
Farmer	0	200
Chex factory	200	500
Distributor	500	800
Grocery store	800	1000

4. What is GNP? How does it differ from GDP?

5. What is the difference between gross investment and net investment?

6. What are the four component of aggregate income?

7. Say the price level rises 10% from an index of 1 to an index of 1.1 and nominal GDP rises from $4 trillion to $4.6 trillion. What is nominal GDP in the second period? What is real GDP in the second period?

8. As pointed out by the quotation that begins the chapter on measuring the aggregate economy, statistics can be misleading. In what way can aggregate economic statistics be misleading? Given your answer, why use them at all?

MATCHING THE TERMS
Match the terms to their definitions

___	1.	depreciation	
___	2.	gross domestic product	
___	3.	gross national product	
___	4.	intermediate products	
___	5.	net domestic product	
___	6.	net foreign factor income	
___	7.	nominal GDP	
___	8.	real GDP	
___	9.	value added	
___	10.	wealth accounts	

a. GDP calculated at existing prices.

b. Aggregate final output of residents and businesses in an economy in a one-year period.

c. GDP adjusted to take account of depreciation.

d. Aggregate final output of citizens and businesses of an economy in a one-year period.

e. Income from foreign domestic factor sources minus foreign factor incomes earned domestically.

f. Nominal GDP adjusted for inflation.

g. Products of one firm used as an input in the production of another firm's product.

h. A balance sheet of an economy's stock of assets and liabilities.

i. The increase in value that a firm contributes to a product or service.

j. The decrease in an asset's value.

PROBLEMS AND APPLICATIONS

1. Using the value added or final sales approach to calculate GDP, state how much the action described has added to GDP:

   a. A used car dealer buys a car for $3,000 and resells it for $3,300.

   b. A company sells 1,000 disks for $500 each. Of these, it sells 600 to other companies for production and 400 to individuals.

   c. A PC and software company sells 50 computers at a retail price of $1,000 apiece and 100 software packages at a retail price of $50 apiece to consumers. The same company sells 25 computers at $800 and 50 software packages at $30 apiece to retail companies. These companies then sell the 25 computers at $1,250 apiece and the 50 software packages at $75 apiece to consumers.

   d. Fred purchases 100 stock certificates valued at $5 apiece and pays a 10% commission. When the price declines to $4.50 apiece, Fred decides to sell all 100 certificates, again at a 10% commission.

   e. Your uncle George receives $600 Social Security income each month for one year.

2. Use the following table showing the production of 500 boxes of Wheaties cereal to calculate the contribution to GDP using the value-added approach.

Participants	Cost of materials	Value of sales
Farmer	$0	$150
Mill	$150	$250
Cereal maker	$250	$600
Wholesaler	$600	$800
Grocery store	$800	$1,000

a. Calculate the value added at each stage of production.

b. What is the total value of all sales?

c. What is the total value added?

d. What is the contribution to GDP of the production of those Wheaties?

3. There are three firms in an economy: X, Y, and Z. Firm X buys $200 worth of goods from firm Y and $300 worth of goods from firm Z, and produces 250 units of output at $4 per unit. Firm Y buys $150 worth of goods from firm X, and $250 worth of goods from firm Z, and produces 300 units of output at $6 per unit. Firm Z buys $75 worth of goods from firm X, and $50 worth of goods from firm Y, and produces 300 units at $2 per unit. All other products are sold to consumers. Answer the following:
a. What is GDP?

b. How much government revenue would a value added tax of 10% generate?

c. How much government revenue would an income tax of 10% generate?

4.

economy:
All figures are in billions of dollars.

Net exports	$10
Net foreign factor income	3
Gross investment	200
Government spending	190
Consumption	550
Depreciation	65

You are asked to calculate the following:
a. GDP.

b. GNP.

c. NDP.

5. You have been hired as a research assistant and are given the following data about another economy (profits, wages, rents, and interest are measured nationally):

Profits	$505
Employee compensation	880
Rents	30
Interest	175

Calculate Aggregate income.

6. Use the following table to answer the questions:

	Real output bils. of 2000 $	Nominal output bils. of dollars	GDP deflator 2000=100
2000	9,817.0	9,817	____
2001	9890.7	10,128	____
2002	10,074.8	____	104.1
2003	____	____	106.0
2004	____	11,735	108.2

a. What is output for 2004 in 2000 dollars?

b. What is the output in nominal terms in 2002?

c. What is the GDP deflator in 2000?

d. Real output grew by 1.9% from 2002 to 2003. By how much did nominal output grow from 2002 to 2003?

● A BRAIN TEASER

1. Why must imports be subtracted in calculating GDP?

● MULTIPLE CHOICE

Circle the one best answer for each of the following questions:

1. GDP is:
    a. the total market value of all final goods and services produced in an economy in a one-year period.
    b. the total market value of all goods and services produced in an economy in a one-year period.
    c. the total market value of all final goods and services produced by a country's citizens in a one-year period.
    d. the sum of all final goods and services produced in an economy in a one-year period.

2. To move from GDP to GNP, one must:
    a. add net foreign factor income.
    b. subtract inflation.
    c. add depreciation.
    d. subtract depreciation.

3. If a firm's cost of materials is $100 and its sales are $500, its value added is:
    a. $100.
    b. $400.
    c. $500.
    d. $600.

4. If you, the owner, sell your old car for $600, how much does GDP increase?
    a. By $600.
    b. By the amount you bought it for, minus the $600.
    c. By zero.
    d. By the $600 you received and the $600 the person you sold it to paid, or $1,200.

5. There are two firms in an economy, Firm A and Firm B. Firm A produces 100 widgets and sells them for $2 apiece. Firm B produces 200 gadgets and sells them for $3 apiece. Firm A sells 30 of its widgets to Firm B and the remainder to consumers. Firm B sells 50 of its gadgets to Firm A and the remainder to consumers. What is GDP in this economy?
    a. $210.
    b. $590.
    c. $600.
    d. $800.

6. If a woman divorces her husband (who has been cleaning the house) and hires him to continue cleaning her house for $20,000 per year, GDP will:
   a. remain constant.
   b. increase by $20,000 per year.
   c. decrease by $20,000 per year.
   d. remain unchanged.

7. The aggregate accounting identity shows that the value of:
   a. aggregate income is equal to the value of final goods plus investment.
   b. aggregate income is equal to the value of final goods plus savings.
   c. aggregate income is equal to the value of final goods sold.
   d. consumption goods is equal to the value of aggregate income.

8. Which of the following correctly lists the components of total expenditures?
   a. consumption, investment, depreciation, exports minus imports.
   b. consumption, investment, government spending, exports minus imports.
   c. rent, profit, interest, wages.
   d. consumption, net foreign factor income, investment, government spending.

9. The largest component of expenditures in GDP is:
   a. consumption.
   b. investment.
   c. net exports.
   d. government spending.

10. The largest component of aggregate income is:
    a. rents.
    b. net interest.
    c. profits.
    d. compensation to employees.

11. Gross investment differs from net investment by:
    a. net exports.
    b. net imports.
    c. depreciation.
    d. transfer payments.

12. While the size of the U.S. federal government budget is approximately $2.7 trillion, the federal government's contribution in the GDP accounts is approximately:
    a. $0.9 trillion.
    b. $2.7 trillion.
    c. $3.9 trillion.
    d. $5.0 trillion.

13. Which of the following factors serves to equate aggregate income and aggregate production?
    a. profit.
    b. depreciation.
    c. net foreign factor income.
    d. value added.

14. Switching from the exchange rate approach to the purchasing power parity approach for calculating GDP generally:
    a. does not make a significant difference for a developing country's GDP relative to a developed country's GDP.
    b. increases a developing country's GDP relative to a developed country's GDP.
    c. decreases a developing country's GDP relative to a developed country's GDP.
    d. changes the relative GDP of developing country's GDP, but not in a predictable fashion.

15. If inflation is 10 percent and nominal GDP goes up 20 percent, real GDP goes up approximately:
    a. 1 percent.
    b. 10 percent.
    c. 20 percent.
    d. 30 percent.

16. Which of the following is the *preferable* measure available to compare changes in standards of living among countries over time?
    a. Changes in nominal income.
    b. Changes in nominal per capita income.
    c. Changes in real income.
    d. Changes in real per capita income.

17. If nominal GDP rises, welfare:
    a. has definitely increased.
    b. has definitely decreased.
    c. may have increased or decreased.
    d. most likely has increased.

18. Estimates of the importance of the under-
    ground economy in the United States
    indicate that it is:
    a. very small—under 1 percent of the total
       economy.
    b. somewhere between 1.5 percent all the way
       to 20 percent of the total economy.
    c. somewhere between 1.5 percent all the way
       to 60 percent of the total economy.
    d. as large as the non-underground economy.

POTENTIAL ESSAY QUESTIONS

*You may also see essay questions similar to the "Problems
& Applications" and "A Brain Teaser" exercises.*

1. Using the circular flow model, explain why any
    dollar value of output must give rise to an
    identical amount of income.

2. How might an economy experience an increase
    in nominal GDP but experience negative growth
    at the same time?

=== ANSWERS ===

SHORT-ANSWER QUESTIONS

1. GDP is the aggregate final output of *residents* and businesses *in* an economy in a one-year period. (157)

2. The four components of gross domestic product are consumption, investment, government spending, and net exports $(X - M)$. (157-159)

3. $1,000. We could use either the value added approach or the final output approach. Summing the value added at each stage of production — the difference between cost of materials and value of sales — we get $1,000. (159-161)

Participants	Cost of materials	Value of Sales	Value Added
Farmer	$0	$200	$200
Chex factory	200	500	300
Distributor	500	800	300
Grocery store	800	1000	200
Sum (total output)			1000

4. GNP is aggregate final output of *citizens* and businesses *of* an economy in a one-year period. GDP is output produced within a country's borders while GNP is output produced by a country's citizens anywhere in the world. Add net foreign factor income to GDP to get GNP. (163-164)

5. Gross investment is expenditures on goods and services used for future production. Net investment is gross investment less expenditures used to replace worn out machinery, also called depreciation. (163)

6. The four components that comprise aggregate income are compensation to employees, rents, interest, and profits. (164-165)

7. A real value is a nominal value adjusted for inflation. So, nominal GDP in the second period is $4.6 trillion, but real GDP is $4.6 trillion divided by the price index, 1.1, or $4.18 trillion. (167-169)

8. Aggregate accounting statistics can be misleading. They are subject to measurement error; they are based on samples of data and assumptions about behavior. For example, the measurement of inflation is widely believed to overestimate true inflation. Also, GDP does not include non-market activities such as housework. It measures economic activity, not welfare; output could rise when welfare falls. Its subcategories are often interdependent; that is, arbitrary decisions were made when determining what goes in which subcategory. Nevertheless, aggregate accounting makes it possible to discuss the aggregate economy. It is important to be aware of the limitations of the data in those discussions. (169-171)

=== ANSWERS ===

MATCHING

1-j; 2-b; 3-d; 4-g; 5-c; 6-e; 7-a; 8-f; 9-i; 10-h.

=== ANSWERS ===

PROBLEMS AND APPLICATIONS

1. a. $300. Only the value added by the sale would be added to GDP, which in this case is the difference between the purchase price and the sale price. (161)

    b. $200,000. Total output produced is $1,000 \times $500 = $500,000$. The intermediate goods are valued at $600 \times $500 = $300,000$. So, the company's contribution to GDP is $(\$500,000 - \$300,000) = \$200,000$. (159-161)

    c. Only that amount that is sold to the consumer is counted in GDP. This is $50 \times 1,000 + 100 \times 50 = \$55,000$ sold by the first company plus the sales of the retailer, which is $25 \times \$1250 + 50 \times \$75 = \$35,000$. Total contribution to GDP is $90,000. (159-161)

    d. Only the commissions of $50 and $45 are counted in GDP. Together they contribute $95. (161-162)

    e. Nothing has been added to GDP. Government transfers are not included in GDP. (162)

2.

Participants	Cost of materials	Value of sales	Value added
Farmer	$0	$150	$150
Mill	$150	$250	$100
Cereal maker	$250	$600	$350
Wholesaler	$600	$800	$200
Grocery store	$800	$1,000	$200

a. The value added at each stage of production is shown in the table above. (160-161)

b. The total value of sales is $2,800. Find this by adding the rows of the value of sales column. (160-161)

c. The total value added is $1,000. Find this by adding the value added at each stage of production. (160-161)

d. The contribution to GDP of the production of those Wheaties is $1,000. Value added at each stage of production is the contribution to GDP. This avoids double-counting. (160-161)

3. a. $2,375: GDP is the sum of the value added by the three firms = 500 + 1400 + 475. (160-161)

b. $237.50: A 10% value added tax would generate (.10)($2,375) = $237.50 of revenue. (160-161)

c. $237.50: A 10% income tax would generate the same revenue as a 10% value added tax because value added equals income. (160-161)

d. $237.50: A 10% sales tax on final output would generate $237.50 of revenue: (.10)(500+1400+475). (160-161)

4. a. $950: GDP = $C+I+G+(X-M)$ = 550 + 200 + 190 + 10 = 950. (157-159)

b. $953: GNP = GDP + net foreign factor income = 953. (163-164)

c. $885: NDP = GDP − depreciation = 950 − 65 = 885. (163)

5. $1,590: Aggregate income = Employee compensation + rent + interest + profits = 880 + 30 + 175 + 505. (164-165)

6. a. $10,845.7 billion in 2000 dollars: Real output = (Nominal output/deflator) × 100 = 11,735.0/108.2 × 100. (167-169)

b. $10,487.9 billion: Nominal output = (real output × deflator) / 100 = (10,074.8 × 104.1)/100. (167-169)

c. 100: Deflator = (Nominal output/real output) × 100 = (9,817/9,817) × 100. (167-169)

d. Real output grew by 1.9% and inflation rose by 2.1%, so nominal output grew by 4.0%. (167-169)

■■■■   ANSWERS   ■■■■

A BRAIN TEASER

1. Government spending, consumption, investment include all expenditures in those categories regardless of where the products were produced. That is, they include products produced in foreign countries. Since GDP measures domestic production, the total value of imports must be subtracted from total expenditures. (158)

■■■■   ANSWERS   ■■■■

MULTIPLE CHOICE

1. a As the text emphasizes on page 157, GDP is the total <u>market value</u> of all <u>final</u> goods and services produced <u>in</u> an economy in a one-year period.

2. a Since GNP is a country's total market value of production of a country's citizens anywhere in the world, and GDP is total market value of production within a country, one must add net foreign factor income to GDP to get GNP. See page 164.

3. b Value added equals value of sales minus cost of materials. See page 160.

4. c As discussed on page 161, sales of used goods do not contribute to GDP except to the degree that they are sold by a second hand dealer. Then the dealer's profit would be the value added.

5. b GDP doesn't include purchases made between businesses, only final sales to consumers. To calculate the answer, calculate total sales for Firms A and B ($600 + $200 = $800) and subtract those goods sold between the firms ($60 + $150 = $210) to get final sales ($800 − $210 = $590). See pages 160-161.

6. b   As discussed on page 162, GDP measures market transactions. The divorce-and-hire changes the housecleaning activities from non-market to market and hence increases GDP.

7. c   The aggregate accounting identity shows that all income (value of aggregate income) equals all expenditures (value of goods sold to individuals). See page 165.

8. b   GDP = C + I + G + (X – M). See pages 157-159.

9. a   Consumption makes up the majority of expenditures. See Table 7-1 on page 159.

10. d   As you can see in Table 7-3 on page 165, compensation to employees is the largest percent of aggregate income.

11. c   Net investment equals gross investment less depreciation. See page 163.

12. a   As discussed on page 158 only federal government spending on goods and services are included as part of GDP. The federal government's entire budget also includes transfer payments.

13. a   Profit is what remains after all firms' other income is paid out. Thus, profit is the key to the income/production equality. See page 166.

14. b   In developing countries, living expenses are generally lower than in developed countries. Thus moving towards a purchasing power parity approach generally increases GDP in a developing country. See pages 166-167.

15. b   Subtract inflation from nominal GDP growth to find real GDP growth as a first approximation. See pages 167-169.

16. d   As discussed on pages 167-169 nominal GDP must be adjusted for price level increases before comparisons over time can be made. Dividing total real income by the population is a good indication of relative standards of living.

17. c   Nominal GDP must be adjusted for inflation to arrive at real GDP before one can even start to make welfare comparisons. And even if real GDP increases, it is not clear that welfare has increased, as discussed on pages 169-171.

18. b   On page 170 the text states that the underground economy in the United States is between 1.5 and 20 percent of the total economy.

ANSWERS

POTENTIAL ESSAY QUESTIONS

The following are annotated answers. They indicate the general idea behind the answer.

1.   Whenever the business community produces some dollar value of output, that dollar value reflects costs of production that were incurred in producing that output level. Those costs of production are all paid out to the resource (input) owners as their income. Hence, any dollar output level (GDP) gives rise to an identical amount of aggregate income.

2.   The price level could have increased by a greater percentage than the decrease in the real quantity of goods and services produced. This would result in an increase in nominal GDP but a decrease in real GDP (negative growth).

GROWTH, PRODUCTIVITY AND THE WEALTH OF NATIONS

8

● CHAPTER AT A GLANCE

This review is based upon the learning objectives that open the chapter.

1. Growth is an increase in the amount of goods and services an economy produces. (177-179)

   Growth can be measured either by increases in real GDP or increases in real GDP per person (per capita growth).

   Remember the Rule of 72: the number of years it takes for income to double equals 72 divided by the annual growth rate of income.

2. Markets create specialization and division of labor and have been empirically highly correlated with growth. The growth rate has increased as the importance of markets has increased. Five important sources of growth are: (179, 182-186)

   ● Institutions with incentives compatible with growth;

   Government policy can help or hinder growth. Regulations have both costs and benefits, but too much regulation definitely hinders growth.

   ● Capital accumulation–investment in productive capacity;

   Can be: (1) Privately owned by business, (2) publicly owned and provided by government– infrastructure, (3) human capital–investment in people, (4) social capital–institutions and conventions.

   Saving is translated into investment in the loanable funds market. The interest rate equilibrates the supply of loanable funds (saving) with the demand for loanable funds (investment).

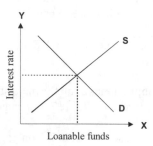

   ● Available resources;

   Technological advances can help overcome any lack of resources.

   ● Technological development;

   Technology not only causes growth, it also changes the entire social and political dimensions of society.

   ● Entrepreneurship.

   This is the ability to get things done. It involves creativity, vision, and an ability to translate that vision into reality.

3. Most growth theories center around the production function: Output = A·f(labor, capital, land). (187-190)

   Returns to scale describes what happens to output when all inputs are increased.

   ● *Constant returns to scale: output rises by the same proportion as the increase in all inputs. (An example: ↑all inputs 10% →↑output by 10%)*

   ● *Increasing returns to scale: output rises by a greater proportion than the increase in all inputs. (An example: ↑ all inputs 10% → ↑output by 15%)*

- *Decreasing returns to scale: output rises by a smaller proportion than the increase in all inputs. (An example:↑all inputs 10% → ↑output by 5%)*

- *Diminishing marginal productivity involves increasing one, not all, inputs. In general, economists assume diminishing marginal productivity—which means the increase in output falls as more of one input is added.*

4a. The convergence hypothesis states that per capita income in countries with similar institutional structures will gravitate toward the same level of income per person. (190)

This hypothesis predicts that the U.S. economy will grow more slowly than developing economies because of technology transfers, learning by doing, and the higher marginal productivity of capital in developing countries.

4b. Convergence hasn't occurred because of (1) lack of factor mobility, (2) differing institutional structures, (3) in-comparable factors of production, and (4) technological agglomeration effects. (190-192)

Technology accounts for a significant portion of U.S. growth. If technology continues to advance more quickly in developed countries, rich countries may continue to grow more quickly than developing economies.

5a. The Classical growth model focuses on the role of capital accumulation. Increases in capital lead to growth. (188-190)

It predicts that the rise in output per worker will eventually slow as additional amounts of capital are less productive. It also predicts that capital-poor countries will grow faster than capital-rich countries.

Focuses on diminishing marginal productivity of labor. Increases in the population beyond N* lead to starvation. Below N* the population grows because of the surplus output.

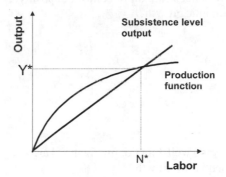

5b. New growth theory focuses on technology. Increasing returns mean growth rates can accelerate over time. (192-195)

Technology and learning by doing often has positive externalities that can accelerate growth.

● SHORT-ANSWER QUESTIONS

1. What are the two ways to measure growth?

2. You've been called in by a political think tank to develop a strategy to improve growth in the U.S. What five things would you recommend they concentrate on to contribute positively to economic growth?

3. Why is a well-functioning financial market essential to growth?

4. Write a production function. Use the production function to explain the difference between diminishing marginal returns and decreasing returns to scale.

5. Which economy does the convergence hypothesis predict will grow faster: Country A with per capita income of $1,000 or Country B with per capita of $10,000? Why might the prediction be wrong?

6. Why did the early Classical model predict that output would gravitate toward a subsistence level?

7. What is the focus of new growth theory?

8. How do the predictions of the Classical growth theory differ from the predictions of the new growth theory?

MATCHING THE TERMS
Match the terms to their definitions

___1.   Classical growth model

___2.   constant returns to scale

___3.   convergence hypothesis

___4.   decreasing returns to scale

___5.   human capital

___6.   increasing returns to scale

___7.   law of diminishing marginal productivity

___8.   learning by doing

___9.   new growth theories

___10.   patents

___11.   per capita growth

___12.   positive externalities

___13.   productivity

___14.   Rule of 72

___15.   Say's Law

___16.   social capital

___17.   specialization

___18.   technological agglomeration

___19.   technology

a.   Output rises by a greater proportionate increase in all inputs.

b.   Producing more goods and services per person.

c.   Legal ownership of a technological innovation that gives the owner sole rights to its use and distribution for a limited time.

d.   The habitual way of doing things that guides how people approach production.

e.   Changes in the way we make goods and supply services and changes in the goods and services we buy.

f.   Output will rise by the same proportionate increase as all inputs.

g.   Model of growth that focuses on the role of capital accumulation in the growth process.

h.   Output per unit of input.

i.   Rule in which you divide 72 by the growth rate of income (or any variable) to get the number of years over which income (or any variable) will double.

j.   Output rises by a smaller proportionate increase than all inputs.

k.   Positive effects on others not taken into account by the decision-maker.

l.   The skills that are embodied in workers through experience, education, and on-the-job training.

m.   Theories that emphasize the role of technology rather than capital in the growth process.

n.   Increasing one input, keeping all others constant, will lead to smaller and smaller gains in output.

o.   The concentration of individuals on certain aspects of production.

p.   Supply creates its own demand.

q.   Improving the methods of production through experience.

r.   Tendency of technological advance to spawn further technological advances.

s.   Per capita income in countries with similar institutional structures will gravitate toward the same level.

PROBLEMS AND APPLICATIONS

1.   According to the Classical growth model how will each of the following events affect a country's growth rate?

   a.   An increase in the percent change in population.

   b.   An increase in the saving rate.

   c.   An improvement in technology.

d The government passes a law extending the time frame in which the holder of a patent has sole ownership of a technological innovation.

2. State the Rule of 72. Answer each of the following questions:

   a. How many years will it take for income to double if a country's total income grows at 2 percent? 4 percent? 6 percent?

   b. If a country's income doubles in 16 years, at what rate is its income growing?

   c. In 2005 per capita output in the United States was about $40,000. If real income per capita is growing at a 2% annual rate, what will per capita output be in 36 years? In 72 years?

   d. If real income is rising at an annual rate of 4% per year and the population is growing at a rate of 1% per year, how many years will it take for per capita income to double?

3. Calculate per capita income for each of the following countries:

	GDP (in mils. of $)	Population (in millions)
Brazil	773,400	164
Ghana	6,600	18
Croatia	20,700	4
France	1,526,000	59

4. The inputs to an economy are labor and capital only. In each of the following state whether the production function exhibits (a) increasing returns to scale, (b) decreasing returns to scale, (c) constant returns to scale, or (d) diminishing marginal productivity.

   a. Output rises by 16% when both labor and capital rise by 16%.

   b. Output rises by 10% when both labor and capital rise by 16%.

   c. Output rises by 10% when labor rises by 16%. (Capital doesn't change.)

5. What prediction did Thomas Malthus make about growth?

   a. Draw a graph that demonstrates his predictions and explain the predictions using the graph.

b. What law are those predictions based upon?

c. According to Classical economists, why didn't his predictions come true?

6. Country A has per capita income of $10,000 while Country B has per capita income of $20,000.

a. According to the Classical growth theory, which country is predicted to grow more quickly? Why?

b. According to the new growth theory, which country is predicted to grow more quickly? Why?

● A BRAIN TEASER

1. How might a country benefit from having misers? How might it be harmed?

● MULTIPLE CHOICE

Circle the one best answer for each of the following questions:

1. Long-run growth analysis focuses primarily:
   a. on demand.
   b. on supply.
   c. on both supply and demand.
   d. on the distribution of output.

2. According to Say's Law:
   a. aggregate supply will exceed aggregate demand.
   b. aggregate demand will exceed aggregate supply.
   c. there will be no relation between aggregate supply and demand.
   d. aggregate demand will equal aggregate supply.

3. If the growth rate is 6%, how many years will it take for output to double?
   a. 4.
   b. 8.
   c. 12.
   d. 16.

4. When earnings are adjusted for inflation, the average worker today earns:
   a. about the same as a worker in 1919.
   b. less than a worker in 1919.
   c. more than a worker in 1919.
   d. more than a worker in 1919 if he/she is unionized, but otherwise less.

5. Suppose output grew at 8% in China and 2% in the United States. Based on this information alone, we can know that:
   a. per capita income grew faster in China.
   b. per capita income grew faster in the U.S.
   c. per capita income could have grown faster in either country. We cannot tell which.
   d. per capita output grew faster in China.

6. Investment relates to capital in the following way:
   a. It is the same thing as capital stock.
   b. It causes a decrease in capital over time.
   c. It causes an increase in capital over time.
   d. It is unrelated to capital.

7. If saving increases from S_0 to S_1:

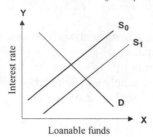

a. the interest rate will rise, investment will rise, and the economy will grow.

b. the interest rate will fall, investment will rise, and the economy will grow.

c. the interest will rise, investment will fall, and the economy will contract.

d. the interest rate will fall, investment will fall, and the economy will contract.

8. Types of capital discussed in the book do *not* include:

a. human capital.

b. social capital.

c. physical capital.

d. investment capital.

9. Available resources:

a. must always decrease.

b. are always constant because of the entropy law.

c. must always increase.

d. may increase or decrease.

10. A production function:

a. shows the relationship between inputs and outputs.

b. is a type of technological manufacturing.

c. is a type of manufacturing technology.

d. is an important source of growth.

11. If there are increasing returns to scale, as:

a. inputs rise, outputs fall.

b. inputs rise, output rises by a smaller percentage.

c. inputs rise, output rises by a larger percentage.

d. one input rises, output rises by a larger percentage.

12. The law of diminishing marginal productivity states that as:

a. inputs increase by equal percentages, output will increase by less than that percentage.

b. inputs increase by equal percentages, output will eventually increase by less than that percentage.

c. one input increases by a certain percentage, output will increase by less than that percentage.

d. one input increases, output will increase by decreasing percentages.

13. The Classical growth model focuses on:

a. technology.

b. saving and investment.

c. entrepreneurship.

d. available resources.

14. Early predictions of the Classical model of growth were that:

a. the economy would grow without limit.

b. the economy will end because of pollution.

c. wages would be driven to subsistence because of diminishing marginal productivity.

d. wages would be driven to subsistence because of decreasing returns to scale.

15. Which of the following is *not* an explanation for why the growth rates of rich and poor countries have not converged?

a. Human capital has increased in rich countries.

b. Technology has increased in rich countries.

c. The law of diminishing marginal productivity is wrong.

d. Both human capital and technology have increased in rich countries.

16. In empirically explaining per capita growth in the United States, the increase in:

a. physical capital is the most important element.

b. human capital is the most important element.

c. technology is the most important element.

d. the quantity of labor is the most important element.

17. Convergence does not rely on:
    a. Similar institutions.
    b. Equal amounts of capital per person.
    c. Mobile technology.
    d. Comparable factors of production.

18. New growth theories are theories that emphasize:
    a. technology.
    b. human capital.
    c. physical capital.
    d. entrepreneurship.

19. In the new growth theory which of the following may be true?
    a. The law of increasing marginal productivity overwhelms the law of diminishing marginal productivity.
    b. Learning by doing overwhelms the law of diminishing marginal productivity.
    c. The law of technology overwhelms the law of diminishing marginal productivity.
    d. The law of QWERTY overwhelms the law of diminishing marginal productivity.

20. QWERTY is a metaphor for:
    a. the invisible hand.
    b. technological lock-in.
    c. the law of diminishing marginal productivity.
    d. the pollution caused by positive spillovers.

21. Growth usually leads to decreased birth rates because:
    a. men and women are too tired to have kids.
    b. the opportunity cost of having children rises.
    c. pollution reduces the fertility of the population.
    d. immigration crowds out endogenous population growth.

22. Which of the following policies will likely *slow* an economy's growth rate?
    a. Increased trade restrictions.
    b. Increasing the level of education.
    c. Increasing saving.
    d. Protecting property rights.

● POTENTIAL ESSAY QUESTIONS

You may also see essay questions similar to the "Problems & Applications" and "A Brain Teaser" exercises.

1. What does the Classical model predict about the growth rates of poor countries relative to rich countries? What accounts for that prediction?

2. How can two countries with equal population sizes have different levels of output?

ANSWERS

SHORT-ANSWER QUESTIONS

1. Growth can be measured either as increases in the amount of goods and services an economy produces (real GDP), or as increases in the amount of goods and services an economy produces per person (per capita real GDP). Increase in per capita output is a better measure of improvements in the standard of living because it tells you how much more income an average person has. (177, 180-182)

2. I would tell them: (1) To promote institutions with incentives compatible with growth. Institutions that encourage hard work will lead to growth. (2) To invest in capital. This would include not only buildings and machines, but also human and social capital. (3) To be creative in recognizing available resources. Growth requires resources and although it may seem that the resources are limited, available resources depend upon existing technology. New technology is a way of overcoming lack of resources. (4) To promote institutions that foster creative thinking and lead to technological development; (5) To encourage entrepreneurship. An economy deficient in the other four areas can still grow if its population can translate vision into reality. Each of these will contribute to growth. (182-186)

3. For saving to contribute to growth it must be translated into investment, which requires a well-functioning financial market. (183-184)

4. A typical production function is: Output = A· f(labor, capital, land), where labor, capital and land are the only inputs. A is a factor that is used to capture changes in technology. Decreasing returns to scale describes the situation where output rises by a smaller percentage than the increase in all inputs. For example, if labor, capital and land all increase by 20%, but output increases by only 10%, the production function exhibits decreasing returns to scale. Diminishing marginal productivity describes what happens to output when only one input is changed—output rises by a percentage that is smaller than the percentage increase in one input (while all other inputs remain the same). (187-190)

5. The convergence hypothesis predicts that, given the appropriate assumptions, Country A will grow faster because it has less capital and therefore the marginal productivity of additional capital is higher. The prediction is likely wrong because the assumptions are not met. A central assumption is that countries have similar institutional structures. Another is that the factors of production are comparable; they may not be; for example, the workers in Country B might be better educated. Another assumption is that technological advances move from country to country. They may not do so because of agglomeration effects, in which technological advances in one country accelerate growth for that country. Another assumption is that technology and capital are free to move; they may not be. (190-192)

6. The early Classical model predicted that output would gravitate toward a subsistence level because they focused on the law of diminishing marginal productivity of labor. As long as an additional worker could produce more than enough for him or herself, the population would grow. But land was relatively fixed. As more and more workers were added to a fixed amount of land, eventually, additional workers would not be able to produce enough additional output to survive. Workers would starve to death and the population would shrink. The equilibrium number of workers was where output was just enough to survive—no more and no less. (188-190)

7. New growth theory focuses on the role of technology rather than capital in the growth process. New growth theory considers the possibility that there are positive spillover effects associated with technological advance so that growth rates can accelerate. It also focuses on learning by doing. Just the process of producing results in lower costs and technological innovation. (192-195)

8. Classical growth theory predicts that the growth rates of poor countries will be higher than the growth rates of rich countries because the law of diminishing marginal productivity of capital is stronger in rich countries. Eventually the incomes of rich and poor countries will converge. New growth theory, because of the

positive externalities associated with technological advance, is consistent with the possibility that rich countries may grow faster than poor countries because they have more technology. Classical growth theory also predicts that growth rates will slow over time whereas the new growth theory is consistent with an acceleration in growth rates. (188-195)

ANSWERS

MATCHING

1-g; 2-f; 3-s; 4-j; 5-l; 6-a; 7-n; 8-q; 9-m; 10-c; 11-b; 12-k; 13-h; 14-i; 15-p; 16-d; 17-o; 18-r; 19-e.

ANSWERS

PROBLEMS AND APPLICATIONS

1. **a.** An increase in the percent change in population will lead to a reduction in the growth rate per capita because each worker will have less capital to produce with. (188-190)
    b. An increase in the saving rate will lead to an increase in the growth rate per capita because saving results in increased investment and more capital for each worker. Eventually, however, the law of diminishing marginal productivity of capital would set in and per capita income would cease to grow. (188-190)
    c. An improvement in technology will increase the growth rate per capita because each worker will be more productive. This will increase per capita output at the time of the technological improvement, but would not result in a lasting increase in the growth rate per capita. (188-190)
    d. Technological innovation is outside the model. Thus government policies to affect technological innovation would not affect the growth rate of an economy. (188-190)

2. The Rule of 72 is, "the number of years that it takes income (or any variable) to double equals 72 divided by the annual growth rate of income (or that variable)." (178)

    a. 36 years if income grows at 2 percent per year; 18 years if income grows at 4 percent per year; 12 years if income grows at 6 percent per year. (178)
    b. Its income is growing at 4.5 percent per year. Divide 72 by 16 to find the answer. (178)
    c. If real income per capita is growing at 2 percent per year, per capita output will double in 36 years. So, real per capita output will be $80,000 in 36 years and $160,000 in 72 years. (178)
    d. Per capita real income is rising at an annual rate of 3% per year (4% - 1%). At 3% per year, real per capita income will double in 24 years (72/3 = 24). (178)

3. Divide GDP by the population to find per capita income: (180-181)
    a. Brazil $4,716
    b. Ghana $367
    c. Croatia $5,175
    d. France $25,864

4. **a.** Since output is rising by the same percentage as the increase in all inputs, the production function exhibits constant returns to scale. (187-188)
    b. Since output is rising by a smaller percentage than the increase in all inputs, the production function exhibits decreasing returns to scale. (187-188)
    c. Since capital is fixed, the correct description involves marginal productivity. Since output rises by less than the percentage increase in labor only, the production function exhibits diminishing marginal productivity. (186-188)

5. Thomas Malthus predicted that since land was relatively fixed, as the population grew, diminishing marginal productivity would set in. The growth in output would not keep pace with the growth in the population and eventually people would starve. (188-189)

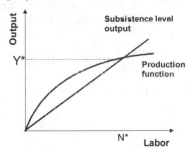

a. The graph above demonstrates Malthus' predictions. The production function is downward bowed because of diminishing marginal productivity. Each additional worker adds less output than the individual before. At population levels below N*, there is surplus output (because output per worker exceeds the subsistence level of output). Because there is surplus output, people have more children and the population grows. Once the population grows beyond N*, per capita output is not sufficient to feed the population (output per worker is less than the subsistence level of output) and some people starve to death. The population declines to N*. (188-190)

b. The predictions of Thomas Malthus are based upon the law of diminishing marginal productivity. (188-190)

c. According to Classical economists, his predictions didn't come true because some output produced is used to increase the amount of capital that workers have to work with. As capital increases, even if land is fixed, output can also increase. The economy can still grow if capital increases at the same rate that labor increases. (190)

6. a. According to the Classical growth theory, Country A is expected to grow more quickly because increases in capital per worker in Country A are more productive than in Country B due to the law of diminishing marginal productivity. (188-190)

b. According to the new growth theory, income doesn't need to converge. In fact, new growth theory stresses the possibility that countries with higher output will grow faster than poor countries because of positive externalities associated with technology and learning by doing. Increases in technology have significant positive externalities that can accelerate the growth rate. Further, as output increases, the benefits from learning by doing also increase. Therefore, greater output can lead to faster growth rates. (192-195)

ANSWERS

A BRAIN TEASER

1. A country might benefit from a miser if the miser's saving in translated into investment, and therefore productive capital that will help the economy grow. In the short-run, however, the miser might hurt by not spending, thereby not creating demand for goods produced. (183-184)

ANSWERS

MULTIPLE CHOICE

1. b On page 177 it states that in the short run economists' analysis focuses on demand; in the long run it focuses on supply.

2. d Say's Law states that supply creates its own demand. See page 177.

3. c According to the rule of 72 on page 178, divide 72 by the growth rate to determine the number of years in which output will double.

4. c As discussed in the text on page 180 the average worker's wages buy many more goods now than in 1919. Whether that makes them better off is debatable, but they definitely earn more.

5. c Per capita income (output) growth equals output growth less population growth. Without knowing population growth, we do not know for which country per capita income (output) growth is greater. See pages 180-182.

6. c As defined in the text on page 184 investment is the increase in capital over time.

7. b When saving increases from S_0 to S_1, there is downward pressure on the interest rate. This leads to higher investment (demand for loanable funds) and, according to the growth model, growth. See pages 183-184.

8. d Investment is the change in capital; it is not a description of capital. See page 184.

9. d Available resources depend on technology. That is why they can increase or decrease. See pages 184-185.

10. a The definition given in the text on page 187 is the relationship between inputs and outputs.

11. c As discussed in the text on page 188 increasing returns to scale refers to the relationship between all inputs and outputs. Increasing returns to scale exist when output increases by a greater percentage than the increase in all inputs.

12. d The law of diminishing marginal productivity refers to one input, not all, and to what will happen to output as that input continually increases, keeping other inputs constant. It is likely that c is true but it is not the law of diminishing marginal productivity. See page 188.

13. b The Classical growth focuses on increases in capital and hence on saving and investment. See pages 188-190.

14. c In the early Classical model, fixed land and diminishing marginal productivity meant that wages would be driven to subsistence. See page 189.

15. c Economists continue to believe in the law of diminishing marginal productivity because there are many other explanations for the lack of convergence. See pages 190-192.

16. c Although increases in technology and increases in the quantity of labor are of almost equal importance in explaining total growth, per capita growth decreases the importance of the quantity of labor. See pages 190-192.

17. b Convergence depends on similar institutions, mobile technology, and comparable factors of production. The initial amount of capital per person doesn't have to equal. See pages 190-192.

18. a New growth theories center their explanation of growth on technology. See page 192.

19. b Choices a, c, and d name "laws" that aren't laws, aren't mentioned in this chapter, and can't overwhelm anything. See pages 194-195.

20. b QWERTY stands for the upper left keys on a keyboard. Placing them there is not especially efficient, but once they were placed there, they were locked in. See page 195.

21. b In industrialized countries, people have chosen to have fewer children in part because the benefits of having children (such as being supported by them in your old age) are reduced. See pages 180-182.

22. a Economists generally believe that trade increases growth, so increasing trade restrictions would decrease growth. See page 179.

─── **ANSWERS** ───

POTENTIAL ESSAY QUESTIONS

The following are annotated answers. They indicate the general idea behind the answer.

1. The Classical model predicts that poor countries with little capital will grow at faster rates than rich countries with a lot of capital. The reason for this prediction is the law of diminishing marginal productivity. Capital that is added in poor countries will be much more productive because the law of diminishing marginal productivity is weaker compared to that in rich countries.

2. Total output in the long run depends upon capital, labor, and land. It could be that the two countries have different levels of capital or natural resources (captured in land). For instance, the United States has many natural resources, but Japan does not. Japan overcomes its lack of natural resources by investing heavily in capital and importing natural resources. If two countries had equal amounts of capital, land and labor, however, their outputs could still differ if they had different amounts of human capital (the skills that are embodied in workers through experience, education, and on-the-job training) and social capital (the habitual way of doing things that guides people in how they approach production).

THE AGGREGATE DEMAND/ AGGREGATE SUPPLY MODEL

CHAPTER AT A GLANCE

This review is based upon the learning objectives that open the chapter.

1. Keynesian economics developed as economists debated the cause of the Great Depression. (202-205)

    In the 1930s, the economy was in a Depression with 25 percent unemployment. Classical economists believed that wages would fall and eliminate the unemployment. Keynesian economists believed that the economy could remain in a Depression unless government did something to increase spending.

2a. The slope of the AD curve is determined by the wealth effect, the interest rate effect, the international effect, and repercussions of these effects. (206-208)

    As the price level falls:
    - *the cash people hold is worth more, making people richer, so they buy more (wealth effect).*
    - *the value of money rises, inducing people to lend more money, which reduces the interest rate and increases investment expenditures (interest rate effect).*
    - *the price of U.S. goods relative to foreign goods goes down. Assuming the exchange rate doesn't change, U.S. exports increase and U.S. imports decrease. (international effect).*

    Repercussions of these effects are called multiplier effects (and make the AD curve flatter than otherwise).

2b. Five important initial shift factors of the AD curve are: (208-210)

- Changes in foreign income.
  A rise in foreign income leads to an increase in U.S. exports and an increase (outward shift to the right) of the U.S. AD curve.

- Changes in exchange rates.
  A decrease in the value of the dollar relative to other currencies shifts the AD curve outward to the right.

- Changes in expectations.
  Positive (optimistic) expectations about the future state of the economy shift the AD curve outward to the right.

- Changes in the distribution of income.
  Typically, as the real wage increases, the AD curve shifts out to the right.

- Changes in government aggregate demand policy.

  Expansionary macro policy (an increase in government spending and/or a decrease in taxes—fiscal policy; or an increase in the money supply—monetary policy) increases the AD curve, shifting it outward to the right.

  Note: Anything that affects the components of aggregate expenditures (AE or "total spending") is a shift factor of AD (aggregate demand). (Recall that $AE = C + I + G + X - M$). Changes in these components of total spending are multiplied by the multiplier effect.

3a. In the short run, the SAS curve is upward sloping. (211)

    The SAS curve is upward sloping for two reasons: (1) Some firms operate in auction markets where an increase in demand leads to higher prices immediately; (2) Firms tend to increase their markup when demand increases. Along an SAS curve, input prices are constant.

3b. The SAS curve shifts in response to changes in the prices of the factors of production (inputs). (211-213)

Shift factors include changes in (1) input prices, (2) expectations of inflation, (3) excise and sales taxes, (4) productivity, and (5) import prices.

The rule of thumb economists use to predict shifts in the SAS curve is:

% change in the price level = % change in wages − % change in productivity.

4. The *LAS* curve is vertical at potential output. (213-214)

Resources are fully utilized at potential output. The LAS curve shifts when potential output rises or falls.

5a. Equilibrium in the short run is determined by the intersection of the SAS curve and the AD curve. (215-216)

Increases (decreases) in aggregate demand lead to higher (lower) output and a higher (lower) price level.

To find the effect of a shift in aggregate demand, start where the AD curve and the SAS curve intersect. Given a shift of either the AD curve or SAS curve, simply find the new point of intersection. This is the new short-run equilibrium. Remember, initial shifts in the AD curve are magnified because of the multiplier effect.

5b. Equilibrium in the long run is determined by the intersection of the LAS curve and the AD curve. (215-218)

If the economy begins at a long-run equilibrium, increases in aggregate demand will lead to changes in the price level only.

If short-run equilibrium output is below long-run equilibrium output, the economy is in a recessionary gap. The price level will fall and the AS curve will shift down until output rises to potential. (See the figure below.)

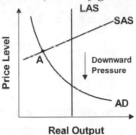

If short-run equilibrium output is above long-run equilibrium output, the economy is in an inflationary gap. The price level will rise and the SAS curve will shift up until output falls to potential. (See the figure below)

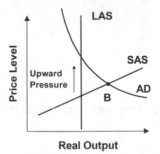

6. Macro policy is more complicated than the model makes it look. (221-222)

Fiscal policy is a slow legislative process and is often determined for political, not economic, reasons.

We have no way of precisely determining potential output, making it difficult to know what is the right policy.

SHORT-ANSWER QUESTIONS

1. How does the Keynesian explanation of the Great Depression differ from the Classical explanation?

2. What effects determine the slope of the AD curve?

3. List some of the important shift factors of the AD curve.

4. What is the slope of the SAS curve? Why does it have this shape?

5. What will shift the SAS curve up or down?

6. What is the slope of the LAS curve? Why does it have this shape?

7. Show graphically the effect of increased government purchases on real output when (a) the economy is far below potential output and (b) the economy is at potential output.

8. Why is the AS/AD model more complicated than it looks?

MATCHING THE TERMS
Match the terms to their definitions

___1.	aggregate demand curve	a.	As the price level falls the interest rate falls, which leads to greater investment expenditures.
___2.	countercyclical fiscal policy	b.	A curve that shows the amount of goods and services an economy can produce when both labor and capital are fully employed.
___3.	equilibrium income	c.	A curve that shows how a change in the price level will change aggregate quantity of goods demanded.
___4.	fiscal policy	d.	Markets in which firms modify their supply to bring about equilibrium instead of changing prices.
___5.	inflationary gap	e.	A curve that tells us how changes in aggregate demand will be split between real output and the price level.
___6.	interest rate effect	f.	Amount by which equilibrium output is below potential output.
___7.	international effect	g.	As the price level falls, people are richer, so they buy more.
___8.	long-run aggregate supply curve	h.	As the price level in a country falls the quantity of that country's goods demanded by foreigners and by residents will increase.
___9.	multiplier effect	i.	Amplification of initial changes in expenditures.
___10.	potential income	j.	Amount by which equilibrium output is above potential output.
___11.	quantity-adjusting markets	k.	Level of income toward which the economy gravitates in the short run.
___12.	recessionary gap	l.	Level of income the economy is technically capable of producing without generating accelerating inflation.
___13.	short-run aggregate supply curve	m.	Deliberate change in either government spending or taxes.
___14.	wealth effect	n.	Government policy to offset the business cycle.

● PROBLEMS AND APPLICATIONS

1. What will likely happen to the shape or position of the *AD* curve in the following circumstances?

   a. A rise in the price level does not make people feel poorer.

   b. Income is redistributed from poor people to rich people.

   c. The country's currency depreciates.

   d. The exchange rate changes from fixed to flexible.

   e. Expectations of future rises in the price level develop without any current change in the price level.

2. What will happen to the position of the *SAS* curve in the following circumstances?

   a. Productivity rises by 3 percent and wages rise by 3 percent.

b. Productivity rises by 3 percent and wages rise by 5 percent.

c. Productivity rises by 3 percent and wages rise by 1 percent.

3. Graphically demonstrate the effect of each of the following on either the *SAS* curve or the *LAS* curve. Be sure to label all axes.

 a. Businesses find that they are able to produce more output without having to pay more wages or increase their costs of capital.

 b. A severe snow storm paralyzes most of the United States.

 c. The country's currency appreciates dramatically.

4. The government of the UK wants to expand its economy through increased spending. Show the likely effects of an activist policy in the short run and in the long run in the following three cases.

 a. The economy is far below potential output.

 b. The economy is close to, but still below, potential output.

 c. The economy is at potential output.

5. Demonstrate the following two cases using the AS/AD model. What will happen in the long run if the government does nothing?

 a. Inflationary gap.

 b. Recessionary gap.

 c. What could government do with fiscal policy in (a) and (b) to keep the price level constant?

● A BRAIN TEASER

1. Suppose the economy has been experiencing a recession for a couple of years with no apparent relief in sight. Currently the unemployment rate is 10%. In response to political pressure "to put America back to work" government policy makers have recently reduced taxes significantly and have dramatically increased government spending on public works projects to rebuild the nation's crumbling infrastructure (roads, bridges, airports...). During a recent press conference the President of the United States remarked that the new government policy of tax cuts and spending programs will be successful in reducing unemployment and there should be no reason to fear inflation either. Because you are a student in an economics course one of your friends has asked you to evaluate the likely success of these recent policy moves. How would you respond?

● MULTIPLE CHOICE

Circle the one best answer for each of the following questions:

1. Classical economists are generally associated with:
   a. laissez faire.
   b. QWERTY.
   c. an activist policy.
   d. their support of low unemployment.

2. Keynesian economics focuses on:
   a. the long run.
   b. the short run.
   c. both the long run and the short run.
   d. neither the long run nor the short run.

3. The term *paradox of thrift* refers to the process by which individuals attempted to save:
   a. less, but in doing so spent less and caused income to decrease, ending up saving even less.
   b. less, but in doing so spent more and caused income to decrease, ending up saving even less.
   c. more, but in doing so spent less and caused income to decrease, ending up saving less.
   d. more, but in doing so spent more and caused income to decrease, ending up saving less.

4. In Keynesian economics equilibrium income:
   a. will be equal to potential income.
   b. will be below potential income.
   c. will be above potential income.
   d. may be different than potential income.

5. In the AS/AD model, the:
   a. price of a good is on the horizontal axis.
   b. price level is on the horizontal axis.
   c. price of a good is on the vertical axis.
   d. price level is on the vertical axis.

6. Which of the following is *not* an explanation of the downward slope of the AD curve?
   a. The wealth effect.
   b. The interest rate effect.
   c. The consumption effect.
   d. The international effect.

7. If the exchange rate becomes flexible so that changes in the price level have little effect on exports and imports, the:
   a. AD curve will become steeper.
   b. AD curve will become flatter.
   c. AD curve will be unaffected.
   d. SAS curve will become steeper.

8. If the multiplier effect is 2 rather than 3, the:
   a. AD curve will be steeper.
   b. AD curve will be flatter.
   c. AD curve will be unaffected.
   d. SAS curve will be steeper.

9. If there is a rise in foreign income the AD curve will likely:
   a. shift in to the left.
   b. shift out to the right.
   c. become steeper.
   d. become flatter.

10. If there is a rise in a country's exchange rate, the AD curve will likely:
    a. shift in to the left.
    b. shift out to the right.
    c. become steeper.
    d. become flatter.

11. Expansionary monetary policy will likely:
    a. shift the AD curve in to the left.
    b. shift the AD curve out to the right.
    c. make the AD curve steeper.
    d. make the AD curve flatter.

12. If government spending increases by 40, the AD curve will shift to the:
    a. right by 40.
    b. left by 40.
    c. right by more than 40.
    d. right by less than 40.

13. The slope of the SAS curve is determined by:
    a. opportunity cost.
    b. the law of diminishing marginal returns.
    c. institutional realities.
    d. the wealth effect, the international effect, and
       the interest rate effect.

14. If productivity rises by 2% and wages rise by
    6%, the SAS curve will:
    a. likely shift up (to the left).
    b. likely shift down (to the right).
    c. become flatter.
    d. become steeper.

15. The LAS curve is:
    a. another name for the AD curve.
    b. another name for the SAS curve.
    c. a vertical line.
    d. a horizontal line.

16. Refer to the graph below. The graph demon-
    strates the expected short-run result if:

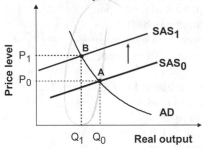

    a. productivity increases by less than wages.
    b. the government increases the money supply.
    c. the exchange rate value of a country's
       currency falls.
    d. there are suddenly expectations of a rising
       price level.

17. The graph below demonstrates the expected
    short-run result if:

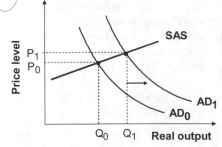

a. productivity increases by less than wages.
b. the government increases the money supply.
c. a country's exchange rate appreciates (gains
   value).
d. wages rise by less than the increase in
   productivity.

18. The graph below demonstrates the expected
    short-run result if:

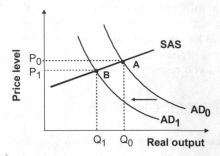

    a. productivity increases by less than wages.
    b. the government increases the money supply.
    c. a country's exchange rate appreciates (gains
       value).
    d. wages rise by less than the increase in
       productivity.

19. Assume the economy is initially at point B.
    The graph below correctly demonstrates an
    economy moving to point C if:

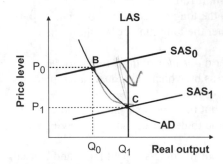

    a. productivity increases by less than the
       increase in wages.
    b. the government increases the money supply.
    c. a country's exchange rate appreciates (gains
       value).
    d. wages rise by less than the increase in
       productivity.

20. Assume the economy is initially at point B. The graph below correctly demonstrates an economy moving to point C if:

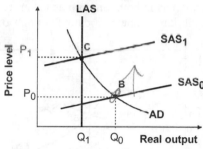

a. productivity increases by less than the increase in wages.
b. the government increases the money supply.
c. a country's exchange rate appreciates (gains value).
d. wages rise by less than the increase in productivity.

21. Which of the following distances in the graph below would represent an inflationary gap?

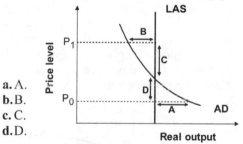

a. A.
b. B.
c. C.
d. D.

22. Expansionary fiscal policy involves:
a. increasing taxes.
b. increasing the money supply.
c. increasing government spending.
d. changing the exchange rate.

23. If the economy has an inflationary gap that it wants to eliminate, the government should use fiscal policy to shift:
a. the *LAS* curve out.
b. the *SAS* curve down (to the right).
c. the *AD* curve out to the right.
d. the *AD* curve in to the left.

24. If an economy has an inflationary gap and the government does nothing, the macro policy model predicts that:
a. the SAS curve will shift up (to the left) as input prices increase, and output will decline.
b. the SAS curve will shift down (to the right) as input prices decline, and output will rise.

c. the AD curve will shift out to the right as individuals collectively decide to increase expenditures, and output will rise.
d. the AD curve will shift in to the left as individuals collectively decide to reduce expenditures, and output will decline.

25. During World War II:
a. expansionary fiscal policy pushed the economy beyond potential and the price level rose tremendously.
b. expansionary fiscal policy pushed the economy beyond potential, but the price level was controlled by legislation.
c. contractionary monetary policy pushed the economy into a depression.
d. increased taxes to finance the war pushed the economy into recession.

26. The U.S. recession in 2001:
a. deepened because of significant increases in Social Security spending.
b. slowed accelerating inflation of the late 1990s.
c. remained mild because of tax cuts passed before the recession began.
d. provided Congress with an opportunity to respond with timely fiscal policy.

27. If the target rate of unemployment falls, potential income will:
a. first decrease, then increase.
b. increase.
c. decrease.
d. first increase, then decrease.

● POTENTIAL ESSAY QUESTIONS

You may also see essay questions similar to the "Problems & Applications" and "A Brain Teaser" exercises.

1. Why is the AS/AD model more complicated than the model makes it look?

2. What was the Keynesians' main argument against the Classical view that the economy will get itself out of the Depression?

3. What is the paradox of thrift and how does it relate to the AS/AD model?

ANSWERS

SHORT-ANSWER QUESTIONS

1. Classical economists focused on the real wage. They explained that unemployment would decline if the real wage were allowed to decline. Political and social forces were keeping the real wage too high. Keynesians focused on insufficient aggregate spending that resulted in a downward spiral. The economy was at a below-potential-income equilibrium. (202-204)

2. The wealth effect, the interest rate effect, the international effect, and the repercussions these effects (the multiplier effect) determine the slope of the AD curve. (206-208)

3. Five important initial shift factors of the AD curve are changes in: (1) foreign income, (2) exchange rates, (3) expectations, (4) distribution of income, and (5) government aggregate demand policy. (208-210)

4. The SAS curve specifies how a shift in the aggregate demand curve affects the price level and real output. A standard SAS curve is upward sloping. That is, increases in aggregate demand lead to increases in output and the price level. Institutional realities about how firms set prices determine the shape of the SAS curve. Faced with an increase in demand, firms generally respond by increasing production. Some firms will take the opportunity to increase their markup over costs, which will increase the price level also. (211)

5. The SAS curve will shift up or down when input prices rise or fall or if productivity rises or falls. The shift in the SAS curve (and therefore the price level) is determined by the following: % change in price level = % change in wages − % change in productivity. (211-213)

6. The LAS curve is vertical. It has this shape because at potential output, all inputs are fully employed. Changes in the price level do not affect potential output. (213-214)

7. If the economy begins at point A, a well-planned increase in government expenditures (plus the multiplier) shifts the AD out to the right from AD_0 to AD_1. If the economy begins below potential output, the price level would

rise slightly from P_0 to P_1 and real output would increase from Y_0 to Y_1. I've drawn it so that the AD curve shifts out enough so that the economy is in both long-run and short run equilibrium at potential output at point B.

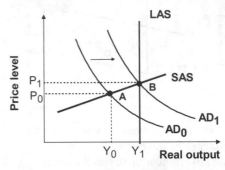

Now suppose the economy begins at point C (graph below) in both short run and long-run equilibrium. In the short-run, when the aggregate demand curve shifts from AD_0 to AD_1, real output rises from Y_0 to Y_1 and the price level rises from P_0 to P_1. Since the economy is now above potential output, however, input prices begin to rise and the SAS curve shifts up. The SAS curve continues to shift up to SAS_1 where the economy returns to a long-run equilibrium at a higher price level, P_2, but the same output level as before, Y_0. (218-219 and Figure 9-9)

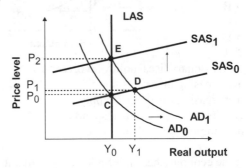

8. The AS/AD model is more complicated than it looks because fiscal policy is a slow legislative process and frequently determined by political, not economic, considerations. In addition, we do not know the level of potential output, which is the key to knowing whether contractionary or expansionary policy is needed. Economists have no sure way of estimating potential output. One method is to estimate the unemployment rate where inflation begins to rise. Unfortunately, this is also difficult to predict. Another way is to add a historical growth factor of 3% to previous levels of real output. This can be problematic if the economy is moving to a lower or higher growth rate. (221-222)

━━━━ ANSWERS ━━━━

MATCHING

1-c; 2-n; 3-k; 4-m; 5-j; 6-a; 7-h; 8-b; 9-i; 10-l; 11-d; 12-f; 13-e; 14-g.

━━━━ ANSWERS ━━━━

PROBLEMS AND APPLICATIONS

1. **a.** This would cause the wealth effect to become inoperative and the AD curve will become steeper. (206-207)
   b. Assuming rich people spend less of an increase in income compared to poor people, the AD curve will shift in to the left. (209)
   c. As the exchange rate depreciates, exports will rise and imports will fall. This shifts the AD curve out to the right. (207)
   d. If the exchange rate was originally fixed and became flexible, increases in the price level will be offset by changes in the exchange rate and the international effect becomes inoperative. The *AD* curve will be steeper. (207)
   e. Expectations of future price increases without changes in the current price level will tend to cause the *AD* curve to shift out to the right. (209)

2. **a.** The SAS doesn't shift at all because rises in input prices are completely offset by increases in productivity. (211-213)
   b. The SAS curve shifts up because the rise in input prices exceeds the rise in productivity. (211-213)
   c. The SAS curve shifts down because the rise in input prices is less than the rise in productivity. (211-213)

3. **a.** The LAS curve shifts to the right as shown below because business people are finding that their productive capacity is larger than they had thought. (214-215)

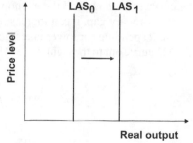

b. The potential output curve shifts to the left as shown below because bad weather will hinder production. Because the storm is temporary, however, the shift in the potential output curve is also temporary. (214-215)

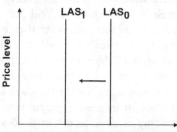

c. The short-run aggregate supply curve shown below shifts down from SAS_0 to SAS_1, because businesses will benefit from the declining import prices to the extent that imports are used in production. The fall in input prices is passed through to the goods market. (212)

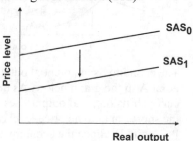

4. **a.** The economy is far below potential output at point A in the graph below. As the AD curve shifts out, the economy moves to point B—the price level rises slightly to P_1, and output increases to Y_1. As I have drawn the LAS curve, Y_1 is potential output, and point B is both a short-run and a long-run equilibrium. (218-219 and Figure 9-9)

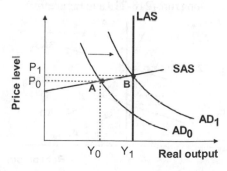

b. The economy is close to potential output at point A in the graph below. The AD curve shifts to AD$_1$. Real output rises to Y$_1$ and the price level rises to P$_1$. Because output is beyond potential, point B is a short-run equilibrium. Input prices begin to rise which shifts the SAS curve up. As the SAS curve shifts up, real output declines and the price level rises even further. The SAS curve will continue to shift up until the economy is at potential output Y$_2$ and a new price level P$_2$—point C. Expansionary fiscal policy will be less effective in increasing output when the economy is close to potential. Real output rises by less than in (a) and the economy experiences much more inflation. (218-219)

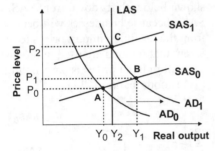

c. The economy is at potential output at point A in the graph below. As the AD curve shifts out, real output rises to Y$_1$ in the short run and the price level rises to P$_1$—point B. Since the economy is above potential however, eventually input prices will rise and the SAS curve will shift up. The SAS curve shifts up until real output falls back to potential output—Y$_0$—and the price level rises even further to P$_2$ (point C). In the long run, real output remains unchanged at Y$_0$ and only the price level increases from P$_0$ to P$_2$. When the economy is at or above potential, government activism is ineffective in the long run. (218-219 and Figure 9-9)

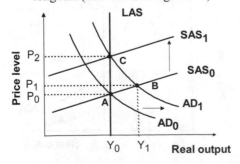

5. a. The graph below demonstrates an inflationary gap—short-run equilibrium output is above potential—point A. If government does nothing, wages will be bid up because there is a shortage of workers. This will shift the SAS curve up to SAS$_1$. Real output will fall to potential and the price level will rise—to point B. (217)

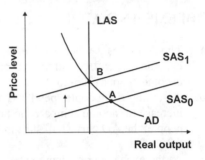

b. The graph below demonstrates a recessionary gap—short-run equilibrium output is below potential—point A. Given the excess supply in the labor market firms will be able to offer workers lower wages. Input prices will fall and the SAS curve will shift down to SAS$_1$. Real output will rise to potential and the price level will fall—to point B. Generally, government intervenes to increase expenditures (shifting the AD curve) before the price level declines. (217)

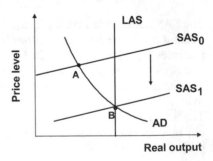

c. To avoid changes in the price level, if the economy is in an inflationary gap, the government can reduce government spending (or raise taxes) to shift the AD curve in to the left. If the economy is in a recessionary gap, it can increase government spending (or lower taxes) to shift the AD curve out to the right. (218-219)

ANSWERS

A BRAIN TEASER

1. My response depends on where I believe the economy is relative to potential output. If we are far below potential output then the President is right—the policy moves will increase the AD curve and the real output (employment) level will rise without creating much inflation. However, if we are close to potential output and the policy pushes the economy beyond potential, then wages will rise pushing the SAS curve up and the price level may rise more. The extent to which wages rise depends on the size of the effect on aggregate demand. It is difficult to predict. Moreover, it is also very difficult to determine how far from potential the economy actually is. (218-220)

ANSWERS

MULTIPLE CHOICE

1. a   Laissez faire is the non-activist policy that Classical economists generally support. See page 202.

2. b   The essence of Keynesian economics is its focus on the short run. See page 203.

3. c   The paradox of thrift is that if individuals increase saving, total income will decline, resulting in lower saving. See page 204.

4. d   Because of coordination problems equilibrium income could be different than potential income in Keynesian economics; it could be higher, lower, or equal to it. See page 204.

5. d   The AS/AD model is different than the micro supply/demand model. It has price *level* on the vertical axis and *total* output on the horizontal axis. See page 206.

6. c   No consumption effect is discussed in the book. See pages 206-208.

7. a   This question refers to the international effect; if the international effect is reduced, the change in the price level will have less effect on AD and the AD curve will be steeper. See page 207.

8. a   The multiplier effect increases the effect of the other effects and hence a smaller multiplier makes the AD curve steeper. See pages 207-208.

9. b   The rise in foreign income will increase demand for exports, shifting the AD curve to the right. See page 208.

10. a   The rise in the country's exchange rate will decrease demand for its exports, shifting the AD curve in to the left. See pages 208-209.

11. b   Expansionary monetary policy will increase aggregate demand, shifting the AD curve out to the right. See page 210.

12. c   The multiplier effect would increase the effect, so the rightward shift would be more than 40. See page 210.

13. c   The SAS curve is not a derived curve; it is an empirical curve determined by institutional realities. See page 211.

14. a   Because wages are rising by more than productivity, the SAS curve will shift up. See page 213.

15. c   The LAS curve shows the amount of goods and services an economy can produce when both labor and capital are fully employed. It is a vertical line since the price level does not affect potential output. See page 213.

16. a   The SAS curve shifts upward when wages rise by more than increases in productivity. Real output will decline and the price level will rise. See page 213.

17. b   An increase in the money supply will shift the AD curve to the right. In the short run, real output and the price level will rise. See pages 210 and 218-219.

18. c   Demand for domestic goods will decline if one's currency appreciates because foreign goods will be less expensive compared to domestic goods. Real output will decline and the price level falls slightly. See pages 218-219.

19. d   Since at point B, the economy is below potential, there will be downward pressure on wages. Or at least wages will rise by less than the increase in productivity.

The SAS curve will shift down until the economy reaches point C. See pages 215-217.

20. a Since at point B, the economy is above potential, there will be upward pressure on wages. Wages will rise by more than the increase in productivity. The SAS curve will shift up until the economy reaches point C. See pages 215-217.

21. a The inflationary gap occurs when the price level is such that the quantity of aggregate demand exceeds the quantity of potential income. See page 217.

22. c Expansionary fiscal policy is the deliberate increase in government expenditures or reduction in taxes. See page 218.

23. d Aggregate demand management policies do not affect SAS, so a and b are out. With an inflationary gap you want to decrease output, so the answer is d. See Figure 9-8 on page 218 .

24. a Inflation results in higher input prices, which shifts the SAS curve up. See page 217.

25. b During WW II, taxes rose, but spending rose even more so that the net result was expansionary. Although the economy exceeded potential, inflation was avoided by price controls. See pages 220-221.

26. c The tax cuts were passed for supply-side reasons, but they became unintentionally timely when the recession began and kept the recession mild. See page 221.

27. b Potential income varies inversely with unemployment. See pages 213-214.

■ ANSWERS ■

POTENTIAL ESSAY QUESTIONS

The following are annotated answers. They indicate the general idea behind the answer.

1.   The macro model is more complicated than it appears because we do not know for sure where potential output is and because fiscal policy is more difficult to implement than is portrayed. Because we have no way of precisely determining how close the economy is to potential output, we don't know precisely by how much we should shift the AD curve.

2.   The Classical prescription for the Great Depression was to do nothing (except remove the obstacles that they argued kept wages and prices artificially high) and wait for the market to work its magic over time.

Keynes believed that equilibrium income was not the same as potential income. He disagreed with Say's Law. Supply does *not* create its own demand. That is, there is no guaranteed equality between savings and investment. Savings could exceed investment so that aggregate expenditures would not purchase all that is produced. Inventories will rise, and output, employment, and incomes would fall creating a further decline in total spending. Keynes doubted whether falling prices could stop this downward spiral. So, we get stuck in a rut.

The policy implications are that insufficient total spending in the economy could result in *an equilibrium* level of output, employment, and income *below potential* output. Therefore, the Keynesian recommendation for a recession: expansionary macro policy. That is, increase government spending, reduce taxes (fiscal policy), and increase the money supply (monetary policy) to stimulate aggregate expenditures. (This would shift the AD curve to the right and increase real output.)

3.   The paradox of thrift is that when people collectively decide to save more and consume less, consumption expenditures fall. If that saving is not immediately transferred into investment, total expenditures falls. Faced with excess supply, firms cut production and income falls. As people's income falls, consumption and saving both fall. It is the paradox of thrift that leads to the multiplier effect. This multiplier effect makes the AD curve flatter than it otherwise would have been and accounts for the multiplied effect of shift factors of aggregate demand.

THE MULTIPLIER MODEL

CHAPTER AT A GLANCE

This review is based upon the learning objectives that open the chapter.

1. Autonomous expenditures are unrelated to income; induced expenditures are directly related to income. (230-231)

AE_0 (autonomous expenditures) can change (shift the AE curve) if there is an autonomous change in any component of aggregate expenditures (AE).

Note: $AE_0 = C_0 + I_0 + G_0 + (X_0 - M_0)$.

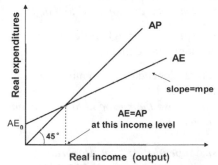

2. To determine income graphically in the multiplier model, you find the income level at which aggregate expenditures equal aggregate production. (234-235)

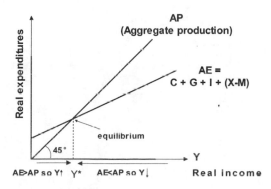

3. To determine income using the multiplier equation, determine the multiplier and multiply it by the level of autonomous expenditures (235-236)

multiplier = $1/(1-mpe)$.

$Y = $ (multiplier)(Autonomous expenditures)

$\Delta Y = $ (multiplier)(ΔAutonomous expenditures)

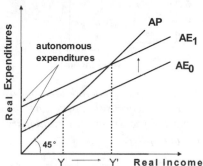

4. The multiplier process works because when expenditures don't equal production, businesspeople change planned production, which changes income, which changes expenditures, which.... (236-240)

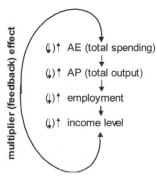

This is the income adjustment process—the multiplier effect on income given a change in spending.

5. Expansionary fiscal policy can eliminate a recessionary gap. It shifts the AE curve up, increasing equilibrium income by a multiple of the shift. (241-244)

If the economy is below potential, at Y_0, in the graph below, expansionary fiscal policy can get the economy out of its recessionary gap by increasing government purchases or decreasing taxes. The AE/AP model assumes the price level is constant, so real output rises by the full amount of the multiplier times the change in autonomous expenditures.

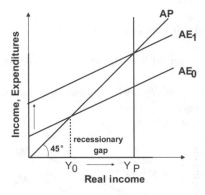

In the model, government knows by how much to increase (decrease) expenditures by dividing the recessionary (inflationary) gap by the multiplier.

The reverse logic explains how contractionary fiscal policy attempts to close an inflationary gap.

6. While the multiplier model is a mechanistic multiplier model, it should be used as a guide to one's common sense. The multiplier model has limitations: (245-246)

- The multiplier is not a complete model of the economy.
  The multiplier is best used as a guide for the direction and rough sizes of shifts in aggregate demand on income.

- Shifts are not as great as intuition suggests.
  Because some saving is brought back into the expenditures flow, a change in autonomous expenditures has less of an effect than the model suggests.

- The price level will often change in response to shifts in demand.
  The multiplier model assumes prices are fixed.

- People's forward-looking expectations make the adjustment process much more complicated.
  Business decisions are forward-looking.

- Shifts in expenditures might reflect desired shifts in supply and demand.

- Expenditures depend on much more than current income.
  People also base their expenditure decisions on future income.

See also, Appendix A: "An Algebraic Presentation of the Expanded Multiplier Model" and Appendix B: "The Multiplier Model and the AS/AD Model."

SHORT-ANSWER QUESTIONS

1. What is the difference between induced and autonomous expenditures?

2. Draw an AP and an AE curve and show how the level of income is graphically determined in the multiplier model. Describe the forces that are set in motion when income levels are above and below equilibrium.

3. In the multiplier model, if autonomous expenditures are $200 and the *mpe* is 0.75, what is equilibrium income?

4. Explain the process by which the economy reaches a new equilibrium income if autonomous expenditures increase by $100. The marginal propensity to expend is 0.5.

5. How does fiscal policy affect the economy? Demonstrate the appropriate fiscal policy for an economy that has an inflationary gap.

6. True or false: The multiplier model is a complete model of the economy. Explain your answer.

MATCHING THE TERMS
Match the terms to their definitions

___1. aggregate expenditures
___2. aggregate production
         curve
___3. autonomous expenditures
___4. expenditures multiplier
___5. induced expenditures
___6. marginal propensity to
         expend
___7. multiplier equation
___8. permanent income
         hypothesis
___9. rational expectations
         model
___10. real business cycle
         theory

a. The hypothesis that expenditures are determined by permanent
     or lifetime income.
b. Expenditures that change as income changes.
c. The theory that fluctuations in the economy reflect real phenom-
     ena—simultaneous shifts in supply and demand, not simply
     supply responses to demand shifts.
d. A number that tells us how much income will change in response
     to a change in autonomous expenditures.
e. $AE = C + I + G + (X - M)$.
f. In the multiplier model, the 45° line on a graph with real income
     measured on the horizontal axis and real production on the
     vertical axis. Alternatively called the aggregate income curve.
g. The ratio of a change in expenditures to a change in income.
h. Expenditures that are unaffected by changes in income.
i. Equation that tells us how much income will change in response
     to a change in autonomous expenditures.
j. Model of the economy in which all decisions are based upon
     expected equilibrium in the economy.

PROBLEMS AND APPLICATIONS

1. Answer the following questions about the
    aggregate production curve.

    a. Draw an aggregate production curve.
        Label all axes.

    b. What is the slope of the aggregate
        production function?

    c. Why is the slope as you have drawn it?

2. You are given the following information about
    the economy:

Income	Expenditures
0	100
500	500
1,000	900
2,000	1,700
3,000	2,500
4,000	3,300

    a. What is the level of autonomous expendi-
        tures?

b. What is the marginal propensity to expend? Explain why it is important.

c. What expenditures function (an equation) corresponds to the table?

3. Putting expenditures and production together:

a. Graph the expenditures function from question 2 on the aggregate production curve from question 1.

b. What is the slope of the expenditures function?

4. Given the following equation, answer the questions: $AE = C_0 + .6Y + I_0 + G_0 + (X_0 - M_0)$ where $C_0 = 1000, I_0 = 500, G_0 = 300, X_0 = 300, M_0 = 400$.

a. Draw the aggregate expenditures curve.

b. What is the slope of the curve?

c. What is the vertical axis intercept?

d. Add the aggregate production curve to the graph.

e. What is the multiplier?

f. What is equilibrium income? Label that point A on the graph.

g. What is the effect of an increase in autonomous consumption of $200 on equilibrium income? Demonstrate your answer graphically.

h. What is the effect on equilibrium income of a change in the *mpe* from .6 to .8? Demonstrate your answer graphically. How does your answer to (g) change with the new *mpe*?

5. Calculate the multiplier in each case.

   a. *mpe* = .7

   b. *mpe* = .6

6. For each of the following, state what will happen to equilibrium income.

   a. The *mpe* is 0.9 and autonomous government expenditures just rose $200 billion. Graph your analysis.

   b. The *mpe* is 0.65 and autonomous investment just fell $70 billion. Graph your analysis.

7. You are hired by the president who believes that the economy is operating at a level $300 billion beyond potential output. You are told that the marginal propensity to consume is 0.5. (Note: assume that the *mpe* = *mpc*.)

   a. The president wants to use taxes to close the gap. What do you advise? Show your answer using the AP/AE model.

   b. The president wants to compare your plan in (a) to a plan using spending to close the inflationary gap. What do you advise? Show your answer graphically using the AP/AE model.

   c. The president's advisers from the council realize that the marginal propensity to consume is 0.75. Recalculate your answer to (b) and show your answer graphically using the AP/AE model.

A1. You've just been appointed chairman of the Council of Economic Advisers in Textland. The *mpc* is .8, and all non-consumption expenditures and taxes are exogenous.

   a. How can the government increase output by $400 through a change in expenditures?

b. Oops! There's been a mistake. Your research assistant tells you that taxes are actually not exogenous, and that there is a marginal tax rate of .1. How can the government change expenditures to increase income by $400?

c. There's more new news which your research assistant just found out. She tells you that not only is there a marginal tax rate of .1; there's also a marginal propensity to import of .2. You have to change your solutions now. How can the government change expenditures to increase income by $400?

B1. What happens to output in the AP/AE model when the AE curve shifts up due to a shift in autonomous expenditures if the economy is at potential output and the price level is flexible?

● A BRAIN TEASER

1. We have all heard about the extent to which local communities go to in attracting and recruiting new businesses, conventions, trade shows, professional meetings, etc., to their area. Sometimes they seem to "give away the farm." They may offer a commitment not to impose property taxes for a particular number of years or offer land at no charge if a company will build a production facility in the area. Why do local governments offer lucrative tax incentives, etc., to attract new businesses to their area—especially considering that there are only a relatively few number of modestly higher paying jobs created?

● MULTIPLE CHOICE

Circle the one best answer for each of the following questions:

1. In the multiplier model:
   a. production is assumed to be fixed.
   b. planned expenditures are assumed to equal actual production.
   c. the price level is assumed to be fixed.
   d. the price level is assumed to be flexible.

2. Autonomous expenditures are expenditures that:
   a. are automatically created by income.
   b. are unrelated to income.
   c. change as income changes.
   d. automatically change as income changes.

3. The marginal propensity to expend is:
   a. the change in expenditures times the change in income.
   b. the change in expenditures divided by the change in income.
   c. the change in expenditures divided by income.
   d. expenditures divided by the change in income.

4. If the mpe is .8, what is the size of the multiplier in the multiplier model?
   a. .5.
   b. 5.
   c. 1.
   d. 10.

5. As the *mpe* rises, the multiplier:
    a. increases.
    b. decreases.
    c. remains the same.
    d. sometimes rises and sometimes falls.

6. Which of the following is the expenditures
    function depicted in the graph below?

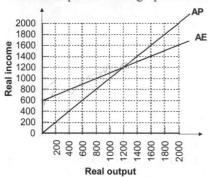

    a. AE = $600 + .5Y.
    b. AE = .5Y.
    c. AE = $600.
    d. AE = $600Y/.5.

7. Refer to the graph for Question #6. Planned
    expenditures exceed production at:
    a. income levels above $1,200.
    b. income levels below $1,200.
    c. income level of $1,200.
    d. no income level since planned expenditures
       equals production.

8. If consumer confidence suddenly falls, you
    would expect:
    a. the aggregate production curve to shift
       down.
    b. the aggregate expenditures curve to rotate to
       the right and equilibrium income to fall.
    c. the aggregate expenditures curve to shift up
       and equilibrium income to rise.
    d. the aggregate expenditures curve to shift
       down and equilibrium income to fall.

9. In the multiplier model, if autonomous expendi-
    tures are $5,000 and the *mpe* equals .9, what
    is the level of income in the economy?
    a. $5,000.
    b. $10,000.
    c. $20,000.
    d. $50,000.

10. In the multiplier model, if autonomous exports
    fall by 40 and the *mpe* is .5, what happens to
    equilibrium income?
    a. It rises by 20.
    b. It falls by 20.
    c. It rises by 80.
    d. It falls by 80.

11. In the multiplier model, if autonomous expendi-
    tures increase by 100, income:
    a. will rise by 100.
    b. will rise by more than 100.
    c. will fall by 100.
    d. may rise or fall. We cannot tell without more
       information.

12. In the multiplier model, if autonomous expendi-
    tures increase by 10 and the *mpe* is .8, what
    happens to equilibrium income?
    a. It rises by 8.
    b. It falls by 8.
    c. It rises by 50.
    d. It falls by 50.

13. In the multiplier model, if autonomous exports
    fall by 40 and government spending in-
    creases by 20, and the *mpe* is .8, what
    happens to equilibrium income?
    a. It rises by 300.
    b. It falls by 300.
    c. It rises by 100.
    d. It falls by 100.

14. In the multiplier model, if people begin to
    spend less of the increases in their income:
    a. leakages out of the circular flow will rise and
       equilibrium income will fall.
    b. because leakages from the circular flow will
       still equal injections into the circular flow,
       equilibrium income will not change.
    c. injections into the circular flow will rise and
       equilibrium income will rise.
    d. the flow of income and expenditures will no
       longer be circular.

15. In the graph on the next page, actual income is
    below potential income. The government is
    planning to use expansionary fiscal policy.
    This will:

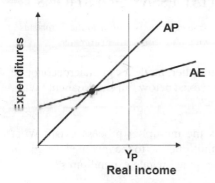

Real income

a. shift the *AP* curve up.
b. shift the *AE* curve up.
c. shift the *AP* curve down.
d. shift the *AE* curve down.

16. The economy has an *mpe* of .5, and a
    recessionary gap of 240. Using the
    Keynesian *multiplier model*, an economist
    would advise government to increase
    autonomous expenditures by:
    a. 120.
    b. 240.
    c. 480.
    d. 620.

17. The economy has an *mpe* of .8 and an inflation-
    ary gap of 500. Assume *mpe* = *mpc*. Using
    the multiplier model, an economist would
    advise government to increase taxes by:
    a. 50.
    b. 75.
    c. 100.
    d. 125.

18. The hypothesis that expenditures are deter-
    mined by permanent or lifetime income
    (making the *mpe* close to zero) implies that
    the AE curve will be close to:
    a. a flat line.
    b. a vertical line.
    c. an upward sloping 45⁰ line.
    d. something economists cannot determine.

19. The interpretative Keynesian macro model
    differs from the mechanistic Keynesian
    model in that the interpretative multiplier
    model:
    a. is essentially a Classical model.
    b. sees the Keynesian model as a guide, not a
       definitive result.

c. integrates the quantity theory into the *AE/
   AP* model.
d. integrates the quantity theory into both the
   Keynesian *AS/AD* and the *AE/AP* models.

20. If there is some price level flexibility, the:
    a. multiplier model is no longer relevant.
    b. results of the multiplier model will be
       reversed.
    c. results of the multiplier model will be
       modified but the central point will remain the
       same.
    d. multiplier model will turn into a Classical
       model.

21. In the real business cycle theory, business
    cycles occur because of:
    a. changes in the real price level.
    b. changes in real income.
    c. technological and other natural shocks.
    d. changes in the money supply.

A1. If the marginal tax rate increases, what would
    happen to the general expenditures multi-
    plier?
    a. It would increase.
    b. It would decrease.
    c. It would remain the same.
    d. One cannot say.

A2. In the multiplier model, if a country has a very
    large marginal propensity to import:
    a. expansionary fiscal policy would be ex-
       tremely effective in expanding domestic
       income.
    b. expansionary fiscal policy would not be very
       effective in expanding domestic income.
    c. The size of the marginal propensity to import
       has no effect on the effectiveness of
       expansionary fiscal policy.
    d. The multiplier model is not relevant to a
       country with a very large marginal propen-
       sity to import.

A3. Assuming the marginal propensity to import is
    .1, the tax rate is .2, and the marginal propen-
    sity to consume is .6, the multiplier will be
    approximately:
    a. 0.
    b. 1.2.
    c. 1.6.
    d. 2.6.

A4. Assume the marginal propensity to import is .1, the tax rate is .25, the marginal propensity to consume is .8, and that the government wants to increase income by 100. In the multiplier model you would suggest increasing government spending by:
  a. 10.
  b. 35.7.
  c. 50.
  d. 100.

A5. Assume the marginal propensity to import is .3, the tax rate is .2, the marginal propensity to consume is .5, and that the government wants to increase income by 200. In the multiplier model you would suggest increasing government spending by:
  a. 87.5.
  b. 100.
  c. 180.
  d. 200.

B1. When the price level falls:
  a. the aggregate expenditures curve remains constant.
  b. the aggregate expenditures curve shifts down.
  c. the aggregate expenditures curve shifts up.
  d. the slope of the aggregate expenditures curve changes.

B2. To derive the aggregate demand curve from the multiplier model, one must:
  a. relate the initial autonomous shifts caused by price level changes on the *AE* curve to the *AD* curve.
  b. relate the *AE/AP* equilibria at different price levels to the *AD* curve.
  c. relate the *AE/AP* equilibria at different quantity levels to the *AD* curve.
  d. relate the initial autonomous shifts caused by price level changes on the *AP* curve to the *AD* curve.

● POTENTIAL ESSAY QUESTIONS

You may also see essay questions similar to the "Problems & Applications" and "A Brain Teaser" exercises.

1. In the multiplier model, can macroeconomic equilibrium exist below full employment? Why, or why not?

2. Why does the multiplier process exist? What does the multiplier do to the income level given any change in aggregate expenditures?

3. What is the major contribution of the multiplier model to the AS/AD model?

SHORT-ANSWER QUESTIONS

1. Induced expenditures depend upon the level of income. Autonomous expenditures are independent of income. (606-607)

2. The *AP* curve is a 45-degree line through the origin. At all points on the *AP* curve, output equals income. The *AE* curve is an upward-sloping line with a slope less than one that intersects the expenditures axis at the level of autonomous expenditures. These curves are shown in the graph below. Equilibrium income is where the two curves intersect. At points to the left, aggregate expenditures exceed aggregate production and businesses find their inventories are being depleted. They increase production, which increases income and expenditures, moving income up toward equilibrium. At points to the right, aggregate expenditures are less than aggregate production and businesses see their inventories accumulating. They cut production, which reduces income and expenditures, moving income down toward equilibrium. (234-237)

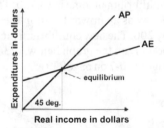

3. To determine equilibrium income, multiply the sum of all autonomous expenditures by the multiplier. In this case the multiplier is $1/(1-.75)=4$, so equilibrium income is $800. (235-236)

4. The initial shock is $100. This increase in expenditures causes aggregate production to increase also by $100, which creates an additional $100 in income. Consumers spend $50 of this additional income on additional goods. Once again aggregate production rises by the same amount as aggregate expenditures rose—$50 increase in this case. Subsequent increases in aggregate expenditures and aggregate production are determined in a similar fashion, each time getting smaller and smaller. Equilibrium income is $200 higher at the end of this multiplier process. This is determined by calculating the multiplier, $1/$

$(1-mpe)=2$ and multiplying it by the initial rise in aggregate expenditures of $100. (236-237)

5. Fiscal policy affects the economy by changing aggregate expenditures, which changes people's incomes, which changes people's spending even more. Expansionary fiscal policy shifts the aggregate expenditures curve up. Equilibrium income rises by a multiple of the increase in government spending. An economy in an inflationary gap is shown below. To avoid inflation, government can reduce government spending by the inflationary gap divided by the multiplier. A decline in government spending shifts the AE curve down and equilibrium income declines by a multiple of that shift. (241-244)

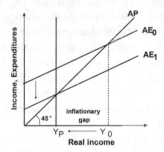

6. False. The multiplier model is not a complete model of the economy. Although it purports to determine equilibrium from scratch, it doesn't because it does not tell us where those autonomous expenditures come from. The multiplier model is best used as a guide for the direction and rough size of the effects of changes in autonomous expenditures on income. (245-246)

MATCHING

1-e; 2-f; 3-h; 4-d; 5-b; 6-g; 7-i; 8-a; 9-j; 10-c.

PROBLEMS AND APPLICATIONS

1. **a.** The aggregate production curve is a 45-degree line as shown below. Production is on the vertical axis and real income is on the horizontal axis. (229)

b. The slope is 1. (229)

c. The slope is one because the aggregate production curve represents the identity that aggregate production must equal aggregate income. That can only be represented by a straight line through the origin with a slope of one. (229)

2. a. Autonomous expenditures are $100. It is expenditures that are independent of income. (230)

b. The marginal propensity to expend is 0.8: This is calculated as the change in expenditures/change in income = 400/500. It is important because it tells us how much of any additional income is re-spent as the economy expands. It is because of the *mpe* that income changes by a multiple of a change in autonomous expenditures. (231)

c. The expenditures function that corresponds to the table is $AE = 100 + .8Y$. The 100 comes from the level of expenditures when income is zero and the .8 is the *mpe*. (232-233)

3. a. The graphs of the expenditures function from question 2 and the aggregate production from question 1 are shown together on the following graph. (229, 233)

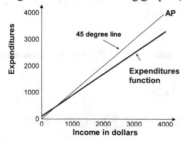

b. The slope of the expenditure function is the *mpe*, or 0.8. (232-233)

4. a. The aggregate expenditures curve is drawn below. The slope of the *AE* curve is the *mpe* and the vertical intercept is autonomous expenditures. (232-233)

b. The slope of the curve is .6. It is the *mpe*. (232-233)

c. The vertical axis intercept is $1000+500+300+(300-400)=1700$. The vertical axis intercept is the level of autonomous expenditures. (232-233)

d. The aggregate production curve is shown in the graph below. It is a 45-degree line through the origin. (229)

e. The multiplier is 2.5. It is $1/(1-mpe)$. (235-236)

f. Equilibrium income is $4,250: autonomous expenditures × multiplier, $1,700×2.5. This is shown as point A on the graph below. (236-237)

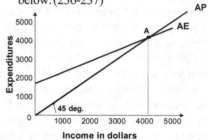

g. An increase in autonomous expenditures of $200 will increase equilibrium income by $500. This is calculated by multiplying $200 by the multiplier, 2.5. The new equilibrium income is $4,750. This is shown below as an upward shift in the AE curve by 200. The new equilibrium income is point B on the graph below. (236-237 and Figure 10-7 on page 239)

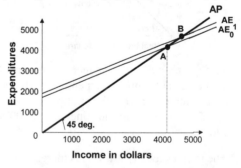

h. The *AE* curve becomes steeper with a slope of .8. The multiplier is now 5 and equilibrium income is now $8,500. This is shown as point C in the graph on the next page. Equilibrium income is calculated by multiplying autonomous expenditures, $1,700, by the multiplier. Since the multiplier is larger, an increase of $200 in autonomous expenditures now increases equilibrium income by $1,000, up to $9,500. (233, Figure 10-5 on page 235, and 235-237)

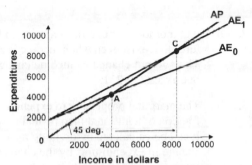

5. a. The multiplier is 3.33: 1/(1 −.7). (236)
   b. The multiplier is 2.5: 1/(1 −.6). (236)

6. a. Income rises by $2 trillion: 200/(1 −0.9). In this case, the aggregate expenditures curve has a slope of 0.9 as shown in the graph below. The increase in government expenditures shifts the *AE* curve up from AE_0 to AE_1 and income increases by a multiple of that amount, in this case by a multiple of 10. (236 and Figure 10-7)

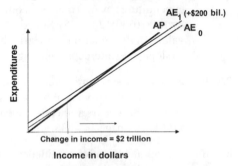

   b. Income falls by $200 billion: $70/.35. In this case the aggregate expenditures curve has a slope of .65 as shown in the graph below. The decrease in investment shifts the *AE* curve down from AE_0 to AE_1 and income decreases by a multiple of that amount, in this case by a multiple of 2.86. (236 and Figure 10-7on page 239)

7. a. The spending multiplier is 2, 1/(1-.5), but only a fraction of the increase in taxes reduces spending. Taxes must be increased by $300 billion to reduce income by $300 billion. We calculate this by solving the following for change in taxes:

change in taxes × *mpc* × [1/(1 −*mpe*)] = $300 billion. The AE curve shifts down by the decrease in consumption spending ($150 billion) as shown below. (244)

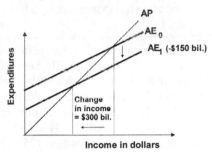

   b. The spending multiplier is 2. Spending must be decreased by $150 billion to reduce income by $300 billion. We calculate this by solving the following for change in government spending: change in government spending × (1/(1 −*mpe*)) = $300 billion. Graphically, the analysis is the same as in part a. (242-243)

   c. The spending multiplier is now 4, 1/(1 −.75). Government spending must be decreased by $75 billion to reduce income by $300 billion. We calculate this by solving the following for change in government spending: change in government spending × 4 = $300 billion. This is shown in the graph below. The *AE* curve is steeper than the *AE* curve in part b. (242-243)

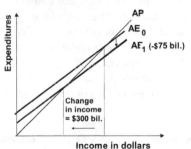

A1. Given an *mpc* of .8:
   a. Increase expenditures by $80. The multiplier is 1/(1 −*mpc*) = 1/(1 −.8) = 5. Therefore, to increase GDP by $400, government spending has to increase $80. (251-253)
   b. Increase expenditures by $112. The multiplier is 1/(1 −*mpc* + *t* × *mpc*) = 1/(1 −.8+(.1 × .8)) = 3.57. Therefore, to increase GDP by $400, government spending has to increase by $112. (251-253)

c. Increase expenditures by $193. The multiplier is $1/(1 - mpc + t \times mpc + mpm) = 1/(1 - .8 + .1 \times .8 + .2) = 2.08$. Therefore, to increase GDP by $400, government spending has to increase by $193. (251-253)

B1. In the multiplier model, a change in autonomous expenditures will be offset entirely by a change in the price level that shifts the AE curve in a direction opposite to the initial shift. If the initial shift causes the AE curve to shift up, prices will rise sufficiently to shift the AE curve back to its initial position. (254-255)

━━━ ANSWERS ━━━

A BRAIN TEASER

1. It may appear that the benefits do not outweigh the costs to the community of "giving away the farm"–especially when one considers that the tax breaks offered to new businesses will likely result in higher property tax rates imposed on other members of the community if the same quantity and quality of local government services are to be provided. However, even though a relatively few number of modestly higher paying jobs are created, because of the multiplier effect, this *can* translate into still more jobs and even more income, etc.–creating "significant growth and opportunities within the community." Next time you read headlines indicating the amount of jobs (or income) created in the city by having the "Pigs are Beautiful" convention in town, you'll know what they mean. (236-237)

━━━ ANSWERS ━━━

MULTIPLE CHOICE

1. c The multiplier model assumes that the price level remains constant and asks how much aggregate equilibrium income will change when aggregate expenditures change. During the adjustment to equilibrium, planned expenditures will not equal actual production. See pages 236-237.

2. b Autonomous expenditures are expenditures that exist even when income is zero. They do not change as income changes. See pages 230-231.

3. b The marginal propensity to expend is the fraction of additional income that is spent. It can be calculated by dividing the change in expenditures by the change in income. See page 231.

4. b The multiplier equals $1/(1 - .8) = 1/.2 = 5$. See page 236.

5. a You can determine this by substituting into the multiplier formula. See page 236.

6. a The graph shows that the y-axis intercept is $600 and the slope is .5. Calculate the slope as rise over run. For example, beginning at the y-intercept, increasing expenditures by 600 means income rises by 1200 (600/1200 = .5). Substitute these values in the equation for a straight line: y = (slope)x + (intercept). See page 233.

7. b Planned expenditures exceed production where the AE curve is above the AP curve. This occurs at income levels below $1,200. See page 234-235.

8. d A drop in consumer confidence would be expected to reduce consumption expenditures. This shifts the AE curve down and leads to a reduction in equilibrium income (output). See pages 240-241.

9. d The multiplier is 10 so the answer is 10 times $5,000. See pages 235-236.

10. d The multiplier is 2 so the answer is $2 \times (-40)$. See pages 235-236.

11. b In the multiplier model, a change in autonomous expenditures will lead to a change in income in the same direction that is a multiple of the change in expenditures. See pages 235-236.

12. c The multiplier is 5 so the answer is 5 times 10. See pages 235-236.

13. d The multiplier is 5 so the answer is 5 times $(-40 + 20)$ or minus 100. See pages 235-236.

14. a   If people spend less of their income, the *mpe* will fall. Because more income leaks from the circular flow, less returns in the form of expenditures and equilibrium income falls. See pages 237-238.

15. b   Expansionary fiscal policy increases aggregate expenditures, which is shown by a shift up in the AE curve. See Figure 10-10(a) on page 242.

16. a   To determine how much to increase expenditures in the *multiplier model* to reach potential income, you divide the recessionary gap of 240 by the multiplier of 2. See pages 242-243.

17. d   Since the multiplier is 5, expenditures need to fall by 100. Expenditures will fall by the *mpc* times the rise in taxes, so taxes need to rise by 100 divided by the *mpc*, or 125. See page 244.

18. a   The permanent income hypothesis suggests that the *mpe* out of current income would be small so, the AE curve would be quite flat. See page 246.

19. b   The interpretative multiplier model views the multiplier model as an aid in understanding. It might integrate the multiplier model with other models but that is not what is distinctive about it. See page 247.

20. c   The multiplier model assumes that the price level is constant. If, however, the price level is not constant, the multiplier model is modified. The central point, however, that an increase in expenditures has a multiplied effect on equilibrium output is still relevant. See page 245.

21. c   Real business cycle theory suggests that fluctuations in output are the result of shifting aggregate supply resulting from changes in technology. See page 246.

A1. b   This is a hard question since it requires some deduction. The marginal tax rate is one of the components of the marginal propensity to consume. It is a leakage from the circular flow, so it makes the multiplier smaller. See pages 251-253.

A2. b   A large marginal propensity to import reduces the size of the multiplier since the marginal propensity to import is one of the components of the marginal propensity to consume. See pages 251-253.

A3. c   The multiplier for the full model is $1/(1-c+ct+m)$. Substituting in gives $1/(1-.6+(.6)(.2)+.1)$ or $1/.62$ or a multiplier of about 1.6. See pages 251-253.

A4. c   First you determine the multiplier. The multiplier for the full model is $1/(1-c+ct+m)$. Substituting in gives $1/(1-.8+(.8)(.25)+.1)$ or $1/.5$ or a multiplier of 2. Dividing 100 by 2 gives an increase of government spending of 50. See pages 251-253.

A5. c   First you determine the multiplier. The multiplier for the full model is $1/(1-c+ct+m)$. Substituting in gives $1/(1-.5+(.5)(.2)+.3)$ or $1/.9$ or a multiplier of about 1.11. Dividing 200 by 1.11 gives an increase of government spending of about 180. The multiplier is very small because the *mpc* is low and the *mpm* is high. See pages 251-253.

B1. c   Since a lower price level makes the cash people hold worth more, people feel wealthier, spend more, and the *AE* curve shifts up. See pages 254-255.

B2. b   As discussed on pages 254-255, especially Figure B10-1, one considers the effect of different price levels on the *AE* curve to derive an *AD* curve.

■ **ANSWERS** ■

POTENTIAL ESSAY QUESTIONS

The following are annotated answers. They indicate the general idea behind the answer.

1.   Yes, because equilibrium exists *wherever* AE = AP. That is, planned expenditures need not equal production at full employment. If there is inadequate spending then the income adjustment process moves the economy to an equilibrium below full employment.

2. A change in spending changes people's incomes, which changes their spending, which changes people's incomes… Because of the induced effects within the income adjustment process, the multiplier magnifies any changes in spending into much larger changes in income. However, given an increase in expenditures, real income increases by a smaller amount when prices are flexible.

3. The major contribution of the multiplier model to the AS/AD model is that it provides an exact number for the shift in the AD curve when autonomous expenditures change and provides the reasoning behind the multiplier effects needed to derive an AD curve.

Pretest
Chapters 6-10

Take this test in test conditions, giving yourself a limited amount of time to complete the questions. Ideally, check with your professor to see how much time he or she allows for an average multiple choice question and multiply this by 30. This is the time limit you should set for yourself for this pretest. If you do not know how much time your teacher would allow, we suggest 1 minute per question, or 30 minutes.

1. All of the following are long-run growth policies *except*:
   a. increasing government spending to spur consumer spending.
   b. reducing tax rates to increase incentives to work.
   c. providing funding for research.
   d. following policies to reduce interest rates and increase business investment.

2. The secular trend growth rate in the United States is approximately:
   a. 1 to 1.5 percent per year.
   b. 2.5 to 3.5 percent per year.
   c. 5 to 5.5 percent per year.
   d. 7 to 7.5 percent per year.

3. Leading indicators include:
   a. manufacturing and trade sales volume.
   b. number of employees on non-agricultural payrolls.
   c. industrial production.
   d. new orders for goods and materials.

4. Keynesians:
   a. generally favor activist government policics.
   b. generally favor laissez-faire policies.
   c. believe that frictional unemployment does not exist.
   d. believe that all unemployment is cyclical unemployment.

5. The level of output that would materialize at the target rate of unemployment and the target rate of capital utilization is called:
   a. nominal output.
   b. actual output.
   c. potential output.
   d. utilized output.

6. To move from GDP to GNP, one must:
   a. add net foreign factor income.
   b. subtract inflation.
   c. add depreciation.
   d. subtract depreciation.

7. If you, the owner, sell your old car for $600, how much does GDP increase?
   a. By $600.
   b. By the amount you bought it for, minus the $600.
   c. By zero.
   d. By the $600 you received and the $600 the person you sold it to paid, or $1,200.

8. There are two firms in an economy, Firm A and Firm B. Firm A produces 100 widgets and sells them for $2 apiece. Firm B produces 200 gadgets and sells them for $3 apiece. Firm A sells 30 of its widgets to Firm B and the remainder to consumers. Firm B sells 50 of its gadgets to Firm A and the remainder to consumers. What is GDP in this economy?
   a. $210.
   b. $590.
   c. $600.
   d. $800.

9. Gross investment differs from net investment by:
   a. net exports.
   b. net imports.
   c. depreciation.
   d. transfer payments.

10. If inflation is 10 percent and nominal GDP goes up 20 percent, real GDP goes up approximately:
    a. 1 percent.
    b. 10 percent.
    c. 20 percent.
    d. 30 percent.

11. According to Say's Law:
    a. aggregate supply will exceed aggregate demand.
    b. aggregate demand will exceed aggregate supply.
    c. there will be no relation between aggregate supply and demand.
    d. aggregate demand will equal aggregate supply.

12. Suppose output grew at 8% in China and 2% in the United States. Based on this information alone, we can know that:
    a. per capita income grew faster in China.
    b. per capita income grew faster in the U.S.
    c. per capita income could have grown faster in either country; we cannot tell in which.
    d. per capita output grew faster in China.

13. If there are increasing returns to scale, as:
    a. inputs rise, outputs fall.
    b. inputs rise, output rises by a smaller percentage.
    c. inputs rise, output rises by a larger percentage.
    d. one input rises, output rises by a larger percentage.

14. New growth theories are theories that emphasize:
    a. technology.
    b. human capital.
    c. physical capital.
    d. entrepreneurship.

15. QWERTY is a metaphor for:
    a. the invisible hand.
    b. technological lock-in.
    c. the law of diminishing marginal productivity.
    d. the pollution caused by positive spillovers.

16. Classical economists are generally associated with:
    a. laissez faire.
    b. QWERTY.
    c. an activist policy.
    d. their support of low unemployment.

17. In Keynesian economics equilibrium income:
    a. will be equal to potential income.
    b. will be below potential income.
    c. will be above potential income.
    d. may be different than potential income.

18. If the multiplier effect is 2 rather than 3, the:
    a. AD curve will be steeper.
    b. AD curve will be flatter.
    c. AD curve will be unaffected.
    d. SAS curve will be steeper.

19. The slope of the SAS curve is determined by:
    a. opportunity cost
    b. the law of diminishing marginal returns.
    c. institutional realities.
    d. the wealth effect, the international effect, and the interest rate effect.

20. Refer to the graph below. The graph demonstrates the expected short-run result if:

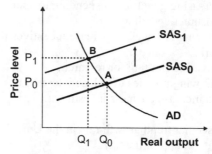

    a. productivity increases by less than wages.
    b. the government increases the money supply.
    c. the exchange rate value of a country's currency falls.
    d. there are suddenly expectations of a rising price level.

21. Assume the economy is initially at point B. The graph below correctly demonstrates an economy moving to point C if:

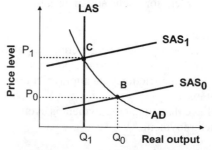

    a. productivity increases by less than the increase in wages.
    b. the government increases the money supply.
    c. a country's exchange rate appreciates (gains value).
    d. wages rise by less than the increase in productivity.

22. If the economy has an inflationary gap that it wants to eliminate, the government should use fiscal policy to shift:
    a. the *LAS* curve out.
    b. the *SAS* curve down (to the right).
    c. the *AD* curve out to the right.
    d. the *AD* curve in to the left.

23. If the target rate of unemployment falls, potential income will:
    a. first decrease, then increase.
    b. increase.
    c. decrease.
    d. first increase, then decrease.

24. In the multiplier model:
    a. production is assumed to be fixed.
    b. planned expenditures are assumed to equal actual production.
    c. the price level is assumed to be fixed.
    d. the price level is assumed to be flexible.

25. If the mpe is .8, what is the size of the multiplier in the multiplier model?
    a. .5.
    b. 5.
    c. 1.
    d. 10.

26. As the *mpe* rises, the multiplier:
    a. increases.
    b. decreases.
    c. remains the same.
    d. sometimes rises and sometimes falls.

27. If consumer confidence suddenly falls, you would expect:
    a. the aggregate production curve to shift down.
    b. the aggregate expenditures curve to rotate to the right and equilibrium income to fall.
    c. the aggregate expenditures curve to shift up and equilibrium income to rise.
    d. the aggregate expenditures curve to shift down and equilibrium income to fall.

28. In the multiplier model if autonomous expenditures increases by 10 and the *mpe* is .8, what happens to equilibrium income?
    a. It rises by 8.
    b. It falls by 8.
    c. It rises by 50.
    d. It falls by 50.

29. The economy has an *mpe* of .5, and a recessionary gap of 240. Using the Keynesian *multiplier model*, an economist would advise government to increase autonomous expenditures by:
    a. 120.
    b. 240.
    c. 480.
    d. 620.

30. If there is some price level flexibility, the:
    a. multiplier model is no longer relevant.
    b. results of the multiplier model will be reversed.
    c. results of the multiplier model will be modified but the central point will remain the same.
    d. multiplier model will turn into a Classical model.

ANSWERS

1.	a	(6:2)	16.	a	(9:1)
2.	b	(6:4)	17.	d	(9:4)
3.	d	(6:8)	18.	a	(9:8)
4.	a	(6:12)	19.	c	(9:13)
5.	c	(6:14)	20.	a	(9:16)
6.	a	(7:2)	21.	a	(9:20)
7.	c	(7:4)	22.	d	(9:23)
8.	b	(7:5)	23.	b	(9:27)
9.	c	(7:11)	24.	c	(10:1)
10.	b	(7:15)	25.	b	(10:4)
11.	d	(8:2)	26.	a	(10:5)
12.	c	(8:5)	27.	d	(10:8)
13.	c	(8:11)	28.	c	(10:12)
14.	a	(8:18)	29.	a	(10:16)
15.	b	(8:20)	30.	c	(10:20)

Key: The figures in parentheses refer to multiple choice question and chapter numbers. For example (1:2) is multiple choice question 2 from chapter 1.

THE FINANCIAL SECTOR AND THE DEMAND FOR MONEY

CHAPTER AT A GLANCE

This review is based upon the learning objectives that open the chapter.

1. The financial sector is central to almost all macroeconomic debates because behind every real transaction, there is a financial transaction that mirrors it. (257-259)

   When you buy an apple for 50 cents, the financial transaction is the 50 cents; the real transaction is the transfer of the apple.

2. The long-term interest rate equilibrates the supply for loanable funds (saving) and the demand for loanable funds (investment). See the graph below. (258-259)

   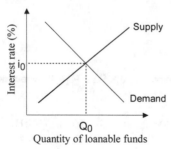

   If the interest rate does not perfectly translate saving (flows out of the spending stream) into investment (flows into the spending stream), then the economy will either expand or contract.

3. Money is a highly liquid, financial asset that is generally accepted in exchange for goods and services, is used as a reference in valuing other goods, and can be stored as wealth. (259-260)

   Money is any financial asset that serves the functions of money.

4. The three functions of money are: (260-262)

   - Medium of exchange;
     As long as people are confident that the purchasing power of the dollar will remain relatively stable over time (by the Fed controlling the money supply) then people will continue to swap real goods, services, and resources for money and vice versa.

   - Unit of account;
     Money acts as a measuring stick of the relative value (relative prices) of things. Therefore, the value of money itself must remain relatively stable over time.

   - Store of wealth.
     Money's usefulness as a store of wealth also depends upon how well it maintains its value. The key is for the Fed to keep the purchasing power of money (and therefore prices) relatively stable over time. Inflation can be a problem!

5a. M1 is the component of the money supply that consists of cash in the hands of the public plus checking accounts and traveler's checks. (262-263)

   M1 is the narrowest measure of the money supply. It is also the most liquid.

5b. M2 is the component of the money supply that consists of M1 plus savings deposits, small-denomination time deposits, and money market mutual funds. (263)

   M2 is the measure of the money supply most used by the Fed to measure the money supply in circulation. This is because M2 is most closely correlated with the price level and economic activity.

   Anything that changes M2 changes the money supply!

6. Banks "create" money because a bank's liabilities are defined as money. So when a bank incurs liabilities it creates money. (265-267)

Banks "create" money (increase the money supply) whenever they make loans. Whenever a person borrows from a bank he/she is swapping a promissory note to repay the loan (the loan is really an IOU; and an individual's IOU is not money because it doesn't meet the criteria of serving the functions of money) in exchange for cash or funds put in his/her checking account. Cash and checking account balances are money! Therefore, the money supply increases. Also Note: When a loan is repaid, the money supply (M2) decreases.

7a. The money multiplier is the measure of the amount of money ultimately created by the banking system per dollar deposited. When people hold no cash it equals 1/r, where r is the reserve ratio. (267-270)

A single bank is limited in the amount of money it may create. The limit is equal to its excess reserves—the maximum amount of funds that it can legally loan out. However, when considering an entire banking system, where any bank's loans, when spent, may end up being deposited back into that bank or another bank, then the entire banking system ends up being able to increase the money supply by a multiple of its initial excess reserves (the initial maximum amount of funds that can legally be loaned out) because of the money multiplier.

Simple money multiplier = 1/r.

(Initial change in money supply) ✕ (money multiplier) – change in the money supply

7b. When people hold cash the money multiplier is (1+c)/(r+c). (270)

Money multiplier = (1+c)/(r+c) , where c is the ratio of money people hold in currency to the money held as deposits.

The money multiplier is less than the simple money multiplier because some of the funds loaned out are held as cash and therefore do not return to the banks as deposits.

8. People demand money for three reaons: (1) transactions motive, (2) precautionary motive, and (3) speculative motive. (272-274)

The transactions motive is the need to carry money to buy things. The precautionary motive is the need to carry money in the event of an emergency. The speculative motive is the desire to hold money instead of another financial asset whose price is falling.

These motives mean people will hold money even if it means forgoing interest payments from holding bonds instead. But, as the interest rate rises, the cost of holding money in terms of lost interest rises, so you hold less money. As the interest rate rises, the quantity of money demanded falls. This explains why the demand for money curve is downward-sloping.

The demand and supply for money in the money market determines the short-term interest rate, as shown in the graph. Notice in the short-term, the supply of money is fixed, that is, the supply of money is independent of the interest rate.

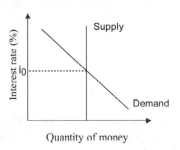

See also, Appendix A: "A Closer Look at Financial Assets and Liabilities" and Appendix B: "Creation of Money Using T-Accounts."

● SHORT-ANSWER QUESTIONS

1. At lunch you and your friends are arguing about the financial sector. One friend says that real fluctuations are measured by real economic activity in the goods market and therefore the financial sector has nothing to do with the business cycle. You know better and set him straight.

2. How does the interest rate regulate the flow of saving into the flow of expenditures during normal times?

3. You are having another stimulating lunchtime conversation, this time about money. Your friend says "I know what money is; it's cash, the dollar bills I carry around." What is your response?

4. You continue the conversation and begin to discuss why we have money. Your friend states that the function of money is to buy things like the lunch he has just bought. Another friend says that because she has money she is able to compare the cost of two types of slacks. Still another offers that she holds money to make sure she can buy lunch next week. What is the function of money that each has described? Are there any others?

5. What are two measures of money? What are the primary components of each?

6. Your friends are curious about money. At another lunchtime discussion, they ask each other two questions: Is all the money deposited in the bank in the bank's vaults? Can banks create money? Since they are stumped, you answer the questions for them.

7. Using the simple money multiplier, what will happen to the money supply if the reserve ratio is 0.2 and the Fed gives a bank $100 in reserves?

8. Using the equation for the money multiplier when people hold cash, what will happen to the money supply if the reserve ratio is 0.2, cash to deposit ratio is 0.3, and the Fed gives a bank $100 in reserves?

9. Because people don't earn interest on the money they hold in their pockets, why do they hold any money at all? (There are three reasons.)

10. Your study partner listens to your reasons why people hold money, but cautions you that even though people hold money despite the opportunity cost of holding it (lost interest), the interest rate does impact how much people hold. You agree and explain the relationship between the demand for money and the interest rate more fully.

11. At lunch you and your study partner are arguing about what market determines the interest rate. One friend says in the loanable funds market; another says in the money market. You know better than both and set them straight.

MATCHING THE TERMS
Match the terms to their definitions

___ 1. asset management	a. Cash that a bank keeps on hand that is sufficient to manage the normal cash inflows and outflows.
___ 2. excess reserves	b. The need to hold money for spending.
___ 3. Federal Reserve Bank (the Fed)	c. Component of the money supply that consists of M_1 plus savings deposits, small-denomination time deposits, and money market mutual fund shares, along with some esoteric relatively liquid assets.
___ 4. financial assets	
___ 5. interest rate	d. Component of the money supply that consists of cash in the hands of the public, checking account balances, and traveler's checks.
___ 6. liability management	e. Assets whose benefit to the owner depends on the issuer of the asset meeting certain obligations.
___ 7. M_1	
___ 8. M_2	f. Holding money for unexpected expenses and impulse buying.
___ 9. money	g. How a bank attracts deposits and what it pays for them.
___ 10. money multiplier	h. How a bank handles its loans and other assets.
___ 11. precautionary motive	i. Measure of the amount of money ultimately created by the banking system, per dollar deposited, when cash holdings of individuals and firms are treated the same as reserves of banks. The mathematical expression is $(1+c)/(r+c)$.
___ 12. reserve ratio	
___ 13. reserves	
___ 14. simple money multiplier	j. Measure of the amount of money ultimately created by the banking system per dollar deposited, when people hold no cash. The mathematical expression is $1/r$.
___ 15. speculative motive	k. Holding cash to avoid holding financial assests whose prices are falling.
___ 16. transactions motive	l. Ratio of cash or deposits a bank holds at the central bank to deposits a bank keeps as a reserve against withdrawals of cash.
	m. Reserves above what banks are required to hold.
	n. The U.S. central bank. Its liabilities serve as cash in the United States.
	o. A highly liquid financial asset that is generally accepted in exchange for other goods and is used as a reference in valuing other goods and as a store of wealth.
	p. Price paid for the use of a financial asset.

PROBLEMS AND APPLICATIONS

1. In each of the following explain the effect on interest rates. (Note: First choose which interest rate is affected – short or long term rates – and then demonstrate in the appropriate market.)

    a. Investment demand rises.

    b. People expect bond prices to fall in the near future.

    c. People begin to save a greater percent of their income.

2. For each, state whether it is a component of M_1, M_2, both, or neither:

    a. Money market mutual funds.

    b. Savings deposits.

    c. Traveler's checks.

    d. Stocks.

    e. Twenty-dollar bills.

3. Assuming individuals hold no cash, calculate the simple money multiplier for each of the following reserve requirements:

  a. 15%

  b. 30%

  c. 60%

  d. 80%

  e. 100%

4. Assuming individuals hold 10% of their deposits in the form of cash, recalculate the money multipliers from question 2.

  a. 15%

  b. 30%

  c. 60%

  d. 80%

  e. 100%

5. While Jon is walking to school one morning, a helicopter flying overhead drops $300. Not knowing how to return it, Jon keeps the money and deposits it in his bank. (No one in this economy holds cash.) If the bank keeps only 10 percent of its money in reserves and is fully loaned out, calculate the following:

  a. How much money can the bank now lend out?

  b. After this initial transaction, by how much has the money in the economy changed?

  c. What's the money multiplier?

  d. How much money will eventually be created by the banking system from Jon's $300?

6. For each of the following determine if it is an example of the precautionary, transaction, or speculative motive for holding money.

  a. You always carry a $10 in your pocket when you go on a date because your mother always said to be prepared for an emergency.

  b. You've lost your ATM card, so you have to carry more money in your pocket for daily purchases.

  c. An entrepreneur who has been "flipping" houses (buying houses, renovating them only to sell them within a short period of time), sees that housing prices are beginning to decline, so he sells his remaining holdings, keeping the proceeds in a money market account.

d It always seems like there is something in the grocery aisle that catches your eye. So you always keep a little extra in your pocket in case you want to buy something.

7. For each of the following, explain the effect on the interest rate in the money market. Demonstrate your answer graphically.

a. The supply of money falls.

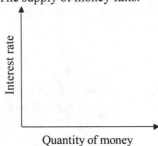

b. A national terrorist attack interrupts the banking system. After banks recover, people decide to hold more money in the event of a recurrence and the need for emergency funds.

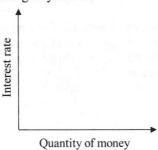

c. People expect bond prices to rise in the near future and move money out of their money market accounts into bond funds.

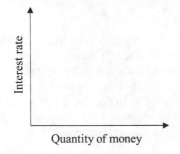

A1. Choose which of the following offerings you would prefer having. (Refer to the present value table on page 657)

a. $1,500 today or $2,000 in 5 years. The interest rate is 4%.

b. $1,500 today or $2,000 in 5 years. The interest rate is 9%.

c. $2,000 today or $10,000 in 10 years. The interest rate is 15%

d. $3,000 today or $10,000 in 15 years. The interest rate is 9%.

A2. A bond has a face value of $5,000 and a coupon rate of 10 percent. (A 10 percent coupon rate means that it pays annual interest of 10 percent of its face value.) It is issued in 2004 and matures in 2009. Using this information, calculate the following:

a. What is the annual payment for that bond?

b. If the bond is currently selling for $6,000, is its yield greater or less than 10 percent?

c. If the bond is currently selling for $4,000, is its yield greater or less than 10 percent?

Chapter 11   THE FINANCIAL SECTOR AND THE DEMAND FOR MONEY   147

d. What do your answers to (b) and (c) tell you about what the bond must sell for, relative to its face value, if the interest rate is 10%? Rises above 10%? Falls below 10%?

A3. For each, state whether a financial asset has been created. What gives each financial asset created its value?

a. Your friend promises to pay you $5 tomorrow and expects nothing in return.

b. You buy an apple at the grocery store.

c. The government sells a new bond with a face value of $5,000, a coupon rate of 8%, and a maturity date of 2016.

d. A firm issues stock.

e. An existing stock is sold to another person on the stock market.

B1. Assume that Textland Bank Balance Sheet looks like this:

Assets		Liabilities	
Cash	30,000	Demand Deposits	150,000
Loans	300,000	Net Worth	350,000
Phys. Assets	170,000		
Total Assets	500,000	Total Liabilities and Net Worth	500,000

a. If the bank is not holding any excess reserves, what is the reserve ratio?

b. Show the first three steps in money creation using a balance sheet if Jane Foundit finds $20,000 in cash and deposits it at Textland.

Step #1

Step #2

Step #3

c. After the first three steps, how much in excess reserves is the bank holding?

d. Show Textland's balance sheet at the end of the money creation process.

● A BRAIN TEASER

1. Whenever new loans are made the money supply expands. Whenever loans are repaid the money supply decreases. During any given period of time new loans are being made and old loans are being repaid. On balance, what happens to the money supply depends upon the magnitude of these conflicting forces. We also know that making loans is the principle source of profits to banks. Having said this, how can bankers' collective lending decisions (whether to give loans or not to give loans in order to maximize their profits, or to avoid losses) destabilize the business cycle, that is, cause recessions to get worse and upturns to become more pronounced?

● MULTIPLE CHOICE

Circle the one best answer for each of the following questions:

1. For every financial asset there is a:
    a. corresponding financial liability.
    b. corresponding financial liability if the financial asset is financed.
    c. real liability.
    d. corresponding real asset.

2. The long-term interest rate is determined in:
    a. the market for loanable funds.
    b. the stock market.
    c. the money market.
    d. the real goods market.

3. If the government runs a deficit and increases its borrowing,
    a. the demand for loanable funds will increase and the interest rate will fall.
    b. the demand for loanable funds will increase and the interest rate will rise.
    c. the supply of loanable funds will increase and the interest rates will rise.
    d. the supply of loanable funds will decrease and the interest rates will rise.

4. Which of the following is not a function of money?
    a. Medium of exchange.
    b. Unit of account.
    c. Store of wealth.
    d. Equity instrument.

5. Which of the following is not included in the M_1 definition of money?
    a. Checking accounts.
    b. Currency.
    c. Traveler's checks.
    d. Savings accounts.

6. Which of the following components is not included in the M_2 definition of money?
    a. M_1.
    b. Savings deposits.
    c. Small-denomination time deposits.
    d. Bonds.

7. In an advertisement for credit cards, the statement is made, "Think of a credit card as smart money." An economist's reaction to this would be that a credit card is:

a. not money.
b. dumb money.
c. simply money.
d. actually better than money.

8. Using a credit card creates a financial:
    a. liability for the holder and a financial asset for the issuer.
    b. asset for the holder and a financial liability for the issuer.
    c. liability for both the holder and issuer.
    d. asset for both the holder and issuer.

9. Modern bankers:
    a. focus on asset management.
    b. focus on liability management.
    c. focus on both asset management and liability management.
    d. are unconcerned with asset and liability management and instead are concerned with how to make money.

10. Assuming individuals hold no cash, the reserve requirement is 20 percent, and banks keep no excess reserves, an increase in an initial inflow of $100 into the banking system will cause an increase in the money supply of:
    a. $20.
    b. $50.
    c. $100.
    d. $500.

11. Assuming individuals hold no cash, the reserve requirement is 10 percent, and banks keep no excess reserves, an increase in an initial $300 into the banking system will cause an increase in total money of:
    a. $30.
    b. $300.
    c. $3,000.
    d. $30,000.

12. Assuming the ratio of money people hold in cash to the money they hold in deposits is .3, the reserve requirement is 20 percent, and that banks keep no excess reserves, an increase of an initial $100 into the banking system will cause an increase in total money of approximately:
    a. $50.
    b. $100.
    c. $260.
    d. $650.

13. If banks hold excess reserves whereas before they did not, the money multiplier:
    a. will become larger.
    b. will become smaller.
    c. will be unaffected.
    d. might increase or might decrease.

14. If you expect interest rates to rise, you will want to be holding:
    a. more money because bond prices will likely fall.
    b. less money because bond prices will likely rise.
    c. more money because bond prices will likely rise.
    d. less money because bond prices will likely fall.

15. If interest rates fall,
    a. bond prices rise.
    b. bond prices fall.
    c. bond prices do not change.
    d. bond prices could either rise or fall.

16. If housing prices are expected to fall by 10 percent, one could say that the interest rate on housing assets is:
    a. 10 percent.
    b. −10 percent.
    c. nothing —interest rates are on bonds, not on other assets.
    d. the answer depends on what the inflation rate in the economy is.

A1. If the interest rate falls, the value of a fixed rate bond:
    a. rises.
    b. falls.
    c. remains the same.
    d. cannot be determined as to whether it rises or falls.

A2. Two bonds, one a 30-year bond and the other a 1-year bond, have the same interest rate. If the interest rate in the economy falls, the value of the:
    a. long-term bond rises by more than the value of the short-term bond rises.
    b. short-term bond rises by more than the value of the long-term bond rises.
    c. long-term bond falls by more than the value of the short-term bond falls.
    d. short-term bond falls by more than the value of the long-term bond falls.

B1. The demand deposits in a bank would go on:
    a. the asset side of its balance sheet.
    b. the liabilities side of its balance sheet.
    c. the net worth part of its balance sheet.
    d. on both sides of its balance sheet.

B2. The cash that a bank holds would go on:
    a. the asset side of its balance sheet.
    b. the liabilities side of its balance sheet.
    c. the net worth part of its balance sheet.
    d. on both sides of its balance sheet.

● POTENTIAL ESSAY QUESTIONS

You may also see essay questions similar to the "Problems & Applications" and "A Brain Teaser" exercises.

1. Why is it important for the macroeconomy that the financial sector operate efficiently?

2. Why aren't credit cards money? What is the difference between money and credit?

ANSWERS

SHORT-ANSWER QUESTIONS

1. The financial sector is important to the business cycle because the financial sector channels the flow of savings out of the circular flow back into the circular flow either as consumer loans, business loans, or government loans. If the financial sector did not translate enough of the saving out of the spending stream back into the spending stream, output would decline and a recession might result. Likewise, if the financial sector increased flows into the spending stream (loans) that exceeded flows out of the spending stream (saving), an upturn or boom might result and inflation might rise. It is this role of the financial sector that Keynesians focused on to explain why production and expenditures might not be equal, resulting in fluctuations in output. (257-259)

2. Just as price equilibrates quantity supplied and demanded in the real sector, interest rates equilibrate quantity supplied and demanded for saving. The supply of saving comes out of the spending stream. The financial sector transforms those savings back into the spending stream in the form of loans that are then used to purchase consumer or capital goods. (258-259)

3. In one sense your friend is right; cash is money. But money is more than just cash. Money is a highly liquid financial asset that is accepted in exchange for other goods and is used as a reference in valuing other goods. It includes such things as checking account balances and traveler's checks. (260)

4. The first friend has described money as a medium of exchange. The second has described money as a unit of account. And the third has described money as a store of wealth. These are the three functions of money. There are no others. (260-262)

5. Two measures of money are M_1 and M_2. M_1 consists of currency, checking accounts, and traveler's checks. M_2 consists of M_1 plus savings deposits, small-denomination time deposits, and money market mutual funds. (262-263)

6. No, banks do not hold all their deposits in their vaults. They keep a small percentage of it for normal withdrawal needs and lend the remainder out. Banks' maintenance of checking accounts is the essence of how banks create money. You count your deposits as money since you can write checks against them and the money that is lent out from bank deposits is counted as money. Aha! The bank has created money. (265-267)

7. The equation for the simple money multiplier is $(1/r)$ where r is the reserve ratio. Plugging the values into the equation, we see that the money multiplier is 5, so the money supply increases by $500. (267-270)

8. The equation for the money multiplier when people hold cash is $(1+c)/(r+c)$ where r is the reserve ratio and c is the ratio of cash to deposits. Plugging the values into the equation, we see that the money multiplier is 2.6, so the money supply increases by $260. (270)

9. People hold money to buy goods (transactions motive); in the event of an emergency (precautionary motive); and to avoid holding other financial assets whose asset prices are falling (speculative motive). (272-273)

10. Since people lose interest when they hold money, holding money has a cost—lost interest. Just like other goods, when the price of holding money (lost interest) rises, people will hold less of it. In other words, the demand for money and the interest rate are inversely related. (274)

11. Both are right. Even though there are many interest rates in the economy, economists divide them into two types: long-term interest rates and short-term interest rates. Long-term interest rates are determined in markets for long-term financial assets such as mortgages. This is the loanable funds market. Short-term interest rates are determined in markets for short-term financial assets such as currency and savings deposits. This is the money market. (258-259, 273-274)

ANSWERS

MATCHING

1-h; 2-m; 3-n; 4-e; 5-p; 6-g; 7-d; 8-c; 9-o; 10-i; 11-f; 12-l; 13-a; 14-j; 15k; 16-b.

ANSWERS

PROBLEMS AND APPLICATIONS

1. a. This would increase the demand for loanable funds and therefore, the long-term interest rate rises. (258-259)

    b. This would increase the demand for money (speculative motive) in the money market and therefore, the short-term interest rate rises. (273-274)

    c. This would increase the supply of loanable funds and therefore, the long-term interest rate falls. (258-259)

2. a. M_2. (262-263)
    b. M_2. (262-263)
    c. Both. (262-263)
    d. Neither. (262-263)
    e. Both. (262-263)

3. a. 6.67. multiplier = (1/.15). (268)
    b. 3.33. multiplier = (1/.30). (268)
    c. 1.67. multiplier = (1/.6). (268)
    d. 1.25. multiplier – (1/.8). (268)
    e. 1. multiplier = (1/1). (268)

4. a. 4.4 = 1.10/(.15+.1). (270)
    b. 2.75 = 1.10/(.3+.1). (270)
    c. 1.57 = 1.10/(.6+.1). (270)
    d. 1.22 = 1.10/(.8+.1). (270)
    e. 1 = 1.1/(1+.1). (270)

5. a. $270. (268)
    b. $270: the increase in loans that are then deposited (.9 × 300) represents the change in money. (268)
    c. 10: 1/r = 1/.1. (268)
    d. $3,000: money multiplier × initial deposit = 10×300. (267-270)

6. a. Precautionary motive. (272)
    b. Transactions motive. (272)
    c. Speculative motive. (272)
    d. Precautionary motive. (272)

7. a. A decline in the money supply shifts the supply of money to the left as shown in the graph. Short-term interest rates rise. (273-274)

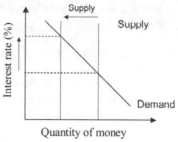

    b. The demand for money shifts to the right as shown in the graph as people hold more cash in the event of an emergency. Short-term rates rise. (273-274)

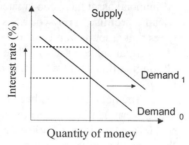

    c. The demand for money shifts to the left as people buy bonds in expectation of their prices rising. Short-term interest rates fall. (273-274)

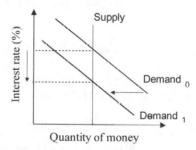

A1. Using the table to calculate the present value of $1 to be received in the future, we find that the better value is

    a. $2,000 in 5 years when the interest rate is 4% is valued today at $1,640. (281)

    b. $1,500 today. $2,000 in 5 years when the interest rate is 9% is worth only $1,300 today. (281)

c. $10,000 in 10 years. $10,000 in 10 years is valued at $2,500 when the interest rate is 15%. (281)

d. $3,000 today. $10,000 in 15 years when interest rate is 9% is worth only $2,700 today. (281)

A2. a. The annual payment for that bond is $500. (280-281)

b. If the bond is currently selling for $6000, its yield is less than 10 percent. (280-281)

c. If the bond is currently selling for $4,000, its yield is greater than 10 percent. (280-281)

d. My answer to (b) and (c) tell me that the bond must sell for its face value if the interest rate is 10%, less than face value if it rises above 10%, and more than face value if it falls below 10%. (280-281)

A3. a. A financial asset has been created. Your friend's promise to pay you $5 is what gives that asset its value. (280)

b. No, a financial asset has not been created, although a financial transaction did occur. (280)

c. Yes, a financial asset has been created. The government's promise to pay you $5,000 at maturity and $400 each year until then are what give that asset its value. (280)

d. Yes, a financial asset has been created. A claim to future profits is what gives that asset its value. (280)

e. No, a financial asset has not been created. The financial asset sold already existed. (280)

B1. a. .2: cash/deposits = 30,000/150,000. (286-288)

b. Step 1: Increase of $20,000 in demand deposits and cash: (286-288)

Assets		Liabilities	
Cash	30,000	Demand Deposits	150,000
Cash from Jane	20,000	Jane's deposit	20,000
Total cash	50,000	Total deposits	170,000
Loans	300,000	Net Worth	350,000
Phys. Assets	170,000		
Total Assets	520,000	Total Liabilities and net worth	520,000

Step 2: Assuming the reserve ratio is .2 as calculated in (a), the bank can now lend out 80% of the $20,000 received in cash. It lends $16,000 to another person, Sherry: (286-288)

Assets		Liabilities	
Cash	50,000	Demand Deposits	170,000
Cash to Sherry	−16,000		
Total cash	34,000		
Begin. Loans	300,000	Net Worth	350,000
Loan to Sherry	16,000		
Total loans	316,000		
Phys. Assets	170,000		
Total Assets	520,000	Total Liabilities and net worth	520,000

Step 3: Sherry uses the loan to purchase a car from John. John deposits the cash in the bank (286-288):

Assets		Liabilities	
Cash	34,000	Demand Deposits	170,000
Cash from John	16,000	Deposit from John	16,000
Total cash	50,000	Total Deposits	186,000
Begin. Loans	316,000	Net Worth	350,000
Phys. Assets	170,000		
Total Assets	536,000	Total Liabilities and net worth	536,000

c. The bank is holding $12,800 in excess reserves. Required reserves for $186,000 in deposits is .2 × 186,000 = $37,200. The bank has $50,000 in reserves, $12,800 higher than required. (286-288)

d. The ending balance sheet will look like this (286-288):

Assets		Liabilities	
Cash	50,000	Demand Deposits	250,000
Loans	380,000	Net Worth	350,000
Phys. Assets	170,000		
Total Assets	600,000	Total Liabilities and net worth	600,000

━━━ ANSWERS ━━━

A BRAIN TEASER

1. An uncontrolled private banking system (where government is not involved in trying to control the money supply) is destabilizing to the business cycle. Why? Because during recessions, bankers are reluctant to grant loans due to the greater probability of default on loans (bankers are simply wishing to avoid losses). Fewer loans made during a recession coupled with the concurrent repayment of old loans (most likely given during the previous upturn in the economy) means that, on balance, the money supply decreases. Less money means less spending. Less spending means the recession gets worse–unemployment rises further and the economy grows even more slowly. Conversely, during an economic expansion, banks make more loans than old loans are being repaid (bankers are happy to make loans when there is a low probability of default–after all, workers are not likely to lose their jobs and businesses' markets and profits are expanding). Therefore, the money supply expands and total spending increases–people spend their loans. The economy expands even more. (265-267)

━━━ ANSWERS ━━━

MULTIPLE CHOICE

1. a The very fact that it is a financial asset means that it has a financial liability, so the qualifier in b is unnecessary. See pages 257-258.

2. a The short-term rate is determined in the money market and the long-term rate is determined in the loanable funds market. See pages 258-259 and 273-274.

3. b When the government runs a deficit, it must borrow, which means that the demand for loanable funds will increase, which will cause the interest rate to rise. See pages 258-259.

4. d Money is not a type of stock so it is not an equity instrument. See pages 260-262.

5. d M_2 includes savings accounts. M_1 does not. See pages 262-263 and Figure 11-3 on page 263.

6. d Bonds are not part of M_2. See page 263 and Figure 11-3.

7. a A credit card is not money and thus *a* would be the best answer. A credit card replaces money, making the same amount of money able to handle many more transactions. See pages 263-265.

8. a One is borrowing money when one uses a credit card, thereby incurring a financial liability. See pages 263-265.

9. c As discussed on page 265, banks are concerned with both asset management and liability management. The second part of answer d is obviously true, but it's through management of assets and liabilities that they make money, so the first part is wrong.

10. d The simple money multiplier is $1/r=1/.2=5$, which gives an increase in total money of $500. See pages 267-270.

11. c The simple money multiplier is $1/r=1/.1=10$ which gives an increase of total money of $3,000. See pages 267-270.

12. c The money multiplier is $(1+c)/(r+c)=1/.5=2.6$, which gives an increase in total money of $260. See page 270.

13. b Holding excess reserves would be the equivalent to increasing the reserve requirement, which would decrease the money multiplier. See pages 267-270.

14. a If interest rates rise, bond prices fall, which means that you prefer to be holding money rather than bonds. See pages 272-274.

15. a Bond prices move inversely with interest rates. See pages 272-274.

16. b The expected percentage change in price of an asset is its implicit interest rate. See pages 272-273.

A1. a   The present value formula tells us that the value on any fixed interest rate bond varies inversely with the interest rate in the economy. See pages 280-281.

A2. a   Since bond values vary inversely with interest rate changes, the answer must be a or b. Judging between a and b will be hard for you at this point unless you have studied present value in another course. However, based on the discussion in the text on pages 280-281, you can deduce that since a long-term bond is not paid back for a long time, it will be much more strongly affected by interest rate changes.

B1. b   Demand deposits at banks are liabilities for those banks and hence go on the liability side. See pages 286-288.

B2. a   The cash that banks hold is an asset for them; hence it goes on the asset side. See pages 286-288.

ANSWERS

POTENTIAL ESSAY QUESTIONS

The following are annotated answers. They indicate the general idea behind the answer.

1.   Recall that for every real transaction there is a financial transaction that mirrors it. The financial sector's role is to ensure the smooth flow of savings out of the spending stream back into the economy. Whenever the financial sector is not operating efficiently then it is quite possible that the flow of savings out of the spending stream could be greater than the amount of money going through the financial sector and back into the economy. If this happens, we will experience a recession. The opposite would create inflationary (demand-pull inflation) problems.

2.   Money is a financial asset of individuals and a financial liability of banks. Credit card balances cannot be money since they are assets of a bank and a liability of the nonbanking public. In a sense, credit card balances are the opposite of money. Credit is savings made available to be borrowed. Credit is not an asset for the holder of the card. However, ready availability of credit through the use of credit cards does reduce the amount of money people need or wish to hold.

MONETARY POLICY

CHAPTER AT A GLANCE

This review is based upon the learning objectives that open the chapter.

1   Monetary policy is a policy that influences the economy through changes in the money supply and available credit. In the AS/AD model, monetary policy works as follows: (290-292)

Contractionary monetary policy shifts the AD curve to the left:
$$M\downarrow \rightarrow i\uparrow \rightarrow I\downarrow \rightarrow Y\downarrow$$

Used during an upturn in the economy to close an inflationary gap.

Expansionary monetary policy shifts the AD curve to the right:
$$M\uparrow \rightarrow i\downarrow \rightarrow I\uparrow \rightarrow Y\uparrow$$

Used during a downturn in the economy to close a recessionary gap.

To increase the money supply (M2), the Fed must first increase banks' excess reserves and therefore bank loans.

2a.   The Fed is a semiautonomous organization composed of 12 regional banks. It is run by the Board of Governors. (292-295)

The Fed (Federal Reserve Bank) is in charge of monetary policy (changing the money supply, credit availability, and interest rates).

The Federal Open Market Committee (FOMC) decides monetary policy.

2b.   Congress gave the Fed six explicit duties. The most important is conducting monetary policy. (296)

Six functions of the Fed:
1. *Conducting monetary policy (influencing the supply of money and credit in the economy).*
2. *Supervising and regulating financial institutions.*
3. *Serving as a lender of last resort to financial institutions.*
4. *Providing banking services to the U.S. government.*
5. *Issuing coin and currency.*
6. *Providing financial services (such as check clearing) to commercial banks, savings and loan associations, savings banks, and credit unions.*

3.   The Fed conducts monetary policy by changing the amount of reserves in the banking system. (296-300)

1. The primary way the Fed changes reserves is through open market operations.
   Open market operations are the Fed's buying and selling of U.S. government securities. This is the most frequently used and most important tool to change the money supply.

2. Changing the reserve requirement and the discount rate also affect reserves.
   The Fed doesn't use these tools often. The reserve requirement affects (1) banks' excess reserves and (2) the money multiplier.
   The discount rate is the interest rate the Fed charges banks for loans.

   If the economy is in a recession, the Fed could increase the money supply (pursue an expansionary monetary policy) by doing any one or more of the following:
   - *Decrease the reserve requirement.*
   - *Decrease the discount rate.*
   - *Buy government securities.*

4. The Federal funds rate is the interest rate banks charge one another for overnight bank reserve loans. The Fed determines whether monetary policy is loose or tight depending upon what's happening to the Fed funds rate. The Fed funds rate is an important intermediate target. (300-301)

The Fed targets a range for the Fed funds rate. If the Fed funds rate goes above (below) that target range, the Fed buys (sells) bonds. These are "defensive" actions by the Fed.

5. The Taylor rule states: (302-304)
Set the Fed funds rate at 2 percent plus current inflation if the economy is at desired output and desired inflation and

- if inflation is higher (lower) than desired, increase (reduce) the Fed funds rate by .5 times the difference between desired and actual inflation.

- if output is higher (lower) than desired, increase (decrease) the Fed funds rate by .5 times the percentage deviation from potential.

Formally, the Taylor rule is:

Fed funds rate = 2 percent + current inflation
+ 0.5 × (actual inflation - desired inflation)
+ 0.5 × (percent deviation of aggregate output from potential)

This rule has described Fed policy since the late 1990s.

Because the Fed targets interest rates, it creates a flat effective supply curve for money at the targeted interest rate.

6. The yield curve is a graph of the interest rate of bonds of various maturities, ordered from the shortest to longest term to maturity. (304-305)

Normally, the yield curve is upward sloping. That is, bonds that mature in a shorter time (for example, 1 year) have lower interest rates than bonds that mature in a longer time (for example 30 years).

The Fed most directly affects short-term interest rates, but monetary policy affects the economy through its effect on the long-term interest rate. Sometimes when the Fed raises the short-term rate and the long-term rate doesn't change, or even fall, the yield curve becomes inverted (downward sloping). When this happens, the Fed is less effective in impacting the economy than it would like.

See also, Appendix A: "The Effect of Monetary Policy Using T-Accounts."

SHORT-ANSWER QUESTIONS

1. You have been asked to speak to the first-year Congresspeople. Your talk is about the Fed. They want to know what monetary policy is. You tell them.

2. Another Congressperson asks how monetary policy can keep the economy from overheating. You reply from the perspective of the AS/AD model.

3. Suppose the economy is below potential output. Now how can monetary policy boost output? You reply again from the perspective of the AS/AD model.

4. To clarify your answer to question 1 you tell them when the Fed was created and what its specific duties are.

5. Another Congressperson asks what monetary policy actions the Fed can take. You answer, mentioning three specific actions.

6. You are asked to elaborate on your answer to question 3. Now that you have told them how the Fed can change the money supply, how does each of the ways to affect reserves work?

7. One Congressperson realizes that the Fed does not have complete control over the money supply. She states that people could demand more cash, which will reduce the money supply. How does the Fed know whether its buying and selling of bonds is having the desired effect? You answer by explaining the Fed's intermediate target.

8. Another Congressperson asks whether there are any rules that they could use to predict what the Fed will do to the Fed's intermediate target. You explain the rule that has described Fed policy since the late 1990s.

9. You take one final question at the conference and it is a difficult one: "It doesn't seem that the Fed is doing a good job. I read in the paper that the Fed has wanted to raise long-term interest rates, but is having difficulty doing so." How do you respond to this concern?

MATCHING THE TERMS
Match the terms to their definitions

___ 1. central bank

___ 2. contractionary monetary policy

___ 3. discount rate

___ 4. expansionary monetary policy

___ 5. Federal Open Market Committee (FOMC)

___ 6. Federal funds rate

___ 7. inverted yield curve

___ 8. monetary base

___ 9. monetary regime

___ 10. nominal interest rate

___ 11. open market operations

___ 12. real interest rate

___ 13. reserve requirement

___ 14. Taylor rule

___ 15. yield curve

a. Interest rate you actually see and pay.

b. Interest rate adjusted for expected inflation.

c. Rate of interest the Fed charges on loans it makes to banks.

d. The Fed's day-to-day buying and selling of government securities.

e. The percentage the Federal Reserve System sets as the minimum amount of reserves a bank must have.

f. A banker's bank; it conducts monetary policy and supervises the financial system.

g. Currency in circulation, vault cash plus reserves that banks have at the Fed.

h. Monetary policy aimed at raising the money supply and raising the level of aggregate demand.

i. Monetary policy aimed at reducing the money supply and reducing the level of aggregate demand.

j. The Fed's chief policy making body.

k. The interest rate banks charge one another for Fed funds.

l. Set the Fed funds rate at 2 plus current inflation plus ½ the difference between actual and target inflation and ½ the deviation of actual output from potential.

m. A predetermined statement of the monetary policy that will be followed in various situations.

n. A curve that shows the relationship between interest rates and bonds' time to maturity.

o. A yield curve in which the short-term rate is higher than the long-term rate.

● PROBLEMS AND APPLICATIONS

1. The Fed wants to change the reserve requirement in order to change the money supply (which is currently $3,000). For each situation below, calculate the current reserve requirement and the amount by which the Fed must change the reserve requirement to achieve the desired change in the money supply. Assume no cash holdings.

   a. Money multiplier is 3 and the Fed wants to increase the money supply by $300.

   b. Money multiplier is 2.5 and the Fed wants to increase the money supply by $300.

   c. Money multiplier is 4 and the Fed wants to decrease the money supply by $500.

   d. Money multiplier is 4 and the Fed wants to increase the money supply by $1,000.

2. How do your answers change for 1 (a) - (d) if instead of changing the reserve requirement, the Fed wants to use an open market operation to change the money supply? Assume the reserve requirement remains unchanged. What should the Fed do to achieve the desired change? (The multiplier and desired change in money supply for each are listed.)

   a. Money multiplier is 3 and the Fed wants to increase the money supply by $300.

   b. Money multiplier is 2.5 and the Fed wants to increase the money supply by $300.

   c. Money multiplier is 4 and the Fed wants to decrease the money supply by $500.

   d. Money multiplier is 4 and the Fed wants to increase the money supply by $1000.

3. Instead of changing the reserve requirement or using open market operations, the Fed wants to change the discount rate to achieve the desired change in the money supply. Assume that for each 1 percentage-point fall in the discount rate, banks borrow an additional $20. How do your answers to questions 1 (a) - (d) change? (The multiplier and desired change in money supply for each are listed below.)

   a. Money multiplier is 3 and the Fed wants to increase money supply by $300.

   b. Money multiplier is 2.5 and the Fed wants to increase the money supply by $300.

   c. Money multiplier is 4 and the Fed wants to decrease the money supply by $500.

   d. Money multiplier is 4 and the Fed wants to increase the money supply by $1,000.

4. Using the Taylor rule, what do you predict will be the Fed's target for the Fed funds rate in the following situations?

   a. Inflation is at the Fed's target of 2 percent, but output is 1 percent below potential.

   b. Output is at potential, but inflation is 5 percent, 2 percentage points above the Fed's target.

   c. Inflation is 4 percent, 1 percentage point above the Fed's target and output is 1 percent above potential.

   d. Inflation is 4 percent, 2 percentage points above the Fed's target and output is 2 percent below potential.

5. Fill in the blanks in the following table:

	Inflation rate	Nominal Interest rate	Real Interest rate
a.	5%	10%	____
b.	____	15%	7%
c.	−3%	____	9%
d.	4%	____	10%

6. Suppose the Fed decides to pursue an expansionary monetary policy. The money supply is currently $1 billion. Assume people hold no cash, the reserve requirement is 10 percent, and there are no excess reserves.

   a. By how much must the Fed change the reserve requirement to increase the money supply by $100 million?

   b. What would the Fed do to increase the money supply by $100,000 through open market operations?

7. The money supply is currently $1 billion. Assume people hold 25 percent of their money in the form of cash balances, the reserve requirement is 25 percent, and there are no excess reserves.

   a. By how much must the Fed change the reserve requirement to increase the money supply by $200 million?

   b. What would the Fed do to increase the money supply by $200 million through open market operations?

8. Given the following yields on Treasury bills and bonds, draw a yield curve.

   a. 3-month 1 year   5 years 10 years 30 years
         2%   3%   5%   5.75%   6.25%

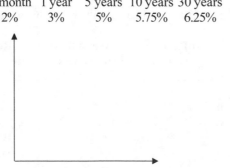

b. 3-month 1 year   5 years 10 years 30 years
      5%   4.5%   3%   2%   1%

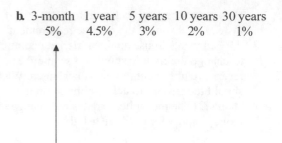

c. Which is a standard and which is an inverted yield curve?

A1. Suppose the money multiplier is 2.5 and there are no cash holdings. Textland Bank is the only bank in the country. The Fed wants to decrease the money supply by $10,000. The initial balance sheet is shown below.

Initial Balance Sheet

Assets		Liabilities	
Cash	20,000	Demand Deposits	50,000
Loans	120,000	Net Worth	100,000
Phys. Assets	10,000		
Total Assets	150,000	Total Liabilities and net worth	150,000

   a. What open market operations must the Fed execute to reduce the money supply by $10,000?

   b. Using T-accounts, show the first two steps of the effects of the Fed open market operation reducing the money supply by $10,000.

   Step #1

   Assets   **Liabilities**

Step #2

Assets	Liabilities

c. Show the final balance sheet for Textland bank.

Final Position

Assets	Liabilities

A2. Using T-accounts, show the effect of a decrease in the reserve ratio from .2 to .1 given the following initial position of Textland. Again, Textland is the only bank, no one holds cash, and there are no excess reserves. Show the first two steps and then the final position.

Initial Position

Assets		Liabilities	
Cash	40,000	Demand Deposits	200,000
Loans	230,000	Net Worth	100,000
Phys. Assets	30,000		
Total Assets	300,000	Total Liabilities and net worth	300,000

Step #1

Assets	Liabilities

Step #2

Assets	Liabilities

Final Position

Assets	Liabilities

A BRAIN TEASER

1. Assume the economy is currently experiencing a recessionary gap of $1,000. Also assume that the expenditures multiplier is 4, the reserve ratio is 0.1, and the ratio of people's cash-to-deposits is 0.4. Investment changes by $100 for every 1% change in the interest rate. The interest rate changes by 1% for every $50 change in the money supply. Generally, what should the Fed do with its three monetary policy tools? By how much would the Fed have to change banks' excess reserves if it wished to close the recessionary gap? (Assume all excess reserves are loaned out.)

MULTIPLE CHOICE

Circle the one best answer for each of the following questions:

1. In the short run if the Fed undertakes expansionary monetary policy, the effect will be to shift the:
    a. AD curve out to the right.
    b. AD curve in to the left.
    c. SAS curve up.
    d. SAS curve down.

2. In the short run if the Fed undertakes contractionary monetary policy, the effect will be to shift the:
a. AD curve out to the right.
b. AD curve in to the left.
c. SAS curve up.
d. SAS curve down.

3. Which of the following is the path through which contractionary monetary policy works?
a. Money down implies interest rate up implies investment down implies income down.
b. Money down implies interest rate down implies investment down implies income down.
c. Money down implies interest rate up implies investment up implies income down.
d. Money down implies interest rate down implies investment up implies income down.

4. The central bank of the United States is:
a. the Treasury.
b. the Fed.
c. the Bank of the United States.
d. Old Lady of Threadneedle Street.

5. Monetary policy is:
a. a variation of fiscal policy.
b. undertaken by the Treasury.
c. undertaken by the Fed.
d. the regulation of monetary institutions.

6. There are seven Governors of the Federal Reserve, who are appointed for terms of:
a. 5 years.
b. 10 years.
c. 14 years.
d. 17 years.

7. Explicit functions of the Fed include all the following *except:*
a. conducting monetary policy.
b. conducting fiscal policy.
c. providing banking services to the U.S. government.
d. serving as a lender of last resort to financial institutions.

8. FOMC stands for:
a. Federal Open Money Committee.
b. Federal Open Market Committee.
c. Fixed Open Market Commitments.
d. Federation of Open Monies Committee.

9. The Fed can conduct monetary policy in all the following ways *except:*
a. changing the reserve requirement.
b. changing the discount rate.
c. executing open market operations.
d. running deficits.

10. If expansionary monetary policy increases real income by 4 percent and nominal income by 6 percent, the price level will rise by:
a. 2 percent.
b. 4 percent.
c. 6 percent.
d. 10 percent.

11. Assuming $c = .2$ and $r = .1$, the money multiplier would be:
a. 1.
b. 2.
c. 3.
d. 4.

12. The discount rate refers to the:
a. lower price large institutions pay for government bonds.
b. rate of interest the Fed charges for loans to banks.
c. rate of interest the Fed charges for loans to individuals.
d. rate of interest the Fed charges for loans to government.

13. The primary way the Fed conducts monetary policy is:
a. open market operations.
b. changing the discount rate.
c. changing the reserve requirement.
d. imposing credit controls.

14. If the Fed wants to increase the money supply, it should:
a. buy bonds.
b. sell bonds.
c. pass a law that interest rates rise.
d. pass a law that interest rates fall.

15. When the Fed sells bonds, the money supply:
a. expands.
b. contracts.
c. Selling bonds does not have any effect on the money supply.
d. sometimes rises and sometimes falls.

16. An open market purchase:
    a. raises bond prices and reduces interest rates.
    b. raises both bond prices and interest rates.
    c. reduces bond prices and raises interest rates.
    d. reduces both bond prices and interest rates.

17. The Federal funds rate is the interest rate:
    a. the government charges banks for Fed funds.
    b. the Fed charges banks for Fed funds.
    c. the banks charge individual investors for Fed funds.
    d. the banks charge each other for Fed funds.

18. Assuming the Fed is following the Taylor Rule, if inflation is 3 percent, target inflation is 2 percent, and output is 1 percent above potential, what would you predict would be the Fed funds rate target?
    a. 4 percent.
    b. 5 percent.
    c. 5.5 percent.
    d. 6 percent.

19. By choosing a monetary rule that targets the short-term interest rate the Fed creates:
    a. an upward sloping yield curve.
    b. a downward sloping yield curve.
    c. an effective supply curve of money that is flat.
    d. an effective supply curve of money that is vertical.

20. In general, the yield curve:
    a. is flat.
    b. is upward sloping.
    c. is downward sloping.
    d. is shaped like a mountain.

21. If short-term and long-term interest rates are currently equal and the Fed contracts the money supply, the yield curve will most likely:
    a. become downward sloping.
    b. become upward sloping.
    c. become vertical.
    d. be unaffected.

22. If inflation becomes expected, and all other things remain as they were, the yield curve would most likely:
    a. become steeper.
    b. become flatter
    c. become flat.
    d. become vertical.

POTENTIAL ESSAY QUESTIONS

You may also see essay questions similar to the "Problems & Applications" and "A Brain Teaser" exercises.

1. According to the AS/AD model, what is considered to be appropriate monetary policy during different phases of the business cycle? What is the cause-effect chain relationship through which a change in the money supply will effect the level of economic activity? How would this cause-effect relationship be reflected graphically?

2. Why do economists keep an eye on the Fed funds rate in determining the state of monetary policy?

3. Explain why the yield curve is important for the implementation of monetary policy.

ANSWERS

SHORT-ANSWER QUESTIONS

1. Monetary policy is a policy that influences the economy through changes in the money supply and available credit. The Fed conducts U.S. monetary policy. (290, 292-295)

2. The Fed should decrease the money supply by increasing the reserve requirement, increasing the discount rate, and/or selling U.S. government bonds. This contractionary monetary policy in the AS/AD model increases interest rates, and lowers investment. This shifts the AD curve to the left and reduces income. (290-292)

3. The Fed should increase the money supply by decreasing the reserve requirement, decreasing the discount rate, and/or buying U.S. government bonds. This expansionary monetary policy in the AS/AD model decreases interest rates, and raises investment. This shifts the AD curve to the right and increases income. (290-290)

4. The Fed was created in 1913. Its six explicit duties are (1) conducting monetary policy, (2) regulating financial institutions, (3) serving as a lender of last resort, (4) providing banking services to the U.S. government, (5) issuing coin and currency, and (6) providing financial services to financial institutions. (296)

5. The three tools of monetary policy at the disposal of the Fed are (1) changing the reserve requirement, (2) changing the discount rate, and (3) executing open market operations (buying and selling bonds). (296-300)

6. Changing the reserve requirement changes the amount of reserves the banks must hold and thus changes the amount of loans they can make. This changes the money supply. Changing the discount rate changes the willingness of banks to borrow from the Fed to meet reserve requirements, thus changing the amount of loans they are willing to make. This changes the money supply. Open market operations change the reserves banks hold by directly increasing or decreasing cash held by banks and simultaneously decreasing or increasing their holdings of government bonds. This changes the amount of loans banks can make and changes the money supply. (296-300)

7. Economists and policymakers keep a close eye on the Fed funds rate, the rate banks charge one another for loans of reserves, as an intermediate target to determine the effect of an open market operation—whether it indeed was expansionary or contractionary. An expansionary action will lower the Fed funds rate and contractionary action will raise the Fed funds rate. In effect, the Fed chooses a range for the Fed funds rate and buys and sells bonds to keep the Fed funds rate within that range. If the Fed funds rate is below (above) the target, the Fed sells (buys) bonds. (300-301)

8. The Taylor rule has described recent Fed policy relatively well. It states: Set the Fed funds rate at 2% plus the rate of inflation plus one-half the difference between actual and desired inflation and one-half the deviation of actual output from desired output. (302)

9. You tell the Congressperson that conducting monetary policy is difficult. The standard discussion of monetary policy is based on the assumption that when the Fed pushes up (down) the short-term interest rate, the long-term interest rate moves up (down) as well. This is based on the relationship between short and long-term interest rates shown in the yield curve. The yield curve is generally upward sloping. But sometimes the shape of the yield curve changes. That is, when the Fed attempts to contract the money supply, the yield curve can become inverted, or downward sloping. Similarly, if the Fed tries to expand the money supply, the yield curve will generally become steeper. (304-305)

ANSWERS

MATCHING

1-f; 2-i; 3-c; 4-h; 5-j; 6-k; 7-o; 8-g; 9-m; 10-a; 11-d; 12-b; 13-e; 14-l; 15-n.

ANSWERS

PROBLEMS AND APPLICATIONS

1. **a.** To find the reserve requirement solve $1/r = 3$ for r. $r = 1/3$. These calculations are based on the formula $M = (1/r) \times MB$, where M is the money supply, r is the reserve ratio, and MB is the monetary base (here it equals reserves). We first find out the cash (monetary base) that supports $3,000 money supply with a money multiplier of 3. It is $1,000. We want the money supply to be $3,300. So the multiplier we want is $3,300/1,000 = 3.3. Again solving $1/r = 3.3$ we find r must be 0.3. (298-299)

   b. To find the reserve requirement solve $1/r = 2.5$ for r. $r = .4$. Cash must be $1,200 to support money supply of $3,000. The Fed must reduce the reserve requirement to .3636 to increase the money supply by $300. Use the method described in (a) to find the answer. (298-299)

   c. To find the reserve requirement solve $1/r = 4$ for r. $r = .25$. Cash must be $750 to support money supply of $3,000. The Fed must increase the reserve requirement to .3 to decrease the money supply by $500. Use the method described in (a) to find the answer. (298-299)

   d. To find the reserve requirement solve $1/r = 4$ for r. $r = .25$. Cash must be $750 to support money supply of $3,000. The Fed must reduce the reserve requirement to .1875 to increase the money supply by $1,000. Use the method described in (a) to find the answer. (298-299)

2. These calculations are based on the formula $M = (1/r) \times MB$, where M is the money supply, r is the reserve ratio, and MB is the monetary base (here it equals reserves).

   a. The Fed should buy bonds to increase reserves in the system by $100. We find this by dividing the desired increase in the money supply by the money multiplier. (296-298)

   b. The Fed should buy bonds to increase reserves in the system by $120. We find this by dividing the desired increase in the money supply by the money multiplier. (296-298)

   c. The Fed should sell bonds to decrease reserves in the system by $125. We find this by dividing the desired decrease in the money supply by the money multiplier. (296-298)

   d. The Fed should buy bonds to increase reserves in the system by $250. We find this by dividing the desired increase in the money supply by the money multiplier. (296-298)

3. These calculations are based on the formula $M = (1/r) \times MB$, where M is the money supply, r is the reserve ratio, and MB is the monetary base (here it equals reserves). Find out how much reserves must be changed and divide by 20 to find how much the discount rate must be lowered (if reserves are to be raised) or increased (if reserves are to lowered).

   a. To increase reserves in the system by $100, the discount rate should be reduced by 5 percentage points. We find how much reserves must be increased by dividing the desired increase in the money supply by the money multiplier. We find how much the discount rate must be lowered by dividing the desired increase in reserves by 20 (the amount reserves will increase with each percentage point decline in the discount rate). (299-300)

   b. To increase reserves in the system by $120, the discount rate should be reduced by 6 percentage points. See introduction to answer number 3 for how to calculate this. (299-300)

   c. To decrease reserves in the system by $125, the discount rate should be increased by 6.25 percentage points. See introduction to answer number 3 for how to calculate this. (299-300)

   d. To increase reserves in the system by $250, the discount rate should be reduced by 12.5 percentage points. See introduction to answer number 3 for how to calculate this. (299-300)

4. **a.** Begin with 2 + rate of inflation, or 4. Since output is 1 percent below potential, subtract 0.5 to get to 3.5%. (302-304)

   b. Begin with 2 + inflation, or 7. Because inflation is 2 percentage points above target, add 1 percent to get to 8%. (302-304)

   c. Begin with 2 + inflation, or 6. Since inflation is 1 percentage point above its target add 0.5 and since output is 1 percent above potential, add another 0.5 to get 7%. (302-304)

d. Begin with 2 + inflation, or 6. Since inflation is 2 percentage points above its target, add 1 but since output is 2 percent below potential subtract 1 to get 6%. (302-304)

5.

Inflation rate	Nominal Interest rate	Real Interest rate
a. 5%	10%	5%

Real rate = nominal - inflation. (305-306)

b. 8%	15%	7%

Inflation = nominal - real rate. (305-306)

c. -3%	6%	9%

Nominal = inflation + real rate. (305-306)

d. 4%	14%	10%

Nominal = inflation + real rate. (305-306)

6. These calculations are based on the formula $M = (1/r) \times MB$, where M is the money supply, r is the reserve ratio, and MB is the monetary base (here it equals reserves).

   a. The money multiplier is $1/r = 10$. Reserves must be $100 million to support a money supply of $1 billion. The reserve ratio to support $1.1 billion money supply with $100 million reserves is about 9.1%. We find this by dividing reserves by the desired money supply. (298-299)

   b. The Fed would buy $10,000 worth of bonds to increase the money supply by $100,000. Calculate this by dividing the desired increase in the money supply by the money multiplier. (296-298)

7. In this case, the money multiplier is $(1+c)/(r+c) = 1.33/(.25+.33) = 2.3$. The cash-to-deposit ratio is .33 since people hold 25% of their money in cash and the remainder, 75%, in deposits.

   a. The reserve requirement must be lowered to about 15%. We find this by first calculating the monetary base: $1 billion / 2.3 = $435 million (money supply/multiplier). For the money supply to increase to $1.2 billion, the money multiplier must be $1.2/.435 = 2.76$. To find the new reserve ratio solve $(1+c)/(r+c) = 2.76$ for r. We find that $r = .15$. (298-299)

   b. The Fed must buy $86.96 million in bonds to increase the money supply by $200 million. Calculate this by dividing the desired increase in the money supply by the money multiplier: $200 million / 2.3. (296-298)

8. a. The graph below shows the yield curve associated with the values given. (304-305)

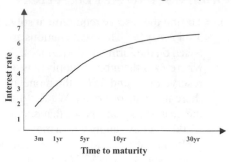

   b. The graph below shows the yield curve associated with the values given. (304-305)

   c. Yield curve a is a standard yield curve. Yield curve b is an inverted yield curve. (304-305)

A1. These calculations are based on the formula $M = (1/r) \times MB$, where M is the money supply, r is the reserve ratio, and MB is the monetary base (here it equals reserves).

   a. The Fed must sell bonds worth $4,000 to reduce reserves by $4,000. We calculate this by dividing the desired reduction in the money supply by the money multiplier. (312-313)

   b. Step 1: An individual or group of individuals buy $4,000 in Treasury bonds from the Fed. Individuals withdraw the funds from the bank. (312-313)

Assets		Liabilities	
Cash	20,000	Demand Deposits	50,000
Payment to		Withdrawals	(4,000)
individuals	(4,000)		
Total cash	16,000	Total demand	
		deposits	46,000
Loans	120,000	Net Worth	100,000
Phys. Assets	10,000		
Total Assets	146,000	Total Liabilities and net worth	146,000

Step 2: Reserves are now too low to meet the reserve requirement of .4. (We calculated the reserve requirement by solving the equation 1/r = 2.5 for r.) The bank must call in $2,400 in loans (46,000×.4 − 16,000). This shows up as loans repaid. But the individuals repaying the loans must get the money from somewhere. Since no one holds cash and Textland bank is the only bank, the individuals must withdraw the $2,400 from the bank. This is shown as a withdrawal on the liability side and a payment to individuals on the asset side. Again reserves are too low, this time by $1,440. (312-313)

Assets		Liabilities	
Cash	16,000	Demand Deposits	46,000
Loans repaid $2,400		Withdrawals	(2,400)
Payment			
to individuals (2,400)		Total demand	
		deposits	43,600
Total Cash	16,000		
Loans	120,000	Net Worth	100,000
Loans called in (2,400)			
Total Loans	117,600		
Phys. Assets 10,000			
Total Assets 143,600		Total Liabilities	143,600
		and net worth	

c. Final balance sheet: The banks continue to call in loans to meet reserve requirements until the multiplier process is finished. The money supply is now $10,000 less. At last, the balance sheet is as shown: (312-313)

Assets		Liabilities	
Cash	16,000	Demand Deposits	40,000
Loans	114,000	Net Worth	100,000
Phys. Assets 10,000			
Total Assets 140,000		Total Liabilities	140,000
		and net worth	

A2. Step 1: The bank makes $20,000 in new loans. This money is spent and deposited into Textland by other individuals. (312-313)

Assets		Liabilities	
Cash	40,000	Demand Deposits	200,000
Payments out (20,000)		New deposits	20,000
Payments in	20,000	Total deposits	220,000
Total cash	40,000		

Loans	230,000	Net Worth	100,000
New loans	20,000		
Total loans	250,000		
Phys. Assets 30,000			
Total Assets 320,000		Total Liabilities	320,000
		and net worth	

Step 2: Textland still has excess reserves (40,000/220,000 > .1) of $18,000 so it makes $18,000 in new loans. Calculate excess reserves by reserves - total deposits×reserve ratio. (312-313)

Assets		Liabilities	
Cash	40,000	Demand Deposits	220,000
Payments out (18,000)		New deposits	18,000
Payments in	18,000	Total deposits	238,000
Total cash	40,000		
Loans	250,000	Net Worth	100,000
New loans	18,000		
Total loans	268,000		
Phys. Assets 30,000			
Total Assets 338,000		Total Liabilities	338,000
		and net worth	

Final position: The previous steps continue until the money creation process ends as shown below. (312-313)

Assets		Liabilities	
Cash	40,000	Demand Deposits	400,000
Loans	430,000	Net Worth	100,000
Phys. Assets 30,000			
Total Assets 500,000		Total Liabilities	500,000
		and net worth	

ANSWERS

A BRAIN TEASER

1. The Fed should undertake expansionary monetary policy: 1) Buy government securities on the open market, 2) decrease the discount rate, and/or 3) decrease required reserves. It should do any one or more of these things to increase banks' excess reserves by $44.64. This is because to close a recessionary gap of $1,000 when the expenditure multiplier is 4 will require an increase in aggregate expenditures

of $250. To accomplish this, investment spending will have to increase by $250. This will require the interest rate to decrease by 2.5%. That will require an increase in the money supply of $125. When the money multiplier equals 2.8, or $[(1+.4)/(.1 + .4)]$, excess reserves will only have to increase by $44.64. (296-300)

ANSWERS

MULTIPLE CHOICE

1. a   Expansionary monetary policy reduces interest rates and investment increases. Hence, AD shifts out to the right by a multiple of the increase in investment. See pages 290-292.

2. b   Contractionary monetary policy increases interest rates which reduces investment, a component of aggregate expenditures. The AD curve shifts in to the left by a multiple of the decline in investment. See pages 290-292.

3. a   Contractionary monetary policy increases interest rates which decreases investment, thereby decreasing income by a multiple of that amount. See page 292.

4. b   See page 292.

5. c   The correct answer is "policy undertaken by the Fed." The last answer, d, involves regulation, which is also done by the Fed, but such regulation generally does not go under the name "monetary policy." Given the accuracy of answer c, answer d should be avoided. See pages 292-295.

6. c   See page 294.

7. b   Fiscal policy is definitely not a function of the Fed. See page 296.

8. b   See page 292 and Figure 12-3 on page 294.

9. d   Deficits are a tool of fiscal policy. See pages 296-300.

10. a   The price level rise is the difference between the change in nominal income (6 percent) and real income (4 percent). 6-4=2 percent. See page 291.

11. d   The money multiplier is $(1+c)/(r+c) = 1.2/.3 = 4$. See page 299.

12. b   The Fed makes loans only to other banks, and the discount rate is the rate of interest the Fed charges for these loans. See page 299.

13. a   Open market operations is mostly how the Fed changes the money supply. See page 296.

14. a   The last two answers, c and d, cannot be right, because the Fed does not pass laws. When the Fed buys bonds, it lowers the interest rate but it does not lower interest rates by law. Therefore, only a is correct. See pages 296-298.

15. b   People pay the Fed for those bonds with money—Fed IOUs——so the money supply in private hands is reduced. See page 298.

16. a   As the Fed buys bonds this increases their demand and their prices rise. Since bond prices and interest rates are inversely related, interest rates will fall. See pages 296-298.

17. d   See page 300.

18. d   The Taylor rule states that the Fed targets the Fed funds rate with this formula: 2 + rate of inflation + one-half the difference between actual and desired inflation plus one-half the deviation of output over its target. Thus, it will set a Fed funds target of 6%, (2+3+.5+.5). See pages 302-304.

19. c   When the Fed targets the interest rate, it adjusts the supply of money so that the quantity of money demanded equals the quantity of money supplied at the targeted interest rate. This creates a flat effective supply curve of money. See page 303.

20. b   The yield curve is generally upward sloping. Interest rates for short-term bonds are generally lower than interest rates for long-term bonds because of the risk premium for long-term bonds. See pages 302-305.

21. a   If the Fed contracts the money supply, the short-term interest rate will rise. This will tend to make the yield curve inverted, or downward sloping. See pages 305-305.

22. a   If expectations of inflation rise, long-term interest rates will likely rise, so other things equal the yield curve will become steeper. See pages 302-305.

ANSWERS

POTENTIAL ESSAY QUESTIONS

The following are annotated answers. They indicate the general idea behind the answer.

1. Use expansionary monetary policy (Fed reduces reserve requirements, reduces the discount rate, and/or buys government securities) during a recession; use contractionary policy during an upturn in the business cycle. Expansionary monetary policy will increase the money supply, which will reduce the interest rate and increase investment spending. This shifts the AD curve out to the right by a multiple of the initial increase in investment spending and brings about a multiple increase in the income level.

2. When the Fed funds rate is above its targeted range many banks have shortages of reserves and therefore money must be tight (credit is tight); and vice versa. The Fed will buy (sell) bonds when the Fed funds rate is above (below) its target and monetary policy is too tight (loose).

3. Economists look at the yield curve because it shows the relationship between short-term and long-term interest rates. It's important to monetary policy because the Fed can only directly impact short-term interest rates. As long as the relationship between short-term and long-term interest rates remains constant, the Fed can also affect long-term interest rates, and therefore investment expenditures, and ultimately output and the price level. But if the relationship changes, the Fed has less control. One possibility is that the Fed raises short-term interest rates and long-term interest rates fall. This might happen if by raising short-term interest rates inflation expectations fall. But if the Fed wanted long-term interest rates to rise, its raising short-term rates will not be effective.

INFLATION AND THE PHILLIPS CURVE

13

CHAPTER AT A GLANCE

This review is based upon the learning objectives that open the chapter.

1. Inflation redistributes income from those who cannot raise their prices or wages to those who can raise their prices or wages. (314-315)

   For example, if inflation is unexpected, income is redistributed from:

   - *workers to firms if workers have fixed wage contracts but firms raise their prices.*
   - *lenders to borrowers since the real interest rate declines when the nominal interest rate is fixed.*

   On average the winners and losers in an inflation balance out; inflation does not make a nation richer or poorer.

2. Three ways expectations of inflation are formed are: (315-316)

   1. *Rational expectations → expectations that the economists' model predicts.*

   2. *Adaptive expectations → expectations based in some way on the past.*

   3. *Extrapolative expectations → expectations that a trend will continue.*

   Expectations can change the way an economy operates. Expectations play a key role in policy.

   Policymakers use the following equation to determine whether inflation may be coming:

   Inflation = Nominal wage increase – productivity growth.

3. The quantity theory of money basically states that inflation is directly related to the rise in the money supply. It is based upon the equation of exchange: $MV = PQ$. (317-319)

   Three assumptions made in the quantity theory of money:

   1. *Velocity (V) is constant.*
   2. *Real output (Q) is independent of the money supply (M).*
   3. *Causation goes from money (M) to prices (P). That is, an increase (decrease) in M causes an increase (decrease) in P.*
   Note: The price level rises because the money supply rises.

   In the 1990s, the close relationship between money and inflation broke down. Economists debate whether this is temporary or permanent. For large inflations, the connection between money and inflation is still evident.

4. The institutional theory holds that institutional and structural aspects of inflation, as well as increases in the money supply, are important causes of inflation. It sees the causation in the equation of exchange going from right to left. That is, changes in the price level result in changes in the money supply. (321-323)

   Firms find it easier to raise wages, profits, and rents to keep the peace with employees and other owners of the factors of production. To pay for those increases, firms raise prices. Government then raises the money supply to make sure there is sufficient demand to buy the goods at those higher prices.

The "insider" versus "outsider" situation creates imperfect markets. Imperfect markets provide an opportunity for "insiders" to increase their wages and prices even when unemployment and excess capacity exist in the overall economy, thereby creating inflation.

In a nutshell: According to the quantity theory, MV → PQ

According to the institutionalist theory, PQ → MV

5a. The long-run Phillips curve is vertical; it takes into account the feedback of inflation on expectations of inflation. (325-327)

In the long run when expectations of inflation are met, changes in the rates of inflation have no effect on the level of unemployment. This is shown as LR in the accompanying graph.

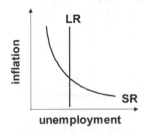

5b. The short-run Phillips curve is downward sloping. Expectations of inflation are constant along the short-run Phillips curve. (323-327)

The short-run Phillips curve reflects the empirically observed trade-off between inflation and unemployment. It is shown as SR in the graph above. Expectations of inflation are constant along the short-run (SR) Phillips curve. Increases (decreases) in inflationary expectations shift the short-run Phillips curve to the right (left).

In the long run we have more time to adjust our expectations to actual inflation. In the short run we may be fooled–we may expect less (more) inflation than actually occurs when inflation is accelerating (decelerating).

6. Quantity theorists believe that inflation undermines long-run growth. Institutionalists are less sure of a negative relationship between inflation and growth. (328-329)

According to the quantity theory, the best policy is a policy that leads to price stability.

Institutionalists believe that low unemployment is an important goal that must be balanced with the risk of inflation.

● SHORT-ANSWER QUESTIONS

1. Your study partner states that inflation is bad because it makes a nation poorer. How do you respond?

2. What are three ways people form expectations of future inflation?

3. If there is a high inflation, most economists are willing to accept that a rough approximation of the quantity theory holds true. Why?

4. What is the quantity theory of money and how does it relate to long-run growth?

5. How does the institutionalist theory of inflation differ from the quantity theory of inflation?

6. Who is more likely to favor a monetary rule: economists who support the quantity theory or economists who support the institutional theory of inflation? Why?

7. Which of the two curves in the graph below is a short-run Phillips curve, and why?

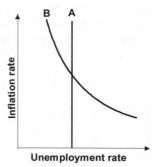

8. Would an economist who supports the quantity theory or one who supports the institutionalist theory of inflation be more likely to see a long-run trade-off between inflation and unemployment? Why?

—————————— MATCHING THE TERMS ——————————
Match the terms to their definitions

___ **1.**	adaptive expectations	**a.**	Expectations based in some way on the past.
___ **2.**	cost-push inflation	**b.**	An institutionalist story of inflation where insiders bid up wages and outsiders are unemployed.
___ **3.**	demand-pull inflation	**c.**	$MV=PQ$.
___ **4.**	equation of exchange	**d.**	A curve showing the trade-off between inflation and unemployment when expectations of inflation are constant.
___ **5.**	extrapolative expectations	**e.**	A curve showing the trade-off (or complete lack thereof) between inflation and unemployment when expectations of inflation equal actual inflation.
___ **6.**	inflation tax	**f.**	The price level varies in response to changes in the quantity of money.
___ **7.**	insider/outsider model	**g.**	Combination of high and accelerating inflation and high unemployment.
___ **8.**	long-run Phillips curve	**h.**	Expectations that a trend will continue.
___ **9.**	quantity theory of money	**i.**	Inflation that occurs when the economy is at or above potential output.
___ **10.**	rational expectations	**j.**	The number of times per year, on average, a dollar goes around to generate a dollar's worth of income.
___ **11.**	short-run Phillips curve	**k.**	Expectations that the economists' model predicts.
___ **12.**	stagflation	**l.**	An implicit tax on the holders of cash and the holders of any obligations specified in nominal terms.
___ **13.**	velocity of money	**m.**	Inflation that occurs when the economy is below potential.

● PROBLEMS AND APPLICATIONS

1. **a.** What are the three assumptions that translate the equation of exchange into the quantity theory of money?

b. State the equation of exchange and show how the three assumptions lead to the conclusion that inflation is always and everywhere a monetary phenomenon.

2. With the equation of exchange, answer the following questions:

a. Nominal GDP is $2,000, the money supply is 200. What is the velocity of money?

b. The velocity of money is 5.60, the money supply is $1,100 billion. What is nominal output?

c. Assuming velocity is constant and the money supply increases by 6%, by how much does nominal output rise?

3. Suppose the economy is operating at potential output. Inflation is 3% and expected inflation is 3%. Unemployment is 5.5%.
    a. Draw a long-run Phillips curve and a short-run Phillips curve consistent with these conditions.

    b. The government implements an expansionary monetary policy. As a result, unemployment falls to 4.5% and inflation rises to 6%. Expectations do not adjust. Show where the economy is on the graph you drew for 3(a). What happens to the short-run Phillips curve? Inflation? Unemployment?

    c. Expectations now fully adjust. Show this on the graph drawn for 3(a). What happens to the short-run Phillips curve?

4. Redraw the long-run Phillips curve and the short-run Phillips curve consistent with the conditions of the economy described in question #3 above and explain the effect of the following on inflation and unemployment using the curves you have drawn.

    a. The government implements a contractionary monetary policy. As a result, unemployment rises to 6.5% and inflation falls to 0%. Expectations do not adjust.

    b. Expectations now fully adjust.

5. For each of the following points that represents the economy on the Phillips curve, make a prediction for unemployment and inflation.

    a.

    b.

    c.

6. Suppose inflation is 12%, unemployment is 5.5%, and the natural rate of unemployment is 5.5%. The president believes inflation and unemployment are both too high.

    a. Assume you are a quantity theorist. What policy would you recommend to improve the situation?

    b. Show the short-run effect of this policy on unemployment and inflation using the Phillips curve analysis. Will the president be satisfied? What is your response?

    c. Show the long-run effect of this policy on unemployment and inflation using the Phillips curve analysis. Will the president be satisfied? What is your response? (In that response, discuss the issue of long-run growth.)

● A BRAIN TEASER

1. Why do countries increase the money supply enormously even though they know that doing so will lead to high inflation?

● MULTIPLE CHOICE

Circle the one best answer for each of the following questions:

1. In an expected inflation, lenders will generally:
a. gain relative to borrowers.
b. lose relative to borrowers.
c. neither gain nor lose relative to borrowers.
d. The effect will be totally random.

2. In an unexpected inflation, lenders will generally:
a. gain relative to borrowers.
b. lose relative to borrowers.
c. neither gain nor lose relative to borrowers.
d. The effect will be totally random.

3. According to the text if individuals base their expectations on the past we say that their expectations are:
a. rational.
b. historical.
c. adaptive.
d. extrapolative.

4. If productivity growth is 2 percent and inflation is 5 percent, on average nominal wage increases will be:
a. 2 percent.
b. 3 percent.
c. 5 percent.
d. 7 percent.

5. If the nominal interest rate is 1 percent and the economy is experiencing deflation of 2 percent, the Fed cannot lower the real interest rate below:
a. 0 percent.
b. 1 percent.
c. 2 percent.
d. 3 percent.

6. Assuming velocity is relatively constant and real income is relatively stable, an increase in the money supply of 40 percent will be associated with an approximate change in the price level of:
a. 4 percent.
b. 40 percent.
c. 80 percent.
d. zero percent.

7. According to the quantity theory:
    a. unemployment is everywhere and always a
       monetary phenomenon.
    b. inflation is everywhere and always a
       monetary phenomenon.
    c. the equation of exchange does not hold true.
    d. real output is everywhere and always a
       monetary phenomenon.

8. The quantity theory is most applicable to:
    a. U.S. type economies.
    b. West European type economies.
    c. developing economies.
    d. Japanese type economies.

9. The inflation tax is:
    a. a tax placed by government on inflators.
    b. a tax placed on inflators.
    c. a tax on the holders of cash.
    d. a tax on holders of goods whose price is
       inflating.

10. Central banks in developing countries such as
    Zimbabwe do not simply stop increasing the
    supply of money to slow inflation because:
    a. the economy is producing goods at a greater
       rate than people can buy them.
    b. they do not believe that rapid money growth
       causes high inflation.
    c. the central bank must purchase government
       bonds to avoid an economic collapse.
    d. black markets are so prevalent, currency is
       disappearing in the market economy.

11. Individuals who hold an institutional theory of
    inflation argue:
    a. the equation of exchange is incorrect.
    b. the equation of exchange should be read
       from right to left.
    c. the equation of exchange should be read
       from left to right.
    d. both the quantity theory and the equation of
       exchange are incorrect.

12. If an economist focuses on social pressures in
    his or her discussion of inflation, that
    economist is likely an advocate of a(n):
    a. quantity theory of inflation.
    b. institutionalist theory of inflation.
    c. insider theory of inflation.
    d. outsider theory of inflation.

13. When there is cost-push inflation, price
    increases:
    a. tend to lead money supply increases.
    b. tend to lag money supply increases.
    c. tend to have no relationship to money
       supply increases.
    d. sometimes lead and sometimes lag money
       supply increases.

14. The Phillips curve represents a relationship
    between:
    a. inflation and unemployment.
    b. inflation and real income.
    c. money supply and interest rates.
    d. money supply and unemployment.

15. The short-run Phillips curve shifts around
    because of changes in:
    a. the money supply.
    b. expectations of employment.
    c. expectations of inflation.
    d. expectations of real income.

16. The slope of the long-run Phillips curve is
    thought by many economists to be:
    a. horizontal.
    b. vertical.
    c. downward sloping.
    d. backward bending.

17. If the economy is at point A in the Phillips
    curve graph below, what prediction would
    you make for inflation?

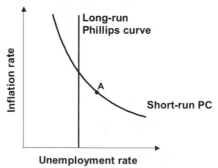

    a. It will increase.
    b. It will decrease.
    c. It will remain constant.
    d. It will explode.

18. If the economy is at Point A in the Phillips curve graph below, what prediction would you make for inflation?

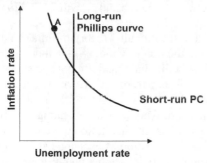

a. It will increase.
b. It will decrease.
c. It will remain constant.
d. It will immediately fall to zero.

19. Stagflation is:
a. a combination of low and decelerating inflation and low unemployment.
b. a combination of low and decelerating inflation and high unemployment.
c. a combination of high and accelerating inflation and low unemployment.
d. a combination of high and accelerating inflation and high unemployment.

20. Advocates of the quantity theory are likely to emphasize a trade-off between inflation and:
a. unemployment.
b. distribution.
c. growth.
d. money.

POTENTIAL ESSAY QUESTIONS

You may also see essay questions similar to the "Problems & Applications" and "A Brain Teaser" exercises.

1. In what way is inflation a tax? Who pays it?

2. What are the differences between the quantity theorists and the institutionalists with respect to unemployment?

3. What role does government play in the Insider/Outsider model?

ANSWERS

SHORT-ANSWER QUESTIONS

1. Inflation does not make a nation poorer. It redistributes income from those who cannot and do not raise their prices to those who can and do raise their prices. On average, the winners and losers average out. An example is lenders and borrowers. (314-315)

2. People formulate expectations in a variety of ways. Three types of expectations are adaptive expectations (expectations based in some way on the past), rational expectations (the expectations that the economists' model predicts), and extrapolative expectations (expectations that a trend will continue). (315-316)

3. The quantity theory is based on the equation of exchange, $MV=PQ$. The quantity theory adds the following assumptions: (1) that velocity is relatively constant; (2) that real output is relatively constant; and (3) that changes in money supply cause changes in prices. In reality, velocity and real output can change sufficiently to make it questionable whether this theory is useful. However, when there is significant inflation—say 100% or more—the relative changes in velocity and real output that are reasonable to assume possible are much smaller than that 100%, leaving a rough correlation between changes in the money supply and changes in the price level.

   The debate between economists does not concern the relationships between money growth and inflation; it concerns the direction of causation. Quantity theorists tend to believe that the causation goes from money to prices, and hence they are willing to accept the existence of a long-run vertical Phillips curve. Institutionalists tend to believe that the causation goes from changes in prices and expectations of prices to changes in the money supply—the government is accommodating the higher prices. Thus they favor more institutionally-oriented theories of inflation. (317-319)

4. The quantity theory of money is best summarized by the phrase "Inflation is everywhere and always a monetary phenomenon." Essentially, it is that increases in the money supply are the cause of inflation, and all other supposed causes are simply diversions from the key monetary cause. According to the quantity theory there is a long-run inverse relationship between inflation and growth. (317-319)

5. The institutionalist theory of inflation differs from the quantity theory in that it is more likely to include institutional and social aspects as part of the theory. The insider/outsider model is an institutionalist model of inflation. Another way of stating the difference is that the institutional theory of inflation sees the equation of exchange as being read from right to left, rather than from left to right. (317-319, 321-323)

6. Economists who support the quantity theory of money are more likely to favor a monetary rule, because they see the economy gravitating toward a natural (or target) rate of unemployment regardless of monetary policy. Thus expansionary monetary policy can lead only to inflation. A monetary rule will limit the government's attempt to expand the economy with monetary policy and hence will achieve the target rate of unemployment and low inflation. Institutional economists are less likely to see the economy gravitating toward the target rate of unemployment, so they would favor some discretionary policy to improve the operation of the macroeconomy. (317-319, 321-323)

7. Curve B is the short-run Phillips curve. The short-run Phillips curve represents a trade-off between inflation and unemployment. It is an empirically determined phenomenon, and based on that empirical evidence, economists generally believe that whenever unemployment decreases, inflation increases, and vice versa. They explain that this empirical occurrence is due to slowly adjusting expectations and institutions. In the long run, expectations and institutions can change and hence the reason for the trade-off is eliminated, making the vertical line represent the long-run Phillips curve—it represents the lack of a trade-off between inflation and unemployment in the long run. (323-327)

8. Institutional economists see institutional and social aspects of the price setting process as more important than do quantity theorists.

They also see individuals as having a cost of rationality, so individuals may not notice small amounts of inflation. These aspects of the institutional theory make it more likely that there is a long-run trade-off between inflation and unemployment since, in their absence, we would expect that money is essentially a veil and real forces predominate. (328-329)

ANSWERS

MATCHING

1-a; 2-m; 3-i; 4-c; 5-h; 6-l; 7-b; 8-e; 9-f; 10-k; 11-d; 12-g; 13-j.

ANSWERS

PROBLEMS AND APPLICATIONS

1.　a.　1. Velocity is constant, 2. Real output is independent of the money supply, 3. Causation goes from money supply to prices. (318-319)

　　b.　$MV = PQ$ is the equation of exchange. Since V is constant and Q exogenous, the only remaining variables that change within the system are M and P. Since the causation runs from M to P, to keep the equation balanced, a rise in M must lead to a rise in P (and only P since Q is exogenous). (318-319)

2.　a.　$V = 10$: $MV = PQ$; $200V = \$2,000$; $V = 10$. (318)

　　b.　$\$6,160$ billion: $MV = PQ$; $(5.6)(1,100) = \$6,160$ billion. (318)

　　c.　By 6%. (318-319)

3.　a.　The long-run Phillips curve is vertical at the rate of unemployment consistent with potential output, here at 5.5%. The short-run Phillips curve is the downward sloping curve shown in the graph below as PC_1. In this case, we drew a short-run Phillips curve where expected inflation equals the 3% actual inflation. It intersects the long-run Phillips curve at 5.5% unemployment and 3% inflation. The economy is at point A. (323-327)

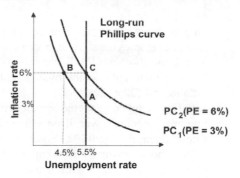

　　b.　The economy moves along the short-run Phillips curve up and to the left to point B. The short-run Phillips curve does not shift since inflation expectations have not changed. At point B, inflation is 6% and unemployment rate is 4.5%. (323-327)

　　c.　Now that expectations fully adjust, the short-run Phillips curve shifts to the right to PC_2 so that it intersects the long-run Phillips curve at an inflation rate of 6%. The unemployment rate returns to 5.5% and inflation remains at the higher 6%. (323-327)

4.　a.　The economy moves along the short-run Phillips curve down and to the right to point B in the graph below. The short-run Phillips curve does not shift since inflation expectations have not changed. At point B, inflation is 0% and unemployment rate is 6.5%. (323-327)

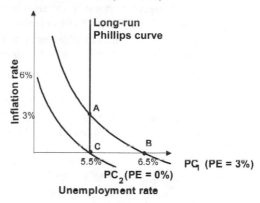

　　b.　Now that expectations fully adjust, the short-run Phillips curve shifts to the left to PC_2 so that it intersects the long-run Phillips curve at inflation rate of 0%. The unemployment rate returns to 5.5% and inflation remains at the lower 0%. (323-327)

5. **a.** Inflation is below expected inflation and unemployment is higher than the natural rate of unemployment. As expectations adjust, the short-run Phillips curve shifts to the left and both unemployment and inflation fall. (323-327)

    b. Inflation is above expected inflation and unemployment is lower than the natural rate of unemployment. As expectations adjust, the short-run Phillips curve shifts to the right and both unemployment and inflation rise. (323-327)

    c. Inflation equals expected inflation and unemployment equals the target rate of unemployment. Inflation and unemployment will not change. (323-327)

6. **a.** I would assume that in the long run, only inflation can be improved, so I ignore the rate of unemployment and focus on fighting inflation. A contractionary monetary policy will improve the inflation rate. (317-319)

    b. The economy begins at point *A* in the accompanying graph, where unemployment is 5.5% and inflation is 12%. Inflation expectations equal actual inflation. With contractionary monetary policy, the economy moves along the short-run Phillips curve down and to the right to point *B*. The short-run Phillips curve does not shift since inflation expectations have not changed. At point B, inflation is lower than 12% and the unemployment rate is higher than 5.5%. The president will be happy that inflation is lower, but disappointed that unemployment is higher. I tell him that in the short run there is a trade-off between the two. Just wait for expectations of inflation to adjust and we will return to 5.5% unemployment. (323-327)

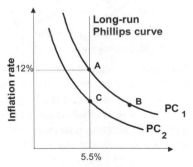

c. Now that expectations fully adjust, the short-run Phillips curve shifts to the left to PC_2 so that it intersects the long-run Phillips curve at inflation rate of below 12% at point *C*. The unemployment rate returns to 5.5%. The president is now pleased because inflation is lower and unemployment returned to 5.5%. But he wanted the unemployment rate to be below 5.5%. I tell him that 5.5% is the natural rate. If he were to follow an expansionary policy, unemployment would fall in the short run, but would return to 5.5% in the long run and inflation would be higher than it currently is. The higher inflation would undermine the economy's long-term growth. (323-329)

ANSWERS

A BRAIN TEASER

1. The reasons are complicated. If a government does not have the capability of either taxing or borrowing to finance expenditures (and if the central bank is not independent) the government may rely on its ability to print money to finance government expenditures. For some countries the choice is between inflation and allowing an economy and its government to fall apart. (320-321)

ANSWERS

MULTIPLE CHOICE

1. c   In an unexpected inflation borrowers gain and lenders lose because the money they are paying back will buy less because of the inflation. In an expected inflation the interest rate will have adjusted to compensate lenders for the decrease in the value of money. See pages 314-315.

2. b   In an unexpected inflation borrowers gain and lenders lose because the money borrowers are paying back will buy less because of the inflation. See pages 314-315.

3. c   Rational expectations are based on models; extrapolative expectations are based on expectations that a trend will continue. Historical expectations are not mentioned in the text. See pages 315-317.

4. d   Inflation is the difference between nominal wage increases and productivity growth. See page 317.

5. c   One of the problems of deflation is that it sets a floor for the real interest rate. In this case, the real interest rate is 3 percent since the nominal interest rate is 1%. The real interest rate cannot fall below 2 percent. See page 315.

6. b   Using the equation of exchange, $MV=PQ$, given these assumptions there is a close relationship between changes in M and changes in P. See page 318.

7. b   The quantity theory directly relates money and inflation. See pages 317-318.

8. c   The quantity theory is most applicable when there are large increases in the money supply and significant inflation. This is most likely to be the case in developing countries. See page 320.

9. c   The inflation tax is a tax on the holders of cash because inflation makes their cash worth less. See page 320.

10. c   Central banks in developing countries often must finance the deficit of the government because no one would buy government bonds, and the government would be unable to continue, which would mean that the economy would likely break down. See page 320.

11. b   The equation of exchange is a tautology; it cannot be incorrect; Institutionalists see price changes causing money and velocity changes so MV=PQ should be read from right to left. See pages 321-323.

12. b   The book describes two general theories of inflation; social pressures definitely fit within the institutionalist theory. One type of institutionalist theory of inflation is the insider/outsider model, but that is not presented as a choice. See pages 321-323.

13. a   As the text discusses on page 323, cost-push inflation is associated with the institutionalist theory of inflation that argues that price increases cause money supply increases, and therefore they lead them. The other answers are possible, but a is clearly the best.

14. a   The Phillips curve is drawn with inflation on the vertical axis and unemployment on the horizontal axis. See page 325.

15. c   The short-run Phillips curve holds expectations of inflation constant. Therefore, it shifts because changes in expectations of inflation cause everybody to build those expectations into their nominal price requests. See pages 324 and 326.

16. b   As discussed in the text, the long-run Phillips curve is vertical. Actually, there is some debate about whether it is downward sloping, but the text focuses on the vertical nature of the curve so that b is the answer that should be given. Remember, one is choosing the best answer relative to what is presented in the text. See page 325.

17. b   Since Point A is to the right of the long-run Phillips curve, actual unemployment exceeds the natural rate of unemployment. Therefore we would expect inflationary expectations to be decreasing, and hence inflation to be decreasing. See pages 323-327.

18. a   Since Point A is to the left of the long-run Phillips curve, actual unemployment is below the natural rate of unemployment. Therefore we would expect inflationary expectations to be increasing, and hence inflation to be increasing. See pages 323-327.

19. d   Stagflation is defined as a combination of high and accelerating inflation and high unemployment. See page 325.

20. c   Quantity theory advocates argue that in
the long run a noninflationary environment is conducive to growth and thus
there is a long run trade-off between
inflation and growth. See pages 328-329.

ANSWERS

POTENTIAL ESSAY QUESTIONS

*The following are annotated answers. They indicate the
general idea behind the answer.*

1. Inflation can be viewed as a tax because it
reduces the value of obligations specified in
nominal terms. A simple way to see this is if
prices rose at a rate of 5 percent a day, a dollar
today will buy only 95 cents worth of goods
tomorrow. The holder of the dollar (or any
obligation specified in nominal terms) pays the
tax.

2. Quantity theorists see a competitive labor
market guaranteeing full employment. Institutionalists see an imperfectly competitive labor
market. Institutionalists also envision a
potential lack of demand for workers because
of a lack of aggregate demand for the goods
they produce. To institutionalists, this can
create some unemployment at any wage.

3. Inflation is a result of *im*perfectly competitive
markets. This allows workers and firms
(especially "insiders") to raise their nominal
wages and prices even during periods of high
unemployment and excess production. Other
groups, feeling relatively worse off, will push
for higher wages and prices too. The government can either ratify this inflation by increasing the money supply or it can refuse to ratify
it, causing unemployment (especially for the
"outsiders").

FISCAL POLICY AND PUBLIC FINANCE

CHAPTER AT A GLANCE

This review is based upon the learning objectives that open the chapter.

1. Ricardian equivalence is the theoretical proposition that deficits do not affect the level of output in the economy because individuals increase their savings to account for expected future tax payments to repay the deficit. (336)

   Basically, the Ricardian equivalence theorem says that increases in government spending are offset by equal declines in private spending. Although this argument is logical, it isn't the reason why economists before the 1930s didn't support activist fiscal policy. They didn't support it for political reasons.

2a. Sound finance is the view of public finance and fiscal policy that the government budget should always be balanced except in wartime. (335-336)

   This view was driven less by economic logic and more by tradition of believing the government should not direct the economy. After the Depression in the 1930s a view called "nuanced sound finance" developed, which supported government involvement under extreme conditions.

2b. Functional finance is the theoretical proposition that government should make spending and taxing decisions based on their effect on the economy, not on moralistic grounds that budgets should be balanced. (338)

   In this view, fiscal policy provides government with a steering wheel with which to direct the economy.

3. Functional finance developed into nuanced functional finance as economists began to recognize assumptions of the *AS/AD* and multiplier models that could lead to problems with fiscal policy: (339-344)

   a. Financing the deficit doesn't have any offsetting effects.

   In reality, it often does. A particular problem is crowding out, which is the offsetting effect on private expenditures caused by the government's sale of bonds to finance expansionary fiscal policy.

   b. The government knows what the situation is.

   In reality the government must estimate what the situation is.

   c. The government knows the economy's potential income.

   In reality the government may not know what this level is.

   d. The government has flexibility in terms of spending and taxes.

   In reality, the government cannot change them quickly.

   e. The size of the government debt doesn't matter.

   In reality, the size of the debt often does matter.

   f. Fiscal policy doesn't negatively affect other government goals.

   In reality, it often does.

4. An automatic stabilizer is any government program or policy that will counteract the business cycle without any new government action. (344-346)

    Automatic stabilizers include:
    - *welfare payments*
    - *unemployment insurance, and*
    - *income tax system.*

    In a recession, government expenditures automatically rise (because of increased welfare payments and unemployment claims). Taxes automatically decrease (because fewer people are earning income). The budget deficit increases and AE (total spending) increases. The opposite occurs during an upturn in the business cycle. Automatic stabilizers help smooth out the business cycle.

5a. The nuanced functional finance view of fiscal policy is that deficit spending can crowd out private investment, reducing the effect of deficit spending on the economy, but deficit spending will increase output in the economy. (339-341)

    In the nuanced view, expansionary fiscal policy shifts the AD curve out to the right from AD_0 to AD_1, although the AD curve might shift back some as investment spending falls if interest rates rise as a result of deficit spending.

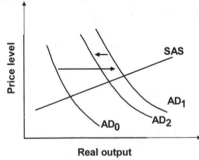

    The nuanced functional finance view suggests government cut taxes and /or increase spending during a recession to increase output in the short run.

5b. The New Classical view is that the Ricardian equivalence theorem is not only theoretically true, it is also true in practice and, therefore, government should not use deficit spending. (346-348)

    The New Classical view is that the AD curve does not shift at all.

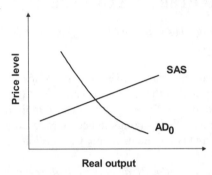

    New Classicals suggest government cut taxes during a recession, not to offset the recession, but to increase output in the long-run (for growth).

● SHORT-ANSWER QUESTIONS

1. What is the Ricardian equivalence theorem?

2. How could Classical economists believe in both sound finance and the Ricardian equivalence theorem?

3. How does sound finance differ from functional finance?

4. How do the six problems of fiscal policy limit its usefulness?

5. Some economists argue that crowding out totally undermines the activist view of fiscal policy. Explain their argument.

6. A country has just discontinued its unemployment insurance program and is experiencing a recession. How will this recession differ from earlier recessions?

7. In the short-run model, you want to lower interest rates and increase income. Would you propose expansionary monetary or fiscal policy? What concerns would you voice about this policy?

8. Suppose you are the featured speaker at a primer for the first-year Congresspeople. You have been asked to speak about fiscal policy. A Congressperson asks what fiscal policy tools Congress has to affect the economy, and what effect they have on the level of output. You tell her.

9. What is the New Classical view of "What to do about a recession?"

MATCHING THE TERMS
Match the terms to their definitions

____ 1. automatic stabilizer

____ 2. crowding out

____ 3. fiscal policy

____ 4. functional finance

____ 5. New Classical economics

____ 6. procyclical fiscal policy

____ 7. public finance

____ 8. Ricardian equivalence theorem

____ 9. sound finance

a. A theoretical approach to macroeconomics that revived many pre-Keynesian theoretical ideas of macro policy.

b. A theoretical proposition that governments should make spending and taxation decisions on the basis of their affect on the economy, not on the basis of some moralistic principle that budgets should be balanced.

c. A view of public finance and fiscal policy that the government budget should always be balanced except in wartime.

d. Government's taxing and spending policies.

e. The changing of taxes and spending to affect the level of output in the economy.

f. The theoretical proposition that deficits do not affect the level of output in the economy because individuals increase their savings to account for expected future tax payments to repay the deficit.

g. Any government program or policy that will counteract the business cycle without any new government action.

h. The offsetting effect on private expenditures caused by the government's sale of bonds to finance expansionary fiscal policy.

i. Changes in government spending and taxes that increase the cyclical fluctuations in the economy instead of reducing them.

● PROBLEMS AND APPLICATIONS

1. Demonstrate your answer to the following question both in words and with graphs:

   a. How does a government deficit affect the long-term interest rate in the loanable funds market?

   b. How does the change in interest rates in *a* impact the effectiveness of fiscal policy in the *AS/AD* model?

2. Demonstrate, using the *AS/AD* model, how the nuanced functional finance view of the effect of expansionary fiscal policy differs from the New Classical View.

● A BRAIN TEASER

1. If someone believed that the Ricardian equivalence theorem was applicable to the real world, could that individual also accept the rules of functional finance?

● MULTIPLE CHOICE

Circle the one best answer for each of the following questions:

1. Fiscal policy is:
    a. the changing of the money supply to affect the economy.
    b. the changing of the money supply to stop any effect of government spending on the economy.
    c. the changing of taxes and spending to affect the level of output in the economy.
    d. a policy of maintaining a balanced budget except in wartime.

2. Sound finance holds that:
    a. government spending is directed toward sound investments.
    b. the government budget should always be balanced except in wartime.
    c. the government budget should be judged by its effect on the economy.
    d. government should always borrow money in a sound fashion when it runs a deficit.

3. The Ricardian equivalence theorem holds that:
    a. government spending is equivalent to private spending.
    b. financing a deficit by bonds will have the same effect as financing it through taxes.
    c. imposing taxes is the equivalent to confiscation of property by government.
    d. all spending in the economy is equivalent.

4. Economists who held that theoretically the Ricardian equivalence theorem was true:
    a. would not support sound finance.
    b. would not support functional finance.
    c. could support sound finance and/or functional finance.
    d. could support either sound finance or functional finance but not both.

5. Functional finance holds that:
    a. budgets should always deal with functional issues.
    b. government should make monetary policy decisions on the basis of their effect on the economy.
    c. government should make fiscal policy decisions on the basis of their effect on the economy.
    d. government's budgets should be balanced.

6. Crowding out is caused by:
    a. government running a deficit and selling bonds to finance that deficit.
    b. government printing money.
    c. the government running a surplus and selling bonds and the people who buy those bonds selling their older bonds to the government.
    d. the tendency for new workers to replace more expensive older workers.

7. Automatic stabilizers:
    a. are government programs to employ workers during recessions.
    b. create government budget surpluses during economic recessions.
    c. are designed to reduce the price level directly.
    d. counteract both recessions and expansions through changes in spending without government action.

8. A state constitutional provision to maintain a balanced budget is an example of:
    a. an automatic stabilizer.
    b. monetary policy.
    c. procyclical policy.
    d. countercyclical policy.

9. New Classical economists differ from old Classical economists in that New Classicals:
    a. believe in the Ricardian equivalence theorem as a theoretical proposition.
    b. believe in the Ricardian equivalence theorem as a practical proposition.
    c. believe in functional finance.
    d. believe in sound finance.

10. In the New Classical view, if the government runs a deficit,
    a. the AD curve will shift out to the right.
    b. the AD curve will shift in the to the left.
    c. the AD curve will not shift.
    d. the AS curve will shift to the left.

11. The New Classical answer to the question, "What to do about a recession?" is to:
    a. impose trade tariffs.
    b. cut taxes and government spending.
    c. cut taxes only.
    d. cut government spending only.

12. If the government borrows money in the loanable funds market, the interest rate will likely:
    a. fall.
    b. rise.
    c. remain unchanged.
    d. rise and then fall.

● POTENTIAL ESSAY QUESTIONS

You may also see essay questions similar to the "Problems & Applications" and "A Brain Teaser" exercises.

1. How do the automatic stabilizers add stability to the business cycle? Are there any time lag (delay) problems associated with the use of the automatic stabilizers?

2. What is the crowding-out effect? What impact does this have on the effectiveness of fiscal policy in stimulating the economy during a recession? How large is the crowding-out effect, according to activist economists? Laissez-faire economists? What does the empirical evidence suggest about the size of the crowding-out effect?

3. Say you are a policy adviser to the government of a country that is growing at 6%, has inflation of 1%, and unemployment of 2%. You are hired by the government to advise them how they can improve the economy. What advice would you give?

4. How have economists' views of what the government's fiscal policy should be when faced with a recession changed over the years?

ANSWERS

SHORT-ANSWER QUESTIONS

1. It is a theoretical proposition that deficits do not affect the level of output in the economy because individuals increase their savings to account for expected future tax payments to repay the deficit. (336)

2. They supported sound finance on the basis of politics; they supported the Ricardian equivalence theorem as a logical proposition that had only limited relevance to the real world. (335-336)

3. Sound finance holds that the budget should be balanced at all times; functional finance holds that spending and taxing decisions should be made on the basis of their effect on the economy. (336-336, 338)

4. The six problems with fiscal policy limit its usefulness in the following ways: (1) Financing the deficit might have offsetting effects, reducing the net effect. (2) The government doesn't always know the current state of the economy and where it is headed, meaning these must be forecast; if you don't know the state of the economy you don't know what fiscal policy to use. (3) The government doesn't know what potential income is, meaning it must be estimated; if you estimated it wrong, you get the wrong fiscal policy. (4) The government cannot implement policy easily; if you can't implement it you can't use it. (5) The size of the debt might matter and since deficits create debt, you might not want to use it. Finally, (6) fiscal policy often negatively affects other government goals; if it does you might not use the policy even though it would change the economy in the direction you want. The bottom line is: In extreme cases, the appropriate fiscal policy is clear, but in most cases, the situation is not extreme. (339-344)

5. If crowding out is so strong that the reduced investment totally offsets the expansionary effect of fiscal spending, the net effect of fiscal policy can be zero. (340)

6. Unemployment insurance is an automatic stabilizer, a government program that counteracts the business cycle without any new government action. If income falls, automatic stabilizers will increase aggregate expenditures to counteract that decline. Likewise with increases in income: when income increases, automatic stabilizers decrease the size of the deficit. Eliminating unemployment insurance will eliminate this stabilization aspect of the policy and will contribute to making the recession more severe than it otherwise would have been. However, it would also make people more likely to accept lower wages and search harder for a job, thereby reducing the amount of unemployment. As usual, the answer depends. (344-345)

7. I would propose expansionary monetary policy. Expansionary fiscal policy would raise interest rates. I would emphasize that while the effect on income may be expansionary in the short run, in the long run, the expansionary monetary policy may simply lead to inflation. (339-340)

8. The tools of fiscal policy are changing taxes and changing government spending. Increasing taxes and lowering spending contract the economy; decreasing taxes and increasing spending expand the economy. (335,344)

9. It is to cut taxes and government spending, not because of the recession, but instead because the tax cuts will encourage growth. (348)

ANSWERS

MATCHING

1-g; 2-h; 3-e; 4-b; 5-a; 6-i; 7-d; 8-f; 9-c.

ANSWERS

PROBLEMS AND APPLICATIONS

1. **a.** A government deficit increases the demand for loanable funds. The following graph shows this as a shift in the demand curve from D_0 to D_1. An increase in the demand for loanable funds increases the long-term interest rate, in the graph, from i_0 to i_1. (339-340)

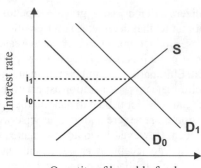

Quantity of loanable funds

b. An increase in the deficit (caused by
increased government spending or a
reduction in taxes) shifts the AD curve to the
right, this is illustrated in the graph below as
a shift in the AD curve to the right from AD_0
to AD_1. The increase in the interest rate
increases the cost of borrowing for investment, which reduces investment expenditures causing the AD curve to shift to the
left by a multiple of the decrease in investment expenditures. This offsets the impact of
fiscal policy on the economy somewhat and
is shown in the graph as a shift in the AD
curve from AD_1 to AD_2 (339-340)

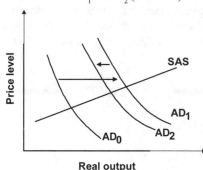

2. In the nuanced functional finance view,
expansionary fiscal policy shifts the AD curve
out to the right from AD_0 to AD_1, although the
AD curve might shift back some as investment
spending falls if interest rates rise as a result of
deficit spending. This is shown in the graph as
a shift in the AD curve to the right from AD_0 to
AD_1, and back to AD_2. Notice, however, that
real output rises, on balance. The New
Classical view is that the AD curve does not
shift at all. Hence, fiscal policy is ineffective in
the short-run. (339-340, 348)

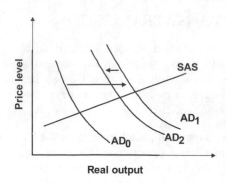

ANSWERS

A BRAIN TEASER

1. Since the rules of functional finance state that
government should make taxing and spending
decisions on the basis of their effect on the
economy, and the Ricardian equivalence
theory states that methods of financing make
no difference to the real economy, they could
accept the rules of functional finance. But, the
functional finance policy they would agree
with would not be what is normally considered
functional financial policy, which is based on
the Keyesian model being the true model. (335-
338)

ANSWERS

MULTIPLE CHOICE

1. c   See how fiscal policy is defined on page
335.

2. b   Sound finance holds the moral stance that
government should stay out of the
economy, that is, the government budget
should always be balanced. See page 335.

3. b   According to the Ricardian equivalence
theorem people will save the money
needed to repay bonds that will come due
in the future, so that financing by bonds
will have the same effect as financing
through taxes. See page 336.

4. c   The Ricardian equivalence theorem states that it doesn't matter if spending is financed by taxes or by bonds. The effect will be the same — none. Sound finance doesn't depend on the Ricardian equivalence theorem, it is a moral position. Functional finance just says that government should make the decision whether to run a deficit based on how it will affect the economy. Someone who holds the Ricardian equivalence theorem to be true would recommend a sound finance of no deficit. See page 335-338.

5. c   Functional finance rejects the moralistic position of sound finance and says government should make decisions based on how fiscal policy will affect the economy. See page 338.

6. a   As discussed on page 339 crowding out is the offsetting of a change in government expenditures by a change in private expenditures in the opposite direction. Answer c, if you could follow it, is nonsensical.

7. d   Automatic stabilizers are welfare payments, unemployment insurance, and taxes that raise income during recessions and lower income during expansions. See pages 344-346.

8. c   State balanced budget provisions mean that states cut spending and increase taxes during recessions and raise spending and reduce taxes during expansions. These actions exacerbate the business cycle and are therefore procyclical. See page 345.

9. b   Although both old and New Classicals don't believe government should use fiscal policy to steer the economy, old Classicals held this belief because of moral principles and New Classicals hold this belief based on the Ricardian equivalence theorem. See pages 346-348.

10. c   According to the New Classical view, a deficit will be exactly offset by a reduction in private spending as people save to pay

for the bonds that were used to finance the deficit. See page 348.

11. b   New Classicals believe that fiscal policy does not affect output, but they do believe that government spending raises interest rates, which will reduce private investment and reduce long-term economic growth. Hence, they advocate a cut in government spending. They also believe that taxes reduce the incentive to produce, so a cut in taxes will also lead to greater economic growth. See page 348.

12. b   When the government borrows money, the demand for loanable funds rises, leading to a rise in the interest rate. See pages 339-340.

ANSWERS

POTENTIAL ESSAY QUESTIONS

The following are annotated answers. They indicate the general idea behind the answer.

1. When the economy is in a recession and total spending is too low, then government spending automatically rises while tax collections automatically fall (the government automatically incurs a deficit). This helps to stimulate total spending and cushion the downturn in the economy. The opposite is true when the economy is expanding. Note that these changes take place while the income level falls and expands. Therefore, there are no time lag problems accompanying the automatic stabilizers.

2. The crowding-out effect states that deficit spending financed by borrowing will increase interest rates and therefore crowd out private spending. Any "crowding out" associated with deficit spending renders fiscal policy less effective in stimulating total spending and therefore the economy during a recession. Activist economists argue that the crowding out effect is relatively small. Committed laissez-faire economists argue that there is a total crowding out effect, which renders fiscal policy impotent in stimulating total spending. Some

laissez-faire economists have argued that the effect of deficit spending may even be negative on the economy if private spending is more productive than government spending. The empirical evidence on the size of the crowding-out effect is mixed and has not resolved the debate. However, everyone agrees that the closer the economy comes to its potential income level, the greater is the crowding-out effect.

3. I would start by pointing out that by most western economy standards the economy is going quite well, and that perhaps they should be satisfied with what they have. If they insist on policy actions, I would try to find out more information about the economy. For example, I would be worried that with high growth and low unemployment, inflation may soon become a problem. Thus I would be very hesitant to use any demand-based policy. With growth of 6%, I would assume that supply incentives are working, but I would consider them carefully to see if a technology or pro-savings policy may make sense.

4. The progression of views regarding fiscal policy can be summarized well by understanding the following terms: sound finance, functional finance, nuanced functional finance, and New Classicals. The sound finance view of the pre-1930s was that the government budget should always be in balance, except in wartime. Although this position is supported by the Ricardian equivalence theorem that fiscal policy has no impact on the economy, sound finance was independent of the Ricardian equivalence theory. Sound finance was a moral position. In the 1930s with the start of the depression, the view changed. Something had to be done to get the economy out of its depression.

The nuanced sound finance developed that stated that expansionary fiscal policy could affect the economy, or would at least be worth a try. In the 1960s another view developed called the functional finance view. This view believed that the government should actively steer the economy with fiscal policy even during small business cycle swings. The moralistic stance of sound finance should not be part of economists' prescriptions. The functional finance view gave way to the nuanced functional view that took the difficulties of fiscal policy, including crowding out, into account. In the 1980s economists came full circle as New Classicals argued that government should not have activist fiscal policy because it would not have any impact because of the Ricardian equivalence theorem.

POLITICS, DEFICITS, AND DEBT

CHAPTER AT A GLANCE

This review is based upon the learning objectives that open the chapter.

1a. A deficit is a shortfall of revenues under payments. A surplus is an excess of revenues over payments. (Surpluses are negative deficits and vice versa.) (355-356)

Surpluses and deficits are flow concepts; all deficits must be financed.

1b. Surpluses and deficits are simply summary measures of the financial health of the economy. To understand that summary you must understand the methods that were used to calculate it. (356)

Different accounting procedures yield different figures for surpluses and deficits.

2. A structural deficit or surplus is that part of a budget deficit or surplus that would exist even if the economy were at its potential level of income. A passive (also called cyclical) surplus or deficit is that part that exists because the economy is operating below or above its potential income. (356-358)

Passive deficit = Tax rate (Potential output −Actual output.)

Passive (cyclical) deficits or surpluses are largely due to the automatic stabilizers.

3. The real deficit is the nominal deficit adjusted for inflation. (358-359)

Real deficit = Nominal deficit − (Inflation × Total debt.)

Inflation wipes out debt. Inflation also causes the real deficit to be less than the nominal deficit. However, inflation means a higher percentage of the deficit (or spending) will be devoted to debt service (paying interest on the debt). Moreover, creditors who do not

anticipate the inflation pay the cost of eliminating the debt through inflation.

4a. Debt is accumulated deficits minus accumulated surpluses. It is a <u>stock</u> concept. (359-363)

Debt is a summary measure of a country's financial situation.

GDP serves the same function for government as income does for an individual. The greater the GDP (income) the greater the ability to handle debt. However, government debt is different from an individual's debt. Government is ongoing; it can pay off the debt by printing money; and much of its is internal— owed to its citizens.

4b. Since in a growing economy a continual deficit is consistent with a constant ratio of debt to GDP, and since GDP serves as a measure of the government's ability to pay off the debt, a country can run a continual deficit. (364-365)

The more you earn, the more debt you can handle.

5. Since World War II, until recently, the U.S. government ran almost continual deficits. From 1998 to 2001, the government ran surpluses, but returned to deficits in 2002. (363-364)

But we still have debt.

6. The Social Security Trust Fund surplus makes the budget deficit look smaller than it really is. Regardless of whether there is, or is not, a trust fund, real output must match real expenditures when the baby boomers retire. (366-371)

Always watch out for political spin when discussing the government budget.

● SHORT-ANSWER QUESTIONS

1. How much importance do most economists give to the budget deficit or surplus?

2. If the U.S. economy is below potential and the surplus is $40 billion, is the structural surplus greater or less than $40 billion?

3. If the nominal interest rate is 6%, the inflation rate is 4%, the nominal deficit is $100 billion, and the debt of the country is $2 trillion, what is the real deficit?

4. If the nominal interest rate is 5%, the inflation rate is 5%, the real deficit is $100 billion, and the debt of the country is $1 trillion, what is the nominal deficit?

5. In an expanding economy a government should run a continual deficit. True or false? Why?

6. If a politician presents you with a plan that will reduce the nominal budget deficit by $40 billion, but will not hurt anyone, how would you in your capacity as an economist likely respond?

7. Are current budget deficits likely to persist?

8. In what way is the trust fund not a real solution to the Social Security problem?

MATCHING THE TERMS
Match the terms to their definitions

___ **1.**	cash flow accounting system	**a.**	An accounting system entering expenses and revenues only when cash is received or paid out.
___ **2.**	deficit	**b.**	A partially unfunded pension system of the U.S.
___ **3.**	external debt	**c.**	A shortfall per year of incoming revenue under outgoing payments.
___ **4.**	internal debt	**d.**	An excess of revenues over payments.
___ **5.**	nominal deficit or surplus	**e.**	Government debt owed to individuals in foreign countries.
___ **6.**	passive deficit or surplus	**f.**	Pension system in which pensions are paid from current revenues.
___ **7.**	pay-as-you-go system	**g.**	That portion of the deficit or surplus that results from fluctuations in the economy.
___ **8.**	real deficit	**h.**	The deficit or surplus determined by looking at the difference between expenditures and receipts.
___ **9.**	Social Security system	**i.**	Government debt owed to its own citizens.
___ **10.**	structural deficit	**j.**	The deficit that would remain when the cyclical or passive elements have been netted out.
___ **11.**	surplus	**k.**	The nominal deficit adjusted for inflation's effect on the debt.

● PROBLEMS AND APPLICATIONS

1. Calculate the debt and deficit in each of the following:

a. Your income has been $30,000 per year for the last five years. Your expenditures, including interest payments, have been $35,000 per year for the last five years.

b. This year your income is $50,000; $15,000 of your $65,000 expenditures are for the purchase of the rights to an invention.

c. Your wage income is $20,000 per year. You have a bond valued at $100,000, which pays $10,000 per year. The market value of that bond rises to $110,000. Expenses are $35,000 per year. Use the opportunity cost approach in your calculations.

2. For each of the following calculate the real deficit:

a. Inflation is 5%. Debt is $2 trillion. Nominal deficit is $100 billion.

b. Inflation is 3%. Debt is $500 billion. Nominal deficit is $20 billion.

c. Inflation is 10%. Debt is $3 trillion. Nominal deficit is $100 billion.

d. Inflation is 8%. Debt is $20 billion. Nominal deficit is $5 billion.

3. Assume a country's nominal GDP is $7 trillion, government expenditures less debt service are $1.5 trillion, and revenue is $1.3 trillion. The nominal debt is $4.9 trillion. Inflation is 2% and real interest rates are 5%. Expected inflation is fully adjusted.

a. Calculate debt service payments.

b. Calculate the nominal deficit.

c. Calculate the real deficit.

d. Suppose inflation rose to 4%. Again, expected inflation is fully adjusted. Recalculate (a) - (c).

4. Potential income is $8 billion. The income in the economy is $7.2 billion. Revenues do not vary with income, but taxes do; they increase by 20% of the change in income. The current deficit is $400 million.

a. What is the economy's structural deficit?

b. What is the economy's passive deficit?

● A BRAIN TEASER

1. How could deficit spending actually reduce the debt burden of future generations?

● MULTIPLE CHOICE

Circle the one best answer for each of the following questions:

1. A deficit is:
   a. the total amount of money that a country owes.
   b. the shortfall of payments under revenues in a particular time period.
   c. the shortfall of revenues under payments in a particular time period.
   d. accumulated debt.

2. If the U.S. government raised the retirement age to 72 starting in 2020, the current budget deficit would be:
   a. reduced.
   b. increased.
   c. unaffected.
   d. eliminated.

3. The nominal deficit is $100 billion; inflation is 4 percent; total debt is $2 trillion. The real deficit is:
   a. zero.
   b. $20 billion.
   c. $80 billion.
   d. $100 billion.

4. If the nominal surplus is $200 billion, inflation is 10 percent, and total debt is $2 trillion:
   a. the real surplus is zero.
   b. the real deficit is $100 billion.
   c. the real surplus is $400 billion.
   d. the real surplus is $2.2 trillion.

5. The real deficit is $100 billion; inflation is 4 percent; total debt is $2 trillion. The nominal deficit is:
   a. zero.
   b. $120 billion.
   c. $180 billion.
   d. $200 billion.

6. If creditors are able to forecast inflation perfectly and there are no institutional constraints on interest rates:
   a. the government will not have to make interest payments.
   b. interest payments will rise by the amount that the real debt is reduced by inflation.
   c. the real deficit will equal the nominal deficit.
   d. the government will be unable to finance the debt.

7. Country A has a debt of $10 trillion. Country B has a debt of $5 trillion.
   a. Country A is in a better position than Country B.
   b. Country B is in a better position than Country A.
   c. One cannot say what relative position the countries are in.
   d. Countries A and B are in equal positions.

8. As a percentage of GDP, since World War II:
   a. debt in the United States has been rising.
   b. debt in the United States has been falling.
   c. debt in the United States has been sometimes rising and sometimes falling.
   d. the U.S. government has had no debt.

9. The portion of the budget deficit or surplus that would exist even if the economy were at its potential level of income is called the:
   a. structural deficit or surplus.
   b. passive deficit or surplus.
   c. primary deficit or surplus.
   d. secondary deficit or surplus.

10. If an economy is $100 billion below potential, the tax rate is 20 percent, and the deficit is $180 billion, the passive deficit is:
    a. $20 billion.
    b. $160 billion.
    c. $180 billion.
    d. $200 billion.

11. One of the reasons government debt is different from individual debt is:
    a. government does not pay interest on its debt.
    b. government never really needs to pay back its debt.
    c. all government debt is owed to other government agencies or to its own citizens.
    d. the ability of a government to pay off its debt is unrelated to income.

12. If there is growth and a country with a debt of $1 trillion has decided it wants to keep its ratio of debt-to-GDP constant:
    a. it should run a deficit.
    b. it should run a surplus.
    c. it should run a balanced budget.
    d. the deficit has no effect on debt.

13. Payroll taxes for Social Security:
    a. reduce the reported deficit and increase the reported surplus.
    b. increase the reported deficit and reduce the reported surplus.
    c. do not affect the budget since it is an off-budget item.
    d. are offset by future obligations in the budget.

14. The "real" problem of Social Security in 2020 could be solved by:
    a. locking up the Social Security Trust Fund to pay for Social Security benefits only.
    b. raising the eligibility age for Social Security so fewer people are collecting Social Security in 2020, raising taxes on workers, reducing Social Security benefits, or a combination of all three.
    c. allowing current workers to divert some of their payroll taxes into private savings accounts to be withdrawn at retirement.
    d. a rise in the value of the stock market that would raise the value of the Social Security Trust fund so that it remains solvent for longer.

● POTENTIAL ESSAY QUESTIONS

You may also see essay questions similar to the "Problems & Applications" and "A Brain Teaser" exercises.

1. What are three reasons why government debt is different from individual debt?

2. How can a growing economy reduce the concern over deficits and the debt?

━━━━ ANSWERS ━━━━

SHORT-ANSWER QUESTIONS

1. While there are differences of opinion, most economists are hesitant to attach too much importance to a deficit or a surplus. The reason is that the deficit or surplus depends on the accounting procedures used, and these can vary widely. Only with much more additional information will an economist attribute importance to a surplus or deficit. It is financial health—the ability to cover costs over the long term—of the economy that concerns most economists. (365)

2. Since the economy is below potential, the structural surplus is larger than the nominal surplus. (356-358)

3. To calculate the real deficit, you multiply inflation times the total debt (4% × $2 trillion), giving $80 billion; then subtract that from the nominal deficit of $100 billion. So in this example the real deficit equals $20 billion. The interest rate does not enter into the calculations. (358-359)

4. To calculate the nominal deficit, you multiply inflation times the total debt (5% × $1 trillion), giving $50 billion, and add that to the real deficit of $100 billion. So in this example the nominal deficit equals $150 billion. The interest rate does not enter into the calculation. (358-359)

5. It depends. In an expanding economy with no deficits, the ratio of debt to GDP will be falling; if the government wants to hold the debt-to-GDP constant it will need to run a continual deficit. If it wants to reduce that ratio, then it need not run a continual deficit. (363-364)

6. TANSTAAFL. I would check to see what accounting gimmick the politician was proposing and what the plan would do to the long-run financial health of the country. (356-359)

7. The Congressional Budget Office predicted in 2005 that the federal government budget will return to surplus in 2012. This projection, however, was based on the expiration of tax cuts implemented in 2001 and does not include

expenditures related to U.S. military activity in Iraq. It is highly unlikely that these tax cuts will be allowed to expire. Current deficits are likely to persist into the indefinite future. (365-366)

8. Ultimately, real expenditures must equal real output in each period. The trust fund provides a financial solution to the Social Security problem, but it does not directly see to it that real expenditures will equal real output in the future. (368-370)

━━━━ ANSWERS ━━━━

MATCHING

1-a; 2-c; 3-e; 4-i; 5-h; 6-g; 7-f; 8-k; 9-b; 10-j; 11-d.

━━━━ ANSWERS ━━━━

PROBLEMS AND APPLICATIONS

1. a. Deficit is $5,000 per year; Debt is $25,000. On page 731, deficit is defined as income less expenditures and on page 735 debt is defined as accumulated deficits minus accumulated surpluses. For each of the past 5 years, you have incurred an annual deficit of $5,000. Total debt is $5,000 times five years, or $25,000. (355, 359)

    b. Deficit is $15,000; Debt is $15,000. Page 732 tells you that what is included as expenses is ambiguous. If you count the purchase of the rights to the invention as a current expenditure, the deficit is $15,000. If you had no previous debt, debt is also $15,000. If, however, you count the purchase of the invention as an investment and include it in your capital budget, then your expenses are only $50,000 and your budget will be in balance. (356, 359)

    c. Surplus of $5,000. Using an opportunity cost approach, a person holding bonds should count the rise in the bonds' market value as revenue. Here, wage income is $20,000 per year, interest income is 10,000, and the bond's value has increased by $10,000. Total income is $40,000. Income of $40,000 less expenses of $35,000 per year yields a budget surplus of $5,000. Unless there was a previous debt, there is no debt. (356)

2. As discussed on pages 358-359, the real deficit is the nominal deficit adjusted for inflation's effect on the debt. The definition of real deficit states: Real deficit = Nominal deficit − (Inflation × Total debt).
    a. $0: $100 billion − .05 × $2 trillion. (358)
    b. $35 billion: $20 billion − (−.03) × $500. (358)
    c. Surplus of $200 billion: $100 billion − .10 × $3 trillion. (358)
    d. $3.4 billion: $5 billion − .08 × $20 billion. (358)

3. a. $343 billion: Debt service payment = nominal interest rate × nominal debt. The nominal interest rate when expected inflation is fully adjusted is the real interest rate plus inflation (5+2). Debt service payment = .07 × $4.9 trillion. (358-359)
    b. $543 billion deficit: The nominal deficit is revenues less government expenditures (including debt service), $1.3 trillion − ($1.5 trillion + $.343 trillion). (358-359)
    c. $445 billion deficit: The real deficit = Nominal deficit − (Inflation × Total debt) = $.543 trillion − (.02 × $4.9 trillion). (358-359)
    d. Since bondholders must be compensated for the loss in the value of their bonds, they demand a nominal interest rate of 9% (5 + 4). Debt service payment is now $441 billion (.09 × $4.9 trillion). The nominal deficit is higher at $641 billion. ($1.3 trillion − ($1.5 trillion + $.441 trillion)). The real deficit has not changed. It is still $445 billion (The real deficit = Nominal deficit − (Inflation × Total debt) = $.641 trillion − (.04 × $4.9 trillion)). (358-359)

4. a. If the economy were at potential, government would collect $160 million more in taxes, reducing the deficit by that amount. There would a structural deficit of $400 − $160 = $240 million. (356-357)
    b. The passive deficit is the deficit that occurs because the economy is below potential. The passive deficit is $800 million × 20 percent, or $160 million. (356-357)

━━━ **ANSWERS** ━━━

A BRAIN TEASER

1. If the deficit spending is used to increase the productivity of the nation, enabling the nation to experience much higher rates of economic growth, the income of the nation could expand faster than its debt. If this happens, the debt-to-GDP ratio gets smaller, the interest expense is less burdensome, and the debt will be easier to pay off. (364)

━━━ **ANSWERS** ━━━

MULTIPLE CHOICE

1. c   A country has a budget deficit if it does not collect sufficient revenue to cover expenditures during the year. See page 355.

2. c   The U.S. uses a cash flow accounting method, so changes affecting the future are not seen in the current budget. See page 366.

3. b   Real deficit = nominal deficit − (inflation × total debt). See page 358.

4. c   Real surplus = nominal surplus + (inflation × total debt). See page 359.

5. c   Real deficit = nominal deficit − (inflation × total debt). See page 358.

6. b   If creditors can forecast inflation perfectly, the interest rate will rise when inflation rises and the subsequent increase in interest payments will match the decline in the real debt due to higher inflation. See page 359.

7. c   Debt must be judged relative to assets and to total GDP. See page 360.

8.　c　See Figure 15-2 on page 363.

9.　a　The passive deficit or surplus is the deficit or surplus that exists because the economy is below or above potential. The structural deficit or surplus is the deficit or surplus that exists even when the economy is at potential. The text doesn't define primary or secondary deficits or surpluses. See page 357.

10.　a　The passive deficit is the deficit that exists because the economy is below potential. The government would collect $20 billion more in revenue if the economy were at potential, so the passive deficit is $20 billion. See page 357.

11.　b　Because government goes on forever it doesn't ever need to pay back its debt. Only about 75 percent of government debt is owed to other government agencies or to its own citizens. The other government debt is owed to foreign individuals. Government is better able to pay off debt when income rises. Both government and individuals pay interest on debt. See pages 362-363.

12.　a　Real growth will reduce the ratio of existing debt to GDP, so to hold the ratio constant a continual deficit is necessary. See page 364.

13.　a　While payroll taxes for Social Security represent future obligations by government to pay social security benefits, they are counted as current revenue today and reduce the reported deficit (increase the reported surplus). See page 367.

14.　b　The real problem is the mismatch between real demand and real supply of goods as the baby boomers retire and the demand for goods and services by retirees outstrips the supply produced by workers in 2020. Real solutions must address this problem and must either reduce benefits to seniors or reduce consumption by workers in 2020. The other solutions address the financial problem only. See pages 369-371.

━━━━━ ANSWERS ━━━━━

POTENTIAL ESSAY QUESTIONS

The following are annotated answers. They indicate the general idea behind the answer.

1.　First, the government's life is unlimited and therefore it never has to settle its accounts. Second, it can pay off debt by creating money (which is not recommended, however). Third, much of the government's debt is internally held and therefore, on average as a group, people are neither richer nor poorer because of the debt (even though it may redistribute income from lower-income individuals to upper-income individuals).

2.　When a society experiences real growth (growth adjusted for inflation), it becomes richer, and, being richer, it can handle more debt. Moreover, since in a growing economy a continual deficit is consistent with a constant ratio of debt to GDP, and since GDP serves as a measure of the government's ability to pay off debt, a country can run a continual deficit. Deficits should be viewed relative to GDP to determine their importance.

Pretest
Chapters 11-15

Take this test in test conditions, giving yourself a limited amount of time to complete the questions. Ideally, check with your professor to see how much time he or she allows for an average multiple choice question and multiply this by 30. This is the time limit you should set for yourself for this pretest. If you do not know how much time your teacher would allow, we suggest 1 minute per question, or about 30 minutes.

1. For every financial asset there is:
   a. corresponding financial liability.
   b. corresponding financial liability if the financial asset is financed.
   c. a real liability.
   d. a corresponding real asset.

2. Which of the following is not a function of money?
   a. Medium of exchange.
   b. Unit of account.
   c. Store of wealth.
   d. Equity instrument.

3. Which of the following is not included in the M_1 definition of money?
   a. Checking accounts.
   b. Currency.
   c. Traveler's checks.
   d. Savings accounts.

4. Assuming individuals hold no cash, the reserve requirement is 20 percent, and banks keep no excess reserves, an increase in an initial inflow of $100 into the banking system will cause an increase in the money supply of:
   a. $20.
   b. $50.
   c. $100.
   d. $500.

5. If banks hold excess reserves whereas before they did not, the money multiplier:
   a. will become larger.
   b. will become smaller.
   c. will be unaffected.
   d. might increase or might decrease.

6. Which of the following is the path through which contractionary monetary policy works?
   a. Money down implies interest up implies investment down implies income down.
   b. Money down implies interest down implies investment down implies income down.
   c. Money down implies interest up implies investment up implies income down.
   d. Money down implies interest down implies investment up implies income down.

7. Monetary policy is:
   a. a variation of fiscal policy.
   b. undertaken by the Treasury.
   c. undertaken by the Fed.
   d. the regulation of monetary institutions.

8. Assuming $c = .2$ and $r = .1$, the money multiplier would be:
   a. 1.
   b. 2.
   c. 3.
   d. 4.

9. The primary way the Fed conducts monetary policy is:
   a. open market operations.
   b. changing the discount rate.
   c. changing the reserve requirement.
   d. imposing credit controls.

10. If the Fed wants to increase the money supply, it should:
    a. buy bonds.
    b. sell bonds.
    c. pass a law that interest rates rise.
    d. pass a law that interest rates fall.

11. Assuming the Fed is following the Taylor Rule, if inflation is 3 percent, target inflation is 2 percent, and output is 1 percent above potential, what would you predict would be the Fed funds rate target?
    a. 4 percent
    b. 5 percent
    c. 5.5 percent
    d. 6 percent

12. If short-term and long-term interest rates are currently equal and the Fed contracts the money supply, the yield curve will most likely
    a. become downward sloping.
    b. become upward sloping.
    c. become vertical.
       be unaffected.

13. In an expected inflation, lenders will generally:
    a. gain relative to borrowers.
    b. lose relative to borrowers.
    c. neither gain nor lose relative to borrowers.
    d. The effect will be totally random.

14. If productivity growth is 2 percent and inflation is 5 percent, on average nominal wage increases will be:
    a. 2 percent.
    b. 3 percent.
    c. 5 percent.
    d. 7 percent.

15. Assuming velocity is relatively constant and real income is relatively stable, an increase in the money supply of 40 percent will be associated with an approximate change in the price level of:
    a. 4 percent.
    b. 40 percent.
    c. 80 percent.
    d. zero percent.

16. The inflation-tax is:
    a. a tax placed by government on inflators.
    b. a tax placed on inflators.
    c. a tax on the holders of cash.
    d. a tax on holders of goods whose price is inflating.

17. Individuals who hold an institutional theory of inflation argue:
    a. the equation of exchange is incorrect.
    b. the equation of exchange should be read from right to left.

c. the equation of exchange should be read from left to right.
d. both the quantity theory and the equation of exchange are incorrect.

18. The short-run Phillips curve shifts around because of changes in:
    a. the money supply.
    b. expectations of employment.
    c. expectations of inflation.
    d. expectations of real income.

19. If the economy is at Point A in the Phillips curve graph below, what prediction would you make for inflation?

    a. It will increase
    b. It will decrease.
    c. It will remain constant.
    d. It will immediately fall to zero.

20. Sound finance holds that:
    a. government spending is directed toward sound investments.
    b. the government budget should always be balanced except in wartime.
    c. the government budget should be judged by its effect on the economy.
    d. government should always borrow money in a sound fashion when it runs a deficit.

21. The Ricardian equivalence theorem holds that:
    a. government spending is equivalent to private spending.
    b. financing a deficit by bonds will have the same effect as financing it through taxes.
    c. imposing taxes is the equivalent to confiscation of property by government.
    d. all spending in the economy is equivalent.

22. Crowding out is caused by:
    a. government running a deficit and selling bonds to finance that deficit.
    b. government printing money.

c. government running a surplus and selling bonds and the people who buy those bonds selling their older bonds to the government.

d. the tendency for new workers to replace more expensive older workers.

23. Automatic stabilizers:
   a. are government programs to employ workers during recessions.
   b. create government budget surpluses during economic recessions.
   c. are designed to reduce the price level directly.
   d. counteract both recessions and expansions through changes in spending without government action.

24. New Classical economists differ from old Classical economists in that New Classicals:
   a. believe in the Ricardian equivalence theorem as a theoretical proposition.
   b. believe in the Ricardian equivalence theorem as a practical proposition.
   c. believe in functional finance.
   d. believe in sound finance.

25. The New Classical answer to the question, "What to do about a recession?" is to:
   a. impose trade tariffs.
   b. cut taxes and government spending.
   c. cut taxes only.
   d. cut government spending only.

26. A deficit is:
   a. the total amount of money that a country owes.
   b. the shortfall of payments under revenues in a particular time period.
   c. the shortfall of revenues under payments in a particular time period.
   d. accumulated debt.

27. If the nominal surplus is $200 billion, inflation is 10 percent, and total debt is $2 trillion:
   a. the real surplus is zero.
   b. the real deficit is $100 billion
   c. the real surplus is $400 billion.
   d. the real surplus is $2.2 trillion.

28. The portion of the budget deficit or surplus that would exist even if the economy were at its potential level of income is called the:
   a. structural deficit or surplus.
   b. passive deficit or surplus.
   c. primary deficit or surplus.
   d. secondary deficit or surplus.

29. One of the reasons government debt is different from individual debt is:
   a. government does not pay interest on its debt.
   b. government never really needs to pay back its debt.
   c. all government debt is owed to other government agencies or to its own citizens.
   d. the ability of a government to pay off is debt is unrelated to income.

30. The "real" problem of Social Security in 2020 could be solved by:
   a. locking up the Social Security Trust Fund to pay for Social Security benefits only.
   b. raising the eligibility age for Social Security so fewer people are collecting Social Security in 2020, raising taxes on workers, reducing Social Security benefits, or a combination of all three.
   c. allowing current workers to divert some of their payroll taxes into private savings accounts to be withdrawn at retirement.
   d. a rise in the value of the stock market that would raise the value of the Social Security Trust fund so that it remains solvent for longer.

ANSWERS

1.	a	(11:1)	16.	c	(13:9)
2.	d	(11:4)	17.	b	(13:11)
3.	d	(11:5)	18.	c	(13:15)
4.	d	(11:10)	19.	a	(13:18)
5.	b	(11:13)	20.	b	(14:2)
6.	a	(12:3)	21.	b	(14:3)
7.	c	(12:5)	22.	a	(14:6)
8.	d	(12:11)	23.	d	(14:7)
9.	a	(12:13)	24.	b	(14:9)
10.	a	(12:14)	25.	b	(14:11)
11.	d	(12:18)	26.	c	(15:1)
12.	a	(12:21)	27.	c	(15:4)
13.	c	(13:1)	28.	a	(15:9)
14.	d	(13:4)	29.	b	(15:11)
15.	b	(13:6)	30.	b	(15:14)

Key: The figures in parentheses refer to multiple choice question and chapter numbers. For example (1:2) is multiple choice question 2 from chapter 1.

INTERNATIONAL TRADE POLICY

16

● CHAPTER AT A GLANCE

This review is based upon the learning objectives that open the chapter.

1. The primary trading partners of the United States are Canada, Mexico, the European Union, and the Pacific Rim countries. (376-381)

    A trade balance is the difference between a country's exports and imports. When imports exceed exports, a country has a trade deficit. When exports exceed imports a country has a trade surplus. Because the United States has had large trade deficits since the 1970s, it is a net debtor nation.

    The nature of trade is continually changing. The United States is importing more and more high-tech goods and services from India and China and other East Asian countries.

    Outsourcing is a type of trade. Outsourcing is a larger phenomenon today compared to 30 years ago because countries where jobs are outsourced today—China and India—are much larger.

2. The principle of comparative advantage states that as long as the relative opportunity costs of producing goods differ among countries, there are potential gains from trade. (381-383)

    When countries specialize in the production of those goods for which each has a <u>comparative advantage</u> and then trade, all economies involved benefit.

    A country has a comparative advantage in producing good "x" if its opportunity cost of producing good "x" is lower.

3. Three determinants of the gains of trade are: (383-384)

● The more competition, the less the trader gets.
● Smaller countries get a larger proportion of the gain than larger countries.
● Countries producing goods with economies of scale get a larger gain from trade.

Also: countries which specialize and trade along the lines of comparative advantage are able to consume more than if they did not undertake trade (they are able to escape the confines of their own production possibility curves).

4. Three reasons for differences between economists' and laypeople's views of trade are: (1) gains from trade are often stealth gains, (2) comparative advantage is determined by more than wages, and (3) nations trade more than just manufactured goods. (384-386)

    The gains from trade in the form of low consumer prices tend to be widespread and not easily recognizable, while the costs in jobs lost tend to be concentrated and readily identifiable. But, the gains outweigh the costs over time. Convincing the public of this remains a challenge, especially for policymakers.

5. Transferable comparative advantages will tend to erode over time, inherent comparative advantages will not. (386-389)

    The U.S. has comparative advantages due to its skilled workforce, institutions, and infrastructure, among other things. Some of these are inherent comparative advantages, while others are transferable comparative advantages. The law of one price and the convergence hypothesis will work to erode any transferable comparative advantages over time. The degree to which, and how quickly, the United States loses some of its comparative advantages depends on how transferable they are.

6. Three policies used to restrict trade are: (389-393)
   - <u>tariffs</u>: taxes on internationally traded goods;
   - <u>quotas</u>: quantity limits placed on imports; and
   - <u>regulatory trade restrictions</u>: government-imposed procedural rules that limit imports.

   Countries can also restrict trade through: voluntary restraint agreements, embargoes, and nationalistic appeals.

   Arguments for restricting trade include:
   - *Unequal internal distribution of the gains from trade;*
   - *Haggling by companies over the gains from trade;*
   - *Haggling by countries over trade restrictions;*
   - *Specialized production; learning by doing; and economies of scale;*
   - *Macroeconomic aspects of trade;*
   - *National security;*
   - *International politics;*
   - *Increased revenue brought in by tariffs.*

   Understand these motives for trade barriers and be able to explain why they may be fallacious.

7. Economists generally oppose trade restrictions because: (398-400)
   - from a global perspective, free trade increases total output;
   - international trade provides competition for domestic companies;
   - restrictions based on national security are often abused or evaded; and
   - trade restrictions are addictive.

   Economists generally argue that the benefits of free trade outweigh the costs—especially over time.

   Trade restrictions limit the supply of an imported good, increasing its price and decreasing quantity. Governments prefer tariffs over quotas because they generate tax revenues, while companies prefer quotas.

8. Free trade associations help trade by reducing barriers to trade among member nations. Free trade associations could hinder trade by building up barriers to trade with nations outside the association. (400-402)

   A free trade association is a group of countries that allows free trade among its members and puts up common barriers against all other countries' goods.

   The WTO and GATT are important international economic organizations designed to reduce trade barriers among <u>all</u> countries.

● SHORT-ANSWER QUESTIONS

1. Who are the primary trading partners of the United States?

2. How has U.S. trade with the rest of the world changed in recent years?

3. What is the principle of comparative advantage?

4. What are three determinants of the gains of trade?

5. What are three reasons laypeople's and economists' views of trade differ?

6. What are four sources of comparative advantages for the United States?

7. Why is the United States losing some of its comparative advantages?

8. In a talk to first-year members of Congress you are asked what they can do to restrict trade. You oblige.

9. You reveal to these first-year members of Congress that you believe in free trade. Hands fly up from people just waiting to tell you why they want to restrict trade. What are some of their reasons?

10. After listening to their remarks, you gather your thoughts and offer them reasons why you generally oppose trade restrictions. What do you say?

11. The first-year members of Congress ask you how the nation joining a free trade association could help and hinder international trade. What do you say?

MATCHING THE TERMS
Match the terms to their definitions

___ 1. balance of trade

___ 2. comparative advantage

___ 3. economies of scale

___ 4. embargo

___ 5. free trade association

___ 6. General Agreement on Tariffs and Trade (GATT)

___ 7. infant industry argument

___ 8. inherent comparative advantage

___ 9. learning by doing

___ 10. most-favored nation

___ 11. quota

___ 12. regulatory trade restriction

___ 13. strategic bargaining

___ 14. strategic trade policy

___ 15. tariff

___ 16. trade adjustment assistance program

___ 17. transferable comparative advantage

___ 18. World Trade Organization

a. A tax governments place on internationally traded goods—generally imports.

b. All-out restriction on import or export of a good.

c. As long as the relative opportunity costs of producing goods differ among countries, there are potential gains from trade, even if one country has an absolute advantage in everything.

d. Costs per unit output go down as output increases.

e. Country that will pay as low a tariff on its exports as will any other country.

f. Demanding a larger share of the gains of trade than you might get normally.

g. Government-imposed procedural rule that limits imports.

h. Group of countries that allow free trade among its members and put up common barriers against all other countries' goods.

i. Periodic international conference held in the past to reduce trade barriers.

j. Program designed to compensate losers for reductions in trade restrictions.

k. Quantity limit placed on imports.

l. An organization whose functions are generally the same as were those of GATT—to promote free and fair trade among countries.

m. With initial protection, an industry will be able to become competitive.

n. You become better at a task the more you perform it.

o. The difference between the value of exports and the value of imports

p. Threatening to implement tariffs to bring about a reduction in tariffs or some other concessions from the other country.

q. Comparative advantage based on factors that are relatively unchangeable.

r. Comparative advantage based on factors that can change relatively easily.

● PROBLEMS AND APPLICATIONS

1. a. State whether there is a basis for trade in the following:

Case 1: In Country A the opportunity cost of producing one widget is two wadgets. In Country B the opportunity cost of producing two widgets is four wadgets.

Case 2: In Country C the opportunity cost of producing one widget is two wadgets. In Country D the opportunity cost of producing two widgets is one wadget.

Case 3: In Country E the opportunity cost of producing one widget is two wadgets. In Country F the opportunity cost of producing one widget is four wadgets.

b. On what general principle did you base your reasoning?

c. Assume that in Case 3 there are constant marginal returns and constant returns to scale. Country E is currently producing 10 widgets and 4 wadgets. Country F is currently producing 20 widgets and 20 wadgets. Can you make an offer involving trade that will make both countries better off?

d. How would your answer differ if each country experiences economies of scale?

2. Suppose Country A and Country B are potential trading partners. Each country produces two goods: fish and wine. If Country A devotes all of its resources to producing fish, it can produce 1,000 fish, and if it devotes all of its resources to producing wine, it can produce 2,000 bottles of wine. If Country B devotes all of its resources to producing fish, it can produce 3,000 fish, and if it devotes all of its resources to producing wine it can produce 3,000 bottles of wine. For simplicity, assume the production possibility curves of these countries are straight lines.

a. Draw the production possibility curve for Country A on the axes below. In Country A, what is the opportunity cost of one bottle of wine in terms of fish?

b. Draw the production possibility curve for Country B on the axes for (a). In Country B, what is the opportunity cost of one bottle of wine in terms of fish?

c. Does Country A have a comparative advantage in producing either wine or fish? Does Country B have a comparative advantage in producing either wine or fish?

d. Suppose Country A specialized in that good for which it has a comparative advantage and Country B specialized in that good for which it has a comparative advantage. Each country would then trade the good it produced for the good the other country produced. What would be a fair exchange of goods?

3. Suppose two countries A and B have the following production possibility tables:

% Resources devoted to Machines	Country A Production		Country B Production	
	Machines	Food	Machines	Food
A	100	200	0	40	0
B	80	160	8	32	40
C	60	120	16	28	80
D	40	80	24	24	120
E	20	40	32	16	160
F	0	0	40	0	200

a. Draw the production possibility curves for Country A and Country B on the axes below.

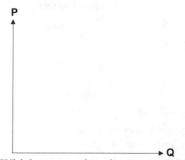

b. Which country has the comparative advantage in the production of food?

c. Suppose each country specializes in the production of one good. Explain how Country A can end up with 50 food units and 150 machines and Country B can end up with 150 food units and 50 machines. Both points are outside the production possibility curve for each country without trade.

4. State whether the trade restriction is a quota, tariff, or regulatory trade restriction.

a. The EU (European Union) requires beef to be free of growth-inducing hormones in order to be traded in EU markets.

b. Hong Kong has maintained rice import controls on quantity since 1955 in order to keep local rice importers in business and to secure a steady wartime food supply.

c. To encourage domestic production of automobile parts, Japan limits the importation of automobile parts according to a rigid schedule of numbers.

d. The United States charges French wineries 10% of the value of each case of French wine imported into the United States.

5. Suppose the U.S. is considering trade restrictions against EU-produced hams. Given the demand and supply curves drawn below, show a tariff and a quota that would result in the same exports of ham to the United States.

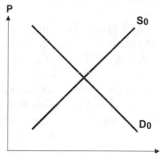

a. Would a tariff or a quota result in higher government revenue?

b. Which would the EU prefer?

c. Which would American ham producers prefer?

d. Which would American consumers prefer?

● A BRAIN TEASER

1. What are the benefits and the costs to a nation of lower trade barriers? Which are greater for the nation: the benefits or the costs of free trade?

● MULTIPLE CHOICE

Circle the one best answer for each of the following questions:

1. If a nation is a debtor nation it:
    a. is currently running a trade deficit.
    b. is currently running a trade surplus.
    c. has run trade deficits in the past.
    d. has run trade surpluses in the past.

2. If a country has a trade deficit, it is:
    a. consuming more than it is producing.
    b. lending to foreigners.
    c. buying financial assets.
    d. buying real assets.

3. Compared to the past, the United States is now:
    a. importing more high-tech goods and services from India and China and other East Asian countries.
    b. importing more goods and services that are lower down the technological ladder.
    c. outsourcing less to newly emerging industrialized countries like China and India.
    d. facing less competition from newly emerging industrialized countries like China and India.

4. Refer to the graph below. Given these production possibility curves, you would suggest that:

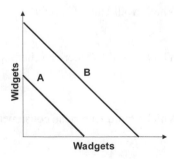

a. Country A should specialize in widgets and Country B in wadgets.
b. no trade should take place.
c. Country A should specialize in wadgets and Country B in widgets.
d. Both countries should produce an equal amount of each.

5. Refer to the graph below. The graph demonstrates Saudi Arabia's and the United States' production possibility curves for widgets and wadgets. Given these production possibility curves, you would suggest that:

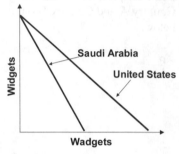

a. Saudi Arabia specialize in widgets and the United States in wadgets.
b. no trade should take place.
c. Saudi Arabia specialize in wadgets and the United States in widgets.
d. Both countries should produce an equal amount of each.

6. If a nation has a comparative advantage in the production of good X then:
    a. it can produce good X at the lowest opportunity cost.
    b. it will import good X.
    c. it can produce more of good X than any other nation.
    d. the opportunity cost of producing an additional unit of good X is greater than for any other nation.

7. A widget has an opportunity cost of 4 wadgets in Saudi Arabia and 2 wadgets in the United States. Given these opportunity costs, you would suggest that:
    a. Saudi Arabia specialize in widgets and the United States in wadgets.
    b. no trade should take place.
    c. Saudi Arabia specialize in wadgets and the United States in widgets.
    d. both countries should produce an equal amount of each.

8. Country A's cost of widgets is $4.00 and cost of wadgets is $8.00. Country B's cost of widgets is 8 euros and cost of wadgets is 16 euros. Which of the following would you suggest?
   a. Country A should specialize in widgets and Country B in wadgets.
   b. Trade of widgets for wadgets would not benefit the countries.
   c. Country A should specialize in wadgets and Country B in widgets.
   d. Both countries should produce an equal amount of each.

9. In considering the distribution of the gains from trade:
   a. smaller countries usually get a larger proportion of the gains from trade.
   b. larger countries usually get a larger proportion of the gains from trade.
   c. the gains are generally split equally between small and large countries.
   d. no statement can be made about the general nature of the split.

10. Which of the following statements correctly summarizes a difference between the layperson's and the economists' views of the net benefits of trade?
    a. Economists often argue that the gains from trade in the form of low consumer prices tend to be widespread and not easily recognizable while the costs in jobs lost tend to be concentrated and readily identifiable.
    b. Economists often argue that most U.S. jobs are at risk of outsourcing while laypeople intuitively recognize that inherent in comparative advantage is that each country has a comparative advantage in the production of some good.
    c. Economists focus on trade in manufactured goods while laypeople also focus on trade involving the services of people who manage the trade.
    d. Economists most often argue that the costs of trade outweigh the benefits while laypeople often argue that the benefits of trade outweigh the costs.

11. Transferable comparative advantages are:
    a. based on factors that are relatively unchangeable.
    b. based on factors that can change relatively easily.
    c. becoming more like inherent comparative advantages with technological innovations.
    d. rarely eroded over time.

12. Trade restrictions tend to:
    a. increase competition.
    b. increase prices to consumers.
    c. benefit consumers.
    d. have economic benefits that outweigh the economic costs.

13. A tariff is a:
    a. tax government places on internationally-traded goods.
    b. quantity limit placed on imports.
    c. total restriction on imports.
    d. government-imposed procedural rule that limits imports.

14. An embargo is a:
    a. tax government places on imports.
    b. quantity limit placed on imports.
    c. total restriction on imports.
    d. government-imposed procedural rule that limits imports.

15. For governments:
    a. tariffs are preferred over quotas because tariffs can help them collect revenues.
    b. quotas are preferred over tariffs because quotas can help them collect revenues.
    c. neither quotas nor tariffs can help collect revenues.
    d. both quotas and tariffs are sources of revenues.

16. Reasons for restricting trade include all of the following *except:*
    a. the existence of learning by doing and economies of scale.
    b. national security reasons.
    c. the increased revenue brought in from tariffs.
    d. the fact that trade decreases competitive pressures at home.

17. Economists generally oppose trade restrictions for all of the following reasons *except:*
    a. from a global perspective, free trade increases total output.
    b. the infant industry argument.
    c. trade restrictions lead to retaliation.
    d. international politics.

18. Free trade associations tend to:
    a. reduce restrictions on trade and thereby always expand free trade.
    b. lower trade barriers for all countries.
    c. replace multinational negotiations, and thereby always hurt free trade.
    d. expand, but also reduce, free trade.

● POTENTIAL ESSAY QUESTIONS

You may also see essay questions similar to the "Problems & Applications" and "A Brain Teaser" exercises.

1. What is the difference between a tariff and a quota? Why do governments prefer tariffs while foreign producers prefer quotas? What is the result of tariffs and quotas on the price and equilibrium quantity of the imported good?

2. What are six ways in which a country may restrict trade? Why do most economists support free trade and oppose trade restrictions?

ANSWERS

SHORT-ANSWER QUESTIONS

1. The primary trading partners of the United States are Canada, Mexico, the European Union, and Pacific Rim countries. (377-379)

2. The kinds of goods and services the U.S. imports has shifted from primarily basic manufacturing goods and raw commodities to high-tech manufacturing goods and services from developing countries such as India, China, and other East Asian countries. In addition, more and more production of more sophisticated goods and services is being outsourced to these countries because their economies are much larger. (377-379)

3. The principle of comparative advantage is that as long as the relative opportunity costs of production differ among countries, there are potential gains from trade, even if one country has an absolute advantage in everything. (381)

4. Three determinants of the gains of trade are (1) the more competition, the less the trader gets and the more will go to the countries who are trading; (2) smaller countries get a larger proportion of the gain than larger countries; and (3) countries producing goods with economies of scale get a larger gain from trade. (383-384)

5. Three reasons for differences between economists' and laypeople's views of trade are: (1) gains from trade are often stealth gains, (2) comparative advantage is determined by more than wages, and (3) nations trade more than just manufactured goods. (384-386)

6. The United States has comparative advantages due to: (1) skills of the U.S. labor force, (2) U.S. governmental institutions, (3) U.S. physical and technological infrastructure, (4) English is the international language of business, (5) wealth from past production, (6) U.S. natural resources, (7) cachet, (8) inertia, (9) U.S. intellectual property rights, and (10) a relatively open immigration policy. (386-387)

7. The United States is losing some of its transferable comparative advantages (as opposed to inherent comparative advantages) because economic forces push to spread technologies, which eliminates transferable comparative advantages. These economic forces include lower wages, a growing entrepreneurial spirit, institutions conducive to production in developing countries and exchange rate adjustments. (388-389)

8. Three policies countries use to restrict trade are (1) tariffs, (2) quotas, and (3) regulatory trade restrictions. There are others. (389-393)

9. Their answers might include: (1) although foreign competition might make society better off, some people may lose their jobs because of foreign competition (unequal internal distribution of the gains from trade); (2) some foreign companies are taking tough bargaining positions, and restricting trade is our only weapon against that (haggling by companies over trade restrictions); (3) some foreign countries are threatening us with trade restrictions (haggling by countries over the gains from trade); (4) trade restrictions will protect new U.S. industries until they learn to be competitive (learning by doing and economies of scale); (5) imports hurt U.S. domestic income in the short run, and the economy needs to grow in the short run (trade can reduce domestic output in the short run); (6) some restrictions are needed to protect our national security; (7) we do not want to trade with countries who violate our human rights standards or whose ideology conflicts with our democratic ideals (international politics may dominate trade considerations); and (8) tariffs bring in revenue for the U.S. government. (393-398)

10. I would say that I generally oppose trade restrictions because (1) from a global perspective, free trade increases total output, (2) international trade provides competition for domestic companies, (3) restrictions based on national security are often abused, and (4) trade restrictions are addictive. (398-400)

11. Free trade associations promote trade among members by reducing barriers to trade among the member nations. However, free trade associations could hinder trade by building up barriers to trade with nations outside the association. (400-402)

■ ANSWERS ■

MATCHING

1-o; 2-c; 3-d; 4-b; 5-h; 6-i; 7-m; 8-q; 9-n; 10-e; 11-k; 12-g; 13-f; 14-p; 15-a; 16-j; 17-r; 18-l.

■ ANSWERS ■

PROBLEMS AND APPLICATIONS

1. a. There is a basis for trade in Cases 2 and 3 because opportunity costs differ. (381-383)

   b. The general principle is that there are gains from trade to be made when each country has a comparative advantage in a different good. (381-383)

   c. I would have country E specialize in widgets and country F specialize in wadgets. Since country E is currently producing 10 widgets and 4 wadgets, I would have it produce 12 widgets and no wadgets, promising that I will give it 5 wadgets for the extra two widgets it produced. I would have Country F produce 28 wadgets and 18 widgets, promising that I will give it 2 widgets in return for 7 of its wadgets. After I made this trade both countries are one wadget better off. I am two wadgets better off. (These two wadgets are the return to me for organizing the trade.) (381-383)

   d. If there were economies of scale, there would be an even stronger argument for trade. (381-383)

2. a. The production possibility curve for Country A is the curve labeled A in the graph below. In Country A the opportunity cost of one bottle of wine is 1/2 fish. Each fish forgone frees up resources sufficient to make two bottles of wine. (381-383)

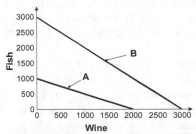

   b. The production possibility curve for Country B is the curve labeled B in the graph above. In Country B the opportu-

nity cost of one bottle of wine is one fish. Each fish forgone frees up resources sufficient to make one bottle of wine. (381-383)

   c. Country A has a comparative advantage in wine because it has to give up only 1/2 a fish for each bottle of wine while Country B has to give up 1 fish for each bottle of wine. Country B must necessarily have a comparative advantage in fish. (381-383)

   d. A fair exchange for B would be giving up one fish for one bottle of wine or better because that is its opportunity cost of producing one fish. A fair exchange for A would be giving up two bottles of wine for 1 fish or better since its opportunity cost of producing two bottles of wine is one fish. Any exchange between these two, such as 2 fish for 3 bottles of wine, would be a fair exchange. (381-383)

3. a. The production possibility curves for Country A and Country B are drawn below. (382)

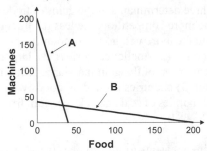

   b. Country B has the comparative advantage in the production of food since it has to give up only 1/5 machine to produce one unit of food while Country A has to give up 5 machines to produce one unit of food. (381-383)

   c. Country A would be willing to supply 5 machines for 1 unit of food. Country A would be willing to supply 5 units of foods for one machine. Let's suppose they trade 1 for 1. Country A would produce 200 machines, selling 50 to Country B for 50 units of foods. Country B would produce 200 food units, and sell 50 to Country A for 50 machines. This way they each reach their higher desired level of consumption. (381-383)

4. a. Regulatory trade restriction because this is a regulation that has the final effect of reducing imports without a tax or numerical limitation. (390-393)

b. Quota. It is a numerical restriction on the amount of rice entering the country. (390-393)

c. Quota because it is a numerical restriction on imports. (390-393)

d. Tariff because it is a tax on imports. (390-393)

5. A tariff would shift the supply curve up by the amount of the tariff. A quota with the same result would be at Q_1. Equilibrium quantity would fall from Q_0 to Q_1. Equilibrium price would rise from P_0 to P_1. This is shown on the graph below. (390-392 and Figure 16-5)

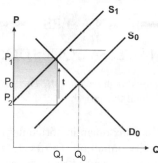

a. The government receives no revenue from the quota, but receives the shaded region as revenue from the tariff as shown on the graph above. (390-392 and Figure 16-5)

b. The EU would prefer the quota since it will receive a higher price, P_1, for the same quantity of goods, Q_1 as it would with a tariff. With a tariff it would receive P_2, for Q_1. (390-392 and Figure 16-5)

c. American ham producers prefer the quota because any increase in domestic demand would be met by domestic supply. (390-392)

d. American consumers do not prefer either since the resulting price and quantity is the same with both. If, however, the tariff revenue were to lead to lower taxes or higher government services, they might prefer the tariff over the quota. They also might prefer the tariff to the quota because any increase in domestic demand will be partially met with imports, keeping domestic producers more efficient than under a quota system. (390-392)

ANSWERS

A BRAIN TEASER

1. The benefits of lower trade barriers are a wider variety of higher quality, lower-priced products made available to consumers. This translates into an increase in the average absolute standard of living for the nation. The costs of lower trade barriers to a nation are the loss of jobs in those industries that find it difficult to compete in the global economy. The economic benefits of free trade outweigh the costs, at least over time. This is why economists generally favor free trade. (398-400)

ANSWERS

MULTIPLE CHOICE

1. c A debtor nation may currently be running a surplus or a deficit. Debt is accumulated deficits. A debtor nation could be running a surplus if it ran deficits in the past. See pages 380-381.

2. a If a country has a trade deficit, it is importing (consuming) more than it is exporting (producing). See pages 380-381.

3. a The U.S. is importing more and more high-tech goods and services that are higher up the technological ladder from India and China and other East Asian countries. The U.S. is outsourcing more to these newly emerging industrialized countries and is therefore facing more competition from these nations. See pages 377-379.

4. b Since the curves have the same slope, no country has a comparative advantage in either good and there is no basis for trade. See pages 381-383 and Figure 16-3.

5. a The opportunity cost for Saudi Arabia of wadgets in terms of widgets is higher than the opportunity cost for the United States. So Saudi Arabia should specialize in widgets and the United States in wadgets. See pages 381-383 and Figure 16-3.

6. a A comparative advantage in the production of X means the nation can produce that good with a lower opportunity cost. Because the nation is relatively more efficient at producing X, it will specialize in its production and export that good. Answer c may be true, but it is also possible to have a comparative advantage in X without being able to produce more of X than any other nation. See pages 381-383.

7. c   The opportunity cost for the United States of wadgets in terms of widgets is higher than the opportunity cost for Saudi Arabia. So the United States should specialize in widgets and Saudi Arabia in wadgets. See pages 381-383.

8. b   The opportunity cost of widgets and wadgets is equal in both countries so neither country has a comparative advantage in either good and there is no basis for trade. See pages 381-383.

9. a   Smaller countries usually find that their production possibilities are changed more, and hence they benefit more. See pages 383-384.

10. a   It is because the costs of trade are more visible than the benefits that many laypeople oppose free trade. Switching "economists" and "laypeople" would make options b through d correct. See pages 384-386.

11. b   Transferable comparative advantages are based on factors that can change relatively easily and will tend to erode over time. Technological innovations are turning inherent comparative advantages into transferable comparative advantages. See page 387.

12. b   Trade restrictions reduce competition and therefore increase prices to consumers. Thus, consumers are hurt. The benefits of trade restrictions go to the domestic producers that do not have to compete as aggressively. The economic costs of trade restrictions (in the form of higher prices consumers must pay) far outweigh their benefits (which go to the protected domestic industries in the form of higher profits and more secure jobs). See pages 389-393.

13. a   A tariff is a tax placed on imported goods. See page 390.

14. c   An embargo is an all-out restriction on the trade of goods with another country. See page 392.

15. a   Governments prefer tariffs because they generate revenues, quotas do not. See pages 390-392.

16. d   Trade increases competitive pressures at home and increases competitiveness. See pages 393-398.

17. b   The infant industry argument is an argument in favor of trade restrictions. Economists' response to the infant industry argument is that history shows that few infant industries have ever grown up. See pages 398-400.

18. d   While free trade associations may work toward lowering trade barriers among member nations, they may result in higher trade barriers for nonmember countries. See pages 400-402.

━━━━ **ANSWERS** ━━━━

POTENTIAL ESSAY QUESTIONS

The following are annotated answers. They indicate the general idea behind the answer.

1.   A tariff is a tax on an imported item. A quota is a quantity limitation. Tariffs are preferred by governments because they raise revenues and are disliked by foreign producers because they require tax payments to the imposing government. However, notice that both tariffs and quotas raise prices and decrease the quantity of imported goods bought and sold.

2.   Countries use a variety of policies to restrict trade. These include:
● Tariffs.
● Quotas.
● Voluntary restraint agreements.
● Embargoes.
● Regulatory trade restrictions.
● Nationalistic appeals.
   Economists generally oppose trade restrictions because: (1) from a global perspective, free trade increases total output—it raises standards of living; (2) international trade provides competition for domestic companies; (3) restrictions based on national security are often abused or evaded, and (4) trade restrictions often become addictive for domestic firms that benefit. Free trade forces domestic firms to be efficient—to provide higher quality goods at cheaper prices. Economists argue that trade restrictions may create some short-run benefits, but the costs (or harm done, which includes higher prices domestic consumers must pay) outweigh the benefits over time.

INTERNATIONAL FINANCIAL POLICY

● CHAPTER AT A GLANCE

This review is based upon the learning objectives that open the chapter.

1a. The balance of payments is a country's record of all transactions between its residents and the residents of all foreign countries. (408-410)

It is broken down into the current account and financial and capital account.

Remember: If it is a minus (plus) sign, money is going out (coming in). Moreover, if foreigners are buying our goods, services, or assets, that represents a demand for the dollar (an inflow) in international exchange rate markets. If we buy foreign goods, services, or assets, that represents a supply of dollars (an outflow).

1b. The balance of trade is the difference between the value of goods and services a nation exports and the value of goods and services it imports. (410)

The balance of trade is often discussed in the popular press as a summary of how the U.S. is doing in international markets. However, it only includes goods exported and imported— not services. Trade in services is just as important as trade in merchandise, so economists pay more attention to the combined balance on goods and services.

1c. Since the balance of payments consists of both the financial and capital account and the current account, if the financial and capital account is in surplus and the current account is in deficit, there can still be a balance of payments surplus. (410-412)

The financial and capital account measures the flows of payments between countries for assets such as stocks, bonds, and real estate. The current (or trade) account measures the flows of payments for goods and services.

1d. A deficit in the balance of payments means that the private quantity supplied of a currency exceeds the private quantity demanded. A surplus in the balance of payments means the opposite. (412-414)

Whenever the exchange rate is above equilibrium (below equilibrium), the country will experience a balance of payments deficit (surplus).

2. Four important fundamental determinants of exchange rates are prices, interest rates, income, and trade policy. (414-415)

A decrease in the value of a currency can be caused by:

- *An increase in the nation's inflation rate.*
- *A decrease in the nation's interest rates.*
- *An increase in the nation's income.*
- *A decrease in the nation's import restrictions.*

3a. Monetary policy affects exchange rates through the interest rate path, the income path, and the price-level path, as shown in the diagram on page 761. (415-418)

Expansionary monetary policy (increasing the money supply) lowers exchange rates. It decreases the relative price of a country's currency. Contractionary monetary policy has the opposite effect.

3b. Fiscal policy affects exchange rates through the interest rate path, the income path, and the price-level path, as shown in the diagram on page 763. (418-419)

The net effect of fiscal policy on exchange rates is ambiguous.

✔ *Be able to explain why!*

4. A country fixes the exchange rate by standing ready to buy and sell its currency any time at the fixed exchange rate. (420-422)

It is easier for a country to maintain a fixed exchange rate below equilibrium. All it has to do is print and sell enough domestic currency to hold the value down.

However, if a country wants to maintain a fixed exchange rate above long-run equilibrium, it can do so only as long as it has the foreign currency (official) reserves to buy up its currency. Once it runs out of official reserves, it will be unable to intervene, and must either borrow, use indirect methods (domestic fiscal and monetary policies), ask other countries to buy its currency (to sell their currency), or devalue its currency.

In reality, because a country has a limited amount of official reserves, it only uses strategic currency stabilization (not a fixed exchange rate policy).

5a. Purchasing power parity is a method of calculating exchange rates so that various currencies will each buy an equal basket of goods and services. (422-423)

The PPP (Purchasing Power Parity) is one method of estimating long-run exchange rates.

5b. A real exchange rate is an exchange rate adjusted for differential inflation in countries. (423-424)

%Δ real exchange rate = %Δ nominal exchange rate + (domestic inflation − foreign inflation).

6a. Three exchange rate régimes are:
- *Fixed exchange rate*: The government chooses an exchange rate and offers to buy and sell currencies at that rate.
- *Flexible exchange rate*: Determination of exchange rates is left totally up to the market.
- *Partially flexible exchange rate*: The government sometimes affects the exchange rate and sometimes leaves it to the market. (424-427)

Which is best is debatable.

6b. Fixed exchange rates provide international monetary stability and force governments to make adjustments to meet their international problems. (This is *also* a disadvantage.) If they become unfixed, they create monetary instability. (424-425)

✔ *Know these advantages and disadvantages!*

6c. Flexible exchange rate régimes provide for orderly incremental adjustment of exchange rates rather than large sudden jumps, and allow governments to be flexible in conducting domestic monetary and fiscal policy. (This is *also* a disadvantage.) They are, however, susceptible to private speculation. (425-426)

✔ *Know these advantages and disadvantages!*

6d. Partially flexible exchange rate régimes combine the advantages and disadvantages of fixed and flexible exchange rates. (426)

Most countries have opted for this policy. However, if the market exchange rate is below the rate the government desires, and the government does not have sufficient official reserves (to buy and increase the demand for its currency), then it must undertake policies that will either increase the private demand for its currency or decrease the private supply. Doing so either involves using traditional macro policy—fiscal and monetary policy—to influence the economy, or using trade policy to affect the level of exports and imports.

7. The advantages of a common currency:
- creates strong political ties
- reduces the cost of trade
- facilitates price comparisons
- creates a larger single market.

The disadvantages of a common currency:
- eliminates independent monetary policy.
- loss of a national currency. (427-429)

✔ *Know the advantages and disadvantages of a common currency.*

The most important disadvantage is loss of independent monetary policy. A country loses the ability to increase the money supply by itself in order to fight a recession.

See also, Appendix A: "History of Exchange Rate Systems."

● SHORT-ANSWER QUESTIONS

1. Distinguish between the balance of payments and the balance of trade.

2. How can a country simultaneously have a balance of payments deficit and a balance of trade surplus?

3. How does each part of the balance of payments relate to the supply and demand for currencies?

4. What are the four fundamental determinants of exchange rates?

5. If a country runs expansionary monetary policy, what will likely happen to the exchange rate?

6. If a country runs expansionary fiscal policy, what will likely happen to the exchange rate?

7. If the demand and supply for a country's currency depends upon demand for imports and exports, and demand for foreign and domestic assets, how can a country fix its exchange rate?

8. How do market exchange rates differ from exchange rates using the purchasing power parity concept?

9. How do inflation rate differentials affect the real exchange rate?

10. Differentiate among fixed, flexible, and partially flexible exchange rates.

12. You are advising Great Britain about whether it should join the European Monetary Union. What arguments can you give in support of joining? What arguments can you give against joining?

11. Which are preferable, fixed or flexible exchange rates?

MATCHING THE TERMS
Match the terms to their definitions

___ **1.** balance of merchandise trade

___ **2.** balance of payments

___ **3.** balance of trade

___ **4.** currency stabilization

___ **5.** currency support

___ **6.** current account

___ **7.** financial and capital account

___ **8.** fixed exchange rate

___ **9.** flexible exchange rate

___ **10.** forex market

___ **11.** official reserves

___ **12.** partially flexible exchange rate

___ **13.** purchasing power parity

___ **14.** real exchange rate

a. A method of calculating exchange rates that attempts to value currencies at a rate such that each will buy an equal basket of goods.

b. A country's record of all transactions between its residents and the residents of all foreign countries.

c. A regime in which government sometimes affects the exchange rate and sometimes leaves it to the market.

d. A regime in which a government chooses an exchange rate and offers to buy and sell currencies at that rate.

e. A regime in which the determination of the value of a currency is left up to the market.

f. The buying of a currency by a government to maintain its value above its long-run equilibrium.

g. The difference between the value of goods and services a nation exports and the value of goods and services it imports.

h. Government holdings of foreign currencies.

i. The part of the balance of payments account that lists all long-term flows of payments.

j. The part of the balance of payments account that lists all short-term flows of payments.

k. The difference between the value of the goods exported and the value of the goods imported.

l. Foreign exchange market.

m. Buying and selling of a currency by the government to offset temporary fluctuations.

n. Exchange rate adjusted for inflation differentials.

PROBLEMS AND APPLICATIONS

1. State for each whether the transaction shows up on the balance of payments current account, the balance of payments financial and capital account, or neither.

    a. An American buys 100 shares of stock of Mercedes Benz, a German company.

    b. A Japanese businessperson buys Ameritec, an American bank.

    c. An American auto manufacturer buys $20 million in auto parts from a Japanese company.

    d. An American buys 100 shares of IBM stock.

    e. Saturn exports 10,000 cars to Germany.

    f. Toyota Motor Corporation, a Japanese firm, makes a $1 million profit from its plant in Kentucky, USA.

2. For each of the following, state who is demanding and who is supplying what currency:

    a. A French person buys a set of china from a U.S. firm.

    b. A U.S. tourist in Japan buys a Japanese kimono from a department store.

    c. An Italian exchange rate trader believes that the exchange rate value of the dollar will rise.

    d. A Swiss investor invests in Germany.

3. Draw supply and demand curves for British pounds, showing equilibrium quantity and price. Price is shown by price of pounds in dollars.

    a. What is the demand for dollars in this case?

    b. Explain a movement up along the supply curve.

    c. Explain a movement down along the demand curve.

    d. What would be the effect on the price of pounds if there were an increase in demand for pounds by Americans? Show this graphically.

    e. What would be the effect on the price of pounds if there were an increase in demand for dollars by the British? Show this graphically.

4. For each of the following, show graphically what would happen to the market for British pounds. Assume there are only two countries, the United States and Britain.

    a. Income in Britain rises.

b. Income in the United States rises.

c. The prices of goods in the United States increase.

d. Interest rates rise in Britain.

e. The value of the pound is expected to fall.

5. State what will happen to the real exchange rate of the dollar in the following instances:

    a. U.S. inflation is 2 percent, Japan's inflation is 5 percent, the U.S. dollar rises 3 percent.

    b. U.S. inflation is 4 percent, Japan's inflation is 1 percent, the U.S. dollar rises 2 percent.

    c. U.S. deflation is 1 percent, Japan's inflation is 1 percent, the U.S. dollar falls 4 percent.

    d. U.S. inflation is 5 percent, Japan's inflation is 2 percent, the U.S. dollar falls 1 percent.

● A BRAIN TEASER

1. What could cause the United States to temporarily experience an increase in its balance of payments deficit even though there is downward movement in the exchange rate value of the dollar? (Hint: Think in terms of demand and supply analysis.)

● MULTIPLE CHOICE

Circle the one best answer for each of the following questions:

1. An exchange rate is the:
   a. rate the Fed charges commercial banks for loans.
   b. rate the Fed charges individuals for loans.
   c. rate at which one country's currency can be exchanged for another country's currency.
   d. speed at which exchange occurs.

2. If a country has perfectly flexible exchange rates and is running a current account deficit, it is running:
   a. a financial and capital account surplus.
   b. a financial and capital account deficit.
   c. a government financial account surplus.
   d. a government financial account deficit.

3. In the balance of payments accounts, net investment income shows up in:
   a. the current account.
   b. the financial and capital account.
   c. the government financial account.
   d. Net investment income is not an entry in the balance of payments.

4. If the government financial account is significantly in surplus, the country is likely:
   a. trying to hold up its exchange rate.
   b. trying to push down its exchange rate.
   c. trying to have no effect on its exchange rate.
   d. sometimes trying to increase and sometimes trying to decrease its exchange rate.

5. In recent years, the United States has:
   a. generally run a balance of trade surplus.
   b. generally run a balance of trade deficit.
   c. sometimes run a balance of trade surplus and sometimes run a balance of trade deficit.
   d. generally run a balance of trade equality.

6. In recent years, the United States has:
   a. generally run a financial and capital account surplus.
   b. generally run a financial and capital account deficit.
   c. sometimes run a financial and capital account surplus and sometimes run a financial and capital account deficit.
   d. generally run a financial and capital account equality.

7. If there is a black market for a currency, the country probably has a:
    a. nonconvertible currency.
    b. fixed exchange rate currency.
    c. flexible exchange rate currency.
    d. partially flexible exchange rate currency.

8. Assuming flexible exchange rates, if the European demand for U.S. imports increases, one would expect the price of euros in terms of dollars to:
    a. rise.
    b. fall.
    c. remain unchanged.
    d. sometimes rise and sometimes fall.

9. Assuming flexible exchange rates, if the U.S. demand for European imports increases, one would expect the price of euros in terms of dollars to:
    a. rise.
    b. fall.
    c. remain unchanged.
    d. sometimes rise and sometimes fall.

    Use the following graph to answer Questions 10 – 12:

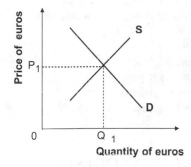

10. If U.S. income increases the:
    a. supply curve will shift out to the right.
    b. supply curve will shift in to the left.
    c. demand curve will shift out to the right.
    d. demand curve will shift in to the left.

11. If European interest rates increase relative to world interest rates:
    a. only the supply curve will shift out to the right.
    b. only the demand curve will shift in to the left.
    c. the supply curve will shift in to the left and the demand curve will shift out to the right.
    d. the supply curve will shift out to the right and the demand curve will shift in to the left.

12. If European inflation increases relative to world inflation:
    a. only the supply curve will shift out to the right.
    b. only the demand curve will shift in to the left.
    c. the supply curve will shift in to the left and the demand curve will shift out to the right.
    d. the supply curve will shift out to the right and the demand curve will shift in to the left.

13. If a country with flexible exchange rates runs expansionary monetary policy, in the short run one would expect the value of its exchange rate to:
    a. rise.
    b. fall.
    c. be unaffected.
    d. sometimes rise and sometimes fall.

14. Expansionary monetary policy has a tendency to:
    a. push interest rates up and exchange rates down.
    b. push interest rates down and exchange rates down.
    c. push income down and exchange rates down.
    d. push imports down and exchange rates down.

15. Contractionary monetary policy has a tendency to:
    a. push interest rates up and exchange rates down.
    b. push interest rates down and exchange rates down.
    c. push income down and imports down.
    d. push imports down and exchange rates down.

16. Refer to the graph below. If the U.S. government wants to fix its convertible currency at exchange rate P_1, it will have to:

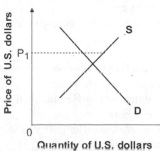

a. supply official reserves in exchange for dollars.

b. supply dollars in exchange for official reserves.

c. disallow currency conversion except at the official rate P_1.

d. supply both official reserves and dollars because excess supply of dollars is so large.

17. Say the Bangladeshi taka is valued at 42 taka to $1. Also say that you can buy the same basket of goods for 10 taka that you can buy for $1. In terms of dollars the purchasing power parity of the taka is:

a. overvalued.

b. undervalued.

c. not distorted.

d. nonconvertible.

18. Suppose inflation in the United States is 3 percent and inflation in Europe is 4 percent. If the U.S. dollar exchange rate falls by 5 percent relative to the euro, the real exchange rate of the dollar relative to the euro has:

a. risen 2 percent.

b. risen 6 percent.

c. fallen 2 percent.

d. fallen 6 percent.

19. If a country has fixed exchange rates:

a. the government need not worry about the exchange rate.

b. governments are committed to buying and selling currencies at a fixed rate.

c. the exchange rate is set by law.

d. the exchange rate has a fixed component and a flexible component.

20. If a country has a flexible exchange rate, the exchange rate:

a. is determined by flexible government policy.

b. is determined by market forces.

c. fluctuates continually, changing by at least 1 percent per year.

d. fluctuates continually, changing by at least 10 percent per year.

21. Compared to a fixed exchange rate system, a flexible exchange rate system:

a. allows countries more flexibility in their monetary policies.

b. allows countries less flexibility in their monetary policies.

c. has no effect on monetary policies.

d. allows countries more flexibility in their industrial policies.

22. A reason why a country might choose to join a currency union is:

a. so that its central bank can monetize the country's debt.

b. to broaden the marketplace by reducing costs of trade.

c. to reduce the demand for the common currency as a reserve currency.

d. to increase its sense of nationalism.

A1. The gold standard is a type of:

a. fixed exchange rate.

b. partially flexible exchange rate.

c. flexible exchange rate.

d. nonconvertible exchange rate.

A2. The gold specie flow mechanism works primarily by flows of:

a. money from one country to another.

b. services from one country to another.

c. merchandise from one country to another.

d. exchange rates from one country to another.

A3. Under the gold standard, if a country has a balance of payments deficit:

a. gold would flow out of the country.

b. gold would flow into the country.

c. the country's exchange rate would rise.

d. the country's exchange rate would fall.

A4. SDRs refers to:

a. Specie Draft Rights.

b. Specie Drawing Rights.

c. Special Drawing Rights.

d. Special Draft Rights.

● POTENTIAL ESSAY QUESTIONS

You may also see essay questions similar to the "Problems & Applications" and "A Brain Teaser" exercises.

1. How are a government's exchange rate policy and the government financial account in the balance of payments related? Is it easier for a government to push the value of its currency up or down? Why?

2. Explain how fixed, flexible (or floating), and partially flexible exchange rates are determined. What are the advantages and the disadvantages of each? Why do most nations have a partially flexible exchange rate policy?

ANSWERS

SHORT-ANSWER QUESTIONS

1. The balance of payments is a country's record of all transactions between its residents and the residents of all foreign nations. It is divided into the current account and the financial and capital account. The balance of trade is one part of the balance of payments—specifically that part dealing with goods. It is not all that satisfactory a measure of the country's position in international markets since it does not include services. Generally, economists pay more attention to the combined balance on goods and services account. (408-410)

2. As discussed in question 1, the balance of trade is one part of the balance of payments. Thus, if other parts of the international payments—for example, the financial and capital account—are in deficit, the balance of trade could still be in surplus. (411-412)

3. The balance of payments records the flow of a currency in and out of a country (1) in order to buy and sell goods and services in the current account, (2) in order to buy and sell assets along with payments resulting from previous purchases of assets in the financial and capital account, and (3) in order to affect the value of a country's currency in government transactions account. To buy foreign goods and assets one must supply domestic currency and demand foreign currency. Therefore, the balance of payments records the demand and supply of a country's currency during a given period of time. (412-414)

4. Four fundamental determinants of the value of a country's exchange rate are (1) domestic income, (2) domestic price level, (3) domestic interest rates, and (4) trade restrictions. (414-415)

5. Expansionary monetary policy tends to push income and prices up and interest rates down. All these phenomena tend to push the exchange rate down. (415-418)

6. Expansionary fiscal policy tends to push income, prices, and interest rates up. Higher income and higher prices increase imports and put downward pressure on exchange rates.

Higher interest rates push exchange rates in the opposite direction, so the net effect of expansionary fiscal policy on exchange rates is unclear. (418-419)

7. The current account and financial and capital account reflect private demand and supply of a country's currency. If the domestic government financial account were zero, then the currency's value is market-determined. If a country wants to fix the value of its currency to maintain its value at the fixed value, the government must buy and sell its currency using official reserves. Buying (selling) one's own currency shows up as a positive (negative) in the U.S. government financial account. (420-421)

8. Market exchange rates are determined by the demand and supply of a country's currency. Since not all goods, services, and assets produced in a country can be traded internationally, the value of an exchange rate may not reflect the relative prices in each country. The purchasing power parity concept adjusts the value of a country's currency by determining the rate at which equivalent baskets of goods can be purchased in each country. (422-423)

9. If inflation is higher in a foreign country compared to the domestic country, and the nominal exchange rate doesn't change, the real exchange rate for the domestic country will fall. This is because the domestic currency will not be able to purchase as many foreign goods as before the foreign inflation. (423-424)

10. A fixed exchange rate is an exchange rate that the government chooses and then holds, by standing ready to buy and sell at that rate. Flexible exchange rates are exchange rates that are determined by the market without any government intervention. Partially flexible exchange rates are exchange rates that are determined by the market but are sometimes also affected by government intervention. (424)

11. It depends. Each has its advantages and disadvantages. Flexible exchange rates give a country more control over domestic policy, but can also cause large fluctuations in the value of the country's currency, hurting trade. With fixed exchange rates, such fluctuations can be avoided. (424-427)

12. The disadvantages of joining the European Monetary Union are that Great Britain would have to give up the pound as its currency, a source of national pride, and it would have to give up independent monetary policy. The advantages are that if the euro becomes an important reserve currency, Britain will enjoy lower interest rates and its producers and consumers will have greater access to a larger market. (427-429)

ANSWERS

MATCHING

1-k; 2-b; 3-g; 4-m; 5-f; 6-j; 7-i; 8-d; 9-e; 10-l; 11-h; 12-c; 13-a; 14-n.

ANSWERS

PROBLEMS AND APPLICATIONS

1. **a.** Financial and capital account. This is a long-term outflow. (411-412)
    b. Financial and capital account. This is a long-term inflow. (411-412)
    c. Current account. These are merchandise imports, a short-term flow. (410)
    d. Neither. It is a domestic transaction. (408-410)
    e. Current account. These are merchandise exports, a short-term flow. (410)
    f. Current account. This is net investment income. (410)

2. **a.** The French person supplies euros and demands dollars because the French person must sell euros to get U.S. dollars to purchase the china. (412-414)
    b. The U.S. tourist supplies dollars and demands Japanese yen because the tourist has to sell dollars to get yen. (412-414)
    c. The Italian trader will supply euros and demand U.S. dollars because he/she wants to purchase the currency that is believed to rise, the dollar. The trader must sell euros to get the dollars. (412-414)
    d. The Swiss investor will supply Swiss francs and demand euros because the

Swiss investor needs euros to invest in Germany. (412-414)

3. A market for British pounds is shown below. Price of pounds in U.S. dollars is on the vertical axis and quantity of pounds is on the horizontal axis. Equilibrium price and quantity is determined by where they intersect. (See Figure 17-1 on page 413)

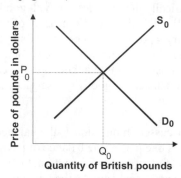

a. If only two countries exist, the United States and Britain, the demand for dollars is the supply of pounds. (412-414)
b. As the dollar value of the pound rises, individuals will supply more pounds. (412-414)
c. As the dollar value of the pound declines, individuals will demand more pounds. (412-414)
d. An increase in the demand for pounds by Americans would shift the demand for pounds as shown in the graph below. The price of pounds in dollars would rise. (412-414)

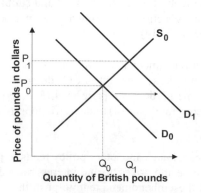

e. An increase in the demand for dollars by the British is equivalent to an increase in the supply of pounds. The supply curve for pounds would shift to the right as

shown in the graph below. The price of
pounds in dollars would fall. (412-414)

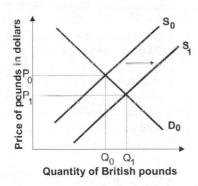

4. **a.** Demand for imports by the British rises;
    hence demand for dollars (supply of
    pounds) rises. This is shown in the graph
    below. (412-414)

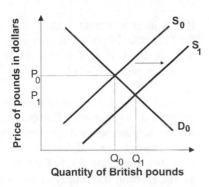

b. Demand for imports by Americans rises;
    hence demand for pounds rises. This is
    shown in the graph below. (412-414)

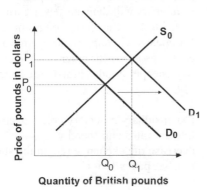

c. Demand for imports by the British falls;
    hence demand for dollars (supply of
    pounds) falls. This is shown in the graph
    below. (412-414)

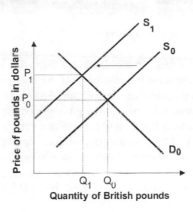

d. Demand for British assets will rise; hence
    the demand for the pound rises. This is
    shown in the graph below. (412-414)

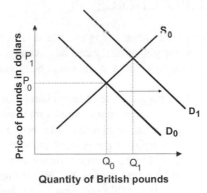

e. The demand for the pound falls. This is
    shown in the graph below. (412-414)

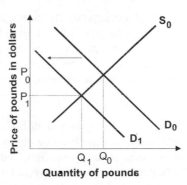

5. **a.** Remains the same $[3 + (2 - 5)]$. (423-424)
    b. Rises 5 percent $[2 + (4 - 1)]$. (423-424)
    c. Falls 6 percent $[-4 + (-1 - 1)]$. (423-424)
    d. Rises 2 percent $[-1 + (5 - 2)]$. (423-424)

━━━━━ ANSWERS ━━━━━

A BRAIN TEASER

1. A decrease in the demand for the dollar and/or
    an increase in the supply of the dollar in
    international exchange rate markets will create
    a temporary balance of payments deficit
    (because the quantity of dollars supplied will
    exceed the quantity demanded—imports will
    exceed exports). The balance of payments
    deficit will also put downward pressure on the
    exchange rate value of the dollar. (412-414)

━━━━━ ANSWERS ━━━━━

MULTIPLE CHOICE

1. c   An exchange rate is the rate at which one
        country's currency can be exchanged for
        another country's currency. See page 412.

2. a   With perfectly flexible exchange rates the
        balance of payments must sum to zero;
        thus the financial and capital account must
        be in surplus if the current account is in
        deficit. The government financial account
        could not be negative because if there are
        perfectly flexible exchange rates, there are
        no net government transactions. See
        pages 408-410 and 425-426.

3. a   Although net investment income might
        seem to many people as if it goes in the
        financial and capital account, it is a return
        for a service and is considered part of the
        current account, as is discussed on page
        410.

4. a   A surplus in the government financial
        account means the balance of payments
        would otherwise be in deficit. The country
        is buying up its own currency. This means
        it is trying to hold up its exchange rate.
        See pages 420-421.

5. b   See pages 411-412.

6. a   Running a financial and capital account
        surplus is the other side of the balance

sheet from the trade deficit. See pages 410-
412.

7. a   All the others allow free exchange of
        currency and hence would not generate a
        black market. See page 410.

8. b   To purchase greater amounts of U.S.
        products, the European Union must
        increase the supply of euros, pushing
        down the value of the euro relative to the
        dollar. See pages 412-414.

9. a   To purchase greater amounts of European
        products, U.S. citizens must increase the
        supply of their currency, pushing down its
        value relative to the euro. That means that
        the value of the euro rises relative to the
        dollar. See pages 412-414.

10. c   If U.S. income increases, the U.S. demand
        for European imports will increase,
        shifting the demand for euros out to the
        right. See pages 412-414.

11. c   An increase in European interest rates will
        increase the demand for European assets.
        As a result, the demand for euros will shift
        out to the right. In addition, Europeans will
        substitute domestic assets for foreign
        assets, shifting the supply of euros to the
        left. See pages 412-414.

12. d   An increase in European inflation will
        reduce the demand for European goods.
        Foreigners will demand fewer euros with
        which to buy European goods and
        Europeans will supply more euros as they
        exchange euros for other currencies to
        buy cheaper goods abroad. See pages 412-
        414.

13. b   Expansionary monetary policy decreases
        interest rates and thereby tends to
        decrease the exchange rate in the short
        run. See pages 415-418.

14. b   See the diagram on page 417.

15. c   See the diagram on page 417.

16. a   At P_1, there is an excess supply of dollars. To keep the value of the dollar from falling, the U.S. will have to buy up that excess using official reserves of foreign currencies. Disallowing conversion except at an official rate would make the dollar a nonconvertible currency. See pages 420-421.

17. b   Since the purchasing power parity exchange rate is lower than the actual exchange rate, the taka is undervalued. See pages 422-423.

18. d   The real exchange rate has fallen 6 percent: $[-5 + (3-4)]$. See pages 423-424.

19. b   To keep the exchange rate at the stated amount, governments must be willing to buy and sell currencies so that the quantity supplied and quantity demanded are always equal at the fixed rate. See pages 424-425.

20. b   There are no predetermined levels of change with a flexible exchange rate. See pages 425-427.

21. a   Under a fixed exchange rate system, countries must use their monetary policies to meet international commitments. Thus flexible exchange rate policies allow them more flexibility in their monetary policies. Flexible exchange rates *may* allow them more flexibility in their industrial policies, but flexible exchange rates *definitely* do allow them more flexibility in their monetary policy, so a is the preferred answer. See pages 424-427.

22. b   A common currency reduces barriers to trade among member nations, thereby broadening the potential marketplace for domestic producers. See pages 427-429.

A1. a.   See pages 433-434.

A2. a.   When there is an imbalance of trade in the gold system, gold—which is money—flows from the deficit country to the surplus country, pushing the price level down in the deficit country and up in the

surplus country. This process brings about a trade balance equilibrium, eventually. See pages 433-434.

A3. a   See pages 433-434 about the flow of gold. The last two answers could be eliminated since the gold standard involves fixed exchange rates.

A4. c   As discussed on page 435, SDRs refers to Special Drawing Rights.

ANSWERS

POTENTIAL ESSAY QUESTIONS

The following are annotated answers. They indicate the general idea behind the answer.

1.   If a country is experiencing a balance of payments deficit (the quantity supplied of its currency exceeds the quantity demanded at the current exchange rate), then its currency will fall in value over time. A country's government could prevent its currency from falling (depreciating) by buying its own currency in exchange rate markets. If it does, then this shows up in the government financial account as a plus sign and we say that the government is supporting the value of its currency. The opposite is also true. Because a country can create and then sell its own currency, it is easier for a country to push the value of its currency down than up.

2.   Notice the "margin list" on page 768. Most nations have opted for a partially flexible exchange rate policy in order to try to get the advantages of both a fixed and a flexible exchange rate.

MACRO POLICY IN A GLOBAL SETTING

18

● CHAPTER AT A GLANCE

This review is based upon the learning objectives that open the chapter.

1a. There is significant debate about what U.S. international goals should be because exchange rates have conflicting effects and, depending on the state of the economy, there are arguments for high and low exchange rates. (437-440)

A high exchange rate (strong value of the $) helps hold down the prices of imports and therefore inflation. However, it creates a trade deficit that has a depressing effect on aggregate demand and therefore the income level.

1b. Running a trade deficit is good in the short run but presents problems in the long run; thus there is debate about whether we should worry about a trade deficit or not. (438-439)

Trade deficit→ imports > exports.

Short-run benefit: We are able to consume more than we would otherwise be able to.

Long-run cost: We have to sell off U.S. assets because we are consuming more than we are producing. All the future interest and profits on those assets will thus go to foreigners, not U.S. citizens.

A country with fixed exchange rates must give up any attempt to target domestic interest rates to achieve domestic goals.

2. Monetary policy affects the trade balance primarily through the income path as shown in the diagram on page 441. (440-441)

Expansionary monetary policy makes a trade deficit larger.

Contractionary monetary policy makes a trade deficit smaller.

✔ *Be able to explain why!*

3. Fiscal policy affects the trade deficit primarily though the income path as shown in the diagram on page 442. (440-442)

Expansionary fiscal policy increases a trade deficit.

Contractionary fiscal policy decreases a trade deficit.

✔ *Be able to explain why!*

4. Governments try to coordinate their monetary and fiscal policies because their economies are interdependent. (442-444)

Each country will likely do what's best for the world economy as long as it is also best for itself.

5. While internationalizing a country's debt may help in the short run, in the long run it presents potential problems, since foreign ownership of a country's debts means the country must pay interest to those foreign countries and that debt may come due. (444)

   The United States has been internationalizing its debt since the early 1980s, which means that it must, at some point in the future, export more than it imports (consume less than it produces) to pay for this.

6. Macro policy must be conducted within the setting of a country's overall competitiveness. (445-447)

   In recent years the U.S. comparative advantage has been in assets, not produced goods. When foreigners cease wanting to purchase dollars or U.S. assets, the U.S. dollar will depreciate.

● SHORT-ANSWER QUESTIONS

1. What should U.S. international goals be?

2. Why can a country achieve an interest rate target or an exchange rate target, but generally cannot achieve both at the same time?

3. Which dominates for a country: domestic or international goals? Why?

4. If a country runs contractionary monetary policy, what will likely happen to the trade balance?

5. If a country runs contractionary fiscal policy, what will likely happen to the trade balance?

6. Given the difficulty of doing so, why do countries try to coordinate their monetary and fiscal policies with other countries?

7. The United States in recent years has run a large current account deficit and has become the world's largest debtor nation. What are some of the potential problems that this presents?

8. If foreigners began to demand fewer U.S. assets, why might U.S. policy makers be forced to consider contractionary monetary and fiscal policy?

9. What would happen to U.S. comparative advantage in production of goods if the U.S. dollar fell?

● PROBLEMS AND APPLICATIONS

1. You observe that over the past decade, a country's competitiveness has improved, reducing its trade deficit.

   a. What monetary or fiscal policies might have led to such results? Why?

b. You also observe that interest rates have steadily fallen along with a fall in the exchange rate. What monetary or fiscal policies might have led to such results?

2. You have been hired as an adviser to Fantasyland, a country with perfectly flexible exchange rates. State what monetary and fiscal policies you might suggest in each of the following situations. Explain your answers.

a. You want to increase domestic income and to reduce the exchange rate.

b. You want to reduce interest rates, reduce inflation, and reduce the trade deficit.

c. You want lower unemployment, lower interest rates, a lower exchange rate, and a lower trade deficit.

A BRAIN TEASER

1. Suppose a country has been running a significant expansionary fiscal policy for many years. Monetary policy has been neutral. What can you expect to have happened to this country's trade balance? What are the benefits and costs of this trade imbalance? If this country wishes to correct for its trade imbalance, what fiscal and monetary policies would you suggest this country pursue now? Will your recommended polices coincide or conflict with any of the country's domestic goals? If so, which goals?

MULTIPLE CHOICE

Circle the one best answer for each of the following questions:

1. Countries prefer:
   a. a high exchange rate.
   b. a low exchange rate.
   c. sometimes a low and sometimes a high exchange rate.
   d. a fixed exchange rate.

2. Countries prefer:
   a. a trade deficit.
   b. a trade surplus.
   c. sometimes a trade deficit and sometimes a trade surplus.
   d. a trade equilibrium.

3. If a country wants to maintain a fixed exchange rate above equilibrium, but does not have the necessary official reserves, it can:
   a. increase demand for its currency by running contractionary monetary policy.
   b. reduce the supply of its currency by running expansionary monetary policy.
   c. increase demand for its currency by running contractionary fiscal policy.
   d. increase supply of its currency by running expansionary fiscal policy.

4. If the trade deficit has gone up, it is most likely that the government ran:
   a. an expansionary monetary policy.
   b. a contractionary monetary policy.
   c. a contractionary fiscal policy.
   d. an expansionary monetary policy and a contractionary fiscal policy.

5. Expansionary monetary policy tends to push income:
   a. down and the trade deficit down.
   b. down and the trade deficit up.
   c. up and the trade deficit down.
   d. up and the trade deficit up.

6. Contractionary fiscal policy tends to push:
   a. income down and imports up.
   b. income down and the trade deficit up.
   c. income down and the trade deficit down.
   d. prices down and imports up.

7. Assume the United States would like to raise its exchange rate and lower its trade deficit. It would pressure Japan to run:
    a. contractionary monetary policy.
    b. contractionary fiscal policy.
    c. expansionary monetary policy.
    d. expansionary fiscal policy.

8. According to the textbook, generally, when international goals and domestic goals conflict:
    a. the international goals win out.
    b. the domestic goals win out.
    c. sometimes it's a toss-up which will win out.
    d. international monetary goals win out but international fiscal goals lose out.

9. When a country runs a large trade deficit, the amount of crowding out that occurs because of fiscal policy is:
    a. increased.
    b. decreased.
    c. unaffected.
    d. sometimes increased and sometimes decreased.

10. A country has the greatest domestic policy flexibility with:
    a. fixed exchange rates.
    b. flexible exchange rates.
    c. a trade deficit.
    d. a trade surplus.

11. A sudden fall in the price of the dollar in terms of other countries' currencies will most likely make policy makers face the possibility of implementing:
    a. capital inflow controls.
    b. import subsidies.
    c. contractionary macro policy.
    d. expansionary macro policy.

● POTENTIAL ESSAY QUESTIONS

You may also see essay questions similar to the "Problems & Applications" and "A Brain Teaser" exercises.

1. If there was initially a trade balance, what kind of trade imbalance would be created by an increase in the exchange rate value of the dollar (a stronger dollar)? Why?

2. What are the benefits and costs to the United States of having a strong dollar–a high exchange rate value of the dollar?

3. Why do domestic economic goals usually dominate international economic goals?

ANSWERS

SHORT-ANSWER QUESTIONS

1. By "international goals" economists usually mean the exchange rate and the trade balance that policy makers should shoot for. There is significant debate in the United States about what our international goals should be, and there are arguments for both high and low exchange rates, and for both trade deficits and trade surpluses. The argument for a high exchange rate is that it lowers the cost of imports; the argument against it is that it raises the price of exports, making U.S. goods less competitive. The argument in favor of a trade deficit is that it allows a country to consume more than it produces; the argument against is that a trade deficit will have to be paid off at some point. (437-440)

2. Because monetary policy affects the value of one's currency, a country cannot target both interest rates and exchange rates simultaneously. Suppose one's currency is at its desired level, but interest rates are too high. Expansionary monetary policy would lower the interest rate, but a lower interest rate reduces foreign demand for the country's interest-bearing assets. The demand for one's currency will shift in to the left and its exchange rate will fall. Likewise, citizens of the country will invest elsewhere and the supply of one's currency will shift out to the right. The value of one's currency will be lower than its target. (437-438, 441)

3. Generally, domestic goals dominate for two reasons: (1) International goals are often ambiguous, as discussed in answer 1 above, and (2) international goals affect a country's population indirectly and, in politics, indirect effects take a back seat. (442-443)

4. Contractionary monetary policy tends to push income down. Lower income means lower imports, lowering the trade deficit. (441)

5. Contractionary fiscal policy pushes income down. This tends to decrease imports and decrease a trade deficit. (441-442)

6. The policies of one country affect the economy of another. So it is only natural that the two countries try to coordinate their policies. It is also only natural that since voters are concerned with their own countries, coordination is difficult to achieve unless it is in the interest of both countries. (442-444)

7. While internationalizing a country's debt may help in the short run, in the long run it presents potential problems, since foreign ownership of a country's debts means the debtor country must pay interest to the foreign countries, and also, that debt may come due. (444)

8. If foreigners begin to demand fewer U.S. assets, the financial and capital account surplus would fall and there would be downward pressure on the price of the U.S dollar. A dramatic decline in the price of the dollar would cause inflation to rise. If that happened policy makers would likely consider contractionary monetary and fiscal policy to stem the decline in the dollar and the acceleration of inflation. (445-447)

9. If the U.S. dollar fell, U.S. goods would be less expensive to foreigners, improving the U.S. comparative advantage in a number of produced goods. (445-447)

ANSWERS

PROBLEMS AND APPLICATIONS

1.   a. An increase in competitiveness and a decrease in the trade deficit are probably due to contractionary fiscal policy. Contractionary fiscal policy reduces inflation, improves competitiveness, and decreases income, which reduces imports. Improved competitiveness and decreased income both work to reduce the trade deficit. Contractionary monetary policy would also reduce the trade deficit, but its effect on competitiveness is ambiguous. (440-443)

     b. If interest rates have also fallen, it is likely that fiscal policy has been very contractionary because contractionary monetary policy would have led to higher interest rates and a higher exchange rate value of the dollar. (440-443)

2. a. Expansionary monetary policy will reduce the exchange rate through its effect on interest rates and will increase domestic income. Expansionary fiscal policy will increase domestic income. The increase in income will increase imports, which will tend to decrease the exchange rate, but higher interest rates will tend to lead to a higher exchange rate. The effect of expansionary fiscal policy on exchange rates is therefore ambiguous. (440-443)

b. Contractionary fiscal policy will tend to reduce inflation and interest rates. The reduction in inflation will improve competitiveness and a reduction in income will reduce imports. Both work to reduce the trade deficit. (440-443)

c. Expansionary monetary policy will reduce unemployment and reduce interest rates. Lower interest rates will tend to make exchange rates fall. Expansionary monetary policy, however, will make the trade deficit higher. Expansionary fiscal policy will also reduce unemployment. Interest rates, however, will rise and so will the trade deficit. This mix of goals is difficult to attain. (440-443)

ANSWERS

A BRAIN TEASER

1. Because of the expansionary fiscal policy, this country will have moved in the direction of a trade deficit. The benefit of the trade deficit is that the country has been able to consume more than it has produced. The cost, however, is that it has had to sell off some of its assets. All the future interest and profits on these assets will now go to foreigners, not the country's citizens.

   To reduce the trade deficit the country should pursue contractionary fiscal and monetary policies. This will reduce imports and increase exports and increase the country's competitiveness in the global economy. That's good. However, even though fewer imports and greater exports should help stimulate aggregate expenditures, the effects of the contractionary fiscal and monetary policies are also simultaneously at play. Aggregate demand may fall on balance. If it does, then you may have created a recession. That's bad. Sometimes, countries can find themselves "in a pickle." (There could be other effects associated with the prescribed contractionary policies.)(438-439,441-443,445-447)

ANSWERS

MULTIPLE CHOICE

1. c The answer is "sometimes a low and sometimes a high exchange rate" because, as discussed on pages 437-438, there are rationales for both.

2. c The domestic economy's needs change over time and as they do, so does the country's preferred trade situation. Both a deficit and a surplus have their advantages and disadvantages. See pages 438-439.

3. a Contractionary monetary policy will increase the demand for one's currency and increase its value. Contractionary fiscal policy will reduce the supply of one's currency and increase its value. Contractionary monetary and fiscal policy are two ways to fix one's exchange rate without intervening in the exchange market. See pages 440-442.

4. a Both expansionary monetary policy and expansionary fiscal policy increase the trade deficit. Thus, only a fits. See the discussion and charts on pages 441-442.

5. d See the discussion and diagram on page 441.

6. c See diagram on page 442 and the discussion on pages 441-442.

7. c The effect of fiscal policy on the exchange rate is ambiguous, so the only sure option is c. See the box on page 443.

8. b   As discussed in the text on pages 442-444, usually, because of political considerations, domestic goals win out.

9. b   Since the trade deficit means capital is flowing into the country, the capital usually ends up buying some government debt, which reduces crowding out, as discussed on page 444.

10. b   When exchange rates are left to the market (flexible), the government does not have to change its domestic policy to meet its international goal for its exchange rate. Therefore, it is freer to follow domestic policy when exchange rates are flexible. See page 440.

11. c   If the price of the dollar falls significantly in the forex market, policy makers will likely be under pressure to slow the fall and prevent inflation, which means that they will have to face the possibility of implementing contractionary policy to keep the dollar from falling too much. The other options are not ones associated with a falling price of the dollar. See pages 438 and 440.

━━━━━ **ANSWERS** ━━━━━

POTENTIAL ESSAY QUESTIONS

The following are annotated answers. They indicate the general idea behind the answer.

1.   A stronger dollar means that a single dollar will now buy more units of a foreign currency. This makes foreign products cheaper to Americans. The United States would import more. At the same time, a stronger dollar means it will now take more units of a foreign currency to buy a single dollar. This will cause U.S. goods to become more expensive to foreigners. The United States would export less. The combined effects of more U.S. imports and fewer U.S. exports means a trade deficit will be created or will get larger in the United States.

2.   A strong dollar holds down the price of imports and therefore inflation. However, the cost is a trade deficit that would have a depressing effect on total spending and therefore on the nation's income level (there would be an especially depressing effect on the nation's exporting industries).

3.   First, there is more agreement on domestic goals. Second, domestic goals affect people within one's country more directly. Finally, pursuing domestic goals is politically more appealing.

MACRO POLICIES IN DEVELOPING COUNTRIES

19

CHAPTER AT A GLANCE

This review is based upon the learning objectives that open the chapter.

1. Seventy-five percent of the world's population lives in developing countries, with average per capita income of under $500 per year. (451-453)

    Be careful in judging a society by its income alone. Some developing countries may have cultures preferable to ours. Ideally, growth would occur without destroying the culture.

2. There are differences in normative goals between developing and developed countries because their wealth differs. Developing countries face basic economic needs whereas developed countries' economic needs are considered by most people to be normatively less pressing. (454-455)

    The main focus of macro policy in developing countries is on how to increase growth through development to fulfill people's basic needs.

3. Economies at different stages of development have different institutional needs because the problems they face are different. Institutions that can be assumed in developed countries cannot necessarily be assumed to exist in developing countries. (455-456)

    Developed nations have stable governments and market structures, which are often lacking in developing countries.

4. "The dual economy" refers to the existence of the two sectors in most developing countries: a traditional sector and an internationally-oriented modern market sector. (456)

    Often, the largest percentage of the population participates in the traditional sector. Tradition often resists change.

5. A régime change is a change in the entire atmosphere within which the government and the economy interrelate; a policy change is a change in one aspect of government's actions. (457)

    A régime change and macro institutional policies designed to fit the cultural and social dimensions of developing economics are what developing economies need.

6. Central banks recognize that printing too much money causes inflation, but often feel compelled to do so for political reasons. Debate about inflation in developing countries generally concerns those political reasons, not the relationship between money and inflation. (458-460)

    Governments in developing economies risk being thrown out of office unless they run deficits and issue too much money.

7. Full convertibility means one can exchange one's currency for whatever legal purpose one wants. Convertibility on the current account limits those exchanges for the purpose of buying goods and services. (460-461)

    Very few developing countries allow full convertibility.

8. Seven obstacles facing developing countries are: (462-471)
    1. Political instability.
    2. Corruption.
    3. Lack of appropriate institutions.
    4. Lack of investment.
    5. Inappropriate education.
    6. Overpopulation.
    7. Health and disease

    ✔ *Know why these are problems!*
    ✔ *The opposite constitutes the ingredients for growth. Remember them!*

● SHORT-ANSWER QUESTIONS

1. What percentage of the population of the world lives in developing countries?

2. What is the average per capita income in developing nations?

3. Why is there often a difference in the normative goals of developed and developing countries?

4. Why do economies at different stages of development often have different institutional needs? Explain.

5. What is the dual economy?

6. What is the difference between a regime change and a policy change?

7. Inflation is simply a problem of central banks in developing countries issuing too much money. Is this true or false? Why?

8. What are two types of convertibility?

9. Economists can't tell developing countries, "Here's what you have to do to grow." But they can identify seven obstacles facing developing countries. What are they?

MATCHING THE TERMS
Match the terms to their definitions

_____ 1. balance of payments constraint

_____ 2. brain drain

_____ 3. conditionality

_____ 4. convertibility on the current account

_____ 5. credentialism

_____ 6. dual economy

_____ 7. economic takeoff

_____ 8. foreign aid

_____ 9. full convertibility

_____ 10. infrastructure investment

_____ 11. limited capital account convertibility

_____ 12. policy change

_____ 13. purchasing power parity

_____ 14. regime change

_____ 15. restructuring

a. A change in one aspect of a government's actions.

b. A change in the entire atmosphere within which the government and economy interrelate.

c. A stage when the development process becomes self-sustaining.

d. A system that allows people to exchange currencies for whatever legal purpose they want.

e. A system that allows people to exchange currencies for the purpose of buying goods and services only.

f. A system that places some limitation on people's ability to exchange currencies to buy assets.

g. Changing the underlying economic institutions.

h. Funds that developed countries lend or give to developing countries.

i. Investment in the underlying structure of the economy.

j. Limitations on expansionary domestic macroeconomic policy due to a shortage of international reserves.

k. Method of comparing income by looking at the domestic purchasing power of money in different countries.

l. Outflow of the best and brightest students from developing countries to developed countries.

m. The degrees become more important than the knowledge learned.

n. The existence of two sectors: a traditional sector and an internationally-oriented modern market sector.

o. The making of loans that are subject to specific conditions.

● A BRAIN TEASER

1. You are the chief economic adviser to a developing country that is politically stable and possesses a culture you believe to be conducive to growth. What economic policies would you recommend to the developing country to enhance its growth and development?

● MULTIPLE CHOICE

Circle the one best answer for each of the following questions:

1. Annual GDP per capita is about _____ in developing countries and _____ in developed countries.
    a. $50; $20,000.
    b. $500; $40,000.
    c. $50; $10,000.
    d. $4,000; $20,000.

2. Two methods of comparing income among countries are the purchasing power parity method and the exchange rate method. Of these:
   a. the exchange rate method generally gives a higher relative measure of the income in developing countries.
   b. the purchasing power parity method generally gives a higher relative measure of the income in developing countries.
   c. the purchasing power parity and exchange rate methods generally give approximately equal measures of the income in developing countries.
   d. sometimes one gives a higher relative measure of income in developing countries, and sometimes the other gives a higher relative measure.

3. The concept "dual economy" refers to:
   a. the tendency of developed countries to have a traditional sector and an internationally-oriented sector.
   b. the tendency of both developed and developing countries to have a traditional sector and an internationally-oriented sector.
   c. the tendency of developing countries to have a traditional sector and an internationally-oriented sector.
   d. the fight, or dual, between developed and undeveloped countries.

4. If a country changes its entire approach to policy, that is called:
   a. a major policy change.
   b. a policy change.
   c. a régime change.
   d. a constitutional change.

5. The inflation tax is:
   a. a tax on those individuals who cause inflation.
   b. a tax on firms who cause inflation.
   c. a tax on both individuals and firms who cause inflation.
   d. a tax on holders of cash and any obligations specified in nominal terms.

6. The "revenue" of an inflation tax:
   a. goes only to government.
   b. goes only to private individuals.
   c. goes to both private individuals and government.
   d. is a meaningless term because there is no revenue from an inflation tax.

7. If you hold a fixed interest rate debt denominated in domestic currency and there is a high rate of inflation, you will:
   a. likely lose.
   b. likely gain.
   c. likely experience no effect from the large inflation.
   d. find that the large inflation could cause you either to gain or to lose.

8. If you hold a fixed interest rate debt denominated in a foreign currency and the exchange rate remains constant, and there is a large domestic inflation, you will:
   a. likely lose some.
   b. likely gain some.
   c. likely lose all your debt.
   d. likely experience little direct effect from the large inflation.

9. Conditionality refers to:
   a. the U.S. government's policy of only making loans to countries who will repay loans.
   b. the IMF's policy of making loans to countries subject to specific conditions.
   c. central banks' policies of making loans to firms only under certain conditions.
   d. the conditions under which inter-firm credit is allowed in transitional economies.

10. Foreign aid is:
    a. the primary source of income of the poorest developing countries.
    b. one of the top three sources of income of the poorest developing countries.
    c. one of the top three sources of income of developing countries who have ties to the United States.
    d. a minor source of income for developing countries.

11. The nickname for economics as "the dismal science" caught on because
    a. the law of diminishing marginal productivity predicted famine.
    b. the law of diseconomies of scale predicted famine.
    c. learning supply and demand economic models is dismal.
    d. it predicted that economic takeoff would seldom be reached.

12. If population grows geometrically, the amount of land is fixed, and there is diminishing marginal productivity, then:
    a. famine is in the future.
    b. income per person will decrease but there will not necessarily be famine.
    c. famine is not in the future if there is technological development.
    d. famine may or may not be in the future.

13. Which of the following best represents the textbook author's view of development?
    a. Optimal strategies for growth are country-specific.
    b. A country's development strategy should include as much education as possible.
    c. Countries should focus on infrastructure investment.
    d. Countries should follow a policy of laissez-faire.

● POTENTIAL ESSAY QUESTIONS

You may also see essay questions similar to the "Problems & Applications" and "A Brain Teaser" exercises.

1. What is the difference between economic development and economic growth?

2. What are some institutional differences between developed and developing countries that make it difficult for developing countries to develop?

3. Why is it that no developing country allows full convertibility?

■ ANSWERS ■

SHORT-ANSWER QUESTIONS

1. 75 percent of the population of the world lives in developing countries. (451)

2. The average per capita income in developing countries is about $500 per year. (451)

3. Developing countries face true economic needs. Their concern is with basic needs such as adequate clothing, food, and shelter. Developed countries' needs are considered less pressing. For example, will everyone have access to a DVD player? (454-455)

4. Economies at different stages of development have different institutional needs because the problems they face are different. Institutions that can be assumed in developed countries cannot necessarily be assumed to exist in developing countries. For example, developing countries often lack the institutional structure that markets require. (455-456)

5. Dual economy refers to the existence of the two distinct sectors in most developing countries: a traditional sector and an internationally-oriented modern market sector. (456)

6. A régime change is a change in the entire atmosphere within which the government and the economy interrelate; a policy change is a change in one aspect of government's actions. A régime change affects underlying expectations about what the government will do in the future; a policy change does not. (457)

7. Any simple statement is generally false, and this one is no exception. The reason why this one is false is that while it is true that inflation is closely tied to the developing country's central bank issuing too much money, the underlying problem behind the central bank's actions is often large government deficits that cannot be financed unless the central bank issues debt and then buys the bonds, which requires an increase in the money supply (printing money to pay for the bonds). (458-460)

8. Two types of convertibility are full convertibility and current account convertibility. Full convertibility means you can change your money into another currency with no restrictions. Current account convertibility allows exchange of currency to buy goods but not to invest outside the country. Many developing countries have current account convertibility, but not full convertibility. (460-461)

9. Seven problems facing developing countries are (1) governments in developing countries are often unstable, (2) governments in developing countries are often corrupt, (3) developing countries often lack appropriate institutions to promote growth, (4) developing countries often lack the domestic savings to fund investment for growth, (5) developing countries tend to have too much of the wrong education, (6) developing countries are often overpopulated so that raising per capita income is difficult, and (7) people in developing countries have limited access to healthcare and face greater incidence of disease. (462-471)

■ ANSWERS ■

MATCHING

1-j; 2-l; 3-o; 4-e; 5-m; 6-n; 7-c; 8-h; 9-d; 10-i; 11-f; 12-a; 13-k; 14-b; 15-g.

■ ANSWERS ■

A BRAIN TEASER

1. Macro institutional policies—those designed to change the underlying macro institutions, and thereby increase output—are what is necessary for development. Although there is some debate about exactly what constitutes the right set of policies for development, all economists agree that developing countries need to get the infrastructure right. That is, they must create a climate within which individual initiative is directed toward production. This requires macro institutional policies and a regime change. (462-471)

■ ANSWERS ■

MULTIPLE CHOICE

1. b   As stated on page 451, b is the closest.

2. b   As discussed on page 453, the purchasing power parity method of comparing income

cuts income differences among countries in half.

3. c   See page 456 for the definition of dual economy. Choice d was put in to throw you off. When the word means "a fight" it is, of course, spelled "duel."

4. c   See page 457.

5. d.   The answer has to be d, as discussed on page 459. The individuals and firms who cause the inflation are gaining from the inflation; they pay no inflation tax.

6. c   The only answer that makes any sense is c. The "revenue" goes from holders of fixed nominal interest rate debt to those who owe that debt. Those who owe the debt include both private individuals and government. See page 459.

7. a   Inflation wipes out the value of fixed interest rate debt. See page 459.

8. d   Because the debt is denominated in a foreign currency and exchange rates remain constant, what happens to the domestic price level does not directly affect you. There could be indirect effects, but d specifies direct effects. See pages 459-462.

9. b   See page 461.

10. d   Total foreign aid comes to less than $14 per person for developing countries. While this does not preclude b or c, it makes it very difficult for them to be true, and in fact, they are not true. See pages 465-466.

11. a   The nickname "the dismal science" was used by Thomas Carlyle in an attack on economists for their views against slavery. It became a popular description of economics however largely because of the writings of Thomas Malthus, whose model of population focused on the law of diminishing marginal productivity and led to the prediction that society's prospects were dismal because population tends to outrun the means of subsistence. See page 470.

12. d   As discussed on pages 470-471, the Malthusian doctrine predicted famine based on the elements of this question. That doctrine did not, however, take into account technological development. Technological growth can offset the tendencies for famine. But technological growth does not necessarily have to offset those tendencies; thus c is wrong, and d is the only correct answer.

13. a   As discussed on pages 471-472, the author believes the problems of economic development are intertwined with cultural and social issues and hence are country-specific. The other answers do not necessarily fail to reflect the author's viewpoint, but he presented arguments on both sides when discussing them. Thus, a is the best answer.

━━━ ANSWERS ━━━

POTENTIAL ESSAY QUESTIONS

The following are annotated answers. They indicate the general idea behind the answer.

1. Growth occurs because of an increase in inputs, given a production function. Development occurs through a change in the production function. Development involves more fundamental changes in the institutional structure than does growth.

2. First, developing nations often lack stable, socially-minded governments with which to undertake policy. Second, developing economies often have a dual economy, that is, a traditional and an international sector. This can create some policy dilemmas. A third difference is the way in which fiscal policy is run. Collecting taxes can be very difficult in developing countries. Expenditures are often mandated by political survival.

3. One reason is that they want to force their residents to keep their savings, and to do their investing, in their home country, not abroad. (Remember that saving is necessary for investment, and investment is necessary for growth.) These citizens usually don't want to do this because of the risks of leaving their money in their own countries; a new government takeover could possibly take it all away.

Pretest
Chapters 16-19

Take this test in test conditions, giving yourself a limited amount of time to complete the questions. Ideally, check with your professor to see how much time he or she allows for an average multiple choice question and multiply this by 22. This is the time limit you should set for yourself for this pretest. If you do not know how much time your teacher would allow, we suggest 1 minute per question, or 25 minutes.

1. If a country has a trade deficit, it is:
   a. consuming more than it is producing.
   b. lending to foreigners.
   c. buying financial assets.
   d. selling real assets.

2. Refer to the graph below. The graph demonstrates Saudi Arabia's and the United States' production possibility curves for widgets and wadgets. Given these production possibility curves, you would suggest that:

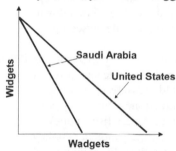

   a. Saudi Arabia specialize in widgets and the United States in wadgets.
   b. no trade should take place.
   c. Saudi Arabia specialize in wadgets and the United States in widgets.
   d. Both countries should produce an equal amount of each.

3. Country A's cost of widgets is $4.00 and cost of wadgets is $8.00. Country B's cost of widgets is 8 francs and cost of wadgets is 16 francs. Which of the following would you suggest?
   a. Country A should specialize in widgets and Country B in wadgets.
   b. Trade of widgets for wadgets would not benefit the countries.
   c. Country A should specialize in wadgets and Country B in widgets.
   d. Both countries should produce an equal amount of each.

4. Transferable comparative advantages are:
   a. based on factors that are relatively unchangeable.
   b. based on factors that can change relatively easily.
   c. becoming more like inherent comparative advantages with technological innovations.
   d. rarely eroded over time.

5. Economists generally oppose trade restrictions for all of the following reasons *except:*
   a. from a global perspective, free trade increases total output.
   b. the infant industry argument.
   c. trade restrictions lead to retaliation.
   d. international politics.

6. If a country has perfectly flexible exchange rates and is running a current account deficit, it is running:
   a. a financial and capital account surplus.
   b. a financial and capital account deficit.
   c. a government financial account surplus.
   d. a government financial account deficit.

7. In recent years, the United States has:
   a. generally run a balance of trade surplus.
   b. generally run a balance of trade deficit.
   c. sometimes run a balance of trade surplus and sometimes run a balance of trade deficit.
   d. generally run a balance of trade equality.

8. Assuming flexible exchange rates, if the European demand for U.S. imports increases, one would expect the price of euros in terms of dollars to:
   a. rise.
   b. fall.
   c. remain unchanged.
   d. sometimes rise and sometimes fall.

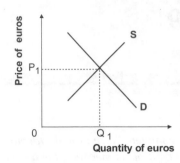

9. Refer to the graph above. If U.S. income increases the:
   a. supply curve will shift out to the right.
   b. supply curve will shift in to the left.
   c. demand curve will shift out to the right.
   d. demand curve will shift in to the left.

10. If a country with flexible exchange rates runs expansionary monetary policy, in the short run one would expect the value of its exchange rate to:
    a. rise.
    b. fall.
    c. be unaffected.
    d. sometimes rise and sometimes fall.

11. Suppose inflation in the United States is 3 percent and inflation in Europe is 4 percent. If the U.S. dollar exchange rate falls by 5 percent relative to the euro, the real exchange rate of the dollar relative to the euro has:
    a. risen 2 percent.
    b. risen 6 percent.
    c. fallen 2 percent.
    d. fallen 6 percent.

12. If a country has a flexible exchange rate, the exchange rate:
    a. is determined by flexible government policy.
    b. is determined by market forces.
    c. fluctuates continually, changing by at least 1 percent per year.
    d. fluctuates continually, changing by at least 10 percent per year.

13. Compared to a fixed exchange rate system, a flexible exchange rate system:
    a. allows countries more flexibility in their monetary policies.
    b. allows countries less flexibility in their monetary policies.
    c. has no effect on monetary policies.
    d. allows countries more flexibility in their industrial policies.

14. If a country wants to maintain a fixed exchange rate above equilibrium, but does not have the necessary official reserves, it can:
    a. increase demand for its currency by running contractionary monetary policy.
    b. reduce the supply of its currency by running expansionary monetary policy.
    c. increase demand for its currency by running contractionary fiscal policy.
    d. increase supply of its currency by running expansionary fiscal policy.

15. If the trade deficit has gone up, it is most likely that the government ran:
    a. an expansionary monetary policy.
    b. a contractionary monetary policy.
    c. a contractionary fiscal policy.
    d. an expansionary monetary policy and a contractionary fiscal policy.

16. Expansionary monetary policy tends to push income:
    a. down and the trade deficit down.
    b. down and the trade deficit up.
    c. up and the trade deficit down.
    d. up and the trade deficit up.

17. Assume the United States would like to raise its exchange rate and lower its trade deficit. It would pressure Japan to run:
    a. contractionary monetary policy.
    b. contractionary fiscal policy.
    c. expansionary monetary policy.
    d. expansionary fiscal policy.

18. A country has the greatest domestic policy flexibility with:
    a. fixed exchange rates.
    b. flexible exchange rates.
    c. a trade deficit.
    d. a trade surplus.

19. Two methods of comparing income among countries are the purchasing power parity method and the exchange rate method. Of these:
    a. the exchange rate method generally gives a higher relative measure to the income in developing countries.
    b. the purchasing power parity method generally gives a higher relative measure to the income in developing countries.

c. the purchasing power parity and exchange rate methods generally give approximately equal measures of the income in developing countries.

d. sometimes one gives a higher relative measure to income in developing countries, and sometimes the other gives a higher relative measure.

20. The "revenue" of an inflation tax:
a. goes only to government.
b. goes only to private individuals.
c. goes to both private individuals and government.
d. is a meaningless term because there is no revenue from an inflation tax.

21. Conditionality refers to:
a. the U.S. government's policy of only making loans to countries who will repay loans.
b. the IMF's policy of making loans to countries subject to specific conditions.
c. central banks' policies of making loans to firms only under certain conditions.
d. the conditions under which inter-firm credit is allowed in transitional economies.

22. If population grows geometrically, the amount of land is fixed, and there is diminishing marginal productivity, then:
a. famine is in the future.
b. income per person will decrease but there will not necessarily be famine.
c. famine is not in the future if there is technological development.
d. famine may or may not be in the future.

ANSWERS

1.	a	(16:2)		12.	b	(17:20)
2.	a	(16:5)		13.	a	(17:21)
3.	b	(16:8)		14.	a	(18:3)
4.	b	(16:11)		15.	a	(18:4)
5.	b	(16:17)		16.	d	(18:5)
6.	a	(17:2)		17.	c	(18:7)
7.	b	(17:5)		18.	b	(18:10)
8.	b	(17:8)		19.	b	(19:2)
9.	c	(17:10)		20.	c	(19:6)
10.	b	(17:13)		21.	b	(19:9)
11.	d	(17:18)		22.	d	(19:12)

Key: The figures in parentheses refer to multiple choice question and chapter numbers. For example (1:2) is multiple choice question 2 from chapter 1.

ANSWERS TO EVEN-NUMBERED END-OF-CHAPTER QUESTIONS

The following answers are meant as guides to answering the end-of-chapter questions, not as definitive answers. The same questions often have many answers; this is especially true of policy-oriented questions. Although we have tried hard to see that mistakes are eliminated, the reality is that, as in any human endeavor, mistakes are inevitable. If you have checked and double-checked your answer and it is substantially different from that found here, assume that our answer is wrong, not yours. If you do come to a different answer, or think an answer misses an important aspect of the question, please check for corrections at my website to see if the answer has changed. If you don't find it there, please e-mail me at Colander@Middlebury.edu with your answer and an explanation of why you think it is better. I will get back to you and if I think you are right, I will post the change on the Web page marked "Corrections," together with your name and a thank-you.

● CHAPTER 1- Questions for Thought and Review

2. The responses will be varied since this question asks individual students about choices they have made. In these responses students should be encouraged to consider all the costs and benefits, and to be clear about the concept of the marginal costs and marginal benefits; sunk costs should not be included in the decision-making process.

4. The opportunity cost of buying a $20,000 car is the benefit we would have gained by using that $20,000 for the next-best alternative, which could be spending it on other goods and services, or saving it.

6. I would spend the $5 million on those projects that provide the highest marginal benefit per dollar spent. The opportunity cost of spending the money on one project is the lost benefit that the college would have received by spending it on some other project. Thus, another way to restate the decision rule is to spend the money on the project that minimizes opportunity cost per dollar.

8. Three ways (among many) that dormitory rooms could be rationed include: administrative decree, lottery, and a market system. In the first, individual behavior would be forced to fit the will of the administrator. Individuals would likely complain and try to influence the administrator's decision. In the second, individual behavior would be forced to fit the luck of the draw; individuals would likely attempt to trade rooms after the draw. In the final example, individual behavior would have already been subject to economic forces, and thus, there will be no tendency to trade after one has "bought" the room one can afford. Because administrative decree is not necessarily an efficient system, some people would likely attempt to trade rooms after the allocation.

10. It suggests that policy should be willing to give up more in possible gains to avoid losses than otherwise would be the case. Economic policies should be risk averse—more committed to maintaining the current standard of living than in risking economic losses by trying to improve it.

12. Two examples of political or legal forces are rent control laws and restrictions on immigration. Both prevent the invisible hand from working. The rent control laws place a price ceiling on rent, causing shortages of apartments, and the immigration restrictions cause the number of immigrants seeking entry to exceed those allowed to enter, which tends to cause wage rates to differ among countries.

14. No; economic theory proves nothing about what system is best. It simply gives ways to look at systems, and what the advantages and disadvantages of various systems will likely be. Normative decisions about what is best can only follow from one's value judgments.

16. Banks are economic institutions. They take a cost-benefit approach to deciding to whom to give loans, and they influence decision making by allowing individuals to spend more money than they either earn or have as wealth.

●1- Problems and Exercises

18. The marginal costs are the additional costs. They are 15 cents per mile for miles above 150 plus the cost of gas. Therefore the marginal cost is $7.50. The initial payment can be forgotten because it is a sunk cost; it is not part of marginal costs.

20. **a, b.** Parts a or b have no "right" answers. Most people would say "no" to a and "yes" to b. If answering this question from the perspective of the economic decision rule alone, one would measure the marginal benefits against the marginal costs of the choice.
   c. People tend to believe that children should be afforded greater protection than afforded to adults and are therefore repulsed by the idea of sacrificing a child even though it would save the lives of other children. A sick person is closer to death and therefore their life tends to be valued less.
   d. Brain imaging suggests that the moral sense behind one's answers does not come from rational thought, but instead from emotion—gut responses. This suggests that a kind of moral intuition exists that is quite separate from reason. If that is the case, opportunity costs were not central to the decision. It was a moral, not an economic decision. Opinions among philosophers and economists differ on this issue.

22. **a.** This is a matter of personal views; there are arguments for and against it. An argument against the practice is that wealthy songwriters would have too much power in promoting their songs. The songs of those songwriters who can afford to share profits will get more play time and become even more famous at the detriment to new entrants into the industry. Arguments for this practice is that it could be used to offset racism as in the example given or, to the extent that new songwriters have the capability of offering such royalty share, to promote new kinds of music.

b. The royalty payment gave Freed a strong incentive to choose what he considered the best song, and to promote that song heavily. The flat payment would have just given him an incentive to play any song, and no long-term interest in whether the song succeeded or failed.

c. Product placement in movies is legal, as are free newspapers to professors for getting your class to use the newspaper. Direct payment to doctors for prescribing a particular type of drug is illegal, although taking doctors to lunch is not.

24. a. It depends. On the basis of cost/benefit analysis, one could figure out cases where most people would say that they should be dishonest, but cost/benefit analysis is not the final arbiter, if you believe that dishonesty is wrong. Additionally, you should consider the effects of dishonesty on your reputation and future interactions.

b. You can make yourself more believable by developing a reputation for honesty. Developing such a reputation usually has a cost because it requires one to be honest even when most people would be dishonest. To encourage the other person to tell the truth, you could use economic incentives. For example, in the kissing situation, tell them you'll kiss them again if they say yes—then they'll have a strong incentive to be honest.

26. a. Micro with macro implications.
b. Micro.
c. Micro with macro implications.
d. Micro with macro implications.
e. Micro.
f. Macro with micro implications

28. a. Positive statement since it is a statement of fact.
b. Normative.
c. This could be seen as a positive statement since it is a statement of fact, although since it deals with normative issues, it could also be interpreted as a normative statement.
d. Since this is relating a normative goal with a decision, this could be statement in the art of economics. It could also be seen as a normative statement if one interprets it as a normative imperative.
e. Positive statement since it is a statement of fact.

1- Web Questions

2. On www.nytimes.com we found an article about the Senate voting to keep a temporary worker program. By allowing thousands of workers to enter the United States to work, this measure helps economic forces become market forces (May 23, 2007). On *The American Prospect* at www.prospect.org we found an article reporting the USDA's recommendation to lower subsidies to farmers (May 23, 2007). This action, if taken, will also help economic forces become market forces.

CHAPTER 2- Questions for Thought and Review

2. If there were decreasing marginal opportunity costs, the production possibility curve would be convex (bowed in) with respect to the origin instead of concave (bowed out). This means that (in terms of the example on page 26 of the text) we would gain more and more guns for every pound of butter we give up. An example of this is found in a situation in which a practice makes perfect; i.e., smaller and smaller numbers of hours devoted to a task, or sport, will result in bigger and bigger gains in performance.

4. If a society became equally more productive in the production of both widgets and wadgets, the production possibility curve would shift out to the right as shown in the accompanying graph.

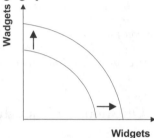

6. This statement can be true or false depending on the implicit assumptions made in the analysis. It is true given that individuals will eliminate all inefficiencies they see through trading. It might be false if not everyone knows all the benefits and the inefficiencies, or does not have the opportunity to correct the inefficiencies, or if the costs of eliminating the inefficiency are too high.

8. If a particular distribution of income is one of society's goals, a particular production technique that leads to greater output, but also an undesirable distribution of income, might be considered an inefficient method of production. Remember, efficiency is achieving a goal as cheaply as possible. Maximizing output is not the only goal of a society.

10. Globalization increases competition by allowing greater specialization and division of labor. Because companies can move operations to countries with a comparative advantage, they can lower production costs and increase competitive pressures. The decreased importance of geographical location increases the size of potential markets, increasing the number of suppliers in each market and thus increasing competition.

12. The wage differential between countries can be reduced by changes in exchange rates. A fall in a country's exchange rate will lower its relative wage, and a rise in a country's exchange rate will raise its relative wage.

2- Problems and Exercises

14. a. See the accompanying graph.

b. As the output of food increases, the marginal opportunity cost is increasing. To illustrate, giving up 4 of clothing (from 20 to 16) results in a gain of 5 food (from 0 to 5), but giving up another 4 clothing (from 16 to 12) results in a gain of 4 food (from 5 to 9), and this pattern continues.

c. If the country gets better at producing food, the place where the production possibilities curve intersects horizontal axis will move to the right.

d. If the country gets equally better at producing food and clothing, the production possibility curve will shift along both axes by the same proportion.

16. a. See the accompanying graph.

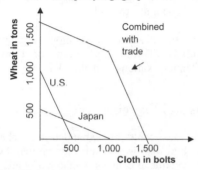

b. The United States has a comparative advantage in the production of wheat because it can produce 2 additional tons of wheat for every 1 fewer bolt of cloth while Japan can produce 1 additional ton of wheat for every 2 fewer bolts of cloth. Japan has a comparative advantage in producing cloth.

c. The United States should trade wheat to Japan in return for bolts of cloth. One possibility is that the United States produces 1000 tons of wheat and Japan produces 1000 bolts of fabric. The United States trades 400 tons of wheat for 400 yards of fabric. The United States ends up with 600 tons of wheat and 400 yards of fabric while Japan ends up with 400 tons of wheat and 600 yards of fabric. Both end up with more of each good.

d. The combined production possibility curve with specialization and trade is shown in the graph. It is the outermost curve.

18. The fact that lawns occupy more land in the United States than any single crop does not mean that the United States is operating inefficiently. Although the cost of enjoying lawns is not included in GDP, lawns are nevertheless produced consumption goods and are included in the production possibility curve for the United States. The high proportion of land devoted to lawns implies that the United States has sufficient food that it can devote a fair amount of land to the production of goods for enjoyment such as lawns.

20. a. Firms may produce in Germany, because (1) transportation costs to/from the other countries may be very high, so that if these costs are included, it would not be efficient to produce there; (2) there might be tariffs or quotas for imports into Germany that will prevent producing elsewhere; (3) the productivity of German labor may be so much higher that unit labor costs in Germany are the lowest; and (4) historical circumstances may have led to production in Germany and the cost of moving production may exceed potential gains.

b. Yes, one would expect some movement from Greece and Italy into Germany, but this is limited by social restrictions such as language and culture and the economic climate in Germany, which currently has high unemployment. Movement in the long run, however, may be substantial.

c. I would need to know the stability of politics, the worker productivity, the infrastructure such as roads, as well as tax differences between the two countries.

● 2- Web Questions

2. a. The IMF supports globalization.

b. The empirical evidence is mixed. But whatever the empirical evidence, the IMF believes that policies should be established to help the poorest nations.

c. It suggests that the poorest countries create the right conditions for investment and saving; engage in structural reform to encourage domestic competition; promote education and training, manage its external debt and create strong institutions and an effective government to foster good governance

d. While there is a tendency toward crisis because of the increased financial complexity that globalization causes, with appropriate institutions, the IMF does not see crises and inevitable.

● 2- Appendix A

2. See the accompanying graph.

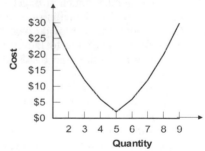

a. The relationship is nonlinear because it is not straight. It is curved.

b. From 0 to 5, cost declines as quantity rises (inverse). From 5 to 10, cost rises as quantity rises (direct).

c. From 0 to 5, the slope is negative (slopes down). From 5 to 10, the slope is positive (slopes up).

d. The slope between 1 and 2 units is the change in cost (30 - 20) divided by the change in quantity (1 - 2), or -10.

4. a. 1 **b.** 3 **c.** 1/3 **d.** −3/4 **e.** 0

6. a. See line a in the accompanying graph on the next page.

b. See line b in the accompanying graph on the next page.

c. See line c in the accompanying graph on the next page.

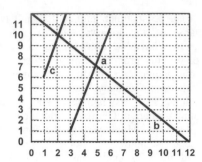

8. **a.** line graph **b.** bar graph **c.** pie chart **d.** line graph

● CHAPTER 3- Questions for Thought and Review

2. The central coordinating mechanism in a centrally-planned economy is the central planners.

4. Centrally planned socialist economies solve the three problems by using administrative control. Central planners decide what to produce according to what they believe is socially beneficial. Central planners decide how to produce guided by what they believe is good for the country. Central planners decide distribution based on their perception of individuals' needs.

6. Markets have little role in most families. In most families decisions about who gets what are usually made by benevolent parents. Because families are small and social bonds strong, this benevolence can work. Thus, a socialist organization seems more appropriate to a family and a market-based organization to a large economy where social bonds don't hold the social unit together. The propensity to look after the common good is much stronger in a family than in an entire economy. The benefits of a market-based economy in a family would be to provide incentives to all members of the family to contribute to family production, although this may undermine the social bonds of families..

8. An economy depends on coordination, and the mechanisms of coordination depend on the people who choose which goods to supply and what to demand. People supply the labor that makes the economy run. Economic growth, and what is considered a resource depend on technology, and people develop new technologies. Even the institutions that oversee the economy are governed by that economy's people. It follows that the economy's ultimate strength resides in its people.

10. Business is dynamic; it involves meeting new problems constantly, recognizing needs, and meeting those needs in a timely fashion. These are precisely the skills of entrepreneurship.

12. The two largest categories of federal expenditures are income security and health and education.

14. The Internet has added competition by increasing the amount of information available to consumers and reducing the importance of geographic location to production and sales. Increasing the amount of information to consumers lowers the cost of comparison shopping, which gives consumers more negotiating power with sellers. Because location doesn't matter, the Internet broadens the potential marketplace for both inputs and outputs, increasing competitive pressures in both factor and goods markets by increasing the number of suppliers. Also, many firms that sell online ask customers to fill out reviews that other potential customers can see before making purchases. This drives firms to provide a better made products.

16. People have made decisions based on the rules that were set up, so changing them after the game has been started may be more unfair than continuing to play by the original rules. Such decisions must be made based on the marginal cost and benefit of changing the rules.

18. Countries coordinate economic relations through membership in a variety of voluntary international organizations such as the United Nations and the WTO.

● 3- Problems and Exercises

20. **a.** Such an idea could be expanded to include college courses, but that is unlikely to happen because the quantity of college courses demanded would decline as people substitute toward recorded lectures. Substitution, however, is not perfect since DVD and CD cannot provide the interaction between student and instructor or among students. Social forces would act against the movement away from college classroom instruction even if the invisible hand pressed action toward it.

   b. Technical problems are virtually nonexistent. Socially, the problems are substantial. A diminishing role of the university would significantly change its role of providing a focal point for intellectual discussion and discovery thus changing the nature of education. There would be great social pressures to maintain this role of American colleges. The economic issues are substantial. A course could be taught once and used over a period of years. This would reduce the demand for professors and create revenues for certifying agencies that would regulate the distribution and quality of the tapes. If these college-at-home courses became an accepted educational credential, the demand for traditional college education would fall, putting major competitive pressure on traditional colleges.

   c. Even though the program is technically possible and cost efficient, it will not necessarily be a success because social forces will play a major role in limiting the market. Social forces are often strong enough to overcome economic forces.

22. **a.** Innovation requires a certain level of freedom of thought and a possibility of profit-making from the innovation. Neither was the case with centrally-planned economies. Government planners directed production with income based on need, so workers had neither the freedom nor the incentive to innovate.

   b. Both freedom and the possibility of making profits provide the means and incentives for innovation in capitalist countries.

c. Schumpeter's argument was based on the idea that profit-making by innovators was necessary for innovation to occur. As firms become larger, however, the individual ceases to become the direct beneficiary of his or her innovations.

d. Since his predictions did not materialize, one must believe that firms have either been able to create incentive structures to foster innovation or that some other venue for innovation has arisen. Firms have large research and development departments designed to promote innovation. In addition, individual innovators have been able to raise enough capital to start their own companies to profit directly from their innovations. In the United States there has been enormous growth in the number of such firms. The U.S. government has been a large motivator of innovation through its strong patent and copyright system, as well as providing subsidies for research at universities and support of military innovations, both of which have large spillovers into private industry.

24. A merit good is a good that government believes is good for you even if you choose not to buy it. An example might be operas. A demerit good is a good that government believes is bad for you even if you choose to buy it. An example is alcohol or drugs. A public good is a good that if supplied to one person must be supplied to all and whose consumption by one does not preclude the consumption by another. An example is national defense. An externality is the effect of a trade on a person not involved in the trade. An example is cigarette smoke.

a. Individuals might disagree as to the categorization of a good as a merit, demerit or public good or a good that involves an externality. In the case of an externality, they may believe that given sufficient property rights, the externality will be solved most efficiently by the market, not government.

b. We discuss the issues of market failure and government failure in the case of operas. There is market failure only if people do not value operas as much as they should. This normative statement is valid only if the "should" can be measured against some absolute truth as to the value of operas, otherwise how would one decide who decides the value of operas? Because it is only through the market that value is revealed, we'd argue that government intervention in this case will likely lead to government failure—the failure of government to accurately value operas. With government intervention, the value will likely reflect the preferences of those with political power, not necessarily those of the general population.

3- Web Questions

2. In the 1930s, government intervened very little in the market. During the Depression, however, as many people became unemployed and needed assistance, the role of government expanded and capitalism's evolution away from a pure market economy began. The Social Security Act was signed into law in 1935. The Act established two programs a pension program for retired workers and an income support program for the unemployed. Both are administered by the federal government.

a. In the late 1990s and early 2000s, there have been proposals to privatize portions of the Social Security system, giving workers more say about where their money is invested.

b. The pendulum is moving back toward a market economy.

CHAPTER 4- Questions for Thought and Review

2. The law of supply states that quantity supplied rises as price increases or, alternatively, that quantity supplied falls as price decreases. Price is directly related to quantity supplied because, as price rises, people and firms rearrange their activities to supply more of that good in order to take advantage of the higher price.

4. A change in the price causes a movement along the demand curve, a movement to a new point on the same curve. A shift in the demand curve means that the quantities will be different at all prices; the entire curve shifts.

6. Shift factors of supply include the price of inputs, technological advances, changes in expectations, and taxes and subsidies. As the price of inputs increase, the supply curve shifts to the left. As technological advances are made that reduce the cost of production, the supply curve shifts to the right. If a supplier expects the price of her good to rise, she may decrease supply now to save and sell later. Other expectational effects are also possible. Taxes paid by suppliers shift the supply curve to the left. Subsidies given to producers shift the supply curve to the right.

8. In the accompanying graph, the demand curve has shifted to the left, causing a decrease in the market price and the market quantity.

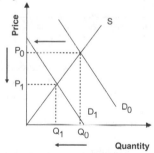

10. Sales volume increases (equilibrium quantity rises) when the government suspends the tax on sales by retailers because the price to demanders falls and hence equilibrium quantity demanded rises. This occurs because the supply curve shifts to the right because suppliers do not have to pay taxes on their sales (cost of production declines).

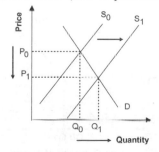

12. Customers will flock to stores demanding that funky "economics professor" look, creating excess demand. This excess demand will soon catch the attention of suppliers, and prices will be pushed upward.

14. Because the price of gas rose significantly, we'd expect people to purchase fewer gas-guzzlers and more fuel-efficient cars such as diesel cars.

16. It suggests that the job is being rationed, which means that the wage is above the equilibrium wage.

18. The fallacy of composition is the false assumption that what is true for a part will also be true for the whole. It affects the supply/demand model by drawing our attention to the possibility that supply and demand are interdependent. Feedback effects must be taken into account to make the analysis complete.

20. The greatest feedback effects are likely to occur in the markets that are the largest. This is most likely to be true for housing and manufactured-goods markets.

● 4- Problems and Exercises

22. **a.** The market demand and market supply curves are shown in the accompanying graph.

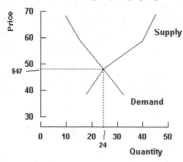

b. At a price of $37, quantity demanded is 32 and quantity supplied is 18. Excess demand is 14. At a price of $67, quantity demanded is 10 and quantity supplied is 46. Excess supply is 36.

c. Equilibrium price is $47. Equilibrium quantity is 24.

24. **a.** I would expect wheat prices to decline since the supply of wheat is greater than expected. Wheat commodity markets are very competitive, so the initial 35 percent increase in output was already reflected in the current price of wheat. It is only the additional 9 percent increase that will push down the price of wheat.

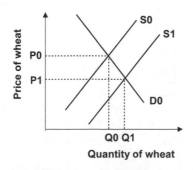

b. This is graphically represented by a shift to the right in the supply of wheat, as shown in the accompanying graph. Equilibrium price falls from P0 to P1 while equilibrium quantity rises from Q0 to Q1.

26. **a.** The tax shifts the supply curve to the left because it increases the cost of supplying the natural gas abroad. Equilibrium price rises while equilibrium quantity declines.

b. The tax will likely reduce the price of natural gas in Argentina as more gas is diverted to the domestic market.

c. It depends; it will have a tendency to push it up, but probably since Argentina is such a small percentage of the world market, the effect would be difficult to distinguish.

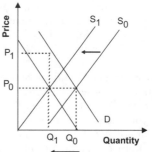

28. **a.** It would likely raise the value significantly – it was estimated that it would raise it to $50,000 a sheet. See the accompanying graph. Demand shifts to the right as people realize the oddity of the stamp. Supply shifts to the left because of the recall.

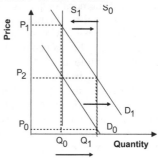

b. It would probably lower the value of the stamps – it was estimated that it would lower the price of the sheet to $100 a sheet. In the accompanying graph, the supply curve shifts back to S0 and the price declines to P2. We've shown the demand curve remaining high, though it might shift back to the left.

c. They would likely sue; they did and they lost.

30. **a.** Because the market for pencils is relatively small, supply/demand analysis would be appropriate without modification. Also, there are no significant political or social forces that would affect the analysis.

b. Because the labor market is very large, supply/demand analysis would not be appropriate without modification. For example, an increase in labor supply will likely lead to greater income and greater demand for goods, which will lead to an increase in quantity of goods produced and therefore an increase in the demand for labor. In this case there are significant feedback effects.

c. Aggregate markets such as savings and expenditures include feedback effects, so supply/demand analysis would not be appropriate without modification.

d. The CD market is relatively small. Supply/demand analysis would be appropriate without modification.

● 4- Web Questions

2. The answers to these questions will depend upon the current "Short-Term Energy Outlook." The answer given here should be used as a guide.

a. Continued problems with local refineries and increased global demand for oil means that oil prices are expected to rise.

b. World oil prices are forecast to rise. The effect of the supply and demand factors on price and quantity are shown in the accompanying graph. Price rises by a lot. What happens to quantity depends on the relative size of the shifts.

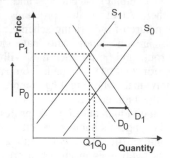

c. Higher crude oil, an input to the production of gasoline, and higher seasonal demand for gas will increase its price in the near term. As the market enters summer, demand for heating oil and natural gas will decline, leading to lower prices.

● CHAPTER 5- Questions for Thought and Review

2. If price fell and quantity remained constant, a possible cause would be a shift out of the supply curve and a shift of the demand curve in to the left. Another possibility would be a shift of the demand curve in to the left with a vertical supply curve.

4. See the accompanying graph. A price ceiling of Pc below Pe will cause a shortage shown by the difference between Qd and Qs

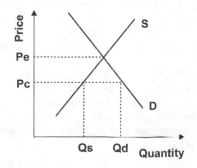

6. See the accompanying graph. A price floor of Pf above Pe will cause a surplus shown by the difference between Qs and Qd.

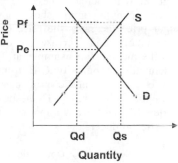

8. A \$4 per unit tax on suppliers shifts the supply curve up by \$4 shown as a shift in the supply curve from S_0 to S_1. Equilibrium price will rise by \$4 only if the demand curve is perfectly vertical. In the case of a vertical demand curve, quantity would not change. Otherwise, equilibrium price rises by less than \$4 and equilibrium quantity falls as shown in the accompanying graph. The price increases from P_0 to P_1 and quantity declines from Q_0 to Q_1

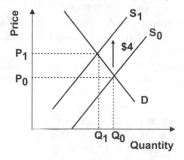

10. Excess supply in U.S. agricultural markets is caused by the government's policy of agricultural price supports, or price floors on agricultural products. Political forces prevent the invisible hand from working.

12. Import disruptions shifted the supply curve for rice to the left. Equilibrium price rose and quantity fell as the accompanying graph shows.

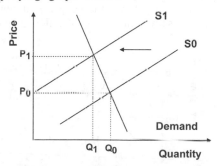

14. Public post-secondary education is an example of a third-party payer market because it is heavily subsidized by state government and in most cases, a student's parents. Those consuming the good, students, do not pay the entire cost of the education they receive. This likely leads to greater expenditures on post-secondary education than if students had to pay the entire cost of their education.

● 5- Problems and Exercises

16. a. An import quota will increase the price of imported sugar. The accompanying graph shows how a higher imported sugar price increases the price that domestic producers can charge and increase the quantity they can supply to the market. For example, at P0, domestic consumers demand the quantity C-B from importers and quantity B from domestic producers After the quotas, the import price is P1. Domestic consumers demand the quantity D-A from importers and quantity A from domestic producers.

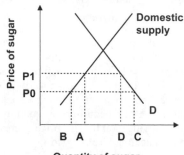

Quantity of sugar

b. The government could have imposed a tariff on imported sugar. This would also have raised the price of imported sugar.

c. A minimum required import level of 1.25 million will limit the ability of the United States to support domestic sugar prices.

18. a. As shown in the accompanying graph, the controlled price is below equilibrium. At this price the quantity of apartments demanded exceeds the quantity of apartments supplied. Since there are more apartments demanded than supplied at this price, apartments are hard to find.

b. Since at the existing quantity supplied, Qs, demanders would be willing to pay Pb, there is a strong incentive to make side payments to existing tenants to acquire the apartment. At Pb, more tenants are willing to supply their apartments than at Pc, so a side payment can induce a tenant to give up their apartments. This is one form of rationing. When market price rationing does not take place, some other form of rationing must take its place.

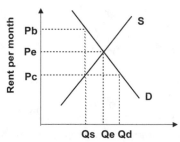

Quantity of apartments

c. Eliminating rent controls would most likely allow the market price of apartments to increase and eliminate side payments. The quantity supplied will rise until it

equals the quantity demanded at the market price. The price, quantity combination is (Pe, Qe) in the graph.

d. The political appeal of rent control is that it benefits those who currently have apartments. Apartment owners are more likely to vote, and this is why it is maintained.

20. a. Computer pricing of roads could end bottlenecks and rush hour congestion by price rationing. Currently at zero price, at certain times, the quantity demanded greatly exceeds the quantity supplied, resulting in congestion. Raising prices, during those times, could eliminate excess demand and reduce the congestion. This technological change will spread out congestions over wider geographic areas and over the day, as individuals with more flexibility with respect to route and timing will choose to demand less of the current high demand route at rush hour.

b. Some of the problems are administrative: disputes may arise over computer accuracy and possibility of cheating the system. Other problems might be the regressive nature of the pricing scheme. If low income individuals are the ones who have less flexibility regarding route and timing then they will be the ones to pay more for the use of roads compared to higher income individuals who might have more flexibility and can avoid the high-cost routes.

c. This is an individual question. A professor in a rural area would change his habits very little because there is no rush hour traffic. A student with a more flexible schedule and who lives in an urban area may be more likely to change driving habits or to use public transportation or carpooling.

22. a. The Oregon Health Plan includes a prioritized list of medical services that determine whether a service is covered. The list is based on comparative benefit to those covered. Those services that have the highest net benefit are ranked highest.

b. Economists should not oppose the Oregon Plan because it involves rationing. The market involves rationing through the price mechanism. Economists might oppose the Oregon Plan because in general they support the market as the least-cost method of providing goods and services. Economists are open to the argument that the market may not distribute goods and services in the way that society wants, which may require government intervention.

c. In the market, the interaction of demand and supply determines the equilibrium price and quantity that is bought and sold. Those who are able to pay the equilibrium price are the ones who receive the health care. The Oregon Plan uses its benefit-ranking system rather than price as the rationing mechanism.

24. a. Equilibrium price is $6 and equilibrium quantity is 300.

b. In a third-party payer system where the consumer pays $2, quantity demanded will be 900. Suppliers require payment of $14 to supply that quantity.

c. Total spending in a is $1,800. Total spending in b is $12,600.

26. a. This is because there are only a limited number of airways in the industry.

   b. No, since they get the money, television networks would have no incentives to produce high definition television.

28. a. The supply curve is vertical at 10,000 tickets. We know there is an excess demand at $130 because there is a secondary market for scalped tickets at a higher price. The graph below on the left shows excess demand of Qd − 10,000.

   b. The people represented by Qd-10,000 will make offers to scalpers for any amount above $130 up to the equilibrium price (if there had been a market) of $2,000. The graph below on the right shows the range of $200 to $2,000.

   c. If scalping became legalized, more people would be willing to sell their tickets when there is no risk of being arrested and fined. The shift of the supply curve for resold tickets to the right will reduce the secondary-market price of Final-Four tickets.

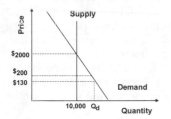 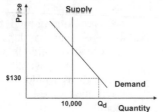

30. a. Japan prescribes many more drugs than the U.S. because Japanese doctors have a financial incentive to do so.

   b. It would lead to many more drugs being produced, even if they were not really innovative, as happened when Japan tried this.

   c. Drug reps would likely provide free samples and other gifts to doctors and have drug lunches for them where they tout the advantages of their drugs.

5- Web Questions

2. a. The minimum wage, adjusted for inflation, has fallen nearly consistently since 1979. It is at its lowest level since 1955. If the inflation-adjusted minimum wage is on the vertical axis, this will reduce the shortage of jobs (number of unemployed) that results from the minimum wage.

   b. According to the article, minorities and women are disproportionately represented among minimum wage earners..

   c. The author says that the job-loss effect is small or minimal. He cites the observation that the 90-cent increase in 1996/97 did not lead to lower employment levels among minorities.

5- Appendix A

2. a. The following are the demand and supply tables after the hormone is introduced:

Price	Quantity Demanded	Quantity Supplied
($/gal.)	(gal./ year)	(gal./ year)
0.00	600	225
1.00	500	125
2.00	400	275
2.50	350	350
3.00	300	425
4.00	200	575
5.00	100	725
6.00	0	875

The hormone (a technological advance) shifts the supply curve to the right by 125,000 gallons, The demand curve is unchanged.

   b. The original supply curve is S0. The growth hormone shifts the supply curve to S1 (to the right by 125). Equilibrium price falls to $2.50 a gallon, and equilibrium quantity rises to 350 million gallons (point B).

   c. The demand curve remains the same at QD = 600 - 100P. The supply curve becomes QS = −25 + 150P. To solve the two equations, set them equal to one another: 600 - 100P = −25 − 150P and solve for P. Doing so, we get P = 2.5. Substituting this value for P into either the demand or supply equation gives us equilibrium quantity of 350.

   d. Quantity supplied would be 425 (−25 + 150 X 3) and quantity demanded would be 300 (600 − 100 X 3). There would be excess supply of 125. The price floor is shown in the accompanying graph.

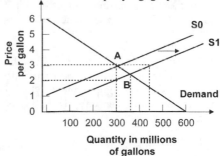

Quantity in millions of gallons

4. a. A demand curve follows the formula $Q_D = a - bP$, where a is the price-axis intercept and b is the slope of the curve. A shift in demand is reflected in a change in a. An increase in demand increases a and a decrease in demand reduces a.

   b. A supply curve follows the formula, $Q_S = a + bP$, where a is the price-axis intercept and b is the slope of the curve. A shift in supply is reflected in a change in a. An increase in supply increases a and a decrease in supply decreases a.

   c. A movement in supply or demand is reflected in the effect of a change in P on either Q_S or Q_D.

6. a. The new supply equation is $Q_S = 150 + 150(P - 1)$ where P is the equilibrium price, or $Q_S = -300 + 150P$.

   b. P = 3.60; Q = 240.

   c. Farmers receive $2.60 per gallon, while demanders pay $3.60 per gallon.

8. a. The new supply equation is $Q_S = -150 + 150(P + 1)$ where P is the equilibrium price, or $Q_S = 150P$.

b. $P = 2.40$; $Q = 360$.

c.   Farmers receive $3.40 per gallon.

● CHAPTER 6· Questions for Thought and Review

2.   The U.S. per capita growth rate of 1.5 to 2.0 percent per year is lower than those of Japan (4.8 percent per year) and China (3.4 percent per year), close to those of Western Europe (2.5 percent per year) and Latin America (1.4 percent per year), and higher than those of Eastern Europe (1.0 percent per year) and Africa (0.8 percent per year).

4.   A representative business cycle is shown in the accompanying graph. Each of the four phases—peak, downturn, trough, and upturn—is clearly labeled.

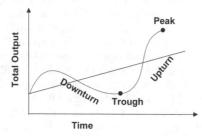

6.   Reducing unemployment to 1.2 percent today is not likely for several reasons. One is that a low inflation rate seems to be incompatible with low unemployment. Another is that today's economy differs from that of the World War II period, when there was an enormous ideological commitment to the war effort and acceptance of strong wage and price controls.

8.   Structural unemployment, because it results from changes in the structure of the economy, is best studied in the long-run framework. Cyclical unemployment, which results from fluctuations in economic activity, is best studied in the short-run framework.

10.   Okun's rule of thumb states that a 1 percentage point change in the unemployment rate will cause income to change in the opposite direction by 2 percent. Thus, a 2 percentage point rise in unemployment will likely cause income to decrease by 4 percent.

12.   Real output rose 13 percent ($15 - 2$).

14.   False. While inflation doesn't make the nation any poorer on average, it does have costs. Its costs include increased transactions costs, capricious distributional effects, the destruction of the informational value of prices, and the breaking down of the institutional structure within which markets work.

● 6· Problems and Exercises

16.   a.   The labor force participation rate is the total number of people employed and/or looking for work (or the labor force) as a fraction of the population over 16 years old. In this instance it is 148,203,000/224,640,000 X 100 = 65.9 %.

b.   The unemployment rate is the total number of unemployed as a fraction of the labor force. In this instance it is 8,047,000/140,156,000 X 100 = 5.4%.

c.   The employment rate is the total number of unemployed as a fraction of the labor force. Since the labor force equals the unemployed plus the employed, we know that in this instance it is (148,203,000 - 8,047,000)/ 148,203,000 X 100, or 94.5%.

18.   a.   Possible explanations include Japanese cultural emphases on tradition, honor, and loyalty. In Japan, firms are less willing to lay off workers in times of excess supply and workers are less likely to change employers in search of higher compensation. Another explanation is the nature of Japanese production. One could suggest that Japanese production does not rely on a changing base of skills so that the skills of workers always match the skills demanded by a particular firm.

b.   It is impossible to say which is better. Each needs to be judged within the broader system of the economy.

c.   The answer to this question depends on the distribution of layoffs and hires in each of the economies. If layoffs in Japan were unavoidable and occurred among mid to-low ranking employees, the average tenure of Japanese employees would decline. If instead the elderly were asked to retire earlier, the average tenure would decline much less. In the United States firms would have to lay off fewer workers than usual due to the booming economy, and average tenure would rise.

20.   a.   4%   b.   5%

c.   It has not increased, Instead, it fell by $120 million

d.   –1%   e.   4%

● 6· Web Questions

2.   a.   The answers to this question will depend upon the current state of the economy. See the accompanying graph. We looked on BEA's web site at <u>www.bea.gov</u> to find the data. The peak and trough are marked.

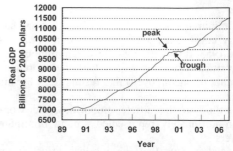

b.   The economy is currently in an expansion.

c.   It has been in an expansion for just a few quarters.

d.   The last recession was in 2001.

● CHAPTER 7· Questions for Thought and Review

2.   A stock concept is the amount of something at a given point in time. A flow concept has a time period associated with it.

A stock is the amount of water in a reservoir; a flow is the amount of water that flows over Niagara Falls every hour.

4. The aggregate value added at each stage of production is, by definition, precisely equal to the value of final sales. Thus, the value-added rate should also be 15 percent. (Technical note: This is assuming the value-added tax is an income-based rather than consumption-based.)

6. It depends on whether more foreign businesses and individuals conduct business in the country relative to domestic businesses and individuals. If more foreign businesses and individuals conduct business in the country relative to domestic businesses and individuals, then GDP will be greater than GNP.

8. Transfer payments are not included in national income, so nothing would happen directly to it.

10. It is difficult to compare GDP over time because prices change. That is, because GDP is measured in prices, a rise in GDP could reflect either a rise in prices or a rise in the amount of goods and services produced. Economists collect data on prices and adjust GDP for those price level increases to create real GDP. A rise in real GDP keeps prices constant and therefore reflects an increase in the amount of goods and services produced.

12. GDP does not measure happiness nor does it measure economic welfare. GDP measures economic activity. Economists talk about GDP because it is measurable and they need something to talk about. Moreover, GDP figures are used to make comparisons of one country's production with another country's and of one year's production with another year's. Besides, GDP does have some relation to happiness.

7- Problems and Exercises

14. Students can search on the Internet to find this information. One source is www.worldbank.org (*The World Development Report*).

16. GDP = C + I + G + (X - M) = 500 + 185 + 195 + 4 = 884.
GNP = GDP + Net foreign factor income = 884 + 2 = 886.
NDP = GDP - Depreciation = 884 - 59 = 825.

18. a. GDP = C + I + G + (X - M) = 485.
GNP = GDP + Net foreign factor income = 488.
Aggregate income = Compensation + Rent + Profits + Interest = 488.
   b. Depreciation = Investment – Net investment = 8.
   c. NDP = GDP – Deprecation = 485 - 8 = 477.

7- Web Questions

2. a. The economic contributions of household and volunteer work.
   b. Crime, depletion of nonrenewable resources, family breakdown and loss of leisure time. The depletion of nonrenewable resources is the largest of these categories.
   c. The GDP has been rising faster than has the GPI in recent years.

CHAPTER 8- Questions for Thought and Review

2. A person living in 1910 is most likely to have worked more to buy a dozen eggs than the person living in 2007. The reason is that, since 1910, the United States real income has been rising, on average, by more than the growth in the population. This means that real income per person has gone up since 1910. Thus, the person living in 2007 had a higher real income than the person living in 1910 and so was likely to work less to buy the dozen eggs. Figure 24-1 supports this.

4. Through free trade, countries can produce the goods in which they have a comparative advantage and trade for those in which they do not, allowing for greater specialization and division of labor, which can result in higher productivity and greater economic growth for the involved countries.

6. Political structure can be viewed as a type of capital if it contributes to production. The longer a country is a democracy, the stronger and more well-developed are the institutions that protect civil liberties and provide secure property and contract rights. These provide the necessary incentives to innovate and produce. A stable political environment also fosters investment in technology because it makes it more likely that the firm will be around in the long term. However, although all the empirical evidence shows a correlation, the causal effects may be from development to democracy. (Source: "Democracy and Growth: A Relationship Revisited," *Eastern Economic Journal*, Winter 2003.)

8. Three types of capital are physical capital, human capital, and social capital. Physical capital includes the buildings and machines that are available for the production process. Human capital includes the workers' skills that are embodied in them through education, experience, and on-the-job training (i.e., through people's knowledge). Social capital includes the habitual way of doing things that guides people in how they approach production in the economy.

10. Two ways in which growth through technology differs from growth through the accumulation of physical capital are: (1) Accumulation of physical capital increases output by simply increasing the amount of the capital available for production whereas technology increases output by making the existing capital more efficient and thereby increasing the marginal return to available capital. (2) Technology can also change the types of goods people buy in an economy by introducing new types of products; accumulation of physical capital does not make such a change.

12. Thomas Malthus based his prediction that population growth would exceed the growth in goods and services on

the law of diminishing marginal productivity of labor. But his prediction did not come true because labor has become more efficient as a result of education and technological progress, which increased the output per worker.

14. According to the convergence hypothesis, Bangladesh is expected to grow faster.

16. New growth theory explains the lack of cnvergence by increasing returns. That is, technological advance will prompt further technological advance, which makes a country that is growing continue to grow, and perhaps at increasing rates. If a country experiences no such increasing returns, its growth rate will slow until it reaches a steady-state.

8- Problems and Exercises

18. a. They will be about the same in about 76 years
b. They will be the same in about 44 years.

20. a. -4.8% from 1994 to 2003.
b. 4.6% from 1994 to 2003.
c. 4% from 1994 to 2003.
d. 2.0% from 1994 to 2003.

22. a. The borrowing circle probably would not work in the United States, because the strong social forces in Bangladesh that eliminate the need for collateral do not exist in the United Statcs. Perhaps there are some minority groups in the United States who do not have the necessary collateral to get loans in the traditional way but whose culture could provide the social forces to make repayment of loans more certain.
b. A possible modification of the program would be to require proof that the "traditional" methods of financing are not open. This would limit the program to those who have few options but do have a good business plan and intention to repay. Another modification would be to require that the business be maintained in the neighborhood where the cosigners live. This would maintain the social forces that ensure repayment.
c. Minorities in the United States often face the same problems because they do not have adequate assets for collateral necessary to gain traditional financing. They also may face discrimination by banks and venture capitalists, or they may not be as trusting of the financial system as their majority counterparts. Nevertheless, they may have good business plans and an intention to repay.

24. a. It exhibits decreasing marginal productivity.

b. If the population is at L_1, it will grow. The surplus food is shown by $Q_1 - S_1$.
c. At L_2 population is declining because there is not enough food to go around.
d. The intersection of the two curves gives the level of population, L^*, at which the economy is in a steady state. It is a steady state because there is no surplus or

shortage—there is just enough to keep people at their subsistence level.

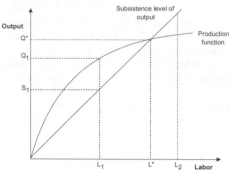

8- Web Questions

2. This question was answered according to the Index of Economic Freedom, 2007. The ratings for the top two are Hong Kong = 89.3; Singapore = 85.7. The ratings for the bottom two are Cuba = 29.7 and North Korea = 3.0.
a. The top two are countries where there is the greatest absence of government coercion or constraint, in the following spheres beyond what is necessary for the citizens' protection: production, consumption, and distribution.
b. GDP per capita growth rates published in the report were as follows: Singapore = 8.7%; Hong Kong = 8.6% . Growth rates arc not available for the lowest two countries, but the assumption is that their growth rates are fairly low. Economic growth and economic freedom do seem to be related, but we would caution that economic upturns and downturns will mask the long-term trends in these economies, which are affected more greatly by economic freedom.

CHAPTER 9- Questions for Thought and Review

2. Classicals felt that if the wage was lowered, the Depression would end. They saw labor unions as preventing the fall in wages, and they saw the government lacking the political will to break up unions.

4. Say there is a rise in the price level. That would make the holders of money poorer (the wealth effect). It would also reduce the real money supply, increasing the interest rate (the interest rate effect). Assuming fixed exchange rates, it would also make goods less internationally competitive (the international effect). All three account for the quantity of aggregate demand decreasing—decreasing spending as the price level rises. These initial increases are then multiplied by the multiplier effect as the initial decrease in spending reverberates through the economy.

6. The LAS curve is vertical because potential output depends on the capacity for production, not the price level. In the long run, output is independent of the price level.

8. This implies that productivity is increasing significantly. If computers are a large portion of the economy, and wages do not rise by the full amount of the productivity increase, the result will be to lower the SAS curve. It can also shift out the potential output curve to the right, increasing equilibrium potential output and lowering the price level.

10. Countercyclical fiscal policy is difficult to implement because it is difficult to assess the condition of the economy at any one time, it takes a long time to enact new government policies, and politically it is difficult to raise taxes when the economy is doing well (or at any time). Oftentimes politics, not the needs of the economy, guide tax and spending decisions.

12. As can be seen in the following diagram, a large increase in potential output (shifting the LAS curve to the right) would cause downward pressure on the price level from P_0 to P_1. As the price level shifts down the output level increases from Y_0 to Y_1. This is the argument some economists used to suggest policy makers didn't need to worry about inflation.

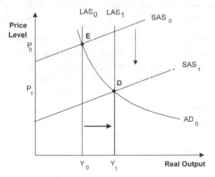

9- Problems and Exercises

14. **a.** Keynes used models not in a mechanistic way, but in an interpretive way. He was a Marshallian who saw economic models as an engine of analysis, not an end in themselves.
   b. It fits in nicely with the "other things constant" assumption since the policy relevance follows only when one has eliminated that assumption and taken into account all the things held at the back of one's mind.
   c. It definitely was primarily in the art of economics since the above method is the method used in the art of economics.

16. **a.** The SAS curve will shift up since wages rise by more than the rise in productivity.
   b. The SAS curve will shift down since productivity rises by more than the rise in wages.
   c. The SAS curve will shift up since wages rise and productivity declines.
   d. The SAS curve will not shift since the wage increase is exactly offset by a productivity increase.

18. **a** We would suggest that the rise in oil prices will shift the SAS curve up and the drop in world income will shift the AD curve in, causing equilibrium income to fall even more below potential (to point B in the accompanying graph).

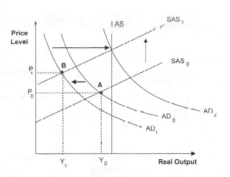

   b. We might suggest expansionary fiscal and monetary policy to shift the AD curve out (from AD_0 to AD_2) and bring equilibrium income to its potential. We would caution the government about the possible inflationary consequences, but since the economy is significantly below potential, we would argue that it is a risk worth taking.

9- Web Questions

2. **a-b.** The level of output and price level are shown in the accompanying graph.

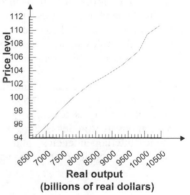

   c. Since the curve involves shifts in both the SAS curve and AD curves, all we can say is that these are points of equilibrium given certain assumptions. It is neither an AD nor an SAS curve. In order to draw one or the other, simplifying assumptions must be made regarding what is held constant.

CHAPTER 10- Questions for Thought and Review

2. If planned expenditures are below actual production, income will decline. Here's how: when planned expenditures are below actual production, firms will see that their inventories are building up faster than they'd like. In response, they cut production. As production falls, so does income. Consumption falls by a fraction of the decline in income, leading to a further decline in planned expenditures. This process continues until planned expenditures equal actual production.

4. The aggregate expenditures curve shifts down by the decline in autonomous expenditures.

6. Equilibrium income is $500.

8. Shocks to aggregate expenditures are any sudden changes in factors that affect C, I, G, X, or M. This includes consumer sentiment, business optimism, foreign income, and government policy. It is possible that people could change their marginal propensities to consume and save, and this could also have an effect on the economy.

10. If the mpe is 0.5, the multiplier is 2. Every $1 increase in autonomous expenditures will raise income by $2. To close a recessionary gap of $200 the government needs to generate $100 of additional autonomous spending. It can accomplish this by increasing government expenditures by $100, or by cutting taxes by somewhat more than that (about $200).

12. The effects of this invention on the economy would be manifold and in many ways unpredictable because such major shocks have social, institutional, and political effects, as well as economic effects. The obvious effect is that the demand for the pill would likely be tremendous (after people were sure it was safe), and so production of the pill would gear up to meet the demand. Market structure and pricing decisions will play a big role in determining the new effect of the change. Alternative forms of transportation would suffer decreases in demand (cars, mass transit, airplanes, etc.), and levels of production of those goods and services would adjust, as would employment in those industries and related industries. Measured GDP might actually fall.

14. A mechanistic model states the equilibrium independent of where the economy has been or where people want it to be. A mechanistic model is used as a direct guide for policy prescriptions. An interpretive model is used as a guide that highlights dynamic interdependencies and suggests the possible response of aggregate output to various policy initiatives.

10- Problems and Exercises

16. If the mpe is .8, then the value of the multiplier is 1/.2 or 5. If autonomous expenditures are $4,200, the equilibrium level of income in the economy is 5 x $4,200 = $21,000. This is demonstrated in the accompanying graph.

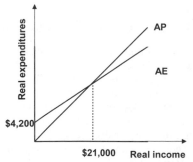

18. a. Given the mpe is 0.8 and autonomous investment has risen by 20, income will increase by 100 (the multiplier is 1/.2 or 5, and 5 X 20 is 100).

b. With an mpe of .8, the multiplier is now only 2 (1/.5), and so the change in investment causes income to change by 40.

c. The decrease in exports and increase in investment cancel each other out so that autonomous expenditures in the aggregate are unchanged.

d. See the graphs below. The graph on the left corresponds to (a) and the accompanying graph corresponds to (b). The graph to (c) would show the AE curve not moving at all.

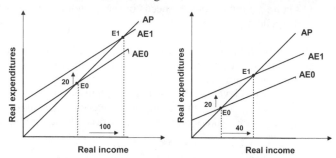

20. a. A likely culprit was a decline in investment spending, partly due to increased bank regulation and Federal Resolution Trust Corporation scrutiny of loans in the wake of the failed S&Ls and liquidity problems of commercial banks in the late 1980s and early 1990s. This was commonly known as the credit crunch, where lower interest rates failed to increase investment spending in the early 1990s. This is shown as a shift down of the AE curve from AE0 to AE1 and a decline in real income.

b. An improvement would be graphically represented by a shift up of the AE curve shown in the graph on the next page as the shift from AE1 to AE2 and a rise in real income. The improvement occurred most likely as a result of expectations of an improving economy and further reductions in interest rates increasing consumption and investment expenditures. Government expenditures did not change much in this period and probably did not contribute to the economic improvement.

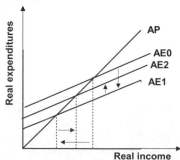

c. President Bush would have had to increase government expenditures or reduce taxes significantly to stop the slowdown, but given the political atmosphere regarding the high deficit and debt, it is unlikely he could have done so.

d. President Clinton faced the same political imperatives to decrease the size of the deficit, so he implemented some policies designed to affect potential output (the supply side). He lowered some taxes, calling them 'supply-enhancing tax cuts,' changed the composition of government spending calling the changes 'supply-enhancing changes', and raised other taxes (discounting their effects on the economy).

22. **a.** If the mpe is .5, the multiplier is 2. Because there is a recessionary gap of $800, government spending would have to increase by $400 to bring the economy back to long-run equilibrium.
   b. If the mpe is .8, the multiplier is 5. Because there is an inflationary gap of $1500, government spending would have to decrease by $300 to bring the economy back to long-run equilibrium.
   c. If the mpe is .2, the multiplier is 1.25. Because there is an inflationary gap of $1,200, the government will want to reduce expenditures by $960.
   d. If the mpe is .7, the multiplier is 3.33. Because there is a recessionary gap of $1,500, the government will want to increase expenditures by $450.

10- Web Questions

2. Answers will depend on the time at which the student answers the question.
   a. Inventories were up 4.3 percent above current levels one year ago.
   b. Rising inventories either mean that consumer expenditures, and therefore aggregate demand, are falling, or that production is rising faster than aggregate demand is rising (or a combination of the two). Either way, production is outpacing expenditures. Unless expenditures pick up, eventually producers will want to cut production. In terms of the multiplier model, it is possible that the economy is going to slow or experience a recession.

10- Appendix A

2. We would recommend increasing expenditures by 80.

4. This makes the multiplier 2.08. This means that we would increase expenditures by about 192 or cut taxes by about 213.

6. This would make the multiplier = $1/(1 - c + ct + m - mt)$. It would be a slightly higher multiplier. (The difference between the two assumptions is whether we are assuming government imports.)

10- Appendix B

2. **a.** The AD curve will become steeper.
   b. An increase in the size of the multiplier makes the AD curve flatter because the effect of changes in the price level on aggregate demand will be augmented even more by the multiplier.
   c. An increase of $20 in autonomous expenditures has no effect on the slope of the AD curve; the increase only affects the position of the curve.
   d. A decline in the price level disrupting the financial market will make the AD curve steeper because it decreases the price-level interest rate effect.

CHAPTER 11- Questions for Thought and Review

2. Loanable funds are financial assets available for lending and borrowing.

4. If the interest rate is higher than the rate that would equilibrate the supply and demand for loanable funds, the supply of loanable funds will exceed the demand and there will be too little investment.

6. Money doesn't have to have any inherent value to function as a medium of exchange. All that's necessary is that everyone believes that other people will accept it in exchange for their goods. This is the social convention that gives money value.

8. Money serves as a unit of account when people compare prices.

10. Two components of M2 that are not components of M1 are savings deposits and small-denomination time deposits.

12. The equation for the simple money multiplier is $1/r$; the equation for the multiplier is $(1 + c)/(r + c)$. Since c is positive, the simple multiplier is larger than the multiplier.

14. People will increase the amount of money they hold, and sell bonds, if they expect interest rates to rise in the future because the price of those bonds will be falling.

16. The demand for money is downward sloping because the interest rate reflects the opportunity cost of holding money. The higher the interest rate, the higher the opportunity cost of holding money. So, people hold less of it when its cost rises.

11- Problems and Exercises

18. **a.** money   **b.** not money   **c.** not money
   d. not money   **e.** money   **f.** not money
   g. not money

20. **a.** No because they are hard to move. In this case, pearl shells were used for small transactions.
   b. It would lower the value of the stones, causing a general inflation in prices.
   c. If they could be distinguished, which in this case they could, the new stones would sell at a discount to the older stones, which they did.
   d. Yes, in some ways money is a marker of individuals' "gifts to the marketplace."

22. **a.** Neither   **b.** Both   **c.** M2
   d. Both   **e.** Neither   **f.** Neither
   g. Both

24. For a deposit of $100 and a reserve ratio of 5 percent,
   a. The bank can lend out $95.
   b. There is now an additional $195 in the economy.
   c. The multiplier is 20.
   d. John's $100 will ultimately turn into $2,000.

26. a. If individuals hold no cash, the simple money multiplier is the reciprocal of the reserve requirement. Thus for the following reserve requirements the simple multiplier is found by dividing the requirement percentage into 1: 5%, 20; 10%, 10; 20%, 5; 25%, 4; 50%, 2; 75%, 1.33; 100%, 1.

b. If the ratio of currency individuals hold to their deposits is 20%, the multiplier becomes $(1+c)/(r+c)$ and so for the following reserve ratios their multipliers are now: 5%, 4.8; 10%, 4.0; 20%, 3.0; 25%, 2.67; 50%, 1.71; 75%, 1.26; 100%, 1.

11- Web Questions

2. a. There is about $820 billion of U.S. currency in circulation today but most of it resides outside of the U.S. Assuming that the world population is about 6 billion, this means that there is approximately $137 per person in the world.

b. People typically withdraw cash at ATMs over the weekend, so there is more cash in circulation on Monday than on Friday.

c. 1.8 years.

d. Most of this is in the form of U.S. government securities owned by the Federal Reserve System. Some of it also consists of gold certificates, special drawing rights, and "eligible" paper such as bills of exchange or promissory notes.

e. Bureau of Engraving and Printing.

11- Appendix A

2. It is a financial asset because it has value due to an - offsetting liability of the Federal Reserve Bank.

4. No, she is not correct. While a loan is a loan, that loan is a financial asset to the one issuing the loan because it has value just as a bond does.

6. $0.50

8. a. Market rates are likely to be above 10 percent because the price of the bond is below face value.

b. Its yield is 12.24 percent.

c. Its price would rise.

10. Substituting into the present value formula $PV = \$1,060/1.1$, we find that the bond is worth $964 now.

12. Using the present-value table, we see that at a 3 percent interest rate, $1 30 years from now would be worth $0.41 now, so $200 in 30 years would be worth $82 now.

14. If the interest rate is still 9 percent, the value of a lump sum of $20,000 in 10 years can be calculated using the annuity table in Table A27-1. You should be willing to pay $20,000 X 0.42, or about $8,400 for this offer.

16. a. Agree/Disagree. Technically, a rise in stock prices does not imply a richer economy. If, however, the rise in stock prices reflects underlying real economic improvement such as finding the cure for cancer or a technological -advance, society will be richer not because of the rise in stock prices, but because of the underlying cause of their rise.

b. Disagree. If both the real and financial asset are worth $1 million, then they have the same value as long as they are valued at market prices. Just as financial assets bear a risk of no repayment, real assets bear a risk of a fluctuation in prices.

c. Disagree. Although financial assets do not have a corresponding -liability, they facilitate trades that could not otherwise have taken place and thus have enormous value to -society.

d. Disagree. The value of an asset depends not only on the quantity but also on its price per unit. The price of land per acre in Japan exceeds that in the United States by so much that the total value of land in Japan also exceeds that in the United States.

e. Disagree. The stock market valuation depends on the supply and demand for existing stock. There is, however, a relationship between relative growth in GDP and the rise in stock prices to the extent that growth in stock prices and GDP growth both reflect economic well-being in a country. Also, many of the companies are multinational companies, and where the company is based may not reflect where its value added is generated.-

11- Appendix B

2. a. The effect on the balance sheet is shown below:

Assets		Liabilities	
Cash	$10,000	Demand deposits	50,000
	-1,000		-1,000
	9,000		49,000
Loans	100,000	Net worth	10,000
Physical assets	50,000		
		Total liabilities and	
Total assets	$159,000	net worth	$159,000

b. The reserve ratio is now 18 percent. This is less than the required 20 percent. The bank must decrease loans by $800 to meet the reserve requirement. But this shows up as $800 less in demand deposits and $800 less in cash. The bank must again reduce loans, but this time by $640. Demand deposits once again decline. This continues until the final position -indicated by the following T-account:

Assets		Liabilities	
Cash	$9,000	Demand deposits	45,000
Loans	100,000	Net worth	110,000
Physical assets	50,000		
		Total liabilities and	
Total assets	$155,000	net worth	$155,000

c. The money multiplier is 5.

d. Total money supply declined by $5,000.

CHAPTER 12- Questions for Thought and Review

2. Contractionary monetary policy shifts the aggregate demand curve to the left. In the short run, this will reduce output and reduce the price level. The long-run effect depends on where the economy is relative to potential output. In the graph on the right, the contractionary monetary policy brings the economy back to its potential.

4. It is neither completely private nor completely public. The Fed is a semi-autonomous agency of the federal government. Although it is owned by member banks, its officials are appointed by government. It is a creation of Congress, but has much more independence than do most public agencies.

6. Six explicit functions of the Fed are: 1) conducting monetary policy; 2) supervising financial institutions; 3) serving as a lender of last resort; 4) providing banking services to the U.S. government; 5) issuing coin and currency; and 6) providing financial services to commercial banks.

8. The money multiplier is $(1+c)/(r+c)$. If the Fed eliminated the reserve requirement, the money multiplier would increase and, without other Fed action, the supply of money would also increase.

10. When the Fed buys bonds the price of bonds rises and the interest rate falls.

12. If we consider the example of an open market sale by the Fed, the initial transaction or "splash" would be the Fed sells a bond, and in exchange a person writes a check to the Fed which the Fed presents to the person's bank for payment. The bank now must adjust to this change, and the "ripples" will show up on its balance sheet. Paying cash to the Fed means that the bank's reserves are too low, and the bank must figure out a way to meet its reserve requirement. It may call in loans to do so, but that in turn could mean that someone paid the loan from a checking account, which has further balance sheet implications. Now that the bank wants to make fewer loans, it will increase its interest rates, which will discourage investment and have further ripple effects on the economy.

14. The Federal funds rate is the interest rate that banks charge one another for Fed funds or reserves. As the Fed buys and sells bonds, it changes reserves, thereby changing the price (interest rate) banks charge for loaning reserves overnight—the Federal funds rate. Other, longer-term interest rates, such as the Treasury bill rate, are only indirectly affected.

16. Throughout this period, the Fed engaged in contractionary monetary policy by raising the Fed Funds Target Rate.

18. The effective yield curve is horizontal because the Fed adjusts the money supply to changes in the demand for money to target a specific interest rate.

20. The nominal interest rate is equal to the real interest rate plus the expected inflation rate. If the nominal interest rate is 6 percent and the expected inflation rate is 5 percent, the real interest rate is 1 percent.

22. Policy makers pay attention to the shape of the yield curve because it will tell them whether their policies are likely to be effective.

24. A policy regime is a predetermined statement about what policies will be followed in various situations. It ties the hands of policy makers. A policy is a one-time action that does not imply the course of future actions.

26. By telling people what the Fed is doing, transparency enhances the credibility of the Fed. With transparency, the Fed tells the people what it is doing and then the people see that in fact, the Fed does what it says it will. This adds credibility to Fed policy.

12- Problems and Exercises

28. a. If people hold no cash, the money multiplier is $1/r$. If this is equal to 3, then the current reserve requirement is 33 percent. To increase the money supply by 200, the Fed should lower the reserve requirement to 32 percent.

b. Lowering the discount rate will encourage banks to borrow. This will increase the amount of reserves in the system so that the money supply increases. If the Fed wishes to increase the money supply by $200, and the multiplier is 3, reserves must be increased by $66.67. If banks will borrow an additional $20 for every point the discount rate is lowered, the Fed should lower the rate by 3.33 percentage points.

c. To increase the money supply by using open market operations, the Fed should buy bonds, thus increasing the level of reserves in the banking system. To achieve an increase of $200 (if the multiplier is 3) the Fed should buy $66.67 worth of bonds.

30. a. Increasing the reserve requirement would lower the multiplier, calculated as $[1/(r + c)]$. To calculate exactly how much, we would need to know the current money supply.

b. The money multiplier is $[1/(r + c)] = 2.5$. If the Fed sold $800,000 worth of bonds it would decrease reserves by $800,000 and so decrease the money supply by $2 million.

c. This part of the question requires information from a local bank. Reevaluate a and b in view of this information.

32. a. This would increase excess reserves enormously.

b. Banks would most likely favor this proposal because they would now earn interest on their assets held at the Fed.

c. Central banks would likely oppose this because it would reduce their superiority to other political institutions and may require that they ask Congress for appropriation to pay the interest, reducing their political independence.

d. This would increase the interest rate paid by banks because the additional interest would increase their profit margin. The initial increased profit margin would shift the demand for depositors out as new banks entered the market and as existing banks -competed for more deposits. This would increase the interest paid to depositors until the normal profits are once again earned.

34. a. This Act will reduce float because money will be transferred almost immediately from bank to bank.

  b. Because checks will be less likely to be transferred by truck or air, weather will be less likely to affect the level of float, so its variability will decline, unless computer glitches arise.

  c. If the variability of float declines so will the level of defensive Fed actions designed to offset this variability.

36. a. The demand for money would decline. The Fed would have to reduce the supply of money as shown in the graph below on the left.

  b. The demand for money would rise. The Fed would have to increase the supply of money as shown in the graph below on the right.

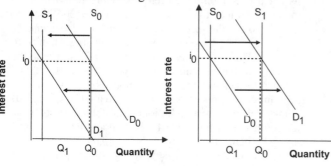

12- Web Questions

2. a. The steepness of the yield curve is a good predictor of recession because high short-term interest rates tend to slow the economy. Also, low long-term interest rates caused by a decline in the expectations of inflation are an indication that people expect the economy to slow.

  b. The economy is more likely to be headed toward a recession if the yield curve is flat or inverted because higher short-term interest rates tend to reduce investment expenditures and slow an economy. Also lower long-term interest rates might indicate that people expect inflation to fall because they expect the economy to slow. Such expectations may be self-fulfilling.

  c. The current yield curve is inverted. That is, the interest rate on the 3-month bill is higher than the interest rate on the 30-year bond. This suggests that people expect the economy to slow or go into recession.

12- Appendix A

2. Let's assume the following initial bank balance sheet:

Assets		Liabilities	
Reserves	$100,000,000	Demand	$1,000,000,00
T-bill holdings	0	deposits	
Loans	905,000,000	Net worth	5,000,000
Total assets		Total liabilities	
	$1,005,000,000		$1,005,000,000

First, individuals sell $2 million in T-bills to the Fed, and deposit the $2 million in the bank. The bank now has more reserves than is required:

Assets		Liabilities	
Reserves	$102,000,000	Demand	$1,002,000,00
T-bill holdings	0	deposits	
Loans	905,000,000	Net worth	5,000,000
Total assets		Total liabilities	
	$1,007,000,000		$1,007,000,000

It has excess reserves of $1.8 million, which it lends out. These loans are redeposited at the bank as demand deposits:

Assets		Liabilities	
Reserves	$102,000,000	Demand	$1,002,000,00
Loans given	-1,800,000	deposits	
New deposits	1,800,000	New	1,800,000
T-bill holdings	0	deposits	
Loans	906,800,000	Net worth	5,000,000
Total assets		Total liabilities	
	$1,008,800,000		$1,008,008,000

It still has excess reserves of 1.62 million, which it lends out. Each round, the amount called in gets smaller and smaller until the bank arrives at its final position with money supply having risen by $20 million.

Assets		Liabilities	
Reserves	$102,000,000	Demand	$1,020,000,00
T-bill holdings	0	deposits	
Loans	923,000,000	Net worth	5,000,000
Total assets		Total liabilities	
	$1,025,000,000		$1,025,000,000

CHAPTER 13- Questions for Thought and Review

2. Adaptive expectations.

4. The three assumptions are that velocity is constant, real income is independent of the money supply, and the direction of causation is from money to prices.

6. Financial institutions have changed enormously and financial markets have become increasingly connected internationally, increasing the flow of money among countries.

8. Governments and central banks sometimes increase money supply even when they know the consequences because sometimes the political ramifications of not -increasing the money supply (which can include a collapse of government) are thought to be worse.

10. Quantity theorists are more likely to support rules -because they have less trust in government undertaking beneficial actions and believe that the long-run effects of monetary policy are on the price level while the short run effects cannot be predicted.

12. The insider/outsider theory of inflation divides workers into insiders and outsiders. It is an example of an insti-tutionalist theory of inflation, which says that social -pressures prevent economic pressures from working. In it, insiders push up wages and outsiders find themselves experiencing unemployment; because the costs of raising wages are not borne by those who make the decision, there is little pressure on insiders not to raise wages

14. The short-run Phillips curve is illustrated on page 696 of the text in Figure 29-3(a). The short-run curve shows the trade-off between inflation and unemployment when expectations of inflation are constant. The long run Phillips curve is shown in Figure 29-4(b) as the vertical curve. The long-run curve shows the trade-off (or lack thereof) when expectations of inflation equal actual inflation.

16. It depends. With short-run, long-run, and shifting curves, just about any combination of inflation and unemployment rates can fit some Phillips curve. So, yes, the Phillips curve is a figment of economists' imaginations. But then again, aren't all models simply structures imposed on reality and doesn't reality only get interpreted through imaginary imposed structures? If so, to suggest that the Phillips curve is "nothing but a figment" is incorrect. Reality is itself a figment of imagination. (If you follow this answer, you might consider shifting to a philosophy major.)

● 13- Problems and Exercises

18. a. Answers may differ. Five goods we buy frequently are newspapers, soda, gas, shirts, and coffee.
    b. This requires research by the student. Answers will depend on goods chosen.
    c. Answer will depend on goods chosen.

20. a. Stopping inflation tends to transfer money from debtors to creditors. Creditors are generally rich, and can golf regardless of their wealth. Debtors, faced with a decrease in their wealth, must cut back on discretionary expenditures, of which golf is one.
    b. Since the exchange rate was fixed, any differential in inflation rates between the two countries could not be offset a change in the exchange rate. The fact that goods in dollar equivalent pesos in Argentina were higher than in NYC suggests that the Argentinean inflation rate remained greater than in the U.S. and the high prices of goods were serving as an anchor on the economy.
    c. In an inflation (with interest rates falling behind inflation), people look for real assets to buy to protect

their wealth. This increases the demand for goods relative to services, increasing their price. When the inflation is stopped, the opposite occurs.
    d. One reason why luxury auto dealers were shutting down was the same as the argument given in (a). A second reason is equivalent to that given in (c). A third reason is that wealthy Argentineans who would most likely purchase such a car also probably had foreign bank accounts denominated in dollars. The car in dollars was cheaper because the peso was overvalued at the fixed exchange rate. The demand for luxury cars fell as Argentincans substituted dollar-denominated luxury cars for peso-denominated cars.

22. a. One would expect real output to decline.
    b. One would expect unemployment to rise.
    c. One would expect inflation to fall.

24. a. Increases in productivity shift the long-run aggregate supply curve to the right as shown below on the left. This allows policy makers to increase aggregate demand (perhaps through expansionary policy, which would keep interest rates low, as desired) without increasing the price level. In this example, the economy moves from point A to point B.
    b. Increase in productivity shifts the long-run Philips curve to the left because it allows a lower unemployment rate at every rate of inflation. This is shown below on the right. Policymakers, therefore are able to increase aggregate demand, shifting the short-run Phillips curve to the left, resulting in lower unemployment and the same inflation rate. In this example, the economy moves from point A to point B.

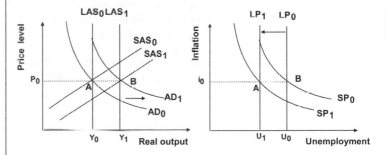

● 13- Web Questions

2. a. Inflation reduces business investment and the efficiency with which productive factors are put to use.
   b. Reducing inflation by one percentage point when the rate is 20 percent may increase growth by 0.5 percent. At lower inflation rates, a one percentage point reduction may increase growth by more than 1 percent.
   c. It affects growth more when inflation is low.
       As the authors point out, their analysis leaves little room for interpretation. Inflation is not neutral, and in no case does it favor rapid economic growth. Higher inflation never leads to higher levels of income in the medium and long run, which is the time period they analyze. This negative correlation persists even when other factors are added to the analysis, including the

investment rate, population growth, schooling rates, and the constant advances in technology. Even when the authors factor in the effects of supply shocks characteristic of a part of the analyzed period, there is still a significant negative correlation between inflation and growth.

Inflation not only reduces the level of business investment, but also the efficiency with which productive factors are put to use. The benefits of lowering inflation are great, according to the authors, but also dependent on the rate of inflation. The lower the inflation rate, the greater are the productive effects of a reduction. For example, reducing inflation by one percentage point when the rate is 20 percent may increase growth by 0.5 percent. But, at a 5 percent inflation rate, output increases may be 1 percent or higher. It is therefore more costly for a low inflation country to concede an additional point of inflation than it is for a country with a higher starting rate. Given their detailed analysis, the authors conclude that "efforts to keep inflation under control will sooner or later pay off in terms of better long-run performance and higher per capita income."

● CHAPTER 14- Questions for Thought and Review

2. According to the Ricardian equivalence theorem, government spending is offset by an equal reduction in private spending because people would increase their savings in anticipation of an increase in taxes in the future to pay for that deficit.

4. Functional finance is difficult to implement because financing the deficit often has offsetting effects, the government doesn't always know how its policies will affect the economy, potential output is not a known quantity, enacting spending and taxing policies is time consuming, government debt can affect private spending, and taxing and spending can negatively affect other government goals.

6. If interest rates have no effect on investment, there would be no crowding out. Crowding out occurs when the government's sale of bonds to finance expansionary fiscal policy causes interest rates to rise, choking off private investment.

8. State balanced budget requirements are pro-cyclical because during downturns, tax revenue generally falls, making it necessary for state governments to raise tax rates and cut expenditures in order to maintain a balanced-budget. Such actions slow the economy even further. The opposite is true during expansions: tax revenues rise so that states accumulate surpluses. They cut tax rates and increase expenditures, contributing to a greater expansion.

10. Automatic stabilizers reduce taxes and raise -expenditures during contractions without additional government -action. They therefore act to offset contractions. Likewise during recoveries, automatic stabilizers -increase taxes and reduce expenditures, which act to slow the recovery.

12. Increasing taxes shifts the aggregate demand curve in to the left, -decreasing income, increasing unemployment and making people less likely to vote for those in office. The maxim holds because people tend to have short memories.

14. While New Classicals do not believe that government spending will affect the economy, they do believe that taxes reduce the incentive to work and produce. Therefore, they promote a policy of reducing spending so that taxes can be cut and incentives to produce, and therefore growth, can increase.

● 14- Problems and Exercises

16. **a.** According to the Ricardian equivalence theorem deficit spending has no effect on the interest rate because people increase their saving (supply of loanable funds) sufficiently enough to offset the increase in the deficit (demand for loanable funds).

   b. According to the Ricardian equivalence theorem, the aggregate demand curve does not shift at all because the increase in government spending is exactly offset by a decline in private spending. This is shown in the graph below.

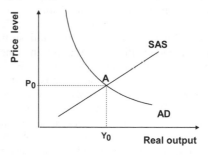

18. **a.** If the economy is truly below potential output, a nuanced functional finance view would be to increase spending enough to bring the economy back to potential as shown in the accompanying graph on the next page, but always be careful to monitor the economy to see that the policy is having the desired effect.

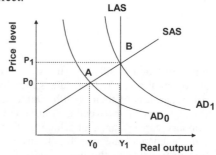

   b. According to the New Classical view, there is no point to activist fiscal policy because it will be ineffective. The only way for the economy to reach potential is for economic forces (such as a decline in the price level) to do it. This is shown in the graph below.

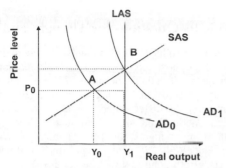

20. a. In the standard AS/AD model, a tax cut will shift the AD curve to the right, leading to an increase in the price level and real output, as shown in the accompanying graph. Congressman Stable's views fit this model well.

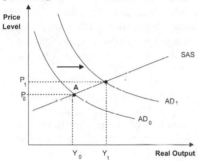

    b. If Congressman Growth is correct, the tax cut will shift the LAS curve to the right. If the economy had previously been in long-run equilibrium, the economy will now be below potential and there will be pressures for factor prices to decline. Assuming nothing else happens in the meantime, the SAS curve will shift down, leading to a lower price level and higher real output, as shown in the accompanying graph.

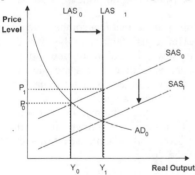

    c. In the short run, Congressman Stable is likely to be correct.

    d. The tax cut will require government to finance a higher budget deficit. This would lead to higher interest rates and lower investment. If there is perfect crowding out, the decline in investment will completely offset the expansionary effect of the tax cut. In this case, the tax cut will have no effect on either the price level or real output.

22. a. In 1995 the unemployment rate fell below the target rate of 6 percent without generating inflationary pressures. He was probably changing his estimates to reflect that reality.

    b. It would shift the LAS curve out.

    c. Using Okun's rule of thumb—which says that for every 1 percentage point rise in the unemployment rate, income falls by 2 percent—a 0.5 percentage point decline in the target unemployment rate would imply a rise in potential income of 1 percent, or $100 billion.

14 Web Questions

2. a. The process starts off by the formulation of the president's budget for a fiscal year. The budget documents are then prepared and transmitted to the Congress. The Congress, after reviewing this budget, develops its own budget and accepts the expenditure and revenue bills. The agency managers then execute the budget in the fiscal year, after which information for the actual spending and receipts becomes available.

    b. It takes about two years. For example, for Fiscal Year 2001 (begins October 1, 2000) the President formulated the budget between February-December 1999, and the data on the expenditures and receipts became available in October-November 2001.

    c. The President and the Congress have to decide upon the discretionary spending, which accounts for one-third of all federal spending. The remaining two-thirds of all federal spending, called mandatory spending, is authorized by permanent laws.

CHAPTER 15 Questions for Thought and Review

2. The two ways the government can finance a deficit is by selling bonds or by printing money.

4. The size of the passive or cyclical deficit will be $200 billion.

6. A structural deficit would exist even if the economy were at its potential level of income, which would be at full employment, or at where the unemployment rate is equal to the normal rate of unemployment. If an economist believed that the normal rate of unemployment was 4 percent instead of 6 percent, then the difference between the economy's current state and the potential income level would be larger, leading to a greater passive deficit and therefore a smaller structural deficit. Thus, Mr. A should also say that the structural deficit is $20 billion.

8. It would not differ; expected inflation does not enter into the determination of the real deficit.

10. Three ways individual debt can be said to differ from government debt are: (a) government is ongoing and therefore never needs to pay back the debt; (b) government can pay off the debt by creating money; and (c) much of the government debt is internal debt owed to its own citizens and agencies.

12. Deficits are only a summary measure of the economy. A government can undertake significant future obligations and therefore get itself into trouble even if it is not running a deficit.

14. Because of the baby boom, there were many people working and relatively few collecting Social Security in the late 1990s. This caused a surplus in the Social Security Trust Fund. Since that Trust Fund is part of the government budget, the Social Security system is a primary -reason for the surpluses.

16. It depends. Clearly, there is some tendency for the deficit to raise the interest rate, thereby decreasing investment and hence future growth. However, to the degree that the government spending is itself productive, not having the deficit could also decrease future growth. The ultimate - effect depends on the relative size of the two effects.

15- Problems and Exercises

18. **a.** The passive deficit must be zero since it is defined as zero at potential output.
   b. The structural deficit is $200 billion.
   c. Now $60 billion of that deficit is passive and $140 is structural since revenue would increase by $60 billion if output rose to potential.
   d. Now there is a passive surplus of $30 billion and a structural deficit of $230 billion because revenue would decline by $30 billion if output declined to -potential.
   e. The structural deficit is likely of more concern to -policy makers because normal stabilization policies will not remove it.

20. **a.** Debt service payments are 0.06 times $360 billion = $21.6 billion.
   b. The nominal deficit is 160 - ($21.6 + 145) = $6.6 billion.
   c. The real deficit equals the nominal deficit ($6.6 billion) - 0.03 X $360 billion = $4.2 billion surplus.

22. To make the deficit look as small as possible, we would do the following:
   a. Enter government pensions when they become payable, not on an accrual basis.
   b. Treat the sale of land as current income rather than spreading it out with the sale of an asset.
   c. Include Social Security taxes as a current revenue - because at this time revenue from Social Security - exceeds payment.
   d. Count prepayment of taxes as current income instead of reserves for future taxes.
   e. Count expenditures on F-52 bombers as capital - expenditures. Do not include their depreciation in the government accounts.

15- Web Questions

2. **a.** 28 percent is held as bills, 49 percent as notes, and 19 percent as bonds; 3 percent is held as inflation-indexed notes and an additional 1 percent as inflation-indexed bonds.
   b. Intragovernmental holdings are securities held by government trust funds, revolving funds, and special funds.
   c. The debt will decline during a year in which there is a budget surplus.

CHAPTER 16- Questions for Thought and Review

2. If Widgetland produces only widgets, it can make 240 of them and the opportunity cost is 1/1. If Wadgetland makes only wadgets, it could produce 720 of them at an opportunity cost of .25/1 (widgets to wadgets). Since the opportunity costs differ, there is a basis for trade in production. Widgetland should produce 240 widgets, and trade 60 of the widgets for 120 wadgets. Wadgetland should produce only 720 wadgets and trade 120 wadgets for 60 widgets. Both countries will be better off.

4. Smaller countries tend to get more of the gains from trade because more opportunities are opened up for them. This is true only under the condition that competition among traders prevails. International traders in small countries often have little competition and so keep large shares of the gains from trade for themselves; hence, the people of the small country may not get the gains from trade.

6. Outsourcing to China and India today differs from outsourcing in the past in two ways: (1) the potential size of that outsourcing is much larger today (those countries have combined population of about 2.5 billion) and (2) China and India are able to compete on a larger number of production levels (China and India have adopted more technological advances).

8. Any three of the following ten would be correct: (1) Skills of the U.S. labor force, (2) U.S. governmental institutions, (3) U.S. physical and technological infrastructure, (4) English as the international language of business, (5) wealth from past production, (6) U.S. natural resources, (7) cachet, (8) inertia, (9) U.S. intellectual property rights, and (10) relatively open immigration policy.

10. The law of one price is that in a competitive market there will be pressure for equal factors to be priced equally. It is important to any discussion of the future of the U.S. economy because relative wages are higher in the United States than in most other countries. The U.S. faces forces that will adjust these wages until the relative prices are equal. This will likely happen by a combination of the following: (1) faster wage growth in other countries, (2) slower wage growth in the United States, and (3) a decline in the value of the dollar.

12. The two methods by which the wage gap between Chinese and U.S. workers will likely narrow are (1) relatively slow wage growth in the United States and relatively faster wage growth in China and (2) a fall in the value of the dollar relative to the Chinese yuan.

14. Tariffs and quotas have similar effects on limiting trade (both shift the supply curve to the left). The big difference is who gets the revenue from the resulting increase in the price of imports. With a tariff, the government gets the revenue. With a quota, the revenues accrue to the foreign producers. You can see this graphically in the margin graph on page 485 of the text.

16. This is a normative question. Some aspects to think about would be your concern about the health of American

consumers, the effect of the price competition on American growers, and the effect of the trade on Mexican farmers.

18. The answer in part will depend on what advice is being given. Most economists would argue that some trade restrictions might benefit a country, but almost no country can limit its restrictions to the beneficial ones. Trade restrictions are additive; most economists would not recommend them, even in a recession.

20. One benefit of Mercosur is more internal competition among the four countries. The danger is that the combination of countries might place stronger restrictions on outside goods, which decreases international competition.

🌑 16· Problems and Exercises

22. a   Since their opportunity costs differ, they can gain from specializing: Nebraska will produce only wheat, and Iowa will produce only corn. If Iowa produces only corn, it can increase its production of corn by 60 million to 180 million. Similarly Nebraska can increase its production of wheat to 180 million. There is now 180 million bushels of both to be divided in whatever way the states decide, making it possible to meet the distribution given in the question.

   b. The states together produce 180 million bushels of both corn and wheat and consume 160 million bushels, so the trader gets 20 million bushels of corn and 20 million bushels of wheat.

24. a.   The gains to domestic producers are shown in the graph. Domestic producers now produce B at Pt instead of A at Pw. Domestic producers gain additional revenue shown by areas FHKG and ABKE.

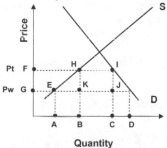

Quantity

   b. The revenue to the government is the quantity supplied by foreign producers, BC, multiplied by the tariff. This is shown in the accompanying graph as HIJK.
   c. The cost to domestic producers to produce additional units is shown by area ABKHE.
   d. The gain to domestic producers is greater than the cost to domestic producers by area FHEG.

26. a.   The countries can move to those points through specialization and trade. Machineland has the comparative advantage in machines and should specialize in them and trade them for food from Farmland. If Machineland produces 200 machines and Farmland produces 200 of food, then they can trade on a 1 to 1 basis to reach points B and D.

   b. At points A and C the total production of machines is 110 and of food is 170. By specialization the total production of each would increase to 200.
   c. Your share should compensate you and still allow for the two nations to gain from trade. Eventually, the above-normal returns will be competed away.
   d. Economies of scale would mean that the production possibilities curves would not be straight lines, and would be a further argument in favor of specialization; the recommendation doesn't change, but the economic case behind it becomes stronger.

28. a.   Three assumptions are that the good is tradable, that transportation costs are minimal, and that taxes between the two countries do not differ significantly.
   b. To the degree that production facilities and labor can move easily, the law of one price should hold for labor, too. Given the wage differentials that exist among countries with seemingly equivalent productivities, it seems that these conditions do not hold for labor.
   c. Since capital is more mobile than labor, the law of one price should have a greater tendency to hold for capital. Financial capital is a great example. Interest rates among countries tend to equate much faster than wages.

30. a.   Yes, if the deductions in lost taxes exceed the amount collected. This is indeed the case. Congressional tax experts have estimated that the deductions exceed the amount corporations pay in taxes by $6 billion a year.
   b. The natural suggestion would be to eliminate the tax, including the accompanying deductions from corporate taxable income. This would have the added benefit of eliminating the administrative costs associated with the tax.
   c. It is likely that the companies want the tax because they benefit from it—in other words, because the tax results in lower taxable corporate income, it is an implicit subsidy, and they will lobby strongly to keep it. The government may keep the tax because it wants to encourage exports. (Source: "U.S. Overseas Tax Is Blasted," *The Wall Street Journal*, May 5, 2004)

🌑 16· Web Questions

2. a.   Three trade barriers listed are biotechnology bans, quotas on lumber, and export control licensing.
   b. The biotechnology bans are implemented because of perceived health risks to genetically modified food. The lumber quotas are to save American jobs in the timber industry. Export control licensing of satellites has shifted from the Commerce Department for security reasons.
   c. The ban on genetically modified food is hurting the U.S. agriculture market. The import quota on lumber has led to a 35 percent increase in the price of U.S. lumber. We are losing business from China due to the change in license control.

4. The answer to this question depends on the country chosen.

● 16- Appendix A

2. **a.** The opportunity cost for Greece of making 1 million olives is 1,000 pounds of cheese. The opportunity cost for France of making 1 million olives is 250 pounds of cheese. The opportunity cost for Greece of making 1,000 pounds of cheese is 1 million olives. The opportunity cost for France of making 1,000 pounds of cheese is 4 million olives.

   b. They are worse off, because France has a comparative advantage in producing olives and Greece has a comparative advantage in producing cheese. Under the new law, France produces 50,000 pounds of cheese and Greece produces 500 million olives—point A. They could have had a greater combination: 100,000 pounds of cheese produced by Greece and 600 million olives (200 million by France and 400 million by Greece)—point B. Their combined possibility curve if they were able to trade is the outermost production possibility curve shown.

   c. See the accompanying graph. All the points in the shaded area were unattainable without specialization and trade.

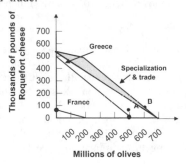

● CHAPTER 17- Questions for Thought and Review

2. When someone sends 100 British pounds to a friend in the United States, the transaction will show up in the component of the current account called net transfers, which include foreign aid, gifts, and other payments to individuals not exchanged for goods or services. It will also appear on the financial and capital account as a receipt of foreign currency just like the purchase of a British stock or bond.

4. A capital and financial account deficit means that financial outflows are more than financial inflows. The excess supply of dollars is balanced by a current account surplus, which means Americans are producing more than they are consuming. In the long run, financial and capital account deficits are nice because you are building up holdings of foreign assets, which will provide a future stream of income.

6. In the early 1980s the U.S. government was pursuing tight monetary policy and expansionary fiscal policy. The high interest rate resulted in a strong dollar. Expansionary fiscal policy failed to stimulate domestic demand as export demand fell sharply due to the high dollar. This, accompanied by the high interest rate that had cut

investment, drove the economy into a recession with twin deficits, but a strong dollar.

8. It was likely increasing because imports are positively correlated with national income.

10. If Japan ran an expansionary monetary policy, it would increase Japanese imports of U.S. goods and make American goods comparatively more competitive, and thereby decrease the U.S. trade deficit. The U.S. dollar would rise relative to the Japanese yen.

12. Since the effect of monetary policy is to push the exchange rate down in all effects, this will not change the effect presented in the chapter, other than to eliminate the effect through income and replace it with the effect through prices.

14. We would use a combination of purchasing power parity, current exchange rates, and estimates of foreign exchange traders to determine the long-run exchange rate of the neverback. This combination approach can be justified only by the "that's all we have to go on" defense. Since no one really knows what the long-run equilibrium -exchange rate is, and since that exchange rate can be -significantly influenced by other countries' policies, the result we arrive at could well be wrong.

16. Both fixed and flexible exchange rate systems have advantages and disadvantages. While fixed exchange rates provide international monetary stability and force governments to make adjustments to meet their international problems, they have some disadvantages as well: they can become unfixed, creating enormous instability; and their effect of forcing governments to make adjustments to meet their international problems can be a disadvantage as well as an advantage. Flexible rates provide for orderly incremental adjustment of exchange rates and allow governments to be flexible in conducting domestic monetary and fiscal policies, but also allow speculation to cause large jumps in exchange rates (and, as before, the government flexibility may be a disadvantage too). Given the pluses and minuses of both systems, most policy makers have opted for a policy in between-partially flexible exchange   rates.

18. They will sell that currency, which will force the government to use reserves to protect the currency. Once the government runs out of reserves, it may be forced to devalue the currency, making the speculators' predictions self-fulfilling.

20. He was advocating significant trade restrictions. These trade restrictions would have likely provoked retaliation by our trading partners, hurting international cooperation, and hurting the world economy.

22. The United States would want to hold up the value of the dollar to help prevent the surge in import prices that would result from the fall in exchange rates, and to keep foreigners from buying our assets cheaply. Other countries would want a higher value of the dollar in order to keep their goods competitive with U.S. goods.

24. Two disadvantages is loss of independent monetary policy for those countries that adopt the euro and loss of national identity because the country must give up its own currency.

17- Problems and Exercises

26. **a.** This suggests that it was running a financial and capital account deficit since the two largely offset each other.

   b. If the private balance of payments was in surplus, China must have a fixed or partially flexible exchange rate regime, because the central bank was selling its currency.

   c. It had to be selling its currency to equalize the balance of payments. In the accompanying graph, the Chinese central bank had to be supplying $(Q_s - Q_D)$ yuan.

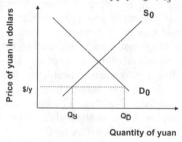

   d. The value of the yuan would likely rise. That is, it would take more dollars to buy a yuan, or alternatively each yuan would get more dollars.

   e. The inflation would increase the price of Chinese goods, increasing the real exchange rate of the yuan, and thereby reducing the pressure on the yuan to rise.

28. **a.** This is an enormous change. In order to bring it about, the Never-Never government would have to run an enormously expansionary monetary policy, -reducing the real interest rate possibly to negative amounts and probably generating significant inflation. As far as trade policies are concerned, the government could eliminate all tariffs or even subsidize imports, causing imports to rise and other countries' currencies to appreciate relative to the neverback. Of course, since there's already a large trade deficit, this may not be a viable option.

   b. Holders of neverbacks will demand foreign currencies (increase supply of neverbacks) since the return on neverback assets has declined. This is shown as a rightward shift in the supply of neverbacks. Likewise, potential foreign investors will demand fewer neverbacks for the same reason. This is shown as a leftward shift in the demand for neverbacks The effect is to reduce the exchange rate value of the neverback to $10 per neverback.

30. **a.** We would suggest buying U.S. dollars and selling - currencies of the EU. (Increased growth in the EU will increase European demand for U.S. goods, thereby causing the dollar to appreciate.)

   b. We would suggest buying U.S. dollars. Since U.S. - interest rates are expected to be higher, the quantity of U.S. assets demanded will rise, and thus the -demand for dollars and the price of dollars will increase.

   c. Since the market will likely already have responded to the higher expected interest rates, the rise will likely have the same effect as a fall in interest rates. Thus, we would suggest selling U.S. dollars.

   d. We suggest selling U.S. dollars by reasoning opposite to that in b.

   e. We would suggest selling U.S. dollars in the - expectation of a decrease in demand for U.S. dollars as U.S. goods become more expensive. Also -U.S.-denominated assets such as bonds will be worth less with greater inflation making foreign assets more attractive to investors.

   f. We would suggest buying because, if the U.S. government imposed new tariffs, the demand for imports would decline, shifting the supply of dollars to the left. This would lead to a higher value of the dollar.

32. **a.** Three assumptions of the law of one price are that (1) there are zero transportation costs, (2) the goods are tradable, and (3) there are no barriers to trade. (There are many others.)

   b. For it to apply directly, labor would have to be - completely mobile and of identical efficiency and ability in all countries. Thus, it does not apply directly. However, assuming capital is flexible, there will be significant indirect pressure toward an equalization of wage rates.

   c. Since capital is more mobile than labor, we would - expect that the law of one price would hold more for capital than for labor.

17- Web Questions

2. The answer to this question depends on the country chosen. We chose Brazil.

   a. The Brazilian currency is the real.

   b. The currency remained virtually unchanged from 2004 to 2005.

   c. Brazil has gotten inflation under control. Unemployment is expected to decline as the economy continues to grow. Fiscal spending is under control. The economy appears to be in good health, which may be contributing to a stable currency.

CHAPTER 18- Questions for Thought and Review

2. At the time that this was written, the U.S. trade deficit had risen to record highs. Still, it is unclear whether we should want to lower the U.S. trade deficit. The trade deficit was in part due to the fact that the economy has been growing for nine consecutive years. As long as the United States can borrow or sell assets, it can have a trade deficit. On the other hand, the more the United States borrows, the more U.S. assets foreigners own. Eventually, the United States will have to run a trade -surplus.

4. A contractionary monetary policy by Japan and China would decrease Japanese and Chinese importation of U.S. goods and would make the U.S. trade deficit worse.

6. If the recession was caused by a fall in domestic expenditures, we would expect that its trade balance was moving toward surplus. If, however, the recession was caused by a fall in exports, we would expect that its trade balance was moving toward deficit. The G-8 countries were trying to get Japan to boost its -economy by increasing aggregate expenditures with -expansionary monetary policy.

8. To finance the debt the U.S. government has to sell more bonds. Because foreigners also demand these bonds (demand is greater), the government doesn't have to pay as high interest rates as it would if only U.S. investors demanded government bonds. Thus, the interest rate doesn't rise as much and crowding out is reduced.

10. If the financial and capital account were balanced and remained balanced, the exchange rate for a country that gained a comparative advantage in most goods would rise because the demand for its currency would rise. Demand for currency would rise because foreigners would want to buy more goods from this country because it could produce goods at a lower cost than other countries and therefore could offer those goods for lower prices. Another way to look at it is that exports would exceed imports, creating a trade surplus, which would not be offset by a financial and capital account deficit, so that there would be an excess demand for the currency.

18- Problems and Exercises

12. a. I'd rather be holding other currencies because their price is expected to rise. I could buy them low and sell them high for a profit.
    b. The same argument doesn't hold for China because it has greater concerns than personal profit, such as the effect of a falling dollar on its economy.
    c. It might want to buy dollars to keep up the dollar's value. In fact, since the government can print yuan, it could theoretically buy as many dollars as it desires. It would want to buy dollars if it feels that the declining dollar would harm its exports. A declining dollar makes Chinese exports more expensive for Americans to buy and falling exports would slow the Chinese economy.

14. a. I would suggest that the IMF require a -contractionary policy for both monetary and fiscal policy. I would, however, suggest a relatively more contractionary fiscal policy so that the exchange rate would also fall while inflation falls, boosting -exports.
    b. This would tend to slow inflation, after an initial burst due to a fall in the exchange rate. The policy, however, would hinder growth and push the economy into a -recession.
    c. I suspect that the country would not be happy about the proposal because its adoption might lead to a deep recession, which is politically unpopular.

16. a. One would expect less stabilization, because when income falls, foreign incomes will likely fall too, and thus decrease exports, which will further decrease income.

    b. This would increase the possibility of a global recession.
    c. Answers on this can differ; an expected answer is that one will need coordinated counter cyclical policy organized through G-8, World Bank, or some other international organization.

18- Web Questions

2. a. Conditionality is the requirement by the IMF that its aid recipients follow certain policies, or conditions, in order to receive aid.
    b. Typical IMF financing preconditions include reducing government spending, budget deficits, and foreign (external) debt, reducing the rate of money growth to control inflation, raising real interest rates to market levels, and removing barriers to export growth. When implemented, these conditions lead in the short term to (a) a devaluation of local currency, (b) a lower trade deficit and (c) domestic problems including slower growth and unemployment.
    c. Mexico, Russia, Pakistan, Thailand, and South Korea are examples of countries that have received IMF financing over the past five years.
    d. Mission creep is the term used to describe the increasing influence of the IMF on domestic policies of its aid recipients. In addition to the enforcement of financial reform in exchange for aid, the IMF has been accused of advocating an agenda in relation to geopolitics and international security, social safety nets, government corruption, the environment, and human rights.

CHAPTER 19- Questions for Thought and Review

2. You can't just judge an economy; you must judge the -entire culture. Some developing countries have cultures that, in some people's view, are preferable to ours.

4. The exchange rate method uses current exchange rates to compare relative incomes while the purchasing power parity method compares incomes by looking at the domestic purchasing power of money in different countries. Because many developing countries' currencies are undervalued, the current exchange rate overstates the income disparity between developed and developing countries.

6. Three ways in which institutions differ in developing countries are that (a) basic market institutions with well-defined property rights do not, in many cases, exist; (b) there is often a dual nature to the economy; and (c) fiscal structures with which to adequately implement fiscal policy often do not exist.

8. An economist might favor activist policies in developed countries and laissez-faire policies in developing countries because the policies one favors depends on the desire and the ability of government to work for and achieve the goals of its policies. Different views of government can lead to different views of policy. Since many economists have a

serious concern about the political structure in developing countries, but less concern about it in developed countries, they can favor one set of policies for developing countries and another set for developed countries.

10. A regime change is a change in the entire structure within which the government and economy interact, whereas a policy change is a change in one aspect of -government action.

12. Governments act to maintain their positions in power, and often feel that in order to do so, they have no choice but to print more money; central banks in developing countries often do not enjoy full independence, and thus cannot resist these pressures (and may not want to, since they also desire to keep the government in power). For those making the decisions, the short-term benefits of the "inflation solution," keeping regimes in power, outweigh any long-term hyperinflationary consequences.

14. Investment and savings are low in developing countries because income is low, and poor people don't have a whole lot left over to save. The rich often put their -savings abroad due to the fear of political instability. As for the middle class, which is usually small in developing countries, the underdeveloped financial -sector leaves them with few opportunities to invest their savings.

16. An investor thinking of making an investment in a -developing country should be concerned about the -country's political stability and its economic condition (inflation, etc.). The existing amount of debt may also be a matter of concern.

18. Corruption limits investment and growth because knowing that payments of graft must be made prevents many people from undertaking actions that might lead to growth. Tax revenues are often diverted to those in power instead of going into legitimate productive investment, and the same is sometimes true of foreign aid money from abroad. But that does not answer the issue, since one must deal with the political reasons why the government increases the money supply.

20. The UN could encourage the development of microcredit banks, like the Grameen Bank, which provide a low-cost alternative to money lenders. There are also significant social and cultural limitations in many areas that limit women entrepreneurs, as well as the lack of day-care alternatives to being a full-time mother.

19- Problems and Exercises

22. This exercise asks you to spend a day living like someone in a developing country, and then to read this chapter and contemplate the degree to which someone in such a situation can pull himself or herself up by the bootstraps.

24. This is a student research question.

26. a. I would want to emphasize those skills that have the highest per-dollar return—those that would lead to development. These would probably be the basic -reading, writing, and problem-solving skills that fit the indigenous culture, as well as technological and computer training.

b. This differs from the ideal educational system in the United States because the U.S. culture is different and U.S. economic problems are different. Thus, in the United States the focus would be more abstract -analysis and becoming generally educated and cultured, while in developing countries the focus would be agricultural science and basic skills.

c. This is an open-ended question. The relevant -question would be: How much would individuals be willing to pay for courses that do not result in a credential compared to how much they would be -willing to pay for a credential without the -coursework?

19- Web Questions

2. a. From their website: "The Bretton Woods Project works as a networker, information-provider, media informant and watchdog to scrutinize and influence the World Bank and International Monetary Fund …. It monitors projects, policy reforms and the overall management of the Bretton Woods institutions with special emphasis on environmental and social concerns."

b. Criticisms about the World Bank and IMF focus on conditions placed on borrowing countries for access to funding (which may include loss of local economic authority) and its dominance by industrialized nations, as well as projects that it has funded that may harm the environment. One recent criticism is the disregard for indigenous people's right to self determination. See forestpeoples.gn.apc.org/index.htm. Another criticism is of human rights violation at a World Bank-supported gold mine. www.leat.or.tz/active/buly